a lion
in the
bedroom

© Pat Cavendish O'Neill, 2004
© Park Street Press, 2004
© Media21 Publishing, 2004

First published in Australia in 2004
as a joint publication between
Park Street Press and
Media21 Publishing (Pty) Ltd

This edition published in
South Africa in 2004 by
JONATHAN BALL PUBLISHERS (PTY) LTD
PO Box 33977, Jeppestown, 2043

ISBN 978 1 86842 209 8

Reprinted twice in 2005

Reprinted once in 2012

Designed by Michelle Wiener and
Sharon McGrath, Australia

Colour reproduction by
Clayton Lloyd, Australia

Printed in the Republic of South Africa
by CTP Book Printers, Dumminy Str, Parow, Cape

a lion
in the
bedroom

BY PAT CAVENDISH O'NEILL

Edited by Shelley Gare

JONATHAN BALL PUBLISHERS
Johannesburg & Cape Town

DEDICATION

To my adored mother. Her love for her children was unconditional and her generosity had no end. She gave me my love for animals, both wild and domesticated, and the result has changed my life.

To my beloved Tana, an unbelievable lioness, who saved my life, who taught me the beauty of Africa.

I also want to dedicate this book to my wonderful staff without whose help and loyalty I could not exist. This is to thank Africa and the people of Africa for my wonderful life. I would not want to live anywhere else.

To my beloved brother Caryll Waterpark who over the years has had to put up with what he considers a psychiatric case as a sister and has renamed Broadlands, Broadmoor. Caryll read my manuscript and firmly red-pencilled many of the more daring stories and many mentions of himself. My editor and I made sure to put them back in. He is a man of remarkable intelligence and courage, and in his youth a great beauty too. So there is no reason I am not going to say so.

To my husband Frank O'Neill, who gave up in despair many years ago the notion of having a normal wife or even a normal life. To Shelagh McCutcheon who helped me with the horses and has dedicated her life to Broadlands and all the animals. To the wonderful Graham Beck family who have come to my rescue as did Sheila Southey and John Kalmanson. With their incredible generosity they have saved my farm and allowed me to continue my life with the animals.

To my beloved animals who are part of myself as I know I am part of them.

ACKNOWLEDGEMENTS

Firstly to John Alexander without whom this book would never have been published. He came to lunch with his wife and friends and got me to tell them some of my stories of Africa. On his return to Australia, he arranged for me to send my manuscript to Craig Osment of Media21 Publishing. Although we have never met, Craig seems like an old friend through his many faxes. Craig also sent an editor, Shelley Gare, over from Australia to spend three weeks with us here at Broadlands. We all adore her, she became part of our family, and she has worked long and hard on my manuscript. I never realised what was involved. How can I thank her enough?

I would also like to thank my dear friend Professor Peter Gray who did mountains of research and retrieved a crucial letter, from Thelma Furness, from the Bodleian Library at Oxford; Norman Bergel, another great friend, who helped me enormously with my recollections of Tangiers and Egypt; and Rod Coupe, who visited Fiorentina every year and reminded me of many stories from there.

Last, but certainly not least, is my beloved friend Elizabeth Wilson who worked so hard on my story of Kenya and was so good about making sure I didn't lose the plot!

Thank you everyone for making a dream come true.

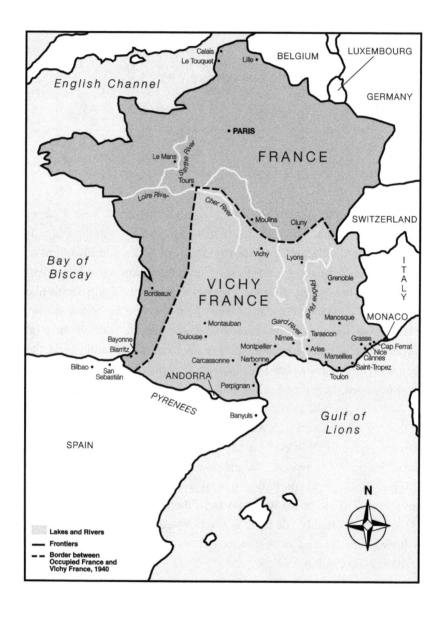

PROLOGUE

This is a story that I heard in Swahili long after my lioness Tana and I had gone to live far out in the Kenyan wilds. It was told to me by one of my dearest friends, Mutete, who was also my cook, and he had been told it by the man I loved, Stan Lawrence Brown, the white hunter. Here is what Mutete said to me: "When you decided to go and live at Meru so that you could be with Tana, *Bwana* Safari was very worried as he realised that you would be living most of the time on your own and there would be no other women around. He wanted to make sure everyone would look after you as he knows how you love walking into the bush and are very forgetful of what happens around you. He said we all know you are very '*bila uangalifu*'. That is, without care. The *bwana* spoke to me about it and this is the story he told to those who were going with you.

"He said that a long time ago, Tana and you were mother and daughter but they got it all muddled up when you went to heaven. They sent you back as a human and Tana was left behind. She walked all over heaven looking for you until the good God couldn't bear her moans any more and sent her back to earth to continue her search.

But they made another muddle and sent her back as a tiny cub. Tana made sure that you found her but realised she would have to grow up fast and become very big and strong so that she could look after you. Her child, her *toto*, was doing lots of crazy things, like driving her at terrible speeds across the face of Africa. As if this were not enough, she would take her for long walks and charge around in the most stupid fashion amongst the elephant and buffalo. Therefore, she could never relax and lie in the shade of a tree for long to recover from the mad drives, before having to get up and follow her crazy *toto* out into the sun and prevent her from going back to heaven before her time.

"Tana then grew into a huge and beautiful lioness and now it was time for her to find her mate, so she is asking all the *toto*'s friends to stay by her side and look after her, so that eventually they can go back to heaven together."

ACT ONE

CHAPTER

1

My Aunt Nanny looked like a bulldog and was such a snob she thought the upper crust Vanderbilt family of New York was nouveau riche. She generally hated women but adored my mother. Mummy was one of the world's six great beauties according to the press of the time. Her hair had turned silver at the age of 28 and this, combined with her extraordinary green eyes, flawless features and skin, made a remarkable impact on everyone.

Aunt Nanny, who had once been striking herself, told me that Mummy literally had stopped New York's traffic. Admittedly, at the time, that consisted mostly of hansom cabs!

Anne "Nanny" Cameron Tiffany was really my older half-brother Rory's American aunt. My mother had married her brother, the shipping broker Roderick Cameron when she was 21. She was just out of her Australian boarding school. He was 24 years older, a millionaire and owned a 16-storey skyscraper in Manhattan. My mother would emerge from the Cameron Building, near where the Empire State Building now is, and, Aunt Nanny said, the cars would come to a halt "the better to view this vision of perfection" as she put it.

Certainly, when my brother Caryll and I were children in London in the 1930s, people would wait outside our townhouse in Mayfair. As the chauffeur and Rolls drew up at the door, a crowd would collect to watch Mummy leaving for lunch, dinner, or the theatre. In the south of France, where we went often, I used to be overwhelmed with embarrassment accompanying her to Antoine, the glamorous hairdresser in Cannes. Ladies would duck from under the dryers to catch a glimpse of her as she walked in, so famous had she become. Alexandre always did her hair; he was young at the time and afterwards he became a name in Hollywood as hairdresser to filmstars like Greta Garbo, Sophia Loren and Elizabeth Taylor. In the 1920s and early 1930s though, there was just a very, very small circle of people who were well-known in England, Europe and America. Society was minute compared to today and beauties like my mother had the same kind of star status that film stars and celebrities have now. What they wore, who they saw, it was all gossiped about and covered by the newspapers.

The story is that the first time Mummy's third husband, Lord Furness, took his new wife to play at the big table at the casino in Monte Carlo, all gambling ceased as she entered the hall. Her tall, perfect figure was draped in a tight-fitting evening dress of white lace over a pale violet-coloured taffeta underskirt that clung to her curves and ended in a slight train. The dress, designed by Molyneux, one of her favourite designers, was appliquéd with lace flowers. In the middle of each flower was sewn a small real diamond. The Furness tiara of large pear-shaped diamonds adorned her upswept silver hair. To complete the toilette, around her neck and falling lovingly over her famous décolletage, was the three-tiered diamond necklace from Cartier that had been one of Furness's wedding presents to her in 1933.

There was, reportedly, a gasp of amazement at this image of perfect beauty. The giant chandeliers overhead picked up the sparkle from the diamonds in which she was smothered and, as she moved, she was caught in a thousand prisms of light. I was told, whether it is true or not, that it was the first time in the history of the casino that gambling had been brought to a standstill.

The Aga Khan, whom she had known for years and who was then one of the richest men on the planet, looked up when she arrived at the main table and commented drily, "My dear Enid, could you not be more discreet with your entrance? Next time come in black...

"No," he apparently corrected himself, "that might be even more disastrous. Allah should have made you a good Moslem and then you would have arrived smothered in veils and I would have been allowed to get on with my game, without the undoubted distraction your presence at my table is going to create."

My mother couldn't help herself: she incited great passion. She married four times. Two of her husbands were millionaires and left her large fortunes, and two of them had titles. She also had numerous lovers and admirers. There is an amusing story about one of her less well-known but equally ardent suitors, a General Erskine. As he was dying, his wife called me up and asked, "Where is your mother going to be buried when she dies?" Rather taken by surprise by her phone call, I said, "I have no idea."

"Well go and ask her," Mrs Erskine said. "My husband has always loved her and as he was not able to be beside her in life, he wants to be beside her in death. Tell your mother, she must make up her mind as I don't intend to keep digging him up."

My mother used to love these stories about herself. Nor was she above adding to them and exaggerating like mad for an appreciative audience. Fact and fiction would merge as she entertained us. She could also tell the dirtiest jokes with her eyes wide and innocent. Indeed, I don't think the harsh realities of life ever really touched on my mother until the very end of her life. She brought us up with three rules which she applied rigorously to herself: never be ill, never be afraid, and never be jealous. Showing any of them, she believed, was a weakness.

Being so generous with her own good fortune, Mummy enabled us, her three children – Rory, my younger brother Caryll and myself – to live our lives fully and each of us made the most of that privilege. She herself was one of seven children, and the grand-daughter of the man credited with being the founding father of the Australian wine industry, Dr Henry John Lindeman. He and my great-grandmother, Eliza, had emigrated to Australia to set up medical practice in the lower Hunter Valley, outside Sydney, but in 1843, he applied for a crown grant of land. He called it Cawarra, which means "running water" in the

Aboriginal dialect of that region. There he launched himself as a vigneron and three of his sons, including my grandfather, Charles, went into partnership with him.

Lindeman is a famous wine name now but then it was still a small family business. My grandfather took over from his father on his death and brought up his family in Strathfield in Sydney. My mother was soon sent away to boarding school to complete her education as a young lady. She had four older brothers though, whom she adored. They were all very good at riding, shooting and fishing. Mummy, being a tomboy, made sure she soon learnt too. The Lindemans were also famous for their looks.

Her first husband Roderick Cameron met her when she was 19. He came to Australia often on business for his company, the R. W. Cameron shipping line, which he had inherited from his father and which traded between the west coast of the United States and Australia. On one trip, he spotted Enid and knew at once that she was the one. Granny refused to let them marry for two years though, saying that my mother was much too young to know her own mind. Years later, I remember Mummy teasing her and saying, "You wicked old woman, you know you were in love with him yourself. That's why you didn't want me to marry."

Cameron took his young bride back to the States where his family lived on a 200-acre estate, Clifton Burley, on Staten Island. He died a year later of cancer in 1914 in a New York hospital, leaving Mummy a young widow, with a fortune of several million pounds, and a nine-month-old baby. This was my much loved half-brother Roderick William Cameron who was always known as Rory and who was born on November 16, 1913.

After her first husband's death, Mummy started an affair with the American financier Bernard Baruch, a liaison that was to last on and off until his death. He was very tall, with grey hair and quite a lot older than her. I know that my mother was the great love of his life because he once told me. Baruch was the elder statesman of the United States from World War I through to World War II and was so enormously rich that during the first war he bought over a million dollars of liberty bonds to help the effort. Later, he used his wealth to help finance the Democrats. My mother had lived for a while with Baruch, who we called Bernie, but even after she left he remained in her life and for years after he handled her finances, something that she was entirely incapable of doing herself.

Another impassioned admirer was Uncle Walter, or Group Captain Walter Carandini Wilson, a director of White City, the greyhound racing stadium in London. Unlike most of Mummy's lovers he was marvellous looking, very Latin with black hair and an olive complexion. He was a hero too. As a Lieutenant-Colonel he was part of the British military mission to Finland and the Baltic states after the Bolshevik revolution. Then, in World War II, he was transferred from the army to the Royal Air Force administration as one of the officers inducted into the RAF without wings.

Baruch and Walter Wilson were my godfathers. When the United States joined World War I, Mummy left Baruch and went to London and then France. It was the fashionable thing to do for rich young women to help the war effort by volunteering for hospital or ambulance work with the soldiers wounded on the battlefields. Sometimes they even supplied their own vehicles or medical units. An ex-boyfriend of hers, the Earl of Derby, who later became British Ambassador to France, was Britain's Minister for War at the time. He adored his beautiful friend but was disconcerted at the havoc she was creating amongst the officers in Paris. One aide was already threatening suicide.

At the time, it was considered best to get rich, young widows safely married and then let them get on with whatever they wanted to do. Deciding a husband was what was needed for my mother, Lord Derby cleverly produced my father. Daddy was known as "Caviar" Cavendish and he was a good-looking cavalry officer and a 10-goal polo player, the highest handicap there is. Contrary to all the gossip since, he was far from rich, only having his army pay to recommend him, but he already had a formidable reputation for bravery and a penchant for lovely ladies. Lord Derby, having decided that they would be an ideal couple, convinced my mother to marry him. At least, that is what my mother told me.

They were married in Paris on June 18, 1917, and Lord Derby gave my mother away. Thereafter my father, Frederick Cavendish, returned to the front and my mother went back to driving her ambulance.

After the war and with many decorations for valour, my father was given command of the 9th Lancers in Egypt. Mummy, as she had done in Paris, now created uproar amongst the officers of my father's regiment. This young colonel's wife, stunningly beautiful and still in her twenties, would spend her day schooling my father's polo ponies. She rode as well as any of the cavalry officers. At night, she would often dress as a man and either play the piano or stand with her Swanee whistle and play in the band of the officers' mess. My mother used to tell a very funny story about this time in Egypt. I don't know if it was absolutely true but it was obviously a regimental tale. Apparently one of my father's troopers was brought before a court martial charged with having had sex with an ostrich. When questioned, the trooper said, "Sir, if I had known there was going to be all this fuss, I would have married the fucking bird!"

Mummy remembered Egypt as being one of the best times of their lives. The war was over and everyone who survived believed there would never be another war again. They now wanted to live life to the full. Egypt was beautiful: there were parties and polo, the races and rides by moonlight in the desert. There were picnics on the Nile and visits to friends who lived in vast sandstone villas surrounded by palm trees. My brother Rory remembered being one of the first to be taken down into King Tutankhamen's fabulous tomb after it was discovered in 1922. Lord Carnarvon, being a great friend of my mother's (and another of her lovers) had arranged for her and her little son to go down to view his wonderful find.

I often wonder if Mummy was ever really in love with any man. She loved their company and her whole life was centred on pleasing men but she certainly never remained faithful to any of them. Five lovers committed suicide over her; I imagine they were not able to take the strain. They also chose the most spectacular deaths.

During her next marriage to Marmaduke "Duke" Furness, who was fabulously wealthy, we went skiing for three weeks every year; St Moritz or Kitzbühl were the favourite places. Furness never went skiing but would spend a few days with us, or just fly in before getting bored and going back to his duties as a coal, steel and shipping tycoon. On one of these occasions Mummy met Franz Meissner, an Austrian scientist. I thought he was quite dreadful but obviously he had something besides a horrible accent that Mummy found attractive.

Furness always had some detective keeping tabs on my mother's activities, even the few days he wasn't there with us. In London, because Furness's townhouse in Lees Place was not large enough to hide us children from his sight as he wished, Mummy used to rent a flat for our entourage and us. It was on Curzon Street in the same building where Rory lived. Franz Meissner was always turning up at our flat, waiting for Mummy's daily visits. They would then disappear for about an hour. I did not like him anyhow, and now I resented the time with her he took away from us. My mother refused to marry him, and broke off the relationship when Furness started getting suspicious, and so, on her birthday, Meissner blew himself up. I was delighted when I heard the news of his demise.

Another threw himself under Le Train Bleu, the luxury train that ran between Paris and the south of France, because he thought my mother would be on it with her new lover. In fact she wasn't; as was usual with her she was so late getting to the station that she missed it.

One besotted young man apparently threw himself overboard as the ship he and my mother were travelling on to Australia went through the heads of Sydney. Mummy had, by the end of the voyage, shown a marked preference for someone else. Leaving a pathetic suicide note of eternal devotion, he threw himself with magnificent abandon to the sharks, never to be seen again.

Certainly those who could bear the stress idolised her until their dying day. After she married Furness, he tried to put a stop to such intimacies: he could never bear other men having any contact with her. I don't know how much success he had.

Peter Coats, a garden designer, writer and man-about-town, once reminisced in a book of memoirs about my brother, that my mother, "the much-married Enid, Countess of Kenmare... had many close and infatuated friends, amongst them a cousin of mine, the rich and glamorous (and slightly second-rate) Jack Coats who, wife and child notwithstanding, left her his fortune, which Enid told me, and I am sure it was true, that she had refused."

My godfather, Captain Walter Wilson, had also been her lover. He took a vow that if she would not marry him then he would never wed again. He left his fortune to my mother on the understanding that it would eventually come to me. My mother, although very impressed by Uncle Walter's commitment, felt that this was not a fair solution. For the last 10 years of his life, he had been living with a very nice woman who had also become a friend of my mother. Unlike my mother however, this lady had very little money of her own. Therefore, Mummy felt that in all fairness, that she and not my mother should be the beneficiary of Walter Wilson's trust. Explaining the reasons to me I was then taken to Uncle Walter's lawyer to sign the necessary documents.

My mother seemed to spend her life at lawyers reversing the outcome of wills! When Mummy married Furness, she signed her entire Cameron fortune from her first marriage over to Rory, as well as giving him the Cameron family flat in Mayfair on Curzon Street. I don't know whether Furness resented the fact that he had married a very rich widow and wanted all the money to come from him instead, or whether my mother realised that Furness would be very jealous of her elder son and she would have to make sure he was looked after. Unfortunately I never asked my mother why she did this.

Her generosity and sense of fair play were truly remarkable. I think again that her faith in human nature and sense of honour had a great effect on men. It always amazed me that my mother, who was brought up by four brothers to become a brilliant shot and who insisted on competing and doing everything as well as her siblings, could so transform herself into the quintessence of femininity for her husbands and lovers. Looking back, I can imagine that one reason men were so passionate about my mother was because she did excel at all the masculine sports like bowls, tennis, bridge, angling and golfing as well as horse-riding and shooting. The contrast between that and her femininity must have been irresistible.

She also devoted herself totally to whichever man was in her life at the time, and her children. She was a chameleon, a foil to everyone around her. With every new lover she would become his ideal woman and his interests would become hers. As she was a perfectionist in anything she took up, maybe that explains her multitude of talents.

All through my life, Mummy showed extraordinary attention to detail. I would accompany her on what, for myself, were long and boring visits to the White House in London. At the time, it was the buying mecca of all things pertaining to the bedchamber. There, the purchase of silk sheets, embroidered silk and lace pillowslips, nightgowns, negligees, all in the most lovely of pastel shades, was a yearly occurrence. A great many of these would also accompany her on her travels.

I remember the nightly rituals of her lady's maids preparing the bedroom for my mother before she retired for the evening. All the bed linen had to be changed every day, and it would always be ironed before being put on the bed in case any wrinkle had appeared from the folding. The negligees and nightgowns were then laid out either to match or complement the sheets. Then, fetching a large bottle of Patou's Joy, which Mummy adored and which cost about three times as much as any other scent of the time, the maid would liberally spray them as well as the bed. Leaving the bedside light burning, she would open the door to the bathroom where she would run the hot water up to a certain level in the bath, and then she would add bath essence. Presumably Mummy, on returning, would only have to add more hot water. Miss Munday or Miss Lane would then open all the cupboards of nightgowns and negligees and once more, with the bottle of Joy, squirt a few drops of perfume into the air inside. When I asked why, I was told that Mummy might want to change during the night.

Looking back, I realise that during my entire life with Mummy and all her husbands and lovers, I never once saw her in bed with a man. I think she would have considered that vastly improper.

She was totally unconscious of the value of money and was the most completely generous being. Later, after Furness's death, she made her fourth marriage to the spendthrift Viscount Castlerosse, Earl of Kenmare, who had vast and magnificent estates at Killarney in Ireland but not the capital to maintain them in their glory. With Mummy's money, Castlerosse blossomed in confidence and the magnificent golf course that he had had laid out around the lakes of Killarney with the aid of the golfing writer Henry Longhurst came into its own. Castlerosse and Longhurst had brought in landscape gardeners with instructions to make it the most beautiful in the world. Mummy and Castlerosse, both being very keen golfers, would spend their time walking the course and planning the future together. He had met her years before, and had been determined to marry her then.

They had been married less than a year before he died of a heart attack. It was a family joke that my mother had murdered all her husbands. The writer Somerset Maugham, who became one of her great friends because they both loved bridge, dubbed her "Lady Killmore", a play on her title from her marriage to Castlerosse, Lady Kenmare. She thought it funny when he invented it, and often teased the press with it later on, but it pained her when others took up the joke and gossiped about it as if it were true.

Mummy, when she was discussing her many husbands much later on, also remarked to me that she had never allowed any of her lovers to break up their marriage for her. And she also told me that Furness was the husband she had loved the most. She said, "There was nothing in the world he was not prepared to give me. Of all the men that loved me, and some were as rich as Duke, he was the one who was prepared to lay the world at my feet."

I remember the conversation so clearly. She was sitting in her bedroom in Fiorentina, our villa on the Riviera in the south of France, with her painting table placed near the balcony while the light of the morning sun bathed her in its radiance. Surrounded by her parrots, she was bending over her tubes of paint, selecting the colours to place on her palette.

I thought, how typical of Mummy. What I remembered was Furness's obsessive jealousy of her, his dislike of us and his coldness towards his own children. But my mother, with her childlike faith in human nature and her fragility, had been sheltered by husbands, lovers, and children, and our love had cocooned her from the mundane. This quality of innocence transcended the beautiful facade and was the essence of her charm and the attribute that drew everyone to her. In return, she was our rock.

CHAPTER

2

It was at the resort of Biarritz in southwest France that I learned of my father's death, on December 8, 1931. I was six at the time. Mummy stood me on a table and, holding my hands, said, "My darling, I have some terrible news. Your father has died and I must leave you and go back to Paris." I remember knowing something dreadful had happened to Daddy, as my mother was hugging me and crying, but I wasn't exactly sure what the word "death" meant. Our father had suffered a cerebral haemorrhage at their apartment in Paris. Found by his valet, he died soon after the doctor's arrival.

I do not remember our father very well. His friends knew him as a fearless officer who loved the good life. My mother, the most incorrigible flirt, told me years later that she had managed to sleep with every officer in my father's regiment. Somebody at the time had dared her and that was something she could never resist. Whether she actually did manage to sleep with every officer one wouldn't know as she never let the truth interfere with a good story. What my father thought of all this, history does not relate. Certainly, as she was a very rich young woman and the soul of generosity, he was now able to indulge in strings of polo ponies, hunters and everything his heart desired, except possibly the love of my mother. I can remember once sitting with my father at Le Touquet station, on the north coast of France, waiting for my mother to arrive from Paris. Mummy regularly visited Le Touquet; it was part of the English aristocracy's social round and it also had a very good golf course. For most of her life, she was a passionate golfer. On this day, she missed the first train and arrived on the second. We must have waited for hours.

My father was a Brigadier-General and commander of the 1st Cavalry Brigade at Aldershot barracks in Hampshire when Caryll and I were born. Our early years were spent at another White House, but this time it was our home in Cove, Farnborough, near Aldershot, and I believe it belonged to the army. I was born in London – on June 30, 1925 – and Caryll was born at home 15 months later. I have dim memories that the White House had a wooden gate at the top of the landing to stop us falling down the stairs. I remember I developed a passion for eating all the heads of the matches and used to rush into the rooms to get them before anyone could stop me. Another delicacy was the pebbles on the front drive. I used to grovel in the dirt and scoop them up quickly, shoving them into my mouth by the handful before Nanny could get there. The first time Nanny Peasley discovered what I had been about, she promptly fainted on the nearest sofa. In her striped uniform, starched white aprons and ruffled cap, she looked like one of my stuffed straw dolls. My pebble-eating is obviously why, years later, I developed such an affinity with my baboons, and if there is such a thing as reincarnation, then I was quite obviously one in a previous existence. This is very baboon-like behaviour!

The other thing I remember of Aldershot is my pony. I learned to ride almost before I could walk properly. As I could only have been two or three at the time, I had a wicker basket-type saddle, which supported me back and front and had holes for my legs and tiny little stirrups. Every day I would go out with my father or my mother or both. There was also a little donkey that I used to ride as well as the pony and they would be led off either Daddy's or Mummy's hunter or polo pony.

As a young lieutenant, my father had led cavalry charges during the Boer War, served in India and with the cavalry on the Belgium front during World War I. He had been badly wounded on several occasions. Towards the end of that war, because he spoke fluent French, I am told he was made liaison officer to Ferdinand Foch, the Marshall of France who became commander of Allied forces for the closing months of the campaign. Certainly, one of the few things I remember about my father is the fact that he always wore the wreathed star of the Legion of Honour in the lapel of his blazer and dress uniform. Daddy was a champion polo player and a steeplechase rider; I still have some of his cups, and a large silver statue of a cavalry officer on his charger. It was presented to him by the regiment, the 9th Lancers, upon his marriage to my mother.

At Le Touquet, I remember my father taking me to what must have been some type of gymkhana which had a steeplechase course. I can still see the grass and the brush jumps. I was probably four or five at the time. He put me on one of his horses and tried to adjust the stirrups to fit my small legs. Finally he put my feet into the leathers, telling me to "hold the reins [which had been knotted short] and grip the martingale, and just remember, don't do a thing except sit tight and grip with your knees. Don't let go of the martingale and my horse will do the rest."

He gave the horse a slap on the quarters and I was sent on my way. I can recall it all so clearly, his instructions, the intense excitement of going over the jumps: it felt like riding a magic broomstick. The jumps looked huge to a tiny child but I can still feel the excitement of sailing through the air. It was the first time I felt like a fairy princess. I was given a prize and my father was so proud of me. I remember him saying, "You would have been a great addition to my regiment." From that day on nobody could keep me off a horse. It became a passion that has lasted me most of my life.

Daddy, apart from always taking me riding, taught me to drive. I would sit on his lap and he'd let me steer the car. One day I had to go to the lavatory, I was desperate. Although he wasn't in uniform at the time, he was intensely embarrassed at having to stop the car and take my pants down as he led me to a ditch on the side of the road. He was obviously not used to the more intimate details of childcare and now being a Brigadier-General was horrified at the thought that someone might come along and see him trying to cope with a piddling child.

Of this period I also remember all the ballet classes I attended, wearing little tutus and ballet slippers. Sometimes Daddy would come and pick up Nanny and myself, or sometimes Mummy, but my disappointment used to be when the driver came. At this time I don't remember much about Caryll, except him burning my wax dolls on a bonfire to which I responded by picking up his toy train and hitting him over the head. He had to be rushed off to the doctor to have stitches while Nanny gave me a severe smacking. I felt he should have been smacked as well for burning my dolls!

Le Touquet was very fashionable at this time because the Prince of Wales, later Edward VIII before he abdicated, was also a keen golfer and liked to play there. The British high society set would follow him every summer, renting large houses for the season and there would be a scrabble for who could rent the best and biggest house. Le Touquet was just across the Channel, the food was better than England's and there was a casino. It became the Monte Carlo of the north. We used to rent too, but later on my mother built a large villa in the forest by the sand dunes overlooking the 18th tee. It was named The Berries and I was to spend happy summers there with my family.

My mother had a large Buick painted in black and white squares. I can still see her, wearing those small cloche hats, her Chanel suits with short pleated skirts and button shoes, showing lots of leg as she placed herself behind the wheel. Not many women drove in those days, so Mama was rather proud of her achievement. The children, the nannies and our Alsatian dogs would scramble into the car and we would set off for picnics, Mummy's favourite pastime. Caryll and I used to loathe them as whenever she had them on the beach, the wind would blow or the dogs would make sure that the food would be filled with sand as they charged around with gay abandon after the balls being thrown for them. "Not another sandy sandwich day," we used to grumble to ourselves as the six Alsatians covered Caryll and myself in clouds of grit. They would invariably skid to a stop just where we were sitting, trying to get the food down our throats. The adults, being so much taller, didn't have the same problem so we could never complain.

What we did enjoy was being taken to La Grenouille (The Frog), a famous restaurant at that time. It had large china frogs, decorating the steps up to it, hence, I suppose, its name. The food meant nothing to us, but what we did enjoy was the terrible effect frogs and toads had on Granny Lindeman on her visits to us. Before going to the restaurant, Mummy used to call up and ask them to cover all the frogs in linen bags before we arrived. One day Rory managed to uncover a large green one and much to our delight, Granny, giving a scream, promptly fainted.

The other thing we enjoyed on the way there was seeing all the tuberculosis patients being taken out for walks on long wheeled stretchers. Lying recumbent and covered in a light sheet, they would be taken for their daily constitutional. We overheard our nannies discussing the fact that most of them were dying, unless of course they were lucky enough to be saved by the healthy sea air of Pas-de-Calais. Rather vague as to what was about to happen to them but knowing it was unpleasant, we used to watch with ghoulish delight as the nurses wheeled them around. In my imagination, I saw wicked witches coming to drag them down to hell as they kicked and screamed and white sheets flew.

Caryll and I shared a twin pram and every afternoon our nanny would walk us and all the Alsatians. The hood of the pram was covered in white gauze net so that the heat of the sun would not spoil our rest. One day, when our grandmother was to push the pram, Rory bundled us into the bushes and put one of the Alsatians into the pram in our place. Telling the dog to lie down, he pulled the net into place, and then accompanied granny while she walked what she thought were her grandchildren. Unfortunately for Rory, after about 10 minutes the Alsatian had had enough of being pushed around. It chose to leap out, sending the netting flying and my grandmother into hysterics. A search party was sent out to find the missing babies.

When Rory turned 17 he was given the latest Ford convertible with a dickey seat at the back. If we were very good, we used to be tied to the open seat to accompany him into the town of Le Touquet. Great excitement!

Another incident that made a big impression was Rory hiding our grandmother's false teeth. In those days dentists were not very sophisticated, so any problems were solved by teeth coming out and false ones being fitted. The false plates were left overnight in a glass of water in the bathroom and it was a common sight of my childhood.

Even our nannies and staff kept their teeth in a tumbler and there were a lot of white and perfect smiles from the elderly. Granny was very proud of her looks; I remember my mother was always teasing her. She was very keen on hats with feathers and veils and would spend her time at the modiste having them specially fitted.

Rory came to our nursery and, showing us granny's teeth, announced he was going to hide them in the garden. There was uproar. The servants searched everywhere. One even had to open all the jaws of the Alsatians to see if they were the culprits. Finally, one of the gardeners found them under a bush. The dogs remained the chief suspects as the "teeth thieves". Rory, rushed up to join us with great glee, howling with laughter.

Every time we were naughty, which was fairly frequently, our nannies would threaten us with the "wicked witches". If we were good, we were told "the angels will bless you". Our nannies brought us up on fairy tales and read from books, which we loved, but they could not tell us the stories that Mummy could.

When my father died, I was driven with my nanny and entourage back to Le Touquet by the chauffeur. I kept crying for Mummy, for in my mind I thought she might now also be "dead", whatever that was, with Daddy. The nurse kept assuring me that he was in heaven. Not that that meant much. I did realise, though, that it was better to be in heaven than dead. But I was terrified that Mummy had gone with him to wherever heaven was.

CHAPTER

3

My mother could never resist rushing to the assistance and rescue of any bird or animal that was wounded or in pain. In fact, in my youth it used to be a continual source of embarrassment. She once came across a crow with a broken wing when we were staying with friends in the south of England. To her delight, my mother then found a large compost heap in the garden and with the help of a charming gardener, raked through the muck-heap looking for worms to feed the ailing bird while it recovered. I made a rapid exit as I saw Mama in her blue and white checked Chanel suit, with her pearls and diamond rings, happily digging through the manure with her bare hands. That crow became the bane of my life for years and my mother's friends loathed it.

When she had to go into the private and luxurious London Clinic on Harley Street for an operation, she somehow managed to persuade her surgeon to let her have both the crow and her pet hyrax, Tikki, with her. A hyrax is like a very large dark brown guinea pig but furrier and my mother used to carry hers around on her shoulder. The crow had to be hastily removed from the hospital after attacking the nurses who were trying to assist my mother. The well-behaved hyrax was allowed to remain. Mummy even had a cradle made that she could put over her feet in bed and there Tikki would sleep. I had to come and make visits through the day to feed him with fresh rose petals and shoots and to take him to the loo. She had trained the horrid little beast to make his doo-doos in the toilet bowl. Mummy used to spend hours in toilets around the world making throaty little noises. That was Tikki's signal and he always obliged, his little feet clinging to the toilet seat and an expression of utmost concentration on his face. He would then be wiped off, given a little spray of Joy and a great many kisses and told what a clever boy he was.

My mother always insisted that he understood everything that was said to him. She had him for so many years that in his old age he had tusks that descended to his bottom jaw which made him more hideous than ever. Therefore he had to be constantly told that he was beautiful, and in my mother's besotted eyes he was. There were other hyraxes after Tikki but as they were called Tikki too, it was as if it was always the same one.

During my younger brother Caryll's school holidays, and whenever Mummy was at home with us in the country, we would always spend the mornings with her. Unless Mummy had been out riding, she would have breakfast in bed at nine o'clock and we used to wait outside the door until the tray went in. By this time, the maid had opened the curtains and Mummy was awake and sitting up in bed. Her animals would have been brought in and taken up their various positions; the dogs, a cheetah she had rescued on safari in Kenya when it was a baby, foxes, the hyrax, a mongoose, parrots, and often there would be a budgie on her other shoulder. Although we had all eaten, we and the various members of the menagerie would then proceed to help her with her breakfast and it was a time of laughter, of hugs and stories. Often Caryll and I would dress up and do plays for her or get her to help with our homework. More often, we would just pretend to be horses and gallop around the room, neighing loudly and leaping over the precious pieces of furniture that we had arranged as a steeplechase course. All this activity was accompanied by the sound of barking dogs and screaming parrots – or our shrieks as we escaped one of the foxes sallying forth from under the bed to nip our heels as we charged by.

Mummy would go off to bathe and dress. She would emerge from the dressing room in one of her beautiful lace slips to sit before her dressing table and put on her false eyelashes for the next hour. They would go on one by one, and then be trimmed to just a bit longer than her own. The effect was very dramatic on her enormous green eyes. Then came her make-up and, last of all, the maid would dress her hair. When she was ready, she would spray herself with scent, and often us and the dogs and animals as well. Another extraordinary facet of her character was that she was devoid of vanity. Having spent so long in the morning surrounded by her maids and toiletries to arrange her appearance, she would then forget about it.

Even as children, there never seemed an age difference between us and her. She was our best friend, could tell us wonderful stories that she made up on the spot and we all adored her. All my childhood, I would take her photograph to bed with me instead of a teddy bear and lie cuddled up to my picture. I once read somewhere that my mother had started life as a chorus girl and there is also a rumour that she had once been an actress. I am sure she would have loved to have been one but she never was. The great studio boss, Louis B. Mayer, did talk her into having a screen test but she was married to the jealous Furness by then and there was no way in the world he would ever have allowed her to remain in Hollywood.

One of the rooms I loved best at Furness's country house in Leicestershire, Burrough Court, was the ballroom. Mummy also used it as a studio for her painting. I spent many hours there, either practising dancing myself, playing with my dogs or watching her paint. When her budgie Joey wasn't flying about, he would land and perch on her shoulder and she was always kissing him on the beak. Meanwhile, the cheetah spent most of its time asleep at her feet. When I was at our house in Mayfair with Mummy, I used to be sent out with the chauffeur, her lady's maid and my governess, to walk the cheetah in Hyde Park, which was just around the corner. Of course, the animal used to cause a sensation and I found it horribly embarrassing. I swore when I grew up that I would never ever have a wild animal. How little did I know. Even as I write I have a baboon lying in my lap.

In those early days, most parents distanced themselves from their children. Children were brought up to be seldom seen and certainly not heard, very unlike the unbearably spoilt children of today. Like all children in those pre-war days, we were very strictly brought up, but on the other hand we were given anything we wanted. I now strongly believe that strict discipline harms no-one as long as they also get that great maternal love. Certainly our mother was unstinting with it and with understanding and we all knew it. The staff or anyone else were also forbidden to ever say to Caryll or myself that we couldn't do something or that it was dangerous. As a result, there were no boundaries and we grew up fearless.

My mother also instilled in us an intense love of family. She was passionate about her own family and various Lindemans from Australia were always coming to stay. From them she had inherited her green eyes and the auburn hair which later turned silver after a serious bout of pneumonia. I gathered through the servants' hall, where I heard all the gossip, that Furness was not too keen on having the Lindemans too often and tried to discourage this influx of relatives. Until I was in my thirties and went to live in Kenya, I never wanted to leave my mother or my family either. Indeed, both of my husbands had to learn to join the family, and to live with my mother and elder brother Rory and join in their adventures. After the last of my mother's husbands died, and as she grew older, she and Rory became inseparable. My half-brother was extraordinarily handsome, tall and of good physique. I remember he was very proud of his legs and it's true that they could easily have belonged to a sculpture of a Greek god. He had an enormous influence on Mummy even when he was still a very young man. They travelled the world together and he would boss her terribly. Until I settled in Kenya I was the spectator to their fantastical life and under their tutelage I got used to seeing anything and everything. It was only Caryll, who went to boarding school and then into the Grenadier Guards, who seemed to grow up outside Mummy's sphere.

She loved people and had an enormous number of friends. At Burrough Court, she was always entertaining. I think that is why Furness used to take her away to Kenya on safari every year for months at a time, so as to have her to himself. My mother had also kept on my father's staff from his old regiment. She used to get very distressed if she saw an ex-serviceman begging on the street and displaying his medals or a couple of them sitting on the pavement beside their pathetic little watercolours in the hope of making a sale. Mummy would get the chauffeur to stop and to my great embarrassment if I was with her, would end up either offering the beggar a job or giving him money. While Mummy was out of the car, the chauffeur would say very disapprovingly, "Her ladyship is much too good, they won't appreciate it. She is wasting her time. They will only go and spend it on drink."

Mummy would sometimes take me on visits, to the suburbs, again much to the chauffeur's disapproval – they were all the most tremendous snobs – and she would visit some of the ex-servicemen for whom she'd found homes. Even my nannies used to disapprove strongly of these visits.

Later in life, my mother was criticised for her lack of discrimination in her friends. Someone once said of our beautiful home in the south of France, Fiorentina, that you never knew if you were sitting next to a hobo off the streets or a Duke, and implied that this was because of my mother's lack of breeding and Australian background. In those days if you were Australian, it was taken to obviously mean you had a convict background and knew no better! Mummy must have heard the gossip that she was the daughter of a convict. After that she never let any conversation about her Australian background go by without finding convicts coming out all over the family tree. None of which was true of course.

She was a terrific gambler and loved the races and the casinos. She carried a large handbag stuffed with notes and she often won. Maybe she had to win sometimes given how much money she lost. She used to like collecting her race winnings in cash. When she lost at the casino, she wouldn't say anything but breakfast the next day would be a very silent affair. If she won though, she was very generous. She was extraordinarily fond of money but it never really meant anything to her except that it allowed her to do whatever she wanted to do and to indulge the people she wanted to indulge. She was very casual about such things, and although she had wonderful jewels she kept her ropes of pearls in Kleenex boxes. Probably because they were the closest thing to hand.

My brother Caryll remembers that after World War II, when you were hardly allowed to take £2 out of England, Mummy was staying at the George V in Paris at the same time as the foreign secretary Ernie Bevin, who was there with his delegation and his detectives for a big post-war meeting. As my mother walked across the foyer of the hotel, rummaging in her big bag, £10 notes kept spilling to the floor behind her under the very eyes of these men who couldn't believe what they were seeing. But Mummy was so charming she seemed to be able to get away with anything. If she ever had to talk her bank managers or trustees into agreeing with one of her schemes that involved spending money, she would get them on the phone and entice and wheedle and convince… and then she'd come off the phone and wink and say, "Piece of cake."

As for me, I grew up being the quiet one in the background, dreaming away while all this was going on around me. Much later on, a former boyfriend of mine wrote in his memoirs that I had told him I had felt miserable as a small child sitting beside my glamorous mother with all her entourage about her and that I had trembled with shyness because of all the people I had to meet. Perhaps that is true but I also always felt that being with her was like being in the bright light. I particularly remember one evening at Burrough Court when I was little and Mummy and Furness were giving a ball. She came into my room dressed in a very tight-fitting satin dress, again by Molyneux, with a train. It was in her favourite colour of pale violet-blue. The dress had a rounded neckline; the low *décolleté* edged with perfect bunches of large embroidered flower buds. Mummy was very tall and slim and her high-heeled satin slippers matched the dress and were decorated with large diamond buckles. My bedroom was dark. When she switched on the lights it seemed to me that all the lights just shone on her. She was late and I didn't want her to leave me.

She was the fairy queen whose wand would wave and transform my world. Her beauty dazzled me. Every evening she would come to the nursery as I was being put to bed so that she could kiss me goodnight and read me a story before going downstairs. Even when there were no guests, she would wear her beautiful evening dresses. I can still see those gowns, the glittering jewels and in winter the long evening capes lined with fur that swirled around her. I would go to sleep and she would fill my dreams.

CHAPTER

4

I do not remember how Duke Furness came into our lives. I don't think we even met him until after Mummy had married him on August 3, 1933. At the time he was reputed to be one of the world's richest men. His father, a shipbuilder, had left a good business behind and an estate worth around £113 million in today's money. He had been knighted and then made a baron in 1910. Duke was also successful at business. He eventually sold out of the Furness-Withy shipping company but kept his interests in various coal, steel and banking companies and also advised the American shipbuilding industry. For the latter service, he was created Viscount Furness in 1918.

My first clear memory of Furness is at Burrough Court. We had been installed in an enormous wing of his Victorian mansion, which was near Melton Mowbray. We arrived from London with our governess, Miss Unger, our nannies and Hannah, a young under-housemaid whom we adored and who was to remain as part of the family until long after the war.

I realised there was a change in our circumstances when Mummy arrived in the nursery at Burrough Court and, kneeling on the floor, took our hands saying something to the effect that we now had a new father. "Darlings," she said, "I do not know what you are going to call him, but I suggest that when I take you to meet him you call him Daddy and do not forget to kiss him on the cheek and do a little curtsey."

I was always made to curtsey to Mummy's friends, and Caryll had to do a little bow. I somehow knew that as far as she was concerned, this was a very important occasion. Mummy and nanny ushered us into the library where Furness was sitting with a drink in one hand and some papers in the other, smoking a cigar. He was a dapper little man, impeccably dressed and with reddish sandy hair that had been brilliantined flat. There wouldn't have been a single strand out of place. In all the time I knew him, I never saw him less than immaculate. My brother Caryll remembers him as being peppery, but to me he was always too cold, too icy to be described like that.

I went and did my curtsey and kissed him as I had been instructed but there was no warmth from him in return. When I addressed him as Daddy, he said, "I am not your father, and do not address me as such." I realised that he did not like me. For the entire time of Mummy's marriage, he was never actively nasty but he kept us at a distance and preferred us to be out of his view.

Viscount Furness, or Marmaduke, was commonly known as Duke and he met my mother while on a visit to Le Touquet. He told friends that from the moment he saw her walk into the casino there he lost all concentration, did not care what cards he held and the result cost him a fortune. "I have seen many beautiful women, but from the moment Enid entered the room my heart stopped," he always said afterwards. Furness, finally losing all interest in gambling that night, left the tables and went to find someone who could arrange an introduction. Mummy told me that from then on he pursued her relentlessly. Flowers and jewellery would arrive daily, only to be sent back. Planes, yachts, and chauffeur-driven Rolls-Royces were put at her disposal. Finally, he found out from Thomas Cook that she was booked on the deluxe train, the Golden Arrow, from Paris back to England. He cancelled her ticket and sent his plane to Le Touquet to pick her up, his Rolls and chauffeur met her at the airport in London and on arriving at her flat in Chelsea she was handed a letter from him. Enclosed was a deed of sale. He had not only bought her the flat she was living in, but the whole building as well.

As she said, at that stage she had never even been to bed with him. That evening, he took her to the Savoy for dinner and their love affair started. From then on, my mother could have virtually anything she wanted. Furness had owned an ocean-going yacht, the Emerald, which he later sold to buy an even bigger yacht, the Sapphire. The only person who had a bigger one than that was the Duke of Westminster, who had had a destroyer converted. Furness used his steam yachts to go around the world. His first wife Daisy had died in 1921 during one of these voyages. There was always a doctor on board and a fully equipped hospital but at the time of her death they were somewhere far out from shore. Daisy was buried at sea, which caused quite a scandal at the time; the *on dit* was that the burial had been unseemingly quick because Furness had really given her an overdose.

I first heard this from the British journalist Godfrey Winn, at the time a famous columnist. I can still hear him addressing the dinner table at large, saying with great glee, "Of course, if it had ever come to trial and he had been found guilty, he would have to have been hanged with a silken cord, being a peer of the realm." I really don't remember for what reason I was in the dining room at Burrough Court. I often used to come down when coffee was being served and stand by my mother's chair. But she was not at the table during this conversation, so presumably one of the guests must have asked for me. Being a child with a vivid imagination I had nightmares about silken cords and dangling bodies for months afterwards.

Years later, I asked my mother. She said, "Darling, don't be ridiculous. He might have been a dreadful stepfather and an even worse father, but he was a man of honour and anyhow, it was impossible to keep a dead body without the proper facilities. It would have been days before the ship could get to land. Of course he had to bury her at sea. People love to talk but there was nothing sinister in that and there was always a doctor on board."

Apart from the yachts, Furness later acquired a private plane and a personal pilot, Tom Campbell Black. When Caryll was home from school, Tom used to allow him to sit on his lap and fly the plane, although not of course when Furness was aboard. Caryll became an absolute flying addict. At the age of seven, he had been sent off to Hawtrey's, the prep school for Eton, and there were always fountains of tears when he had to go back at the end of the school holidays. Even I felt sorry for him, that pale little face, sick with the trauma of departing from Mummy – and his bloody aeroplanes.

Furness's first plane was a single-engined Puss Moth. He had met Tom in Kenya when he was the pilot who used to fly all the supplies in to Furness's safari camps. On his advice, Furness rapidly bought a De Havilland Dragon, then a De Havilland Dragon Rapide in which he and Mummy often flew to Baden Baden for the racing and the casino. They would be met by German Nazis in full uniform; they were dead keen for English people like Furness to visit Germany at the time. Finally, Furness acquired the ultimate in flying machines available in those days, the Lockheed 12 Electra. He always had to have the best and the latest as it came off the assembly lines. The 12E was a high-powered, scaled-down version of the twin-engined 10 Electra in which the American woman pilot Amelia Earheart made her last fatal flight, a bid to circle the globe which ended in the Pacific. I believe it was also an Electra, the model 14, that took the Prime Minister, Neville Chamberlain, for his historic flight to meet Adolf Hitler in Munich in late 1938 to negotiate Germany's annexation of Czechoslovakia. And it was from the steps of this plane that Chamberlain, on his return to Britain, triumphantly waved his piece of paper, and later declared infamously, "I believe it is peace for our time… Go home and get a nice quiet sleep."

Furness had an obsession with neatness. Even his shoes had to have new laces every day. There was a special room for all the shoes and riding boots, next to the butler's pantry. A boot boy spent his whole day polishing and cleaning them but the final shine was left to one of the valets. With a green apron over his uniform, he would apply the finishing touches. It was a daily ritual that I used to watch with amazement. Even new shoelaces were ironed before being taken up to "His Lordship".

Furness was one of the richest men in the world at the time and he certainly lived like one. We children became used to a style of living that was very different from that of most children of our age. Apart from the yacht, plane and his private train carriages, and an utterly distinctive Rolls Royce, which had room for two chauffeurs, solid silver door knobs, the Furness crest on the doors and a very long silver bonnet with a maroon body, Furness entertained a lavish lifestyle. He had two valets, Mummy had four lady's maids, and there were six cooks in the enormous kitchens, plus butlers, footmen, masseurs, boot boys and maids by the score.

The livery of the Furness footmen was plum knee breeches with yellow stockings for eveningwear and long plum-coloured trousers for daywear. They also wore long plum tailored cutaway jackets with yellow waistcoats. At dinner parties, footmen in the livery would stand behind each chair; a butler and two footmen would escort in every dish. The dining room had lovely paintings by George Stubbs and John Frederick Herring and overlooked a large topiary garden, its box hedges cut into designs of peacocks, pyramids and columns with ball tops. There were innumerable other gardens, all divided up by large clipped hedges; water gardens, rose gardens, vegetable gardens, herb gardens and so on.

Burrough Court itself was a very large house covered in ivy creeper, with two large courtyards. The front entrance in one of the courtyards had columns over the front door at which stood a butler flanked by two footmen to greet his lordship or any new arrivals. The gate lodge would notify them so they had time to be in place when the car drove up.

The mile-long avenue leading to the house, the stable yard, and the pathways in the gardens were of small white pebbles and had to be raked twice a day. Six gardeners were employed to keep them pristine; any staining and the pebbles were immediately replaced. When Furness rode or drove out, he wanted no sign of hoof prints or tyre tracks to mar the road's surface.

We children were expected to keep out of the way, and with such a huge house that wasn't difficult. One wing was kept for myself and Caryll. We had our own staff and our own staircase. There was a large nursery, rooms for Miss Unger who looked after us and also for our various other governesses, Nanny Peasley, and the nursery maid. There were also several empty rooms for any friends who came to stay. Our staircase led into the staff quarters next to which we had our own dining room. We had very little contact with the rest of the house. Furness himself we hardly ever saw. At the beginning, Mummy asked us to go and say goodnight to him in the evenings before we went to bed but the dreadful experience of having to kiss goodnight to that coldly proffered cheek soon came to an end.

Rory, being so much older, seldom came to Burrough Court. He was *persona non grata* with Furness. When he did come during the holidays he had to stay in our section of the house. He was 14 years older than I was and was studying architecture in Germany. He would have been about 20 when Mummy married Furness. Even in his teens, Rory had a great influence on Mummy. He was the one who told her that he did not see any reason for me to go to school and it was his suggestion that I be educated at home. Rory laid out the studies in which he wanted me to become proficient. A lot of ancient history and not much arithmetic. From the age of 10 I had two governesses and a tutor. Miss Unger, who was German-Swiss, was in charge of us and also of my French lessons.

Miss Unger, who was to remain with us until the war, was a strange woman. A lady who had fallen on hard times, she was a better-looking replica of Thelma Furness, Duke's second wife who had had an affair with the Prince of Wales, Edward, before the future king took up with Wallis Simpson. Miss Unger even did her black hair the same way, parted in the middle with a bun at the back. Miss Unger, Thelma Furness and Mrs Simpson were indeed all look-alikes and that was another reason why Furness could not bear to see any of us. Miss Unger once escorted me down to pay a visit to my mother and her friends at teatime. I had duly made my curtsey to the guests and was sitting in Mummy's lap. Meanwhile, Miss Unger in departing had run into Furness who arrived on the teatime scene in a fury. "Enid, get rid of that fucking bitch. She looks just like that other fucking bitch. I finally managed to get rid of that bloody cow, now get rid of this one." His choice of language was always exceptional. In all the years she was with us Miss Unger was never seen in the front of the house again. Furness was paranoid about us and Miss Unger, and even, as it later turned out, his own children.

I spent my early childhood alternately adoring my little brother

Caryll and hating him because of Miss Unger. He was so beautiful with his blond hair and bright blue eyes that everybody made a fuss of him. That made me immensely proud to be his sister but it also had its drawbacks. Miss Unger loved him and disapproved of me. Caryll and I were dressed like twins, brown and white tweed coats and hats in winter and in summer, the same coloured shirts. I would wear a skirt and he would wear shorts but of the same colour. When we were in public places, I was made to walk behind. In London, when Miss Unger was in a bad mood, I dreaded crossing streets, as she could not leave me to negotiate the traffic on my own. On joining them for the safe passage, she would grab my arm and pinch it. What a relief when once more I could fall back so that she could pretend I was not with them. In spite of Miss Unger's unpleasantness, I felt sorry for her. Unconsciously I must have realised she was a very lonely woman, she had no friends and she did not fraternise with the staff.

I don't think she actually disliked me but she was a great disciplinarian and I think I was a wilful child. I can only be intensely grateful now for the fact that she was so strict with me. Without her I would have become the most ghastly spoilt brat. Instead, through the discipline she meted out, I became a model of good behaviour. I was much too frightened not to be. Any major misdemeanour and I was lashed around the legs with a horsewhip. Any rudeness on my part and she would pull my hair and slap my face or pinch my nose. If I ever chatted away to anyone and tried to take over the conversation when she was present she would say, "Be quiet, nobody is interested in what you have to say." Which of course gave me a great complex, not only at the time but also later on in life.

When Caryll and I were playing games and we did anything wrong, I was the one that got punished. Then I would slyly try and get back at him by slamming his fingers in the door when nobody was looking. One day Miss Unger caught me and I realised that something terrible was going to happen. I was sent to my room. Mummy was away and in desperation I got down on my knees and, weeping, I prayed to my father and to God to help me. There were double doors between Miss Unger's room and mine and while still on my knees I heard Miss Unger opening her door. Then she came to a halt. I waited terrified, expecting my door to open any moment. Then to my amazement, I heard her turn away. I wasn't punished and that incident was not mentioned. From then on, I have always used my father as an intermediary in my prayers.

I had another experience with her that I won't forget. I had two crooked front teeth and the dentist had fitted me with a plate with a wire in front and two hooks around my back teeth. I was always sucking it up and down as it was a bit loose. One day having breakfast, I half swallowed it; Nanny went to get Miss Unger because when she had tried to extricate it, it hurt. Miss Unger had a look and pulled hard whereupon I screamed with pain. I got my face slapped and told not to be such a cry-baby. She then tied the front section of the plate to the dining room door and slammed it. Of course the plate came out but I poured blood as well. She told me to keep my head down and gave me a towel, which was soon soaked. How I did not bleed to death I don't know. Years later when I went to a doctor in Australia for all my sore throats, he remarked that part of one of my tonsils had been torn out. My plate had obviously got hooked around it.

Looking back, I am sure Miss Unger must have had cancer. During the time she was with us, she had to go back to Germany for three breast operations. The last time, they removed her breast entirely, which upset her greatly. Miss Unger, being very psychic, always knew when she was about to have another operation. She used to sit in front of the fire staring at the flames and she would pick at a small mole on her chin. She told me she could see the operating theatre in the embers. She also used to read cards and teacups very well.

Miss Unger earned £10 a month, which were good wages in those days. She also had the use of the children's car and a chauffeur, as she could not drive. Still, she used to worry about the cost of the operations. I used to get very good pocket money and lots of £5 notes were handed to me for birthdays and Christmas, so I was extremely well off. As I had every conceivable thing that money could buy, I saved a lot of my pocket money and hid it in her bag so I could help towards her expenses. In a strange way, I was quite fond of her. Although I was a child, I was the only person she had to talk to and she used to tell me her dreams and ambitions. Sitting in front of the fire, she would treat me as if I were her greatest friend and confidante. Whether she ever suspected that I used to put the notes into her bag

I don't know, but she would act very surprised when she found them there and mention that the good angels were looking after her, that she had forgotten she had so much.

Caryll and I used to charge around playing horsey, followed by my dogs. It was my favourite game. I called myself Best and he was Second Besty, and I used to give him hell when I would turn round and find him with his little arms outstretched pretending to be an aeroplane instead of a horse. I even used to walk like a horse when nobody was looking.

At Burrough Court there was an enormous Tudor stable yard, all black and white gables. Built in a square with cobblestones, the entrance was through an archway with a large clock tower. There must have been 100 loose boxes. On the right hand was the magnificent tack room and up the middle of it were glass display cabinets with silver cups and trophies. Along the side were the saddles and bridles on their racks, each one looking as if it were new and never used. The blankets and sheets lay on their shelves, just below the bridles, and were washed and ironed after every use so that no stain would blemish their pristine beauty. To ensure that there were no marks, each horse had four of everything, all in the Furness colours of plum and gold. As with all Furness's belongings, nothing was left to chance; all was kept in the most immaculate condition. Not a speck of dust, everything polished to a high shine. The tack room smelled of saddle soap and lavender wood polish. One hardly dare tread on the floor in case one left a mark on its gleaming surface. Neatness was carried to such extremes that the bedding in the stable boxes had to be plaited at the entrance to the stable doors so that no stray bits of straw would hang untidily. Then an area in front of the doors was freshly painted with white chalk each day, before the evening inspection tour began.

Next door to the tack room was the smithy and large furnace. I used to watch fascinated as the blacksmith hammered away at the shoes. Holding them on long tongs, he would inspect their fiery red surface, hammer away some more, sparks flying, then finally the shoe would be plunged in a bucket of cold water. Still smoking, it would be fitted on to the hoof of the patiently waiting horse. Never satisfied, the smithy would repeat this procedure until he considered the shoe a perfect fit.

The blacksmith had been in my father's regiment and he had a very battered book about the regiment that he proudly used to show me. There was a photograph of my father and he would tell me of his heroic deeds. My mother had also kept Sergeant-Major Higgins, who was now my full-time riding instructor.

Apart from the main house and the stable yard, there were various cottages housing the senior members of the staff. The lands stretched as far as the eye could see, set in lovely rolling countryside, with fields surrounded by hawthorn hedges, spinney and coppices. Furness had several farms, including a dairy farm and a cattle farm. He liked seeing cattle on the rich pastureland – Aberdeen Angus and Scottish longhorns. I think he used to enjoy looking out of the windows to see their yellow shaggy coats and long horns emerging from the early morning mists. The dairy farm consisted of jerseys, all with names and excessively tame. I used to love putting my arms round their necks and burying my nose in their soft, sweet-smelling coats. The head dairyman used to allow me on occasion to help with the grooming and washing of their tails. It was done every morning at 6am so they would be in immaculate condition in case his lordship rode up during his daily rounds of the farm.

There was another farm and stable block for the percherons, the strong draught horses originally from France. Furness loved these huge grey horses and he won many prizes at the shows. Again, all their equipment and the horses themselves, with their shining silver manes and tails and their feet beautifully polished, looked as if they were about to leave for the show ring, not as if they were to work in the fields.

There were also enormous kennels for the various types of dogs: Rhodesian ridgebacks, beagles, hounds, and 50 poodles that belonged to my mother. Each section had its own kennel boys and maids. Occasionally, I would go to the shows and watch them perform for the judges.

Furness and my mother would go out riding most mornings, surrounded by a pack of dogs. They were always accompanied by the head stud groom and various outriders. A tour of the farm would take place. Until he started out, nobody knew which section of the farm he would be visiting that morning. I can still see him in beautifully tailored, tight-fitting jodhpurs, immaculate shining boots, a tweed jacket and waistcoat and tweed hat. My mother would ride sidesaddle, either in navy blue or black, with a felt hat to match. Of course, when she went out hunting she wore a top hat and veils.

Furness loved cobs and the stable yard consisted mostly of cobs of various colours. I couldn't bear it when one of his agents found him a new one, as on arrival it would have its tail docked. Mummy's hacks of course were left with their tails as were the hunters and all my ponies.

It was, apart from the occasional punishments from Miss Unger, a fabulous life for a child who loved animals. I had a gym instructor who would come twice a week and give me a workout in the gymnasium and we had a permanent German masseur. I would also be driven into Leicester for ballet lessons twice a week. My daily lessons had to fit in around my riding activities. Sometimes, I would be ready for lessons at 6.30 in the morning and they might last for the two hours before breakfast. At other times, they would go into the late afternoon. Apart from Miss Unger, there was another governess, Miss Carruthers, and various nannies. I also had a German tutor but I couldn't stand him, so I loathed learning German. I had an enormous nursery where I did all my lessons and it was filled with toys.

When breakfast was finished I would rush to the stable yard and spend the rest of the morning riding out with Higgins, who was never without a bowler hat. There was an indoor and an outdoor arena. Higgins's idea of schooling was cavalry-style. Before saddling up, he would make me do a round of jumps without saddle or bridle and with my arms crossed. "Grip with your knees and lean into your horse. Learn to feel him," he would say. It was a daily litany. "Feel your horse. Feel your horse." Gradually one did. Through one's legs and body, one could read almost every thought and so become an extension of the horse. I could never resist in later years climbing onto any horse that was supposed to be unrideable. I never found one that was. Not in Ireland, in Texas nor Australia. I found that as soon as I could feel them, I could ride them. The feeling was euphoric, and it was thanks to Sgt Higgins and his cavalry training that I gained such a wonderful understanding of horses. It has remained with me all my life and, although I do not ride any longer, it was that knowledge that enabled me in later years to take over the training of my mother's racehorses in South Africa and become so amazingly successful. I am also sure this training with horses in my youth taught me how to become part of my wild animals later on. I can feel their emotions and read their thoughts to such a degree that when I eventually shared my life with my lioness Tana, I did not even have to be in the same room to know what she was feeling and thinking.

My friends and companions at Burrough Court were the stable boys and the staff. There were dozens of them, so I was never lonely but unless Caryll was home I had virtually no other real playmates. So, naturally, in my mind I became a horse. When I was not riding I played horses. At night, I made up stories about them to send myself to sleep. I had numerous 14.2-hand thoroughbreds, the size considered right for a child. As long as it was a thoroughbred and beautiful, it was bought for me, and each horse had to be exercised every day. There was a very beautiful skewbald pony called Joseph that had a problem I soon discovered. It used to rear very badly. As soon as something upset it, it would go straight up on its hind legs. "Drop your reins, put your arms round its neck and go with it," Sgt Higgins used to shout. It became second nature.

Caryll came home for the holidays and, being a boy, was considered perfectly competent to handle rearing horses. It was good training for the army. In spite of Sgt Higgins's instructions though, Caryll, who was no horseman, ended on the ground. I remember being unspeakably cross, for he was letting the side down.

"What are you doing crawling on the road? Get up at once," I said.

"I am not getting on that horrid creature. I would rather walk home," said my mewling brother.

"Stop crying. You should be ashamed of yourself," I barked. "Get on the horse or I will never speak to you again."

In spite of all our efforts, Caryll never showed the slightest real interest in horses. He was brilliant at trick-cycling and we used to practise for hours in the back courtyard. Of course his biggest thrill of all was when Campbell Black allowed him to fly the plane. He could not talk of anything else. I found it extremely boring. Also, one of the drivers used to allow us to practise our car-driving skills on the airstrip, which was on top of the rise of a fairly steep hill. A large field

Enid Lindeman couldn't help herself: she dazzled men and incited passion.

Roderick Cameron, a shipbroking millionaire from New York, became Enid's first husband.

Enid's father, Charles Lindeman, above, shared her fine mouth and firm jawline. Right, Frederick "Caviar" Cavendish, known for his bravery, with his two childen, Caryll, front, and Pat and stepson Rory.

Egypt after World War I was bliss, remembered Enid, centre, with Frederick, left.

Walter Carandini
Wilson, far left,
adored Enid,
next to him, and
tried to leave her
his fortune.
Below, Enid with
Lord Furness in
Baden Baden.

Enid, at Burrough Court, could shoot and ride as well as any man.

Marmaduke Furness liked Enid to himself and took her to Africa on long safaris each year. On one trip, she shot a massive elephant and the tusks, above, went back to Burrough Court. Left, the ubiquitous hyrax, Tikki. Below, one of the Nile houseboats that took rich tourists.

Furness was called "Champagny Lordy" because of his opulent safaris, left. Below, Enid with either Idina or Joss, her two pet porcupines.

Top, Enid and Furness, right, flying into Baden Baden. Tom Campbell Black is centre.
Above, Miss Unger with Caryll and Pat.

The famous letter of apology from Thelma Furness now kept among Sir Walter Monckton's papers at Oxford. Thelma had insinuated that Enid caused Furness's death.

Telephone· Terminus 7566

DOLLMAN & PRITCHARD

GEORGE PRITCHARD M.A. B.C.L. OXON

COMMISSIONER FOR OATHS

37, Mecklenburgh Square,

London, July 10th 19 46.
W C I

Dear Sirs,

I write in reference to my letter dated 6th September 1945 addressed to the Procureur of the Republic of France.

Now that I know the real facts of this matter I desire to take this the earliest opportunity of apologising for having written such a letter. I now know that there is not the slightest justification for any of the allegations and insinuations the letter contains. That letter was written by me under an entire misconception of the true facts of this case and I hope your client will accept this apology and in asking her to accept it, I wish to express my deep regret for having made these charges.

This letter has been shown to my client, Lady Thelma Furness and I have her full approval and authority for writing it.

Yours faithfully,

George Pritchard

Thelma Furness.

Messrs Theodore Goddard & Co.,
5 New Court,
W.C.2.

Enid kept as many as 50 poodles at Burrough Court.

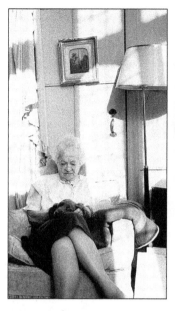

Pat's childhood revolved around horses, right, and she rode almost before she walked. Aunt Nanny, above, thought Pat an unbearably spoiled little girl.

Caryll and Pat joined Enid on one life-changing journey to Kenya.

Among the film stars Enid knew was Gary Cooper, here with Pat.

Enid in her robes for King George VI's coronation in 1937.

Enid's third marriage was to the brilliant Castlerosse. Caryll and Pat attended their mother.

Suddenly, at age 18, shy Pat was allowed her freedom. Her best friend was Peggy Mathewson, right, and the two girls, who used to help out at the wartime canteens, went dancing most nights with glamorous American soldiers.

Pat, left, wth Peggy, at her marriage to war hero Christy Mathewson.

Lord Castlerosse encouraged a timid Pat to believe in her beauty.

Pat posed for Harlip, a famous London society photographer of the time.

had been turned into the runway with a hangar over which flew the air sock.

I remember one evening when Mummy and Furness were coming back from Kenya from one of their regular safari trips there. It was sunset when the plane circled low over the house. I can still see the red-streaked sky outlining the dark plane and how it picked up flashes of light from the setting sun as it roared overhead. It was the usual signal to let the staff know to send the cars to the airfield. Miss Unger looked up and announced that we had better go up there as the plane was going to crash. She called our chauffeur and we arrived just as the plane was landing.

Furness, who was always a fairly heavy drinker, had been imbibing too much champagne on the voyage home and perhaps Campbell Black had indulged as well. Campbell Black, brilliant a pilot as he was, misjudged the runway and hit a hedge with one of the wheels. The plane slewed sideways on landing, ending up with its nose on the runway, tail in the air and a buckled wing. How Campbell Black managed to land at all with one wheel gone was a miracle. The steward told Miss Unger afterwards that Mummy was amazing. Furness had been smoking a cigar and as the plane was about to crash-land, Mummy reached across, took the cigar out of his mouth, saying, "Darling, I am going to put this out or the plane might catch fire."

Furness, of course, was furious, and blamed Campbell Black who really was the best pilot you could have. Tom was also a great lady's man and it was he who taught the brilliant aviatrix Beryl Markham to fly. They had met on one of the roads of Kenya where Beryl had grown up. His car had broken down and this stunning blonde on horseback came to his rescue. He became her lover and taught her to fly, the pupil becoming even more famous than her mentor. She was later to make history being the first person to fly the Atlantic alone from east to west, in 1936. It was at Burrough Court that I first saw Beryl. She had flown back from Kenya with Campbell Black and when I saw her she was still dressed in a glamorous all-white flying suit, which made a lasting impression on me.

As much as Sgt Higgins made an impact on my life through his knowledge of horses, so Tom Campbell Black and his knowledge of aircraft impacted upon the lives of Beryl and also Caryll. Tom

Campbell Black and Charles William Anderson Scott flew a de Havilland Comet in the MacRobertson International Air Race from Suffolk to Melbourne in 1934 and won, making them world-famous. Tragically, two years after this victory and just days after Beryl's Atlantic feat, Tom Campbell Black was killed at Speke Airport, Liverpool, when an aircraft landed on top of him while he was taxiing onto the runway. I remember how the whole of Burrough Court went into mourning, as he was so immensely popular. Caryll was in despair. Although he wasn't even quite 10 at the time, he already knew how to handle the controls of an airplane, thanks to Tom.

CHAPTER

5

Furness was famous for his foul language, his temper, and his drinking. He carried a silver hip flask filled with neat brandy and he continually took swigs. Everything was "fucking this" or "bloody that". Not that I saw that much of him but when I did, these words were the most frequently used. It was just his normal way of speaking.

I must have been eight years old when, standing on Victoria Platform in London, waiting for a train, very tidy and beautifully dressed in coat, hat, gloves and shining shoes, I turned to one of my governesses and piped in a loud childish voice, "Why is the fucking train so late?" You could have heard a pin drop. Everyone turned to look. Both Miss Unger and my governess Miss Carruthers were puce in the face with embarrassment. One of the bystanders said, "Disgusting. That child is indecent and should not be allowed on the station."

Another lesson learned. Miss Unger on our return took the horsewhip and, lashing me around the legs, screamed at me, "Never let me hear that filthy language again. You are a disgusting child and I am ashamed to be associated with you." When she calmed down, she explained that gentlemen used those words but never ladies or children.

Furness did not often use his private railroad cars as by this time he had his aeroplane and much preferred to fly. Very occasionally we went with my mother and him on his train. His carriages would either be attached to the regular train, which would stop at his private railway station at Burrough Court, or there would be a special engine for them alone. I remember that he would dispense large tips like confetti to the stationmaster and porters. He did the same to his staff, and he paid them extremely well too, which is why there wasn't a large turnover in spite of his demands for perfection.

Our retinue rode in one carriage and Furness went in the other, so he would not have to see us. On arriving at our destination, we would have to wait until Mummy and Furness had left. The same thing happened on departure; we had to be all installed before they arrived. I remember a particular journey. Furness had his own very grand toilet that I had been shown on one occasion. It had a wooden seat with gold chain and ivory handle, nothing but the best for Furness. Unfortunately, this time the train steward must have forgotten to put enough toilet paper in the container. To Furness's fury, it ran out while he was on the loo. He always carried two things on his person though. One was a specially made, very thin silver flask that was curved to fit snugly and invisibly into the back pocket of his beautifully tailored trousers or jodhpurs. And the other thing he carried was a gold clip containing £500 in £5 notes. In those days, the £5 notes were very large and I imagine at today's rate of inflation they would have been the equivalent of £200. Furness, in this *moment critique* used his £5 notes to replace the non-existent loo paper. I remember that his under-valet had the kitchen and staff at Burrough Court entranced with this tale. He announced, "If only there had been a station, I would have rushed back and cleaned off the shit myself."

I heard, again from the servants, that as his Lordship emerged from the toilet there were roars of rage. He summoned the steward, poor man, and sacked him on the spot.

I received five shillings a month pocket money, and on birthdays and Christmas, as well as all my presents, there were several £5 notes. With my pocket money, I was allowed to go to Battersea Dogs' Home in London and buy two abandoned dogs every year. I acquired the most beautiful dogs this way. These were traumatic visits and I was always reduced to tears at seeing the hopeful and desperate eyes of those that had to be left behind. Mummy had given a black poodle to me as a puppy and I worshipped him. I named him Mickey and he went with me everywhere. I even had a basket put on the front of my bicycle and the only time I left him behind was when I went riding. At night he slept beside me in bed. When we went to France for the holidays Mummy would smuggle him over in the plane with her own special pets. Private aircraft in those days were not considered much of a customs risk because they were so few and far between and all their owners were famous millionaires. With Mummy and the mountains of luggage she and Furness took, a few more suitcases with undetectable air holes went unnoticed. Mummy would give the animals a bit of a sleeping pill before leaving and there was a maid and a valet to accompany them during the flight. It was their duty to see to the baggage and the welfare of the various smuggled pets. My mother's pet cheetah also used to go with them. How that was achieved I really don't know; I suppose on a trolley.

After the war, when Furness was no longer in our lives, my mother didn't have her own plane or train to make animal transporting quite as easy. It was sheer hell for the maids and me for we were left to cope with all these extraneous animals and to smuggle them in and out of customs. Once, after a trip to India and its marketplaces, we had to smuggle several rescued parrots through French customs. An obliging ship's captain, clearly besotted by my mother, had already helped her get them off the ship at Brindisi and through Italian customs. We then had to get them over the border at Menton. Mummy had already sailed ahead in her car, so it was left to her maid and me to stuff a lot of blankets over the parrots, which had been packed into our car to muffle their screeching. The French lady's maid was almost hysterical with fear and even our chauffeur who was used to our household was looking harassed. I could see sweat trickling down his forehead and under his peaked cap. Fortunately, the customs officers had just done a thorough search on the car in front so once all our passports had been stamped, they were only too glad to get rid of us.

I promised myself time and again, that never, but never, would I have wild animals or parrots. How little did I know! Blood is obviously thicker than water. If anything, I suppose I have proved to be a great deal worse than Mummy. Caryll assures me that our mother at least was sane, thus implying that his totally mad sister is not!

When I turned 10, my mother thought that maybe I should go to day school in spite of having Miss Unger for French lessons, a German tutor, and an English governess. I found their lessons endlessly boring and could not wait to get back to the horses.

The dreadful day came when I was sent off to a convent in Leicester. I fancied myself as Marie Antoinette on the tumbril going off to the guillotine; the thought of leaving my horses and dogs was unbearable.

I was treated as some sort of a freak. The fact that I used to arrive each day in a chauffeur-driven Rolls-Royce, escorted by a governess or a nanny, and was only interested in horses made me very different from the rest of the girls. The famous occasion arrived when my beautiful mother came to collect me. For days, nobody could talk about anything else. After a month, the novelty of school had completely worn off for me. I started to loathe everything about it. The food was inedible, and the smell of sweat and unwashed bodies permeated the classrooms. Above all, I was now only able to ride on weekends. The girls were not interested in anything that interested me – mainly horses. One day I decided that enough was enough and, seizing my opportunity, I locked the girls and the nuns into one of the classrooms and took off on foot for home. Burrough Court was a long way from Leicester but after a while I got a lift from a delivery van.

When I arrived back home, I found the place in an uproar. I had in fact timed my escape for when I knew my mother would be there. She was frantic with worry; I was enveloped in Joy and hugs and kisses and she promised I would never have to go back. Bursting into giggles in typical Mummy fashion she said, "Darling, I am also quite convinced you would be the last person in the world the poor nuns would want to take back. You are much too headstrong and dreadful for those poor gentle women in a convent to handle." Even Miss Unger, from whom I expected a thrashing, did nothing. Secretly I think she must have been delighted. Possibly, had I remained at school, her job might have been at risk.

Life returned to normal, back with my lessons, horses, and dogs.

During the hunting season, I used to go out all day escorted by Sgt Higgins with either the Cottesmore Hunt based in Rutland or the Quorn which stretches between Nottingham, Leicester and Melton Mowbray. A horsebox with a change of horses would meet us at midday. Whenever Joseph the skewbald rearer appeared, I knew I was in for a rough ride. He was not a bold horse and certainly no jumper. In fact, when he wasn't on his hind legs trying to topple over, we spent the rest of the time crashing to the ground. It was very good training and as I got so used to him I hardly ever came off. I grew quite attached to him and his dreadful ways. It was not his fault he kept rearing or falling over the jumps. I begged Sgt Higgins not to tell on him because Furness was ruthless; if any animal did not live up to his high standards, it was shot.

His attitude to family wasn't too different as far as I could understand. Furness had three children, two by his first wife Daisy: Dick and Averill. I never met his daughter Averill. She had married a white hunter in Kenya called Andrew Rattray with whom Furness had hunted on safari and did not consider good enough for his only daughter. As she did not match up to his expectations, he disinherited her. Rattray did try and patch up their differences. As usual, I heard all the gossip from the servants' hall. Arriving from Kenya to see his father-in-law, he had turned up at the front door of Burrough Court and given the butler his calling card. This was duly delivered on a silver tray to Furness in his office. He, in a rage at the man's supposed effrontery, gave orders that he was to be shown to the back door. "I do not receive fucking tradesmen," Furness had instructed. "Get my steward to see what the bugger wants." Rattray's mission failed.

There was another tragedy. One of our great delights was when Furness's eldest son, Dick, came to stay. He was a cavalry officer, an intrepid horseman, and a very good steeplechase rider. Good looking, tall, fair and with a moustache, he was wonderful with us and filled every day with excitement. One Christmas, he took us walking in the deep snow, following the tracks of a fox until we found its earth. There we sat on a dead tree branch and watched the fox and its family as they played.

Other days Dick would take me riding, looking for impossible jumps, anything to test the capabilities of our horses. With him, we never opened a gate or skirted a wall. It was always "Tally-ho!" and over the top. I remember on one occasion taking a huge wall but as we went over I saw, to my horror, that there was a steep drop and a plough parked underneath. How our horses managed I will never know; one could feel them in mid-air gathering themselves for that extra effort. Everything with Dick was fun and as Furness did not seem to like him very much, he would spend a lot of time with us instead. Mummy adored him and his lovely girlfriend who unfortunately did not like riding. Instead, Mummy would drive her in the car and we would meet up at various places and have tea and scones while the grooms held our horses.

As I grew older, Dick always left two of his steeplechasers at Burrough Court for me to exercise and school over the brush fences. He had built a proper steeplechase course through the paddocks. One day I was on one of Dick's horses when Furness rode up with his stud manager and one of the grooms. I saw them waiting by one of the fences and just as I was about to take off he lashed my horse round the hocks with his riding crop. The poor horse went berserk. I heard later from the groom that Furness had said to them, "The bloody little bitch is getting much too cocky; it's time she learned a lesson." I somehow knew that his anger was really directed at my mother, for loving us so much.

Sometimes, while at Burrough, Dick would throw wild parties. I used to hear that Furness was always complaining about his orgies and drunken companions. Furness himself was a heavy drinker but although he would drink all through the day and most of the night, he never got drunk.

Furness and Mummy were away when Dick gave another of these parties. This time it ended in disaster. At Burrough Court there was a billiard room with walls lined with enormous fish tanks. There were all sorts of exotic, beautifully coloured fish, as well as salmon and trout. I could spend hours watching them when Furness was not at home as the underwater decoration was so beautiful. There were huge rocks, caves, coral and every kind of lovely plant swaying in the bubbles with shoals of fish swimming in and out. At night-time, the tanks were lit up, and if the light over the billiard table was not on, the room became a fairyland.

I knew nothing about Dick's party, but heard endless tales of what had occurred from the servants' hall. Champagne had been flowing when some wag suggested all the guests go fishing in the tanks. Well! When Furness arrived home and found the dreadful results of this fishing expedition, he was livid. Apparently screaming that he was going to disinherit the fucker, he also decreed that Dick was never to be allowed back to Burrough Court. According to Furness's valet, it was my mother who finally persuaded him not to disinherit Dick. His valet told the other servants: "At one stage, her Ladyship turned to me and said, 'Get hold of Lane and ask her to pack my bags.' She told his lordship that if he disinherited Master Dick, she was also leaving."

Mummy might have managed to save Dick's inheritance but she never managed to persuade Furness to have Dick back at Burrough Court. Mummy and I would meet up with him at the Dorchester Hotel in London and have lunches with Dick and his girlfriend. I heard her say to him, "Leave it to me. We will start with Sandley House and Gilltown [Furness's stud farms in Dorset and Ireland] then gradually get you back to Burrough." Dick did go to Gillltown and Sandley House but he never got back to Burrough. Then World War II broke out and Dick was killed at Dunkirk on May 24, 1940, commanding the Carrier Platoon, First Welsh Guards, which was part of the garrison at Arras. In typical Dick fashion, he brought out a hunting horn and, shouting "Tally-ho!" yet again, stood in the open hatch of his troop carrier and charged a machine-gun position that was wreaking havoc on the evacuation of the men to the beach. Dick died as he lived, a hero, and was awarded the Victoria Cross. Furness wept and wept on hearing the dreadful news and Mummy was inconsolable. To make it worse, Dick's sister Averill had died four years earlier, also without her and her father being reconciled.

Furness had another much younger son by his second wife Thelma. I know he did not like children, even his own, but he really hated Tony. He was referred to as "the bastard" if he was ever spoken of at all. Being so close to her own family, my mother could not bear the thought that Furness had a son whom he refused to see even though he was living in England. I so clearly remember Mummy coming to us. We had our own dining room at Burrough Court and we were having lunch at the time. She was so seldom serious about anything and the fact she was discussing important news and our behaviour remained etched in my memory. "Darlings," she said, "I have persuaded Duke to let his son Tony come and spend a week with us. I want you to be very nice to him. He is only a baby and a lonely little child, so give him lots of love and Pat, during his visit, don't spend the whole day on a horse. Make time to show him all the beautiful gardens and flowers and animals and, above all, make him feel wanted."

Tony arrived. He must have been about six at the time and he had the most horrible governess. Tony was a very well-behaved, silent child who I think very seldom got love from anyone, certainly not from the governess. He was a sad little figure and, following my mother's instructions, I spent a lot of time hugging and kissing him. One afternoon, when I was cuddling him, his governess fixed me with an icy stare and said, "Tony is a boy. You are a big girl now and must not treat him like one of your dolls. Leave him alone."

I gather from the servants that when Mummy took him to see Furness, he said, "I told you; I do not want to see the bastard. Get him out of here."

Mummy spent a lot of time with Tony that week and invented all sorts of games for us to play with him, but in spite of her I don't think Furness saw him again. According to servants' gossip, Furness would have nothing to do with him because he was rumoured to be the Prince of Wales's bastard, even though the dates don't match up. When Thelma had her affair with the prince, the enraged Furness was unable to get a divorce as he would not have wanted to cite a member of the royal family as a co-respondent. Furness did finally divorce Thelma and never forgave her.

During Thelma's royal affair but after her divorce from Furness, she had to return to the United States in early 1934 for two months, and then again later in the year. The case that would see her twin sister Gloria Morgan Vanderbilt sued for the custody of her daughter Gloria Laura Vanderbilt (who had inherited $4 million on the death of her father Reginald Vanderbilt) by little Gloria's paternal aunt, Gertrude Vanderbilt Whitney was already being put in place. Thelma's sister was accused of being an unfit mother because of her partying and highly social lifestyle. The aunt won custody after a bitter battle, although it turned out to be a sad childhood for Gloria.

Very foolishly as it turned out, Thelma had introduced her prince to her great friend Wallis Simpson at a house party at Burrough Court in 1931 and the prince had taken an interest in Wallis and her husband Ernest after that. Just before her first trip in 1934 to America to be with her sister, Thelma sought her friend's help. Knowing the prince's weakness for good-looking women, she asked Wallis to look after him while she was away and to make sure he did not stray. The rest of the story became a *cause célèbre*.

CHAPTER

6

It's amazing how innocent children were in those days. When we were very tiny and on holiday in Biarritz, we went for endless walks in the beautiful forest surrounding the hotel. There were toads everywhere, all walking around, one on top of the other. I suppose they were mating but at the time I was told they were tired and the ones on top were being carried by their mothers. After that, I spent my time trying to pick them up and carry them so they wouldn't be tired any longer. My nanny, much to her horror, would look back to see why I was dawdling and find me with an armful of toads, all trying to leap to freedom.

Later on, when I was still quite small, we had some American friends to stay at Sandley House. These were the Johnsons (of Johnson & Johnson baby products fame). The children were our age and Mummy, with her usual love of picnics, had decided to have one down by the river. As it was a very hot day, all of us children were in bathing suits which consisted of little pairs of trunks. Caryll was six and I was seven. Nanny suddenly descended on me saying, "You must come out of the water at once." I was dragged off to the house and had to remain there until a suitable top could be found for me. She said, "Her Ladyship is most upset that you are not wearing a decent bathing suit, although I do not see what her ladyship objects to. You are as flat as a little pancake." As nobody ever explained anything in depth, I was left wondering why I was always the one causing social disasters, never Caryll.

There was a colonel managing Sandley House and his daughter, Georgina, became a great friend of mine; we spent a lot of time together as she also loved riding. She was the first to tell Caryll and me about sex. We were up in one of the hay barns when she said that she had gone into her mother and father's bedroom and, she said, they were mating. We had often seen horses mating and now we were old enough to have it explained to us that what they were doing was making babies. We never associated it with human beings though. In fact, when I first used to ask Sgt Higgins what the cattle out in the paddocks were doing, he would still get very embarrassed and say, "They are going for a ride." When I saw a ram I wanted to know what that big sack was. Again an embarrassed Sgt Higgins told me, "That is where they carry their babies." As a result I was a mine of misinformation!

Georgina said her parents were mating but lying flat and we discussed this extraordinary activity on the part of her parents. Georgina said she was sure this was what all grown-ups did to make children. I was highly indignant and said, "My mother would never do anything like that." I must have been about 11 at the time and had not the foggiest idea about anything.

There was a Swedish countess also staying at Sandley House. She was a sculptress and was doing a life-sized bronze of one of Furness's mares, Rosy Legend, later the dam of famous Derby winner Dante. The countess had a daughter with her who was quite a bit older than us and she wanted to play the strangest games called "operations". These consisted of her lying naked with her legs open while we performed operations all over her private parts. After several of these sessions, I told Miss Unger about the funny type of games this girl wanted us to play. Well! All hell broke loose.

Miss Unger had always told us proudly that she was a 36-year-old virgin. We didn't understand what a virgin was, although we were made to realise it was something special. Now Miss Unger, in spite of my having told her about "operations" in all innocence, was furious with me. She told me I was disgusting and a shameful child. Caryll had also played these games and had happily driven his toy aeroplane and cars all over the exposed parts but she didn't berate him. Instead of hitting me, Miss Unger then gave me a large dose of castor oil. "To clean out my system," I was told. The result was that I couldn't leave the bathroom. That evening Mummy came to the schoolroom to find out why I had not been to see her and discovered me glued to the toilet seat. I explained that it was the castor oil but didn't tell her that it was for a punishment. Thank goodness Miss Unger was told never to give me castor oil again.

I didn't understand what was so terrible about any of this, although I did realise that one was not supposed to look at naked bodies, either one's own or someone else's. In fact I was 18 before I realised that a man kissing a woman did not produce babies. I had been brought up not to kiss anybody on the lips. Even as a child.

There was another big step in our understanding of such things when we were at Le Touquet. Caryll and I used to spend a lot of time climbing around the roof of The Berries. There was a flat section outside Rory's bathroom that was a great vantage point for watching the arrival and departure of guests. One day we were on our roof when through the window we espied Rory having his bath. We rushed down to Mummy in great excitement: "Mummy, Mummy, Rory is in his bath, come and see, he has a big thing that looks like an ugly water lily, and it floats." I remember Mummy, nearly hysterical with laughter, explaining that was his "wee-wee". Caryll was most upset, saying, "I don't want an ugly wee-wee like that when I grow up."

Fascinated by Rory's wee-wee, we then used to spend our time when nobody was looking lying outside the guest toilet, trying to peer through the crack, hoping to find out whether other grown-ups had wee-wees like Rory's. We also must have heard guests talking about Mummy's lovers, not that we knew what it meant, but obviously from what we gathered they visited her at night-time. So one night when everybody had gone to bed and we were supposed to be asleep, we crept out and stationed ourselves in the linen cupboard, and tied some cotton thread to her door. We hoped that, whatever a lover was, one would visit her. The fact that Furness was in residence at The Berries at the time, and that there could be no possibility of a lover did not register. Needless to say we fell fast asleep and were found by the maid in the morning – who did not tell Miss Unger.

Back at Burrough Court, Furness never hunted any more but Mummy often used to go with Sgt Higgins and me. During the early years of her marriage to Furness, she had had a very nasty fall and fractured one of the discs in her back. She had been bedridden for ages and was left with a huge knob on one of her vertebrae. Furness made his decision not to hunt again after that and tried very hard to stop my mother. He was worried that she, being so fearless, would have another accident. Finally, he was successful and Mummy wasn't even allowed to spend the day going with Sgt Higgins and me.

But it may also have had something to do with the fact that he was getting suspicious of the hunt master's attentions to my mother. He was a major, and a master of the Quorn and had fallen madly in love with my mother. Mummy now rode side-saddle at Furness's insistence and an instructor had even been called in to teach her the refinements of this form of riding. I used to be so proud of her as I rode out with her to the hunt. She was always mounted on the most beautiful hunters, her clothes were immaculate and she would mount from a block. Once on her horse, her maid would adjust her jacket and skirt and give a final polish to her boots. In a top hat and veil, she looked to my mind like a fairy queen on a magical steed. On our arrival at the meet, I used to love the way everyone would turn and look at her. As always, men soon surrounded her.

I do not know whether the major ever managed to have an affair with Mummy but we children saw quite a lot of him. He also gave several children's parties; I imagine it was an excuse for him to see her, for he had no children of his own and I don't think he was married. One of our nannies used to give him letters from my mother. Once I was taken up to his bedroom to spend a penny and there was a large photo of her beside his bed. When I came downstairs I said, "Why do you have a photograph of our mother?" To this day, I can still feel his embarrassment. Sitting down, he took my hands and said, "Darling Pat, you must promise me, that you will never ever tell anyone that I have your mother's picture. This will be our secret. I know you love her and so do I. So never mention this to anyone."

CHAPTER

7

After she married Marmaduke Furness, my mother would spend at least three to four months of every year in Kenya on safari. Furness was known as "Champagny Lordy"; empty crates and empty bottles of Dom Perignon were stacked like a hill at his permanent campsites. Mummy was a teetotaller but Duke and Tom Campbell Black, their white hunters and friends used to get through a substantial amount of alcohol. It was never a problem when supplies ran out as airstrips would have been hacked out of the bush and Tom Campbell Black would simply fly back to Nairobi to replenish the store. If Duke felt the occasion warranted it, Tom would be sent all the way back to Scotland for grouse or salmon or whatever else was in season at the time. Or he would be sent backwards and forwards for caviare, masseurs, hairdressers or whatever other luxury was considered necessary to keep the safari in comfort.

A Furness safari was like no other. He had two Rolls-Royces for east Africa which had been used by the British General Edmund Allenby in the desert during World War I. They had been fitted out with specially built safari bodies. Each had a fully stocked pull-out bar fitted out in silver. When Mummy travelled, she was always accompanied by her silver foxes, by Tikki her hyrax and her cheetah which, purring loudly, used to recline in the utmost luxury on the heavily padded maroon upholstery.

In Kenya, Furness's chauffeurs' cockaded caps and black uniforms changed to cockaded white caps and white dustcoats. The year before the war, 1938, saw the last of these safaris, but for many years later you would come across a Furness Rolls on the roads of east Africa. They always filled me with nostalgia.

When I was 10 and Caryll nine, Mummy decided we were old enough to travel, although how she persuaded Duke to let us come I will never know. We might have been young but we fully realised that Furness could not stand children.

The excitement was intense. First of all we had to travel to London, where we were outfitted for Africa. Army & Navy Stores was the huge emporium near Victoria station where intrepid travellers, explorers and adventurers came for all that was considered essential for life in the merciless tropics. They were suppliers of all British colonial needs with their array of heavy green tents and the endless stacks of black tin trunks in all sizes and shapes. There were rolls of sun-resistant safari materials, specially woven for maximum resistance to the harmful rays of the tropical sun, and trousers and bush jackets were made from these. There were racks of pith helmets and double terai hats; the whites in Africa were convinced that without them, they would die of sunstroke. Safari boots provided protection from the snakes and there were mosquito nets to fit all types of beds and cots, from the exotic to the practical. And last but not least there were fly swats and mosquito repellent.

We were measured and fitted and so were my governess Miss Unger and one of Mummy's lady's maids Miss Munday. Finally, the long awaited day arrived. The Thomas Cook's representative, in his smart uniform and peaked cap, met us at Waterloo. This was to be the start of many such journeys with Cook's around the world. I think in the days of my youth, nobody of any consequence thought of undertaking even a channel crossing without their assistance.

There followed the usual total confusion which was to become the pattern of our voyages. Mummy never travelled without 50 to 60 trunks, suitcases, hatboxes, and bags of all descriptions containing all the requirements of a world-famous beauty. When the various animals that used to accompany us were added as well, total bedlam ensued. Mummy would swan through and I, along with the lady's maids, butlers, footmen, chauffeurs and Thomas Cook, would be left to deal with the pandemonium.

Finally we were on our way, leaving the grey and rainy skies of London behind as the train hurtled through the dripping countryside on its way to Southampton. From there sailed all the ships bound for the great and far distant ports of the world. The British India Steam Navigation Company shipping line was a name conjuring up all the romance of the far-flung countries of the empire. The ships were floating hotels of colonial splendour. A fairy palace to a child's eye, full of sweeping staircases and enormous gilded mirrors reflecting the lights of great crystal chandeliers. Ballrooms, lounges, verandahs, bars, and miles of endless shiny linoleum passages leading to the staterooms and cabins. There was huge excitement as we walked up the gangplank and peered down from a vast height into the sea below, that narrow width of ocean with its slight sheen of oil that showed between the vast hull and the quayside. With continual strictures not to fall overboard and drown, we watched the milling crowd, entranced. A lot of the crew were lascars in red fezzes, khaki uniforms and bare feet, and we watched them and the porters struggling up the swaying gangway with the luggage. There were several tiers of decks, all lined with passengers amongst whom the crew were striving to make their way. Above everything was a line of funnel smoke already beginning to show against the yellow sky of winter.

The whistle blew; there were the last minute tearful farewells, with some passengers still rushing to board before the gangway was lifted while visitors were jostling back to land. There was a great deal of *va et viens* and the sound of voices and running feet. The last hooter sounded and we were under way. It was the start of a voyage that was to have a profound effect on my life.

Never the best of sailors, as the ship got up steam and started to roll, I retired to bed. The Bay of Biscay was at its usual violent best and I lay on the tiled bathroom floor clutching the loo and wishing I were dead. In the Mediterranean, we were hit by a gale. The wind screeched, the ship plunged, rolled, shook, and shuddered and the seas pounded my porthole. On the second night we passed a ship in distress. I could see it quite clearly from my cabin, some distance away, being battered by the storm. I know we did not go to its rescue; I think our Captain did not dare risk his passengers by answering their SOS. What the eventual fate of the cargo vessel was I do not know. My dreams became filled with sinking ships and passengers drowning under tumultuous seas.

By morning, the wind had died down and the sea was empty of life. I stood in the bow watching the endless horizon and towards evening I was the first to see the sandy shoreline of North Africa. I can still see that nebulous ridge of land that gradually took shape rising out of the sea. Africa at last. We were asleep when we docked that night but all the noise and the padding of feet along the decks and the faint bump as the ship settled into its berth woke Caryll and me. We spent our time at the porthole watching little boats ferrying people to and fro. The men seemed to be wearing long nightshirts and there was a lot of shouting and gesticulating as they swarmed around, vying for attention from the upper decks.

The following day, a Thomas Cook representative in a striped jellaba and the ubiquitous red fez met us. In antiquated cars we were soon on the road to Cairo. It meant sand and heat and large men on tiny donkeys and our first sight of a camel train. As we approached the city, there was tremendous congestion with people and donkeys and camel carts. We slowed to almost walking pace and the children crowded at our windows with hands outstretched asking for baksheesh. To my amazement, I saw an Arab pulling up his rather dirty white dress to defecate beside the corner of a wall. My excitement at this discovery, which I tried to share with Caryll, was the cause of a sharp lecture from Miss Unger. But even her bad temper could not spoil our first sight of the pyramids outside Cairo and our ecstasy when Said, the Thomas Cook's man, put us up on the patiently waiting camels. Lines of them, with their camel boys waiting by, were lying or standing chewing their cud and belching nauseous fumes into people's faces. Being children, we were on a level for this to have the maximum effect. In the background, we could see the towering pyramid of Cheops. What with the noise and bustle of the passengers who had arrived en masse and were bargaining for their camels – and being instructed how to stay on when this enormous beast lurched to its feet – we were kept fully occupied. Then the confusion of background noises fell away and we were out on the desert. To my delight Miss Unger refused to go, so, accompanied by our guides and Miss Munday who was much more adventurous, we spent an enthralling hour riding around the pyramids and the Sphinx which, in those days, was half buried in the sand. Then we came back and had delicious lime drinks on the verandah of the Mena House Hotel.

Our next stop was Port Said with its tree-lined avenues and giant statue of the French engineer Ferdinand de Lesseps at the entrance to the Suez Canal. I little realised, as a child gazing up at his statue that stood so proudly overlooking his vision, this great waterway, that as a young girl and later as a young woman I would fall in love with his relative, Guy de Lesseps.

Being a lonely child, I was an avid reader and spent my life in a dream world where my fantasies were more substantial than reality. Port Said was all I had ever imagined. Hundreds of small boats surrounded our ship selling their wares. Ropes with leaded weights landed on the deck and in no time a selection of kimonos in brilliant blues, reds and greens, embroidered with dragons, surrounded us. Miss Unger and Miss Munday were being cajoled from the boats: "Missy, missy, just look!" Gulli-gulli men, conjurors, had also arrived on board, and mesmerised us with live chickens coming out of their fezzes and from around our necks. There were snake charmers and fortune-tellers; it was more exciting than any fairy tale. I held Caryll's hand, entranced by the cobra rearing its head and swaying in time to the monotonous tune of the pipe. I was also terrified that my brother might get lost in all the hustle and excitement or that someone might steal him because he was so beautiful. When I was not trying to kill him I loved Caryll to distraction. I would wake in the night and climb up to look into his bunk above mine to make sure he hadn't fallen out of the porthole and drowned.

We were taken ashore in a launch with white awnings and dark-skinned Egyptian sailors in the white starched uniforms, navy blue fezzes and black tassels of the Royal Navy. The sun shone in a cloudless blue sky and its reflection danced off the ripples in the water. The dark green palm-lined banks rose to meet us and beyond were the buildings, the noise, the people, the camels and donkeys, the general commotion attendant on one of the most famous ports in the world, Port Said, the colonial gateway to the east.

Dominating the port was the famous emporium Simon Artz, its name emblazoned in large letters. Once through its great doors, Aladdin's Cave was put to shame. There were leather pouffes dyed in every bright colour and heavily embossed, camel seats, rugs, carpets, kimonos, silks, satins, scarves, jewellery, scent, and toys. It was all there, the visual magic of the east flaunting its voluptuous colours and exotic wares, each object brighter, more dazzling than the next. Colours intermingling, they flowed on the shelves, floors and ceiling. Above our heads were arrays of incandescent saris that hung, shimmering and fluttering in the breeze of the giant slowly turning fans overhead. I stood under the portals of Simon Artz, lost in wonder, and knew that Africa was the land of my dreams.

In the future, I was to do this trip so many times and, while I always loved it, I never quite recaptured the pure magic of my first voyage. In later years I still enjoyed rummaging around but by then their displays and their goods seemed slightly tawdry and my Aladdin's Cave a childhood memory.

The canal itself was also to become a familiar stamping ground over the decades, whether we were going by ship or in *dhows*, driving along its banks on the way to Cairo, or on horseback with our syces, the grooms, in attendance, picnicking on the bank and watching the liners steam by. Mummy and I would eat cucumber and sardine sandwiches. After a long hot ride, the oiliness of those sandwiches always made me feel slightly nauseous. The Suez, for me, became synonymous with sardines.

To our intense excitement, our ship now proceeded down the canal. Caryll and I sat on deck all that day fascinated by the scenery unfolding on either side of the ship. It was an effort to get us down to meals, so anxious were we not to miss anything. We were enthralled by the buildings of mud blocks that rose out of the water, the lushness of the banks and the desert beyond. Donkeys were trotting along, their owners sitting on their quarters driving them with a stick on their neck. Oxen were plodding endlessly around, harnessed to a giant wheel and the villagers with their gourds were coming for water while the *fellahin* in white loincloths stood on one leg, the other tucked in above the knee. Still as dark statues, they would stand by their furrows and watch us sail by. We could see villages of baked mud bricks in the coconut palms and, as evening fell, the pictures in my childhood books came alive as the camel caravans passed, black silhouettes against the lemon sky.

From Port Said down the Suez and through the Red Sea to the heat of Aden, the town built into the side of a blazing volcanic rock face. Even when the sun went down, the stone walls acted like an oven. The ship lay at anchor in translucent pale green water not far from an ugly coal-black lighter. On board was a swarm of young boys, all shouting to the passengers on our ship to throw them pennies. We watched for hours as their black eel-like bodies dived into the clear waters after the gleaming coins. We had a vicarious thrill of horror at the thought of the shark-infested sea in which they were so happily swimming.

Once more the Cook's representative met us and we were taken ashore into the merciless heat. First of all, a walk along the main street to see the shops. There I was desperate to buy a gazelle that had been tied by a collar and lead to a stanchion in the bright white sun. The memory of its sorry plight is still with me. Then there was the obligatory tourist drive to the old salt-pans where again the heat reflected off the desert sand and the mountain engulfed us. The air through the open car windows brought little relief and the millions of flies simply crawled as if they also were stunned. I watched one in a torpor climb up our guide's white robes before giving up the effort and dropping to the floor.

By the time we arrived in Mogadishu, I had a high temperature and a very sore throat. Miss Unger as usual refused to recognise any ailments except her own. As a child, I had had measles, mumps, and whooping cough without benefit of doctor, nurse or medicine. Three days in bed with aspirin was the cure for everything. Each school holiday, Caryll invariably brought back the latest epidemic and we used to keep a proud count. All I can say is thank goodness that

A LION IN THE BEDROOM

Mummy was at home the time Caryll got appendicitis or he would probably have died left to Miss Unger's lack of concern.

I used to suffer from croup as a child and now my chest had closed up. Being much too frightened to wake Miss Unger, I had lain for ages trying to get relief by holding my hands over my throat and chest. Finally I took my hot water bottle, which I always kept for this purpose, and went down the long corridors in search of a stewardess. I hadn't had the courage to ring as I knew I would get into trouble for being a nuisance. At night, the endless corridor was very dimly lit and creaking in the most ghostly way. I kept thinking of ghoulies and all things that went bump in the night. My relief when I finally found the pantry was indescribable.

In sign language, as my voice was almost gone, I was able to convey my problem and the stewardess returned me to my cabin, clutching a hot water bottle to my chest. She remained most of the night cradling me against her large and maternal bosom.

The following morning, we were docked in the harbour. In a haze of pain I remember the heat and the terrible smell of sweat and excrement. The ship was swarming with Somalis with long matted fuzzy hair and filthy stained loincloths. They invaded the ship, working under the pitiless sun on the cargo. All the cranes were going and the cargo was being unloaded from the hold and guided over the sides of the ship, looking as if at any moment all the contents would be disgorged on deck. I was made to go ashore but hated the intense heat. The sun dazzled and burned and there was no shade and no relief. Even my eyeballs hurt, added to which was the smell, the poverty and the dirt. Feeling like death I dragged myself around and when we returned on board I received a hiding for "sulking". I have hated Mogadishu ever since.

One of the passengers on board was exquisite and the first of Caryll's great loves. She must have been about 16 at the time. Always beautifully dressed, she would walk around the deck in white shorts and top, showing a lot of lovely tanned leg. With her black hair and exotic colouring, she had a coterie of ardent admirers, ship's officers and all the unattached male passengers, amongst them my little brother Caryll. Being a very affectionate child, Caryll would cling to her side. She was very kind and gentle, listening to his stories, buying him ice-creams, hugging him and playing endless deck games with him to the intense annoyance of the ardent swains who were unable to get as close to her as this blond and blue-eyed child. When he was not with her, Caryll mooned around the ship, telling me endlessly how he was going to marry her when he grew up.

If he were not circling the decks looking for his love, he would be lying on his bunk staring at the ceiling and sucking the corner of his sheet which he invariably did in times of stress. There was very little comfort I could offer except to listen to his dreams of the future. In later years, when his magnificent looks enchanted a great many ladies, I was either comforting him from the torments of frustrated love and jealousy or trying to soothe the heartbroken women whom he had discarded.

CHAPTER

8

Our first glimpse of Kenya was sailing through the heads of Mombasa harbour. Deep forested hills rose on either side of the ship, and there were no houses. A thick jungle of trees towered above us, interspersed here and there with the fronds of giant coconut palms outlined against the deep blue sky. Although tigers have never existed in Africa, I was not aware of this and I imagined the forests teemed with these magnificent, tawny beasts. This was how I had pictured Africa and Kenya never disappointed me, the reality always far exceeding the dream.

Mombasa itself I only vaguely remember. It was the railway station that enchanted, with its tin roofs and fretwork columns and everywhere enormous luxuriant green leaves, banana trees and bright tropical flowers that spilled over onto the platform in their exuberance. The platform itself was crowded, a sea of white figures. The men were all dressed in starched white tropical suits and topees and the women all seemed to wear white cotton dresses and the invariable topees or terais. Obviously white cotton was de rigueur for colonial living. Maybe there were other fashions but my impression was of white and lush green, of heat, and the excitement of the train with its attendants standing by the open doors to the carriages, the steam curling up from under the wheels as if the train were impatient to get going. Then there was the excitement of boarding and the novelty of having to purchase the bedding, tickets being issued by our attendant for sheets, blankets, pillows and mattresses.

On top of this there were dining car tickets to collect, and being young we were allotted the first sitting. From our dinner table we were able to watch our steady climb up the thickly wooded hillside. The train wound upwards and upwards, through the mango swamps of the lowlands then past the banana and pawpaw plantations that surrounded the clearings formed by villages of round palm-thatched huts. Children rushed to stand waving vigorously at all the white faces peering at them through the train windows.

As dusk descended, we passed through another such village, its inhabitants clustered around a fire. Giant flames threw the black figures into relief; the women with their naked bodies, the first I had ever seen, and large rush thigh-length skirts. The men wore loincloths that did not always hide the parts that were never mentioned in front of us children. The smoke swirling around the figures gave them a disembodied effect and I was sure they were cooking a missionary for dinner. Having whispered this to Caryll, we both almost fell out of the window in our efforts to catch a glimpse of his last struggles, and I think equally to try to get a closer look at all the unmentionable parts of the human anatomy that might be on display.

Miss Unger, looking up from her Tournedos Rossini to see what the excitement was about, firmly shut the window and fixing us with an icy glare told us we were disgusting children and we should just wait until she got us back in the compartment. I knew I could not be punished in the dining car and realised her temper would have cooled somewhat by the time we retired anyway, so I was able to sit sedately and eat a delicious meal. At intervals, fascinating glimpses of the faraway ocean appeared. The tropical night fell fast and the trees of the jungle through which we were passing turned from dark green to black. From then on, like well brought-up children, we remembered to keep our eyes downcast if any more naked or semi-naked bodies hove into sight.

Caryll and I shared a compartment and were once more at our window during the night when the train shuddered to a halt to fill up with water. We could see the large funnel being attached. Did we imagine or did we see the giant shape of an elephant? Certainly we were there for a long time, with the engine hissing, the creaking of the wheels gradually subsiding and only the occasional voice speaking in soft Swahili. Suddenly the gentle silence of the night was broken by the roar of a lion and from the distance came an answer. It was the voice of Africa, the challenge, the defiance, and it sends the blood rushing through one's body.

When we woke the next morning, we were out on the plains. Our steward, collecting our bedding, told us that while filling up with water at Voi, the train had been held up by a herd of elephant that was grazing along the railway line. As a result, we would be late coming into Nairobi. We did not mind. We sat entranced at our window watching Africa unfold with its game – buffalo, zebra, rhino, lion, antelope, wildebeest, gazelle, giraffe – as far as the eye could see.

Our windows were open to let the cool air in but although the mosquito-netting frame was up, it still didn't protect us from the film of red dust that eventually settled over everything. It is invasive and an accepted part of travelling in Kenya. In the 1930s, the colonial ladies draped silk veils over their topees, which swathed their faces. I doubt that even this protection, uncomfortable as it must have been, kept the dust out for long. The starched white clothes that had been so distinctive in the pristine cleanliness of the tropical Mombasa platform were now wilted and soiled and the pretty *memsahibs* drooped as a hot dry wind carried the dust and toyed with their thin cotton dresses. Even the station was red. The gharries with their thin tired horses, the taxis, the large and welcoming crowd, all were covered with a permanent film of dust. No wonder that khaki in all its shades was the uniform of the up-country settler.

My mother however was dressed in pale apricot silk with strings of pearls. She wore a large-brimmed hat in a contrasting dusky rose with lots of large apricot ribbons and an apricot sunshade. The ribbons and the dress floated in the breeze and she looked spectacular on that dusty platform with Chui on a lead (inappropriately named as it turned out, as he was a cheetah and "*chui*" is Swahili for leopard). As usual, all heads were turned in her direction, a fact of which she was supremely unaware.

There were the two distinctive Furness Rolls-Royces waiting and as usual they were packed with an excessive amount of luggage, plus all of us and the cheetah. There wasn't enough room for every suitcase, so poor Miss Munday had to stay behind to wait for one of the cars to return. Caryll and I, discussing this later, were sure she had arranged this so that she would have an extra few minutes with her lover.

Tall and always beautifully tailored, but painfully thin and with a flat chest and grey hair cut in a bob, this English spinster had fallen in love. We had all travelled first class and one of the settlers coming out to Kenya had paid her assiduous attention during the voyage. I used to listen as she spoke to Miss Unger of her love and hopes for the future. Caryll and I, hidden behind a lifeboat, watched their first embrace with fascination. To our minds he was old and ugly with his grey hairy legs and knobbly knees and we watched for some sign that he would transform into a figure of romance. But this stick-like figure in khaki shorts and hairy legs and a bristly grey moustache never did become our heroic prince. In fact, he became the intensely irascible old Colonel Jameson. I even remember his name, so terrified were we when he caught us hiding under their deck chairs. They had been lying side by side sipping their hot consommé, which was offered around by a steward in thick white china cups in a daily noon ritual. I loved it beyond all things but on this day I had even forgone this pleasure to take up our prime position on the upper deck. We had decided that this was going to be the marriage proposal and we could hardly contain our curiosity as to how he would proceed and what would be the outcome.

Whether this was the plan or not we never did find out as he was so enraged at discovering us that we were marched down to Miss Unger. She meted out her usual punishment to me and we were then locked in our cabin for the rest of the day.

Miss Munday had not told her suitor that she was a lady's maid. He duly proposed and she accepted without our being there to monitor events. She only gathered courage to tell him of her status the night before arrival. The stigma of a maid for a wife was too much for this pillar of the British Empire and we heard her come sobbing to Miss Unger's cabin weeping that "her heart was breaking". We watched her intently over the next few days for any signs of this phenomenon but there was no physical evidence, much to our disappointment. That night we sat outside the door to her cabin, which was next to ours, and listened to her sobs and the pacing footsteps. We huddled together, our hearts aching, and we wept for her misery but we dared not enter: a grown-up's grief was no place for a child and we knew there would be no welcome if we did. We climbed back into my bunk clinging to each other for comfort and sharing a grief of which we had no real comprehension.

We were getting into the car with all the attendant flurry and confusion when we saw the colonel for the last time on the Nairobi station platform, an upright figure in military khaki, doffing his topee as he passed Miss Munday. Then he was gone, leaving her a solitary figure surrounded by suitcases and with her broken heart.

Furness had rented what is now the old Shell House in Muthaiga, a district of Nairobi. Because of my propensity to carsickness, I was in the back seat next to the open window on the drive from the station. Mummy had her arm around me and Chui the cheetah was lying next to her with its head on her lap. She had long slender hands with pink varnished nails, and around her wrist she had her favourite three-strand pearl bracelet with an enormous diamond clasp. It matched her engagement ring which was a large exquisite pearl. She was caressing Chui's neck who was purring so loudly it sounded like a dry rasp. What with the smell of leather and the fragrance of Joy with which my mother used to liberally spray herself and all her clothes, I was beginning to feel my usual hot sweat and watery mouth and I desperately tried to quell the urge to throw up. I stuck my head out of the window and feasted my eyes on the wonderful lush vegetation and flowering trees. The earth on the sides of the roads was bright red. We were passing through the Indian quarter and the women were like exotic butterflies in their beautiful silks and cotton saris, all the colours of the rainbow on display. They contrasted so beautifully with the rich ochre, the brilliant green and the vibrant pink of the bougainvillaea hanging from every tree and hedge and vying with the yellow flowers of the tipuana trees, the pinky-cream of the bauhinia and the tecomaria with its orange-red spiky flowers and deep green leaves.

On arrival, we were greeted by a vast and glamorous array of African staff dressed in the Furness colours, with yellow kanzus and wide plum-coloured cummerbunds and fezzes. They had beautiful skins, white smiles and gentle voices, and there were a million dogs plus Joss and Idina, the porcupines. My mother on an earlier visit had rescued the porcupines from an old African who had been sitting on the side of the road. He had the two babies in a cardboard box and offered them for sale as my mother and Duke were driving by, on their way to a lunch in the White Highlands, in the Wanjohi Valley, the centre of the infamous Happy Valley crowd. Part of the massive Rift Valley, the White Highlands were named for the early white settlers who had colonised this beautiful rich uplands area. It even looks like Scotland or England in parts. The Happy Valley lot was the fast-living aristocratic set immortalised in the book and film *White Mischief* and virtually created by the Earl of Errol, Joss Hay and his first wife, Lady Idina when they came out to Kenya from England in 1924. Hence my mother's decision on what to name the porcupines that day.

By the time we arrived in Nairobi, the porcupines were fully grown and very tame. They loved being scratched under the chin and had the run of the house and garden. To our intense delight, we would watch the female visitors utter shrieks of dismay as either Joss or Idina rubbed themselves against the guests' elegantly stockinged legs. In moments of fury they would back up with a great rattle, their quills on end. This was usually displayed for an over-familiar dog but basically there was respect between the animals and they lived in harmony. There were six young lion dogs or Rhodesian ridgebacks that were extremely boisterous and when Caryll and I were running, they would join in our games. We were always being sent for six. We spent most of our time in that lovely garden being flattened by those overgrown puppies. When the safari was over, all the dogs were flown back to Burrough Court along with the porcupines.

The house in Muthaiga, which was nearly opposite the back of the Muthaiga Country Club, became a meeting place for beautiful women in chiffon dresses, large hats and the scent of Chanel No 5, and men, often in polo breeches and boots. Great friends of my mother at this time were the American-born Alice de Janzé and Lady Idina and in fact all the members of the Happy Valley set. I remember years after, Mummy telling me about life in Kenya during the 1920s and 1930s and how incredibly promiscuous that group all was. One of her friends, said my mother, had two sons by a previous husband who had remained in England. Therefore she had never really known her sons until they were in their twenties and had come to see her in Kenya. Finding them very attractive, she had gone to bed with them both.

Whether this was true or not, I don't know as my mother was a great one for embroidering on a good story. She also told me that she and Duke had once stayed with the much-married Idina Erroll in the early 1930s. On their return from a dinner out, my mother, being thirsty, had gone to the sitting room to get a drink. Opening the door, she found a seething mass of naked bodies. Terrified that Duke would see what was going on, she swiftly closed the door and went to bed without her lemonade. My mother also decided that, as this was possibly the general behaviour at Idina's house parties, they would have to find some excuse to leave; it was more than her life was worth to risk Duke's possessive anger. In all probability, he would have accused her of instigating the scandalous behaviour.

Lady Idina had no less than five husbands. Joss Hay, later Lord Erroll, was the third and said to be the best-looking man in Kenya. He was later murdered, supposedly by a former Irish Guardsman and coffee plantation owner, Sir Delves Broughton, because Broughton's own wife, the beautiful Diana Caldwell, had fallen in love with Erroll. At the trial in 1941, which became the talking point of Kenya for many years, Broughton, who had a large estate in Britain and had inherited a huge amount of money on the death of his father (and then spent much of it), was found innocent.

Years later in South Africa I met Douglas Penwill, a wonderful raconteur. I was fascinated by the story of his arrival in Kenya. Douglas had been in the army and had then become a district commissioner after World War II. Needing a manservant, he interviewed several gentlemen who applied for the job. Amongst the Africans was a very tall Luo from west Kenya who had come highly recommended by Broughton. Although he was with Douglas for years the Luo never spoke of the famous murder of Lord Errol even though

Douglas tried to question him on the subject once or twice. Then Douglas had to go on business to Mombasa on the coast and he took his manservant with him. One day he came to Douglas saying, "*Bwana*, I must speak to you on a matter of urgency." Penwill was a fluent Swahili speaker; being a scholar he had learned the correct Kiswahili, scorning our up-country kitchen Swahili efforts. The manservant wanted to warn Douglas that he must hurry back to Nairobi. Douglas, who himself was a marvellous-looking man, had a very lovely young blonde wife who he had left behind at the Muthaiga Country Club. Now, said the Luo, the *memsahib* was being assiduously courted by two young army officers.

"Not to worry," said Douglas. "My wife loves me and I know she would never be unfaithful."

A week later, his manservant came once more. "Please *Bwana*, let us go back to Nairobi. You might be confident of the *memsahib* and her love for you, but I do not want to get involved in another murder case!" Trying to convince Douglas that he must return to protect his wife from the attentions of the officers, he told him how Broughton had entrusted to him the job of making a bonfire and burning all the bloodstained clothes. "So you see, *Bwana*," he repeated, "I would not like to get involved in another murder."

Caryll and I were now taken on our first safari; it remains indelibly printed on my memory and was to establish the future pattern of my life. The tents, the dark blue lorries, the smell of smoke, the crackling of the camp fires, the flames illuminating the thick forest, the roaring of lions and the howling of hyenas; our nights were filled with beauty and the drama of the unknown. I don't think Caryll and I ever got over the glamour of Africa and it is why we always wanted to come back. Those early days were a continual adventure. When the cars could no longer continue, porters would be hired to carry the equipment. The long line of men would move through such high grass that at times only the large bundles they carried on their heads would be visible. We went in dugout canoes, often surrounded by hippo. Other times, having been told to remain noiseless whatever happened, we would follow our mother and the safari's white hunter up to herds of enormous elephant. In our presence, Mummy never allowed anything to be killed, although she herself was a first-class shot and used to spend a lot of time going after trophies. The tusks from an elephant she had shot were displayed at Burrough Court and were so huge we could walk underneath them. Later on, she told me that her love of animals prevented her from continuing this sport that she was so passionate about because the thought of taking a life sickened her. That is when she started collecting animals instead.

CHAPTER

9

One day, not long before the coronation of King George VI and Queen Elizabeth in May, 1937, I was with my mother at Burrough Court admiring her coronation robes and having a marvellous time trying them on, much to the lady's maid Maureen's amusement. I was prancing around the room with the ermine-lined crimson robes trailing behind me, delicate high-heeled slippers falling off my feet and the diamond tiara, much to big for my small head, falling over one eye. I was convinced that I was the Queen of England and the room full of animals my subjects, "To the tower, to the tower and off with their heads!" I kept ordering the dogs in what I imagined was a queenly and authoritative voice, pointing my mother's rolled-up umbrella at my disobedient courtiers. One of my mother's silver foxes was being particularly recalcitrant in not wanting to leave the room. In my effort to stop him going under the bed, I tripped over the cheetah and went sprawling. "Darling," said my mother, having suddenly realised the havoc I was creating in her bedroom, "I don't think that the Queen would wave her wand around so energetically. Just sit on your throne and your henchman [Maureen] will carry out your orders and escort them from the room and into the tower. You will soon be 12. Teenage years are a wonderful time in a girl's life, so darling, think of a suitable present and please, not another dog or a horse."

Forgetting all about being Queen of England, I leapt to my feet and hugging my mother asked, "Can I have anything I want? Please will you take me to America?" I had been reading all the Zane Grey western novels and lived in a dream world of cowboys and cow ponies and the vast plains of America.

Mummy gave a groan of despair: "I do not for one moment see Duke allowing me to go to the States. I've changed my mind. How about two horses and a couple of dogs? Or anything else you want, but no trips please."

I was adamant; I wanted to go to America.

As it turned out, I eventually got my wish, two years later and in time for my 14th birthday. Mummy and Furness had a major row before the coronation. Furness accused my mother of having an affair with Bendor, Duke of Westminster, one of the few men in England richer than Furness. Westminster owned most of the best bits of London's West End and spent his time travelling the world in pursuit of pleasure. He was a tremendous playboy and had had a long affair with the couturier Coco Chanel in the 1920s. Again, I heard it all from servants' hall gossip. The result was that Furness refused to go to the coronation, although all his magnificent ceremonial robes had been fitted and were hanging in the special wardrobe on display. Mummy's was a white, heavily embroidered dress with a train and there were scarlet cloaks trimmed with white ermine collars. Diamond coronets, diamond necklaces and bracelets were locked away in a special safe. Mummy then infuriated Furness even more by threatening that if he refused to accompany her, she might go with someone else. The someone else she meant turned out to be none other than Westminster. This caused a total uproar; I learned from the servants that the screams of rage could be heard all over Grosvenor Square.

Unfortunately, the rowing over Westminster continued until eventually there was such an explosion Furness simply departed overseas. It was the first and only time he left my mother. Furness had always been terrified that unless she was glued to his side she would find the opportunity of casting her eyes elsewhere. After this, Mummy became very ill; I know that she suffered terribly with her back as a result of her hunting accident but one of my mother's principles was that one never discussed ailments or illnesses. This time it was some complication resulting from her back and serious enough that she was taken off to the London Clinic. When she returned home, after quite some time, she was accompanied by a private nurse, Miss Sedgwick. Mummy decided that now she could give me my birthday wish and without the presence of Furness to get in the way of her plans, she got Furness's office to book us all on the Queen Mary to New York and she started organising a six-month trip away.

To prevent any accusation of her taking a lover, my mother asked the formidable Aunt Nanny Tiffany to accompany us on the ship and also across the States. I had never previously met Rory's aunt, Mrs Cameron Tiffany, and found her quite the most terrifying woman. Not only did she look like a bulldog, as I got to know her she behaved like one. She took an instant dislike to me, fixing me with a baleful glare from her drooping eyes under which, with childish fascination, I could see the pink membranes exposed by sagging bottom lids. She also had a bristly grey moustache and was the most hideous woman I had ever seen. Aunt Nanny and my mother together were the most extraordinary combination; I used to think of them as Beauty and the Beast, hardly flattering to Aunt Nanny. In fact, she and her two sisters had been considered fine-looking in the late 1880s. Rory eventually inherited an enormous painting that had been left to him in Aunt Nanny's will. The tall beautifully elegant young woman pictured was a far cry from what she looked like when I first encountered her.

The Camerons, with their big Staten Island estate, could trace their lineage back to Scotland to the 16th century, to the clan chief Cameron of Lochiel, and the Cameron clan is one of the most ancient. Of course, Aunt Nanny never let anyone forget that. She was an appalling snob. At this time the only redeeming feature I could find in her, although I tried very hard, was that she obviously adored my mother.

We set off on the Queen Mary – my mother, myself, Aunt Nanny, Miss Sedgwick the nursing sister (who later married one of her elderly patients and became Lady something-or-other and a regular visitor to Lees Place), Mummy's maid Maureen and Nanny Peasley, as Miss Unger was having another operation on her breast. There was also a young chauffeur sent over by Furness's office, whom Maureen said was a private detective. Furness was making sure of his wife's fidelity. Whether Mummy realised this or not, I don't know, but as usual, Maureen, my source of information, was convinced of the fact.

The Queen Mary was full of film stars, including Gary Cooper who was a friend of my mother, and one evening I was allowed to join them all for dinner. Everyone was in full evening dress. Being a child, I had on a short silk dress and sandals and Nanny Peasley had put a large bow in my hair to dress me up a bit. In spite of my unprepossessing appearance, Gary Cooper, with his wonderful manners, took pity upon me and asked me to dance. I was so thrilled that I never wore that dress again, kept it for most of my life, and refused to wash the hand that he had held on the dance floor. For days thereafter, in spite of nanny's displeasure and being taken to Mummy's stateroom for a serious talking to, I refused to wash. Instead, I would tuck the offending and smelly hand under my face at night while I dreamed of Gary Cooper. When we were in Hollywood later, Mummy asked him to have a photograph taken with me which I still have to this day.

The 1939/40 World Fair was on when we arrived in New York and I spent every day wandering around with Nanny Peasley looking at the amazing displays. She was not nearly as thrilled as I was by all the sights. I had only been in America a few days, we had not even gone west, but I realised that it was a country even more magical than I had dreamed.

We left New York to drive across country to California. Mummy felt that as I loved America so much, I should be given the opportunity of seeing as much of it as possible. We set off, Mummy, Aunt Nanny, myself and Miss Sedgwick in one car and Maureen, Nanny Peasley and the chauffeur in the other. I remember spending a few days in Hollywood. We went to watch Joan Crawford and Norma Shearer on the set of the new film, *The Women*, and to another where Gary Cooper was acting a jungle scene. We spent a lot of time with him sitting around in canvas-backed chairs. While he was chatting up my mother, I was devouring him with my eyes so that I could memorise every little change of facial expression. I was desperate when we left.

We then went to stay a weekend with the newspaper proprietor

William Randolph Hearst and his companion, the actress Marion Davies. All the guests stayed in individual cottages and a chauffeur-driven Rolls-Royce would appear at meal times to drive one to the main house. I remember San Simeon, with its 165 rooms and 127 acres of gardens, being a large copy of a medieval castle, grey stone walls and all very dark and dreary. The first night at dinner we sat down at an enormous dining room table laden with gold plates and golden goblets. I was amazed that I was sitting with all the grown-ups and then realised that there were several other young girls of my age but they were so sophisticated (and already wearing make-up) that I hadn't realised that they also were in their early teens. We, of course, had nothing in common. They could only talk about boyfriends and the latest parties. None of them was interested in dogs or horses. Instead, they eyed this plain, thin, flat-chested teenager wearing socks and flat heels, with no make-up and no conversation, with complete derision. Nor did they try to hide the fact that they considered me some sort of freak. The great attraction the first night was that my mother had a title but when they found out that titles did not necessarily mean that one was related to the king or that one spent one's time at Buckingham Palace, they very soon lost interest.

Dorothy Parker wrote a very funny verse about her stay at San Simeon:

> *Upon my honour*
> *I saw a Madonna*
> *In a thirteenth-century niche*
> *Above the door*
> *Of a Hollywood whore*
> *And a notorious son of a bitch*

After dinner each night we had to watch endless films of Marion Davies. Obviously she adored herself and was conceited about her looks but to my mind she was not beautiful at all, just a common-looking peroxided blonde.

Mummy arranged for me to have my 14th birthday in the Grand Canyon on horseback. I will never forget the excitement of the ride down that small twisting trail that wound around the mountains, following our guide in single file. There was no room for two horses abreast. Our horses and the pack mules behind spent their time right on the edge of the cliff. As there were no barriers, it meant one false step and there was nothing to stop us plunging thousands of feet into the valley below. It was magnificent scenery, although a boiling hot day in the middle of summer with the heat reflecting off the granite rocks. We arrived at the bottom of the canyon about midday, by which time I was so thirsty that I climbed off my horse and rushed to drink from the muddy river. It was dark yellow-brown but no water ever tasted so good. We had a wonderful picnic lunch, Mummy, myself, our guide and two cowboys who had led the pack mules from their cow ponies. The mules had been tied to one another on long reins and were obviously old campaigners on this hazardous trail. It was my dreams come true; the cowboy guide was tall and beautiful and I was lost in a haze of love.

We camped out that night and left as dawn broke. The magnificent splendour of the sunset was unforgettable, as was the sun rising the next day, lighting up the valley and turning the mountains bright pink and mauve.

Back once more to Aunt Nanny who immediately read my mother a lecture on what a terrible mistake parents made in spoiling their children. This was a theme that followed us throughout the trip. She thought it horrifying that all this journey and all the effort put into it should be to satisfy the whim of an awful, over-indulged child. At the time she really seemed to hate me and would glower at me in the car's rear-view mirror. I could not have believed that one day, instead of hating Aunt Nanny, I would grow to love her. With bad grace and a lot of sulking, I put up with her disapproving glares and nasty speeches.

After that, we drove through the redwood forests and on up into the Canadian Rockies. There was wonderful scenery all the way and it was one breathtaking view after another. We stayed a few nights in a lodge on a lake in Alberta which was just bliss, with lots of brown bears. At one stage, when Mummy had parked at the side of the road so we could go off and explore the park, a bear climbed into our car. Mummy, with her love for picnics, had packed a basket. Of this there was soon nothing left and we had to wait and watch from a distance while the bear consumed the last morsel of the sweet biscuits. It was ages before it deigned to amble out of the car and let us back in.

The colour of the lake was an extraordinary ice-blue and surrounded by incredible mountains and forests. We went riding every day. There is nothing else to compare when exploring. Being so much higher than on foot, one can see so much more. I am so grateful that Mummy gave me the opportunity to discover so many countries and foreign lands in this fashion: England, Wales, Scotland, the States, Canada, Mexico, the Yucatan, Guatemala, France, Portugal, India, Pakistan, the Himalayas, Ceylon, Egypt and Africa. On a horse one has the freedom to cover miles of virgin country a day.

We returned to England just before the summer holidays began. Caryll was to join me at Burrough Court and then we were to move on to the Berries for our annual vacation. Furness was still unhappy about the trip we had taken and so my mother finished off her absence by taking this golden opportunity to have a face-lift. The famous plastic surgeon at that time was Sir Archibald McIndoe, from New Zealand, who also treated disfigured airmen. Killing two birds with one stone, Mummy then let it be known through the grapevine that she had tried to commit suicide. Furness, in dire distress, came rushing back only to find that his beloved thought it all a huge joke and, looking 20 years younger, was happily luxuriating with maids, nurses and her pet cheetah in the London Clinic.

Not so thrilled, I believe, was Sir Archibald, who on one visit to his famous patient arrived to find a cheetah sprawling across her bed and a silver fox emerging from under the sheets.

CHAPTER

10

We all left for France just weeks before England went to war with Germany. We were unconcerned by whatever was happening in central Europe. As far as everyone in our circle was concerned the Maginot Line, the defensive fortifications and guns along the border between France and Germany, was impregnable and England was a world power. Hitler, we believed, was just a little German upstart prancing about with his storm troopers in Munich and he needed taking down a peg or two. Any war over Hitler's ambitions for Poland and the rest of Europe would be firmly dealt with in a couple of months. This is what I heard from my governess. Looking back, I realise we must have been either very naïve, or very arrogant, or both.

My mother loved her golf at Le Touquet and Furness loved the casino. On this occasion, we were to fly over. Mummy and Furness were already there and so we were allowed to use the plane. As our chauffeur drove the Rolls down the pebbled drive to the landing strip from the back gate – we children didn't use the front entrance – Miss Unger said, "Look out of the window at Burrough Court, you will never see it again." She was right. We never did see our glorious Burrough Court again.

Caryll never much liked it at The Berries. When we were younger, we had had an English governess-cum-riding teacher who used to shut us in the laundry cupboard when we were naughty. Thank goodness I was not claustrophobic. When I got locked up, I was perfectly happy to sit and dream away of being a fairy princess shut in the tower by an evil witch and so I was hardly conscious of being punished. I was also definitely the favourite with this governess as I adored my horses and riding. Poor Caryll, however, was once left in the cupboard on his own for hours. Our new governess was probably busy with the horses and forgot. This experience left my little brother very wary of the dark and he would often appear at my bedroom door, when everyone had gone to sleep, clutching his little blanket. Even as a grown man, I used to find him asleep at night with one corner of the sheet in his mouth. As a small child his blanket never left him. I would hear this pathetic little voice, "Pat, are you asleep? I have had a nasty dream. Can I climb into your bed?" I would turn on the bedside light and there he would be, sucking his blanket, his enormous blue eyes wet with tears and I would feel my heart bursting with love.

I loved the Berries. There was a marvellous head housemaid called Emilienne and her husband Gaston was in charge of the garden. Later, Gaston was killed in the garden in the war during a bombing raid on Le Touquet and Emilienne eventually came to Fiorentina, our villa in the south of France and was with us until she retired.

The Berries was not a huge place like Burrough Court but we had our own wing and I was able to go riding every day, either in the forests, on the sand dunes or along the beaches. Rory had also joined us this time, which made life more interesting. He would take us for wonderful drives around the countryside and to restaurants and visits to lovely chateaux. Rory always wanted to see beautiful things and places. It did not matter if it was furniture, flowers, or houses. He would take us with him when he went exploring and it was magical. Rory was the apple of Mummy's eye. Furness never ever got used to her love of her children, and particularly her love of Rory because he was so much older than us. He remained jealous.

I used to ride along the beaches and see the planes overhead but thought nothing of it until the day I saw one crash. It fell in flames, not far from where we were, and to our horror we saw the pilot running towards us burning like a torch. We galloped towards him and although my groom tried to smother the flames with the jacket he had taken off, it was too late. We were left with a blackened and smouldering body. For many years I associated his death with flying and it became the one thing that terrified me.

The author, P. G. Wodehouse, creator of Jeeves and Bertie Wooster, lived in a villa nearby with his wife Ethel and they were great friends of my mother. They had a young and attractive secretary who was very sweet to me. I remember her taking me out to lunch in one of the restaurants with a whole lot of RAF pilots stationed nearby – a Hurricane Squadron. Unless I had gone with them, they would have been 13 and none of them was prepared to take the risk. This is the first time I had heard of this superstition.

Two things happened during this period at Le Touquet that made me loathe Furness. I had always disliked him but I now hated him. I had a beautiful Harlequin Great Dane. I was running with him in the garden one day when in play he leapt on me, tearing my jacket and tumbling me to the floor. It was only exuberance because he was young but Furness had just come out onto the terrace and saw this episode. The next thing I knew, a van had come to collect my beautiful dog and he was taken off to the vet to be put down. I will never forget his big mournful eyes looking at me through the wire mesh as he was driven away. I was quite hysterical. It took ages before Mummy could calm me. She called up the vet and told him not to say anything to her husband but he was not to put the dog down and he was to find him a good home and she would pay for his keep. This helped to a certain extent but to this day I can still see him being driven away.

At this time, I also had a corgi, two poodles and a Yorkshire terrier. The Yorkshire terrier was practically impossible to house-train and one day he did a wee on Miss Unger's handbag, which she had left lying on the floor. Miss Unger was furious and blamed me for my "horrid" dog. She then came to me with great delight saying that she had sent a message to Furness and had his permission to have the dog shot. Miss Unger had taken it on a lead to the forest where Gaston shot it. I never forgave her or Furness. This had come so soon after my terrible experience with the Great Dane that it had a huge psychological effect on me.

Meanwhile, Furness had left The Berries for Monte Carlo, a favourite haunt of his because of the casino. He took Mummy and his entourage with him and later we joined them, accompanied by our governess Miss Carruthers and the nannies. Miss Unger stayed behind to look after the house. It was when she was saying goodbye to me that she said, in her psychic way, "I will not be seeing you again, and I am sorry for not having been nicer to you in the years we were together. I must tell you of an amazing occurrence when I was coming to punish you once at Burrough Court. Your father stood in the doorway and would not let me through."

That was the time I remember so well when I had prayed to him, and I had heard her come to the communicating door but no further.

Again Miss Unger was right; we never did see her again. She stayed at The Berries, which was commandeered by the Germans after they invaded France, formed a relationship with the German officer sequestered there, and then, after the Allies stormed the French coastline in 1944 on D-Day, went back to Montreux in Switzerland where she died in the early 1950s.

In Monte Carlo, in the Hôtel de Paris, there was a large portrait of my mother displayed on an easel at the bottom of the main staircase. I often used to sit near it because I loved hearing the gentlemen discussing her beauty. I don't know what triggered Furness's possessiveness on this occasion but having just arrived at Monte Carlo, he challenged some would-be lover of my mother to a duel in a fit of rage. I believe, according to the staff gossip, that they were to meet at dawn with pistols. When I asked Mummy about it, she said that for once she wasn't guilty. The gentleman in question was a well-known gambler and ladies' man and from the time he had set eyes on my mother he had pursued her relentlessly. I had heard from the valet that Furness had got his pistols ready and sat there saying, "I'm going to shoot the bugger. I'm going to shoot the bugger."

Furness was apparently a very good shot and intended to wound his opponent but Mummy said that his hands were shaking so much as he practised with the pistols that she was seriously worried as to what would be the outcome. Seeing that she was getting nowhere with her pleas for him to desist, my mother finally gave him an ultimatum. She said that she was taking her children and leaving Monte Carlo. He could choose to stay and carry out his ridiculous duel, in which case she did not want to see him again, or he could come with her. She also wrote to the gentleman in question telling him of her ultimatum to Furness and that, furthermore, even if she left Furness, he should never expect to have a place in her life as she never wished to speak to him again. This must have satisfied Furness as our whole entourage packed up and left the Hôtel de Paris.

CHAPTER
———
11

After this episode, Furness shifted Mummy into a house at St Jean Cap Ferrat, the Villa La Fiorentina that he had just bought, although she had chosen it. It was on a peninsula, the Cap St Hospice, which curved to face the mainland over the Bay of Beaulieu. Not content with just the one house, a huge Florentine-style mansion, he had bought all the neighbouring houses as well. According to my mother, this was to prevent incidents like the Hôtel de Paris one. No would-be lovers would be able to buy or rent a villa nearby. He had virtually bought the whole end of the point with the four big houses and their attached cottages on it.

We arrived along with governesses, nurses and maids, and my dogs, but I had had to leave the horses behind at The Berries. I never did find out what happened to them, although I was told that all the animals that were left at Burrough Court were still there after the war. Burrough Court itself was burned down accidentally by the Canadian Air Force who had been billeted there. Mummy had rented a house in St Jean for Rory, us and our retinue. It sat high up off the road and had a verandah that overlooked the harbour. Furness by this time was not well and Mummy was worried that we and our staff would upset him. Fiorentina was a huge villa but it was not set up with enough staircases and dining rooms to keep us out of the front of the house, and therefore out of his line of sight.

I loved our house in the village. I had my bicycle and my dogs and there were baskets to attach to the bicycles so that they could come riding with me and whoever was accompanying me. We used to cycle up to Fiorentina every morning to spend time with Mummy and in the afternoons I spent a lot of time sitting on our verandah under the grapevines, watching the life of the village. Hannah, the young maid, often sat with me and flirted with the local fishermen. I was only 14 at the time, and was experiencing my first crush. My hormones had started working and telling me that there were other things besides horses to be fascinated by. There was a particularly good-looking young fisherman who used to pass by each day. He would look up and give me messages for Hannah, who did not speak French. I was fascinated by his beautiful black eyes and his strong Basque accent and made sure I was always on the balcony when he was passing. He was a tremendous flirt because it was not long before he was telling me that I had the most beautiful eyes, and as the months went by, he transferred his affections to me. Although there was never any contact, for I was much too strictly chaperoned, he had turned the full charm of his Latin good looks on to winning the heart of this young English girl. Which of course he succeeded in doing! I felt like Juliet looking down on her Romeo. Ever since I had turned 12, I had been reading not just Zane Grey but the romantic novels of writers like Jean Plaidy and Georgette Heyer. And I loved the books about the Scarlet Pimpernel by Baroness Orczy. I immersed myself in these books; they were a refuge for a shy girl in a household with such larger than life figures as Furness, my beautiful mother and my bossy and sophisticated brother Rory. I have been a true romantic ever since.

At the end of the Christmas holidays, in 1939, Caryll went back to England, to school, on the Blue Train with Furness's man of affairs, who had come over for business meetings with Furness. It was almost three years before I saw my little brother again. England and France had declared war on Germany four months before, Poland had been invaded by Hitler, ships were being sunk by German submarines and over 150,000 British troops had crossed the channel onto French soil, but we were protected from it all by being in the south of France. By May, the Germans had pummeled Belgium and Holland, crossing their borders and dragging them into the war. Alone with my novels and fantasies, I was blissfully unaware of just how very serious things were getting. Perhaps we all were.

Rory had been busy getting the Clos ready for our bit of the family to move in. The Clos, an 18th-century, pink-washed three-storeyed cottage, was the original house on Cap St Hospice and the largest of the other three houses that Furness had bought with Fiorentina. When it was ready, Rory, the staff and I moved in and also Phyllis Satherswaite, a great friend of Rory's and a competition-standard tennis player. Fiorentina had a good hard court and Phyl persuaded my mother to get a professional to give me lessons. He used to bicycle over from Monte Carlo twice a week to teach me, a most reluctant pupil. I was miserable. I had no horses and running about after a ball was not my idea of enjoyable exercise. Poor man, it must have been dreadful trying to earn one's living having to put up with a sulky rich English girl.

Also staying at the Clos were a very nice, very good-looking young Belgian couple, a count and countess. They played tennis well and I liked them enormously as they spent a lot of time trying to encourage me to take an interest in the tennis court. They had come south to escape the German army. Mummy was a great friend of the young wife's mother. By now, even we were becoming aware that the war was going to affect all of us. There was no petrol available for transport, although there was always some available on the black market at a vast expense. Everybody bicycled everywhere. Food was getting very short. Mummy bought some goats but Furness and I were the only people allowed to have the milk, butter and cheese that she made from the three goats.

There was eventually a terrible row; Phyllis Satherswaite kept going to the kitchen and snaffling the cheese and butter. Finally one of the maids told my mother. Phyl had hidden a whole supply of food and cheese under her corsets. Mummy was very upset, and apparently said to Phyl: "You are stealing food from a sick man and a child. I and everybody else go without and I am not having one of my guests disobeying the rule. Therefore you must find somewhere else to stay!" The maid, with great delight, came to tell me. None of them liked Phyl anyway.

The other incident involving guests had a lasting effect on my life. One day I came back to the Clos to find the young Belgian countess in the sitting room, acting like a madwoman. I had noticed her becoming more moody and strange every day. Now she was crawling around the walls and looking in every corner, saliva coming out of her mouth, mumbling, "*Mon Dieu, Mon Dieu, c'est caché.*" I rushed to find someone to help. I saw the doctor arrive, and she was taken off to hospital. I could not really find out what had happened to her but as usual one of the maids told me. She was an addict and her supply of morphine had run out.

From that day on, I haven't even taken a sleeping pill I became so terrified of getting hooked on anything. No matter what one tells a very young teenager, they always think a grown-up does not understand the ways of youth. It is the shattering effect of seeing for oneself that forces one to face the horror of reality.

We also saw a lot of Leonor Fini, the Argentinian surrealist who had been a pupil of Salvador Dali. She was very glamorous and always arrived to stay accompanied by two boyfriends, one fair and one dark. There was a lot of giggling amongst the staff as they organised the rooms. She had a voluptuous figure and amazing legs which she showed off by wearing short shorts. Dark-haired and sun-tanned, she used to like wearing long white dresses for evening that clung to every curve and she would walk from one mirror to another she was so in love with herself. She thought I had a marvellous face for painting, with great big cat's eyes. Once she did a glamorous portrait of me in a medieval green velvet gown, with my long hair flowing down my back and my face turned up to the moon against the backdrop of an old ruined castle. She framed it in green velvet, the same colour as the dress. It was so beautiful that she gave it to me, but I don't know what happened to it as I didn't see it again after the war. She also did a lovely one of my mother which I still have, as well as a sketch of myself.

One day, Rory and his friends were discussing Nora Auric, the wife of the famous French composer Georges Auric, and Nora's boyfriend,

Count Guy de Lesseps. They were saying he was the best-looking man in France, 20 years younger than Nora, and how romantic it was that they lived in an old castle near the sea. Rory invited them to lunch. I was almost 15 and the thought of meeting a descendant of the famous de Lesseps who had built my Suez Canal was tremendously exciting. Especially as he was supposed to be such a great beauty and living in a castle. I couldn't wait to meet this romantic couple.

My first sight of Guy de Lesseps still lives in my memory. Tall, fair and deeply sun-tanned, he was wearing tight gaucho pants, obviously made specially for him, and a terracotta-coloured linen shirt that was opened almost to his navel and which showed off his beautiful tanned chest with its gold St Christopher medallion. Even his feet were beautiful and he wore no shoes. I was standing with my back to the sea on the verandah and he was laughing at something someone had said as he came towards me. His teeth were very white and his feline elegance was breathtaking. As he was introduced, he kissed my hand. Nobody else had yet done that, even though I lived in France, because I had been considered too young. As he bent over my hand, he smiled at me; even his blue eyes were laughing. I felt as if I were drowning. For ages after I did not wash the back of my hand and, just as with Gary Cooper's imprint, I used to hold it out of the bath so as not to erase the touch of that beautiful mouth. I was in love and I remained in love with him in my dreams for years. He became the prince of all my romantic thoughts.

Guy sat next to me at lunch and, although I was speechless for most of the meal and broke out into a deep blush every time he bent towards me, it did not deter him. He carried on a light flirtation with me as if I were the only female at the table. For the first time in my life a man sat next to me and behaved as if I were fascinating.

The second time I met Guy was in Cannes. I had gone with Mummy and Rory to a concert. To get to the boxes, one had to climb a narrow twisting iron staircase. It was impossible to buy clothes at that time, so Mummy had altered one of her glamorous evening dresses to fit me. It was made of white taffeta, and flared from a tight waist. Being one of my mother's dresses, it had a low décolleté which had to have a lot of alteration for I was still very immature in that department. Mummy had allowed me to have a little make-up for the first time, blackening my eyelashes with mascara, which had a wonderful effect on my eyes, always my best feature. A powder and light pink lipstick transformed me. I felt quite grown up and could not stop looking at myself in the mirror. I could now understand how Leonor Fini felt!

Mummy and Rory were so busy talking to their friends that as we mounted the narrow and crowded staircase, I went ahead. As I looked up, I saw Guy de Lesseps just in front of me. If possible, he looked even more beautiful. He was wearing tight black trousers and a white dinner jacket and was still shoeless. He was the original hippie who never worried about fashion but dressed to show off his wonderful figure. As I came up behind him, he looked down just as he was about to take the step up. Catching sight of me, he was so intrigued by my transformation that he tripped and nearly fell over. Laughing he said, "*Tu vois ce que tu fais*" and, bending low in a mime of a courtly bow said, "*Chapeau! Mais tu es belle.*" Taking my hand, which was gripping the banister, he took it to his lips and kissed the palm. I was scarlet with embarrassment once more and at the same time transported with love. Nora, who was just in front of him, said, "Guy, she is only a child. Behave yourself." I did not see Guy again until after the war, but in all those years I never forgot him. He was later to become my lover and one of the great loves of my life.

CHAPTER

12

The war was going very badly for our side. Hitler wasn't going to be stopped after all. Belgium and Holland had surrendered. Our troops were driven back towards the channel and then evacuated from Dunkirk. With German bombs falling around them and amid deadly machine-gun fire, they made it to the ships, ferries, fishing boats and even dinghies that had come over from England and were waiting for them. Paris fell on June 17, 1940. France was split into two: occupied France in the north with the Germans in power and Vichy France in the south, which was supposed to be independent but which collaborated with the Germans. Rory had already decided to return to the States because he felt, as an American citizen, he should be ready to join up if his country went to war. He eventually enlisted as a G.I. and then, after serving in Nebraska as a sergeant in the army, was transferred to the Office of Strategic Services. It was the forerunner of the CIA and Rory was useful because he spoke fluent French and German. He was later sent to London, on loan to British Intelligence where he worked with Hugh Trevor-Roper. After the war, Rory worked on Trevor-Roper's book *The Last Days of Hitler*.

Meanwhile, Mummy moved me over to Fiorentina, for Furness now kept mainly to his room. Mummy had hired a trained nurse to help look after him and there were daily visits from the doctor. Nobody discussed his illness and I never saw him. Food was very scarce. As I was growing and getting very tall, Mummy had to keep altering her dresses to fit me, but shoes were a problem. I ended up with wooden clogs made for me by one of the gardeners and so, rather like Guy de Lesseps, I went barefoot instead. I kidded myself it was because of the lack of shoes but secretly it made me feel a bit closer to him when I copied his eccentric style of dress.

Mummy and I would often bicycle to Monte Carlo or Nice. Any petrol was kept for Furness, although now he hardly ever went out because he was so frail. I remember walking barefoot around Monte Carlo, pretending I was with Guy instead of my mother, and feeling as if I were starving. There was always a terrible shortage of food, and in spite of a thriving black market there was not that much available. I wanted to go into one of the restaurants but Mummy would not allow it; she said that everyone was telling her that they were now using dogs, cats and even rats to make their soups and stews. Therefore, they would not get a penny of her money. She bought me some horrible-looking biscuits, for all the bread had been sold out.

We could feel the presence of the Germans even though we were in Vichy France or what was called the Free Zone. Supposedly, we were in a French state, led by Marshal Henri Pétain who had been a great French hero of World War I, but we all knew that the Germans were really pulling the strings and that it was only a matter of time before they took over this bit of France as well. A few days after the fall of Paris, England organized for a refugee ship to bring all the British citizens home from the south of France. Somerset Maugham, whose villa La Mauresque was close by and who was one of Mummy's bridge partners whenever he was on the Côte d'Azur, came to see her and tried to persuade her that, in spite of Furness's ill health, we would have to risk the journey. It would be the last chance for English citizens escaping France. Anyone left behind would almost certainly end up in a concentration camp, he said. All the English staff had left long before.

Furness by now had a night and a day nurse and my mother was very worried about him. I was seeing less and less of her as he was continually demanding her presence. Mummy had a marvellous lady's maid, Mademoiselle Jeanne, who adored the dogs and my mother in that order! And she was wonderful to me. She tried to console me for the lack of my mother's attention but I resented the fact that Furness was taking all of her time now. There were no more bicycle rides and romps in the morning. Mummy was either playing bridge with friends or was with Furness. She never even went out any more in case Furness might need her. This was not the laughing, joking mother I knew.

On the day we left for Cannes and the evacuation ship, Furness was so sick he had to be carried into the Rolls by the butler and one of the footmen. He always carried a hip flask and having been settled in the back of the car, he took his flask out and had a quick slug of brandy. His hand was shaking so much though that he spilled some on his shirt. It was so little that it would have been unnoticeable to anyone else but Furness, who was used to being immaculate, got in a terrible tizz. He would not move until his valet had been summoned, and a newly ironed shirt and a matching tie produced. This was the first time I had seen Furness in months and I was shocked by the difference in him. It was also the first time in my life that I had been in the same car as him.

We went to the Carlton hotel in Cannes to await the boat's departure. The pier was piled high with luggage, and desperate people, terrified of being left behind, were camping out on the quayside next to their luggage. The next startling occasion came when I had lunch with Mummy and Furness in the dining room of the Carlton. Again, it was the first time I had ever eaten a meal with Mummy when Furness was present. Furness had beautiful hands and three times a day one of his valets would buff his nails until they shone. His right hand was lying on the table and was shaking so much that all the china rattled. Mummy had tucked a large white napkin over his shirt and had started feeding him his soup. Mummy placed her hand over his trembling hand and said, "Darling, don't get so upset. Once we are on board, it won't be so bad. At least we shall be amongst friends."

"They're not my fucking friends," Furness exploded. "They are all your bloody friends and that is not a ship. It is a fucking cargo boat. If you are so worried about your safety, you can go with your bloody friends and take that bloody little bitch with you" – meaning me – "but I am not going!" Mummy did her best to calm him down; he also kept insisting that she get his nurse as he needed another "*piqûre*" [injection].

At the time it meant nothing to me. I was used to hearing his foul language whenever I was around and it was only years later that I realised he probably wanted some morphine.

For the impeccable Furness who was only used to his own transport – I doubt in the whole of his spoilt life he had ever been on public transport of any kind – the very thought of getting on a refugee ship, a collier which looked like a big tramp steamer, with a horde of people in cramped conditions was more than he was prepared to consider. Mummy, when Furness started getting so worked up, turned to me and said, "My darling go to your room and wait for me. I will come and see you later."

When she did finally arrive, she said to my horror, "Darling, you must understand I cannot leave Duke. He is too ill to travel and I do not think he would survive the trip. I have arranged with Willy Maugham to take care of you on the boat and to see you get safely back to Burrough Court. When you get to England, there will be everyone there to look after you and Caryll will be able to come and spend the holidays with you."

I went into screaming hysterics. The thought of being taken care of by the terrifying Willy Maugham while at the same time having to leave my beloved mother was more than I could bear. I clung to her in such a frenzy of despair that Mummy in the end had to agree to let me stay. Once she had promised I could remain, nothing else mattered.

I do not remember if it was at this stage or at some other time when we were staying at the Carlton that a German bomber came over and dropped some bombs in the harbour. I went on the balcony to watch and was absolutely amazed at the reaction of the crowd on the waterfront. They rushed around like chickens with their heads cut off. Two women were so hysterical that they stripped their clothes off as they raced down the street. What that was supposed to accomplish I do not know. When I went downstairs in the lift, the lobby was full of terrified people, fainting and screaming. During the whole of the time I later spent in London during the constant air raids, I was not to see any such signs of panic and I could never get over the fuss that was being made about a few bombs dropping in the harbour.

We returned to Fiorentina where life became more difficult. Furness, as I now learned from the nurses, was fatally ill. He was suffering from cirrhosis of the liver. Although Mummy never spoke about it, she was getting thinner and thinner as she was now saving all her food for Furness and myself. I was hungry all the time. I used to dream of Guy de Lesseps and lovely fresh loaves of bread dripping with butter. Mummy seemed to be the only one who knew how to milk the goats, or maybe she wanted to make sure that we got the benefit and so wouldn't allow anyone else to do it. She also used to boil down candles to make a sort of dark furry soap. I don't know what other ingredient she used and I suppose it kept one clean but it never lathered. This soap was mainly kept for Furness so that the nurses could bathe him twice a day.

I was with Mummy in the kitchen at Fiorentina late one day when someone came to get her. The kitchen was huge and dark because it was in the basement and Mummy was melting the candles as usual. I think it was Mlle Jeanne who came to say the doctor had arrived. Mummy turned to me and said, "Duke needs me, I must go up. Darling, keep an eye on the saucepans and make sure the grease does not boil over onto the stove."

She left me in this dark kitchen with these enormous pots bubbling away. It was very creepy for a young girl. There was almost no electricity because of the shortages and everything was lit by candles. It was so dark it must have now been evening but I had been given a responsibility and so I sat keeping my eye on the boiling pots. Talk about witches' cauldrons. I even trod on the cat when I went to lower the gas, and it immediately started screeching. Trying to pacify the cat and look after the boiling candles kept me occupied, but as time went on, it got colder and colder and then darker and darker as the candles gradually burnt down. Nobody came back.

Furness died during the night, on October 5, 1940. The nurses left, there were no more daily visits from the doctor and for me, life had not changed that much. But Mummy now always dressed in black, got even thinner and never laughed. One morning when I came into her room, she was sitting in bed, her arms wrapped around her knees, her head bent, and the tears pouring down her face. Lost in misery, she did not hear me come in so I tiptoed out again. I knew she would hate anyone to witness her despair. She was a great believer in never showing a weakness.

There was a big detention camp near Eze. Any Allied military still in Vichy France had had to give themselves up for internment once the new government was declared. I often used to sit on the rocks with my dogs and wonder what kind of life the prisoners were enduring in that formidable fortress of La Revère. I used to sit on the harbour wall and try and signal to them with my hand mirror. It was not long before we started housing the escaped ones who were trying to make it back to England. Sometimes they stayed a day, or sometimes two, then disappeared as quietly as they had come. Rory told me much later that the American racing driver and pilot Whitney Straight had been flying for the RAF when he was downed by ground fire and captured. He managed to escape from Nice via the French underground movement and our mother had been involved. But, according to Rory, Mummy was hurt when she met him later; he didn't mention the fact nor thank her.

Mummy never really discussed these prisoners with me, but on one occasion she asked me to accompany one into Nice. We set off on our bicycles with him dressed in clothes from one of our gardeners and wearing a beret. I think he must have been ill or sick with fright as I remember wondering why he was such a funny colour. His skin was a yellowish white. We had to pass quite a few patrols on the way. We arrived at the address my mother had given me, in one of the back streets of Nice, and there I left my prisoner and joined Mlle Jeanne, who was waiting for me on a bench under one of the palm trees.

Mummy never explained why I had been sent this time and I never thought to ask her. It is only as I write this that I wonder what the reason was. The next prisoner stayed for a few days. The Vichy police arrived and searched the house but he was disguised as one of the maids. It was not long after this episode that we left ourselves. I suppose the authorities were getting very suspicious of my mother's activities. I do not remember much of our departure, except that my mother spent hours taking my long hair and rolling it up into curls on top of my head, and in each curl she had pinned notes. By the time she had finished I was a walking bank. Travelling on Mummy's American passport from her first marriage, we then caught the train across the border and into Spain.

What I do remember is the nightmare journey in the train across Spain. We definitely were not travelling first class but were in a crowded compartment where there was hardly room to move. Even the loo was crowded with women sitting with their chickens. There was no way that I could get to the toilet, it was too embarrassing, and the women had no intention of moving. I suppose there was no place for them to move to. But I was in agony. I managed to rush out at one of the stations while Mummy made sure the train did not leave without me. There was also a soldier on board who was squashed up on the seat next to me and in the dark, he started fumbling around, trying to stroke my leg. For a while I did not realise what he was trying to do until he got a bit bolder. Even then, as I had no idea of sex, I could not understand why his hands were getting higher and higher. I said to Mummy, "That man is trying to do funny things with his hands." So for the rest of the journey, my mother moved over and I had to half-sit on her lap which made this nightmare journey even more uncomfortable.

The relief when we arrived in Portugal and were once more cocooned in luxury and under the aegis of the British Embassy was immense. We spent a couple of weeks there, being shown Portugal by the most charming and lovely young girl from the embassy who was madly in love with the naval attaché. She made a great confidante of my mother and I was intrigued listening to her passion for this very nice-looking young man – in my mind he was no Guy de Lesseps – because it was the first time I had heard a girl talking of the uncertainties of love and whether he would marry her.

I was fascinated by my mother's advice. Never let a man know how much in love you are; never show any signs of jealousy, for it gives them too much confidence. If they are going to flirt with other girls, your jealousy will not stop them. Instead, it just makes for a continual conflict and in the end will drive a man away. Nothing brings a man to heel quicker than to keep him totally uncertain. I remember Mama giggling and saying, "A man is a predator, he enjoys the uncertainty of the chase; so never let him feel sure of his prey." I never forgot this conversation and as I am only attracted to womanisers, it has worked like a charm.

We were in Portugal about two weeks before my mother used her influence to get us onto the regular flying boat service that went between Lisbon and England. It flew almost on top of the water with no lights on to evade the guns. Everything was in darkness. I can still clearly see the moon's reflection on the black sea below. The next year, making a similar flight, the actor Leslie Howard died when his plane was shot down.

CHAPTER

13

We arrived back in England in 1942. Mummy had decided to live in London, so we stayed at Claridges while the townhouse in London was made ready. Lees Place was a Georgian red brick house set back in a courtyard, with the stables converted into garages and at the back, a small garden. It was just off Grosvenor Square.

While we were still at Claridges, Mummy went to see either the Prime Minister, Sir Winston Churchill, or the foreign secretary Sir Anthony Eden and their staffs for a series of interviews about the situation in the south of France and the prisoners there. My mother at that time must have been one of the last Englishwomen to leave that country.

When we finally moved back into Lees Place, we were left with only Collins the butler as all the footmen had been called up. He was probably in his sixties, very tall and upright with terribly swollen, arthritic hands. He was forever trying to put on white gloves that had to be large enough to fit over his deformed knuckles.

The rest of the staff were women, mostly Irish. I adored Mummy's lady's maid Maureen. She was always joking and laughing, which was remarkable when I look back, as she had been buried alive when a bomb hit the building she and her sister lived in. They managed to dig her out of the ruins, but her sister was killed. I used to listen with horrified fascination to this dreadful story and picture her feeling of suffocation as she lay there in the dark, inhaling thick dust with every breath, and listening to the moans of her sister which finally ceased, and the sound of water from a burst pipe trickling down the wall. What had saved Maureen's life was the fact that on hearing the sirens she had crawled under the bed, which kept most of the bricks from falling on her.

Hannah, by now the head housemaid, was a great favourite and she had a wonderful singing voice. A very tall girl in her twenties, I can still see her in her striped grey and white uniform and mobcap singing as she wielded the brush on the yellow carpeted staircase. I used to sit below the ones on which she was working and join in the chorus. Apart from Hannah, there was an under-housemaid from County Cork who had a thick Irish accent and a penchant for the American G.I.s. It was not long before she got herself pregnant, and nine months later an illegitimate baby boy joined the household. From then on, the kitchen was filled with nappies, both clean and very dirty. More often than not the dirty ones were left lying on the kitchen table as, quite understandably, Mary found it happened to be the most convenient place on which to change him. Those that were not littering the kitchen table were left drying over the large Aga stove. The baby screamed a lot and the cook, who was very maternal, kept cooing to him and shoving food down his throat.

It was a good thing my mother was not used to coping with the daily running of a household. All her life, an efficient and elderly head housemaid had done this for her. Now it was different. Each morning my mother used to discuss the menus with the cook who, in a clean apron and book to hand, would present herself in the bedroom to receive the orders for the day. Mummy would lie in bed with her beautiful nightgowns and feather-trimmed satin negligées, having her coffee and scrambled powdered egg. Everything was rationed and there were no such thing as fresh eggs but her tray had starched linen, Dresden china, silver cutlery and always a beautiful fresh flower arrangement. Mummy had absolutely no sense of time; she was invariably several hours too late for everything. After Furness's death and the disappearance of his private transport we spent the rest of our lives missing trains, planes and even ships. Therefore, she certainly never left herself enough time to descend to the basement. As a result, the total lack of hygiene in the kitchen went unnoticed.

The final female members of the household were my Nanny, Nanny Peasley, whom my mother summoned out of retirement to come and look after me, and a very young girl who helped the cook. She was the grocer's daughter from just around the corner. We only had one footman. He had been the scullery boy at Burrough Court but now he was elevated in status. One of his legs being shorter than the other, he had a decided limp. The other remaining male was the chauffeur. There had always been five but the others were young and long gone. Arthur stayed and, as far as I could see, spent his life polishing the Furness Rolls until it shone like a mirror. On account of petrol rationing, it and the Buick were up on blocks in the garage and never moved.

Life in London settled down to a routine, although nothing with my mother remained routine for long. Her new boyfriend, Lord Brownlow, positively haunted Lees Place. He had a job somewhere in the Aircraft Production Ministry and was usually in air force uniform. It was his suggestion that I be sent to secretarial college as I was still too young for the army. Nanny Peasley's duties were to see that I did not go anywhere unaccompanied. She and I would walk every morning to the secretarial college in Victoria Street. Nowadays with all the traffic it would be a long journey but in those days the streets were practically deserted and a morning and evening constitutional was good for the health. She would take a bus home and return in time to pick me up at 4pm. Then we used to go to a YMCA, near Victoria Station, which served tea, sandwiches, Yorkshire pies and scones to the armed forces, and we would wash dishes for an hour. The days we did not go to the canteen, I would be taken to Miss Vacani's dancing classes where we did ballroom dancing and were made to practise endless sweeping curtsies. I had a passion for dancing and had regularly attended ballet classes from the age of five. Miss Vacani and the beautiful waltzes, foxtrots, polkas and Charlestons she taught, were the highlights of my week.

At the weekend, when school closed, we used to go to the canteen for most of the day. Never a word of complaint was allowed about sore chapped hands. Only Maureen would come to my rescue, when Nanny had retired for the evening, and massage them with Vaseline.

Meanwhile, Mummy had found herself a job at an armaments factory and it involved the use of a welding iron. She had moved on to a new lover, an eminent, very good-looking and ardent American. Consequently, I presume getting up in the mornings to get to the factory on time was becoming more and more difficult. By the time she was dressed, which took hours, she would have to speed across the city. As half the morning would have already gone, I could never understand why she bothered to rush. Before the war, Mummy rarely got up before 11am and now she returned to this familiar pattern. The only difference was that she would bring the welding – or maybe it was a soldering – machine home from the factory so she could catch up on her work at night in her bedroom.

There she would have a tray full of bits and pieces of ironwork from the factory, and in the darkened room – because of the blackout no light was allowed to show – Mummy would sit up in bed totally absorbed in fusing together these various pieces. Flying sparks would light up the dim room. To my imagination, she looked like a fairy queen, surrounded by fireflies. So beautiful! One night going up to my room, I passed her bedroom and as the door was slightly ajar, I caught a glimpse of her. There she was, lying in bed, bathed in a glow from the dimmed bedside lights, wearing a pale blue lace nightgown and negligée trimmed with blue dyed ostrich feathers that floated in the breeze from the open window and caressed the long, delicate neck and expanse of white skin exposed to their touch. The welding mask was pushed to the back of her head, the adored machine clasped in one hand, and, kneeling on the floor beside the bed and tenderly raising the other hand to his lips, was none other than the exalted American. I fled past the room terrified that one of them might look up and see me.

My mother was nothing if not enthusiastic about any new project that she undertook and she could not contain her enthusiasm for her new skill. She started soldering around the house as well. Having been told that the guest room door handle was loose, Mummy, convinced her machine would remedy the fault, went to work. Unhappily for the guest inside, Lady Drogheda, Mama welded the door handle into the lock position, and poor Kathleen was imprisoned for the rest of the day. I remember Billy the footman climbing the extension ladder in the hope of bringing her down by way of the window. But in spite of Billy's coaxing, the height and the rickety ladder were not conducive to a mountaineering feat and our guest firmly decided against this method of escape. Finding a handyman to let her out was, in wartime London, like looking for a needle in a haystack. Therefore she remained incarcerated until nightfall.

Kathleen Drogheda was my mother's closest friend. She had been a great beauty, tall and slim, with dark auburn hair. Very vivacious, she still looked like a magnificent gypsy and dressed accordingly in marvellous bright colour combinations and trailing scarves. She and her husband, the Earl of Drogheda, had had their marriage dissolved in 1922 and she had been one of Furness's lovers prior to his marriage to my mother. It was thanks to her that he had such a wonderful collection of Chinese artefacts. Kathleen Drogheda had made Furness take her to China in one of his huge ocean-going steam yachts, the Emerald. There they had visited Peking and come away with enough treasures to furnish two houses, Burrough Court and Lees Place, not only with carpets but an incredible collection of Tang Horses from large to larger. There were also camels, figurines, vases, pots and plates and Kathleen herself had furnished her entire flat in Curzon Street from this expedition. Celadon, Ming, Tang, Famille Rose, there was no treasure that had been overlooked and in what abundance had they been collected! The holds of the Emerald had been filled for, as Kathleen explained, "It was no point leaving empty spaces when there were so many beautiful things to choose from, so I made Duke keep on buying until most of the guest rooms on the yacht had also been used for storage."

Caryll was now at Eton. While we had stayed in France, he had gone back to his school and because of the war he had remained in England. Now it was Eton's traditional June 4 celebration and speech day and we were going to see him. I remember Mummy's excitement and for days beforehand Lees Place came to a standstill as everybody's concentration focused on preparations for the picnic that was to accompany us. Mummy determined that her adored son, being a growing boy, must be dying of starvation and made our lives hell. All our ration cards were saved up. I decided that I was a growing girl and equally starving but I couldn't persuade my beloved parent of this no matter how hard I tried. Our rations went on a selection of food for Caryll. I remember looking at the collection on the kitchen table and in spite of the dirty nappies my mouth literally watered.

On the day, which was cool, Mummy looked magnificent in a long grey astrakhan coat and hat. (Nowadays I would die if any member of my family wore a fur but then it was very much "*à la mode*".) As it was summer, Mummy had put on underneath a pale violet taffeta silk tailored coat and skirt, with dark violet trim and matching silk blouse, which her great friend Coco Chanel had designed for her before the war. My mother, wanting to look her best for this, her first visit to her son in so many years, had changed as many times as the English weather. With her two lady's maids in attendance, she had tried on dress after dress.

As for myself, Mummy had said, "Darling, do try to look your best. You must make sure that your brother will be proud to introduce you to his friends." I was only just 17 and my life had been spent with my mother, my brothers, nannies, governesses, tutors, grooms and the servants. I was very naïve about life and the romantic novels I read hadn't helped. Mummy and I used to spend a lot of time seeing all the latest movies, given we had just come back from the austerity of France. We had recently seen Lana Turner in a film where she had worn a very tight sweater. Now my one ambition was to look like her. I still built my dreams around the great romantic prince who was Guy de Lesseps. Mentally I transformed myself into a Lana Turner look-alike with whom Guy was madly in love.

I was tall and had a very good figure with an 18-inch waist, but I had no chest development, although Mummy insisted I wore a bust bodice, the restriction of which I hated. I kept trying to convince her it was unnecessary, telling her, "I am not like you, Mummy. I have no bosom to put in it." She insisted that it was very vulgar to go without corsets and without bust bodices, saying, "Darling, that is not the behaviour of a lady." The only blessing was that as it was practically impossible to get stockings, she allowed me to wear corset pants. Thank goodness she did insist. These passion killers were to stand me in very good stead a little later on when I started being escorted around town. I had been brought up by governesses and nannies on the precept that one never argued or disagreed with one's elders and betters, that one should always be polite and well behaved. As a result of this excellent teaching, I found it not only difficult but intensely embarrassing to ever say no to all these so-called officers and gentlemen who began to take me out, in case I hurt their feelings. Almost to a man, they would spend the end of an evening with me, frantically trying to up-end me either on the Lees Place's sofa or in their respective rooms.

Now, with Lana Turner as my role model, I went and bought cotton wool and put the hated bust bodice to good use. Fully padded I looked, to my great delight, like a woman and not a young gangly girl. Mummy would simply say, "You have a lovely figure; you don't need a large bosom." But I couldn't help remarking with glee how, now on my walks to Victoria, men's heads would turn. Nanny, not noticing how her charge had blossomed, would complain bitterly about the licentious behaviour of the soldiers in the canteen. "You are only a child. It's disgusting the way they are trying to paw you and get you out on dates." I was thrilled. At last people were starting to notice me and I was getting the attention that so far had been reserved for my mother and brothers.

For this, my first visit to Eton, I therefore wore a bright red skin-tight dress that showed to perfection my lovely new chest development. I had always been told that I had incredible eyes so I had started using mascara heavily. Not content with the mascara, I had also discovered that my leg tanning fluid, rubbed on my face as well as my legs, gave me an instant sun-tan which I felt showed up my eyes to even better effect. The finishing touch was my manicure. I wore my nails very long and lacquered them bright red. Knowing that my mother was going to be late as usual, I kept well away until she had already entered the hired car, the picnic baskets had been packed and Arthur and Billy were safely installed in front. Only then did I make my appearance. I had put on a jacket over my dress but even so, the reaction to my get-up from my mother was, as I knew it would be, one of horror.

"Darling, you look like a tart! What have you done to yourself?"

It was too late to send me off to change and Mummy with her usual sense of humour burst out laughing, declaring, "At least no other Etonian is going to have a sister who looks like you. Whether Caryll will appreciate the fact or not, I hesitate to guess." Whereupon, she could hardly contain her giggles. Thinking to myself that she was terribly old-fashioned and knew nothing of the modern world, I sat and sulked all the way while my mother, in between her giggles, tried to keep a conversation going.

On arrival at the famous playing fields of Eton, Arthur and Billy started unloading the large wicker hampers. One contained the lovely silver cutlery and beautiful Royal Worcester porcelain. I remember the trouble Collins had gone to in preparing these picnic baskets which were lined with velvet. I had followed him to the china room which consisted of cupboards from floor to ceiling filled with the various types and periods of porcelain. Each cupboard was marked with the contents. I remember him hesitating between the Royal Worcester or the Crown Derby cupboard, deciding which would be more appropriate for that so English institution, Eton. As we passed the blue and white Meissen, he snorted with disgust.

The hampers were so heavy it took both men to carry them from the car. Once the baskets were installed at a site that Arthur had decided would be suitable for the picnic, the tables were laid out with their white starched and embossed linen cloths and napkins. Even the flowers, in their beautiful porcelain vases, were arranged by Billy, acting on strict instructions from Collins. Next came the champagnes and ice buckets, the red and white wines, although neither my mother nor myself ever touched alcohol. Even to this day, I do not like the taste of wine, no matter how much I have tried. But as Collins said, "I must give Master Caryll's guests the choice."

Mummy went to sit on one of the white-backed canvas chairs that had been unfolded, and was soon surrounded by an admiring court of uniformed men. Most of the fathers who were home on leave had managed to get down to their son's speech day. Apart from the top hats, striped trousers and black jackets of the Etonians, nearly everyone else seemed to be in uniform of one type or another, as were most of the mothers.

There was still no sign of Caryll and Mummy kept saying anxiously, "Darling do go and find him and tell him we are here." Looking at that vast crowd of strangers, there was no way I was prepared to venture forth. Caryll finally arrived looking quite magnificent. Dressed in running shorts and top, over which he had put his Eton blazer and long scarf, he came jogging up. Now 6ft 3ins he was tanned and very fit. Not only did my mother cause heads to turn, I could see the effect my brother was having on the young female population as they followed his progress. Giving Mummy a hasty kiss, he explained that he was now captain of athletics and would not be able to spend the day with us after all, as he was very busy arranging the sports activities for the following week. He was now off to reconnoitre the cross-country course for the next day's event.

Mummy and I were left with this vast picnic and nobody to share it. I thought of all the food we had gone without so that Collins would have coupons for the elaborate menu. I felt so sorry for my mother. I knew how much she had wanted to impress her son and the excitement she had built up at the thought of spending an afternoon with him. Feeling weepy and resentful, I stuffed myself with all I could cram into my mouth and was vastly relieved when, after about an hour, Mummy decided to go home.

Fifty years later, Caryll and I were walking in the garden of my home in South Africa, as usual surrounded by dogs and baboons, and we were reminiscing about our youth. He said that one of the most embarrassing moments of his life was the first (and only time) that Mummy and I came down to Eton. He had heard about the arrival of the large hired car and the picnic hampers, the butlers and the footmen and the girl with large tits and long red nails and the beautiful woman who must be a film star. He said his heart sank as he realised that his mother had arrived. At that time, he used to long for her to be a normal, tweedy matron. Caryll also said his life was made miserable at Eton by the number of his friends' fathers who had been her lovers and the gossip this had caused. That is why on this day he had made excuses to keep away in the hope that the rest of his friends would not associate him with us.

In later years, we accepted with pride the knowledge that our adored and famously beautiful parent would, with her legions of distinguished lovers and husbands as well as her eccentric lifestyle, always be a subject of gossip and hearsay. After the war, Caryll decided to study at the Royal Agricultural College at Cirencester. I went to visit him one weekend. Sitting in a pub having lunch with friends, one of the girls at the table said to Caryll, "You travel a lot. Have you ever come across this fabulously beautiful countess who has two footmen to help her in and out of her bath?"

"Oh yes," said Caryll, with great aplomb, "that's my mother, but it is four, not two. She is always so worried the floor might be slippery." There was a dreadful silence and the girl went scarlet with embarrassment. Afterwards, when Caryll and I were laughing about the reactions of his friends, he said if they want to believe gossip, one might as well make it worthwhile.

The truth was somewhat different. Mummy's lady's maid, Jeanne, finally retired and the job was offered to Walter, one of the footmen at Fiorentina. Walter was a divine young man and Mummy consulted Rory before offering him the job. I remember her giggling and saying, "I bet I will be the first woman to have a male lady's maid." Rory said, "Yes darling, very eccentric of you but you can hardly call him male."

Walter was thrilled with his new job and took my scatty mother firmly in hand, helping to choose her clothes, advising her on hair styles, on her jewellery, and also instituting himself as unpaid secretary, running errands, bossing the other staff around and, when he thought it necessary, even getting bossy with me. He seemed to think we were his family and became the most dreadful fussy old woman. We all adored him.

Knowing my mother, one thing was certain. Walter would never have seen her unclothed. She was very Victorian in her upbringing and one did not display one's naked body. In all the years we were with her, we never did and I remember, after the age of five, Caryll and I were never allowed to bath together.

CHAPTER

14

When Mummy had arrived back in Britain from France, she had bought a house in Wales on the river Wye next to her great friends, the Stapleton Cottons. As Mummy said, she needed a place in the country to take Caryll for his school holidays and for our animals. They went down there with Miss Lane, who had been left at Burrough Court during the war. It was the same Miss Lane who later came with all the dogs and us to Kenya and then to South Africa. She worshipped my mother and bossed her about in the most incredible fashion. She had the idea that my mother could not look after herself and she was not far wrong. Bertie Stapleton Cotton had been in my father's regiment and was probably one of my mother's old boyfriends. Now the pair of them would spend hours in waders standing in the middle of the river fishing for salmon. On other days they would go off trout fishing. If Mummy caught anything while I was there I would make her put it back. I had got very squeamish about killing after I saw and heard about the effects of bombing and war. Until then, I had not thought much about life or death. I became *persona non grata* on the river.

There were war clouds of another kind that also threatened our security and happiness, although I didn't find out about it until several years later. Thelma Furness, Duke's second wife, had determined to get her hands on the Furness fortune. She was now a thoroughly embittered woman, having lost a fantastically wealthy husband as well as her royal lover, and she was determined on vengeance. Prior to the war, morphine was the panacea for all excessive pain and freely administered by doctors. Furness had become addicted and Thelma thought she could prove that Mummy had kept Furness drugged and got him to change his will, cutting out her son Tony. The gossip turned that into a story about Mummy actually administering a fatal overdose of the drug. Thelma decided to launch a probate suit against my mother. She even produced an affidavit signed by one of the nurses who had been with us in France. How in wartime she had managed this was a mystery. Thelma engaged the services of one of the most famous barristers in England, Sir Walter Monckton, to represent Tony and her interests. Theodore Goddard, who looked after all Mummy's affairs, asked an equally famous defence counsel, Sir Patrick Hastings, to represent my mother if the case ever came to court.

Thelma's actions must have tied up Mummy's inheritance until after the war, and so she had to borrow money against it to get through to finance our household and her lifestyle. I think my godfather Bernard Baruch helped her. The strain must have been dreadful but I knew nothing of any of it until one day shortly after the war ended when Collins came to tell me there was a gentleman waiting to see me. To begin with, I never saw strangers. People I did not know terrified me. A few days previously, I had been crossing the hallway just as Collins was opening the front door to admit the Sitwells, Sir Sacheverell, poet and art critic and brother of Edith, and his wife, Lady Georgia. I was so frightened I rushed to hide under the hall table.

Unfortunately, I was wearing my bright red dress at the time and apparently they saw my behind disappearing under the tablecloth. I heard afterwards from Collins that they had questioned him about who was hiding under the table. "That is her Ladyship's daughter, Miss Pat, she is very shy with strangers," he replied. They of course thought he was being polite on a sensitive subject and it was soon around London that I was a halfwit.

Now I was being asked to meet a stranger! So, begging Collins to come with me, we went into the sitting room. A man in uniform came forward and introduced himself. He was from Theodore Goddard, one of their senior partners, and he was still waiting to be decommissioned. He started questioning me about Furness and in particular the day of his death. I explained to him that I was in the kitchen with Mummy helping her make the soap. He couldn't believe that Mummy would be making soap; how little he knew my mother. He kept asking me what the time would have been but I had no idea. All I knew was that it was dark, for that enormous kitchen was lit by only two or three candles. And that at some stage Jeanne had come to call my mother.

He kept questioning me in the most ferocious way as if every word I said was a lie. He kept saying, "You must tell the truth. You must have had some idea of the time. You must have known the date. Why would your mother make soap when she had a house full of servants? Did she tell you to make this story up?" I felt he was not attacking me so much as attacking my mother and I didn't understand what was happening. I began to feel that my story of the soap was somehow betraying my mother and I started to get panicky. Everything started going black, I couldn't breathe and I passed out.

I came to with Collins fussing over me, saying he had sent that dreadful man away. Collins did not seem to be any the wiser over the visit than I was. My beloved parent had forgotten to tell me that I was going to be questioned as a possible defence witness. After all, I was the only person with her in France. In fact, she never even thought to mention that there was the possibility of a case against her, so it came as a terrible shock when this man kept trying to get me to admit that I must have seen my mother giving Furness injections at some stage. He told my mother there was no way I could be a witness as I did not know truth from fiction and was obviously mentally handicapped. I remember that fainting episode clearly, as it became the first of many such embarrassing moments in my youth. The first time I was kissed, the first time I made love, when I got engaged, the list of faintings was endless and highly embarrassing. Not only for me but for everybody else.

Some time later, I found a large Bentley and chauffeur parked outside the door on arriving home one evening. I asked Collins who had arrived and he said, "Sir Walter Monckton." Collins was fussing about saying, "I just hope he is not going to upset her Ladyship." He and I awaited anxiously, imagining all sorts of dreadful things.

He had hardly shown Sir Walter out of the door before we rushed into the sitting room to know what dreadful events the visit portended. Mummy said, "Sir Walter Monckton was the most charming man. He has discovered that the nurse who was Thelma Furness's witness was bribed. Therefore, he had immediately refused to have anything more to do with the case and felt it his duty to come and apologise to me in person. He has also made Thelma Furness write a letter of apology." (This letter from Thelma and her solicitor, George Pritchard, dated July 10, 1946, is amongst Sir Walter Monckton's papers given to the private archive at Balliol College, Oxford University, now released to the Bodleian Library, and is reproduced on page 57.)

The way was then clear for Mummy to inherit Furness's fortune (although Tony did receive a considerable share in the out of court settlement). I don't think she ever doubted she would inherit it. Furness had left almost £4 million, which in today's money is worth around £150 million. Mummy had a wonderful way of assuming that everything would always work out. And she certainly believed that whatever money she needed would be there.

CHAPTER
___
15

My shorthand and typing course lasted six months but I graduated in four. I loved every moment. Mummy bought me a typewriter and when I got home I would sit at my desk, surrounded by dogs, and practise, often until the early hours of the morning.

When I came out of the secretarial college, I was offered a job with a law firm in the city. I had been with them just a few months when my mother informed me that she had managed to get me a job just across the square in the American Embassy. At the time, she was still seeing her American who turned out to be very high up and able to pull strings. I was delighted, but begged my mother to arrange with the embassy for permission to take my dog. I couldn't bear the thought of leaving my adorable poodle Mickey behind. I remember Mummy saying, "Darling, I somehow don't think the embassy will be particularly charmed by such an unusual request." But I knew my mother could fix anything.

The necessary permission was given and on my first day of work, accompanied by Nanny, I walked across Grosvenor Square, giving the dog time to be clean in the park on the way. Having arrived at the reception desk, Nanny abandoned me, leaving me in the hands of a uniformed guard. I was terrified and almost turned tail and ran in the opposite direction. Worse was to follow. I was given a job as junior filing clerk. Obviously they had to think of something to keep me occupied. My newly acquired secretarial skills were forgotten; I had never seen a file in my life. It took days of patient explanations before I had even the foggiest idea of what I was doing. The embassy staff must have been horrified at having to employ such a pathetic excuse for a secretary. Looking back, it can only have been Mummy's influence that kept me there originally. Later though it was to become my second home and I remained at the embassy until the end of the war. By that time I was head of my section and in charge of the other secretaries and filing clerks, most of whom were a great deal older than myself.

This is how it happened. One day almost four months after I had been buried in the filing cabinets, a visitor who urgently needed a secretary to take dictation arrived. It was late on a Saturday morning and most of the staff had left. Getting anywhere in wartime London was difficult but as I lived so close I always remained later than others. Thank goodness, more by luck than good management, someone remembered that there was a very junior staff member who in this time of crisis could at least type and take dictation. So I was shunted up to the third floor. Luckily for me, there I was to remain.

By the time I had been at the embassy about six months, I was firmly established with my own desk plus dog on the third floor, in the typing pool. One of the elderly secretaries came to confide in me. Not only was she old but she wore no make-up and always dressed very severely. (And remember, when one is young anyone over the age of 30 is ancient.) "Pat," she said, "I need to speak to you. Will you come to my office before you leave?" Filled with curiosity, as I hardly knew her, I went along to her office on the corner of the building. The last thing I expected was to find her in tears. "I desperately need advice," she said. "You must help me. I'm pregnant and I don't know where to go. I need an abortion."

I obviously looked such a tart with my tight dresses, false bosom and heavy make-up, that she had decided that even though I was a great deal younger than most of the other secretaries, I must be very much *au fait* with all forms of sexual activities! Pride would not let me say that I had not the first idea.

Comforting her as best I could I said, "I am sure I can arrange it for you. Please don't worry any more." The next few days were dramatic; I knew the only person who would be able to help in this situation was my mother. The problem was I always left before she awoke in the mornings and because of her busy social life, I often couldn't get near her in the evenings either. Mummy was now on to yet another lover, an old flame Valentine Castlerosse, Earl of Kenmare. This one was serious though and he was soon to be her fourth husband and so was occupying all her spare time. I finally managed to seize an opportunity and rushed through my little speech before we could be interrupted.

I will never forget the deathly silence and look of total horror on her face. It suddenly dawned on me that my beloved parent thought that it was me who was pregnant. I couldn't believe how long it took me to disabuse her of this assumption. I was getting frantic. Mummy could now see sex maniacs popping out from under every desk in the embassy. The more I tried to explain, the more suspicious she got.

But in a funny way, that abortion did me a great service at the embassy. Word must have leaked out and it got around that Patricia Cavendish, the lowly typist in the embassy, was the daughter of a peeress and world-famous beauty, and the acquaintance of the great Castlerosse, who was well known for his sharp and funny newspaper column in Lord Beaverbrook's *Express*. In no time my typing skills were being demanded by all and sundry and I skipped up the embassy ladder at a rapid rate, not as a result of my ability but my mother's name. I would have liked to think it was for my skills; I was at the time one of the few secretaries who could take dictation in both French and English, which came in useful at times. I was really good at my job, or I thought I was, and I certainly loved the challenge.

Most of my evenings were spent either going to the cinema or watching German bombers attacking London. We were lucky to have missed the terrible blitzing of 1940 and early 1941 but there were still enough raids to keep people nervous. Mummy invented a game. As soon as the air raid sirens sounded, instead of rushing to the shelter we dashed to the balcony and whoever counted the most bombs leaving the bays won money. Looking back I think it was her way of making a game out of something that would otherwise have been frightening. The planes used to look so dark against the night sky, the bays would open, and the bombs would descend while I counted furiously. I invariably won and Mummy would dole out handfuls of pound notes, hugging me and saying, "You horrible little cheat, you just couldn't have counted that many!" We used to count out loud and I would dance up and down with excitement as I managed to squeeze out one or two more than her.

Once when we were playing our game, we watched a bomb coming down. It looked as if it was coming straight at us and we ducked as it hurtled past. Instead, to Arthur's horror, it landed on the garage, which was now almost empty of cars. There were now only two left, including the Rolls, but what was even more miraculous is that the bomb didn't explode.

Mummy forgot that it was there and didn't think to notify the bomb squad. It was only after she and Valentine were married, in January 1943, and he had come to live with us that she told him the story of what she now referred to as "our bomb". Valentine made such a fuss that in no time the whole of Grosvenor Square was evacuated and Valentine departed in all haste to the safety of Claridges. Mummy, as usual, refused to leave. So once again from our balcony we watched the whole proceedings.

It was an enormous bomb, and in order to disconnect the warhead, one of the bomb removal squad had to climb up and sit astride it. The bomb was so large that his feet didn't even touch the ground. Mummy's theory was that the danger of the bomb exploding was minimal, the removal squad being extremely efficient, and if British soldiers were going to risk their lives to disconnect "our bomb", she and her family were not going to take the coward's way out and abandon them to it. Even Maureen joined us on the balcony, which was amazing when one thinks of the trauma she had already lived through.

What I found more sinister than the bombing raids were the doodlebugs that came later in the war, in mid-1944. One had become used to the nightly droning of the bombers overhead and the sirens. The doodlebugs, which were unmanned jet-propelled missiles launched from across the Channel, arrived mostly by day, as far as I can remember, and looked like flying torpedoes. There would be very little warning before they were overhead. The noise of the engine would suddenly stop, then silence. One had time to count to 12, then would come the explosion and a pall of black smoke and flames as buildings collapsed. Once we came out of a cinema, just after a bus had been hit. It was horrific; heads, arms and bodies were lying in the gutter and were being collected and put into bags.

CHAPTER

16

Mummy's new husband, Valentine Castlerosse, was a very tall and excessively large gentleman who strongly and loudly objected to climbing the narrow staircase at Lees Place. He complained to all who cared to listen that, having a bad heart, if sex didn't finish him off, the staircase certainly would. As far as I was concerned, he was quite terrifying and I kept out of his way as much as possible at the beginning. This was not easy as he had taken up residence. He was not like the others who only used to visit. This one moved in and, rather soon after the marriage, moved out. First of all to Claridges, which made life inconvenient, and so then to a large flat in Grosvenor Square that my mother rented from the Duke of Westminster's third wife, Loelia. There he and Mummy lived. The apartment took up the whole of the first floor and the rooms were enormous. It was just round the corner from Lees Place where we stayed on.

The Earl of Kenmare, better known as Castlerosse, was a splendid figure of the 1930s and '40s. The Canadian-born press baron Max Aitken, Lord Beaverbrook, who owned *The Daily Express* and *The Evening Standard* and was also minister for aircraft production during the war, was his greatest friend and mentor. They were inseparable and not only did Lord Beaverbrook pay his debts, which were always considerable, he was the one who discovered and recognised Castlerosse's formidable writing talent. Castlerosse, apart from being a hero in World War I, where he almost lost an arm, was a famous dilettante, a gambler, a reckless spender, a lover of women and a great wit. Beaverbrook finally convinced Valentine to put his talents to good use and write a column for his newspapers. Thus came into being the "*Londoner's Log*".

With his arrival in my mother's life, there were now constant dinner parties, all given at Lees Place. The world and his wife seemed to converge there. Valentine had an enormous circle of friends and while he and my mother were in London there was a continual procession of lunches and dinners. One day, I was sent in with a message for Mummy and found Sir Hugh Dowding sitting at the table with his signet ring dangling from a piece of string. He seemed to be in a trance. Later, when I questioned Mummy about the extraordinary happenings in the dining room, she explained that the former Air Chief Marshal was communicating with some of his pilots who had been killed. He had been commander-in-chief of Fighter Command during the Battle of Britain in the summer of 1940, when our pilots had stopped thousands of German bombers from destroying the country and preparing it for Hitler's invasion. He told my mother that his pilots found death difficult to accept in the beginning but he had found that he was psychic. By tuning in to them, he could help them to understand and to come to terms with death. I remember thinking – unfairly as it turned out – that he was quite cuckoo and was amazed to think he had been in charge of the fighter squadrons.

For me, these dinners were the worst as Valentine entertained an endless list of petrifying people. He had a mind like a rapier and would fix his little cold eyes on some unfortunate guest and make him or her the butt of his satirical humour. Or so it seemed to me. But everyone adored him and his friends kept coming back for more; they seemed to enjoy the sport.

I used to watch those eyes pass over me as I sat in frozen silence. I realised that in spite of my mother my turn would have to come. From then on, no matter how much Mummy tried to get me to join them, I took all my meals in the kitchen. From my peephole with the maids I used to watch the rich and famous who looked so perfect against the Tang and Ming.

Professor Lindemann – Lord Cherwell, the physicist, close friend and advisor to Churchill on special weapons – was a frequent visitor as well. He used to call my mother "cousin Enid", making a joke of their similar surnames. Lord Cherwell was very worried that the world was going to be dominated by communist Russia and as he had a great influence on the prime minister, it may have been his misgivings at the time of the Yalta Conference in early 1945 that influenced Churchill's concerns about Stalin and post-war Europe. He was also worried that all the coupons would eventually run out and there would be no more clothes and no more shoes and that England would end up dying of starvation. Apparently, he was very funny on the subject and Valentine couldn't resist greeting him thus, "I see, Frederick, that unfortunately you are still not dead of starvation and, my God – don't tell me those things on your feet are shoes!"

Often there were musical evenings and Lord Cherwell would play the piano and Mummy the flute. Other frequent visitors were the Westminsters, Bendor and his wife Loelia. They usually came separately. It was Westminster whose friendship with Mummy had caused such ructions with Furness. Mummy was also a great friend of his former lover, Coco Chanel. After one of his visits, I heard Mummy complaining, "Bennie just lets his dogs wee all over the beautiful curtains. He doesn't seem to worry about the stains or the smell."

At the time Mummy married Valentine, he was writing a biography of Tolstoy. He seemed in many ways to have so little in common with my mother except for a passion for golf. Mummy, like myself, was no intellectual. And I think, unlike myself who was openly terrified, she was secretly nervous of Valentine's brilliant friends. Valentine had fallen in love with my mother many years ago during World War I, and at the time had been one of my mother's lovers. Later on they had met again on Le Touquet golf course and he was furious when she chose to marry Furness. Now he was back in her life and before long I was being maid of honour at their wedding, which took place at the Brompton Oratory in South Kensington. The next day they left on their honeymoon.

Valentine owned the vast estate of Killarney, including the lakes. All that was left of the original Castle Rosse was a tower crumbling into the lake. It was very romantic, like a dejected lover, its sad image forever reflected in the beautiful clear water. The ruins of Killarney House stood in solitary splendour amongst the heather on the hill above. It had been burnt to the ground many years before, in 1913. One evening, I saw a stag, its head raised, its antlers in sharp delineation against the fading pink of a setting sun and against the black ruins. Valentine now lived in its large replacement, Kenmare House, almost on the lake. Our holidays, after Mummy's marriage, were spent at Killarney and we would only go to the house on the Wye in Wales on the weekends when we were in England. Valentine Kenmare was a true Edwardian, a flamboyant man who did everything to excess. Like Furness though, he was an immaculate dresser. In the country he wore beautifully cut plus-fours in vivid colours and, like Furness, he was proud of his small feet, particularly as he was such a large man.

In London, Valentine was an extravagant dresser with a variety of waistcoats and, to match, a selection of tie-pins with enormous diamonds and fob watches. (I now wear Mummy's ring, which Rory designed, made from Furness's signet ring and one of Kenmare's tie-pins. Cartier set the two diamonds in heavy gold.) On the death of his father, when he succeeded to the Kenmare title and estates, it did not take Valentine too long before he went through the Kenmare fortune. He had first married a woman almost as flamboyant in her lifestyle as himself, Doris Delavigne. She eventually died of barbiturate poisoning after many break-ups with Valentine. Then he married my mother, another famous beauty and great eccentric.

Now that he was with my mother, who was about to inherit an enormous fortune once the Thelma Furness case was dealt with, he persuaded her to let him make the most of it. His great ambition had been to build the best golf course in the world on the banks of the Killarney Lakes and he was already well started. Mummy was nothing if not enthusiastic about his plans for a resort which would bring tourists to his estate.

My memories of Killarney are of lovely peaceful days, far from the noise of war and from sudden death and destruction. The sun would illuminate the still waters of the lake, the blue hills of Kerry were home to herds of deer and lovely tumbling waterfalls would splash their way through the ferns and bracken. Valentine in his bright tweeds and plus-fours and surrounded by his pack of Shetland collies would spend his days with his friends and my mother, discussing plans and walking the course.

Caryll, two of his friends from Eton, Sandy Radcliffe and Colin Fyfe-Jameson, and I were there for a short break. I remember we were all on the golf course when Valentine said, "Today, you are going to meet one of the most beautiful girls in Ireland. I have invited her for lunch." We were coming around the lake towards the house when the dogs started charging up the hill. How clearly I remember our first meeting with Averil Knowles, a vision of beauty, dressed in a lovely violet and mauve tweed jacket and skirt. A tall, slim girl, she came walking across the heather towards us.

Averil had enormous eyes and a face like an Italian Madonna by Raphael, framed by hair cut short and falling in soft curls onto her neck and cheeks. Within 10 minutes of her arrival, she had turned the boys into her adoring slaves. As we headed for the house, with Averil's arm through Valentine's, I could hear her gay laughter as she teased him about something he had written about a friend of hers. I watched the effect she was having on my brother and his companions as she appealed to them for help. By the time lunch was over, I could tell my Caryll was in the throes of an unholy passion.

Averil was 26, married to a much older Colonel Knowles and they had two small children. But she also had a stepson and daughter only a few years younger than Caryll, who was 16 at the time. That night Caryll came to my room and lay on my bed for hours, sucking his handkerchief distractedly. Caryll was in love. With some amusement I had to listen to his rapturous descriptions of her beauty, of the perfection of her voice, of her laughter and soft Irish charm. She is married, he moaned, she can have any man in the world she is so beautiful, and with a groan of anguish and much working of the handkerchief, he tormented himself with the fact that he was a schoolboy, that he could never be anything in her life and that probably at some stage he would have to watch her walk off with some equally beautiful lover.

From my vast age of 17, but with far less knowledge of the world than Caryll, I tried to offer him comfort. As far as I was concerned, there was no young man in the world who could compare with him in looks or character. Caryll and Mummy were the beauties of this world and I was immensely proud of them. I had so much faith in the magic that they wove that I think I was the only one who was not in the least surprised at the outcome of this meeting between Caryll and Averil.

A few days later there was a big fancy dress ball being held at the hotel in Parknasilla. Mummy dressed Caryll as an Indian maharajah. Turning one of her beautiful silk scarves into a turban, she decorated it with a white ostrich feather fastened with a huge diamond clip. She altered one of her long Schiaparelli evening coats which had a high collar and pearl buttons down the front. Caryll wore white trousers and, to complete the picture, she festooned him with her jewellery, long necklaces of diamonds and pearls. Mummy went as a maharanee and was equally magnificent. Valentine had risen to the occasion and almost outshone them both with his enormous girth and beak of a nose. Mother had found a hairpiece that she had made into a beard and this was combined with a white turban and more of her pearls. Valentine now looked as if he had just stepped out of a Moghul portrait.

Their arrival at the ballroom, was unforgettable; one could almost hear the gasp of amazement. The jewellery around their necks alone must have been worth a king's ransom. To my delight, by the end of the evening Averil was in love with Caryll. It was the start of an affair that lasted a good many years. I wrote a poem about it with which to tease him:

My brother is a lover bold,
He emulates the knights of old.
He has caused plenty of trouble,
He will insist on sleeping double.
At gay 16, he had his fling,
Without the aid of a wedding ring.
But he gave her lots of joy,
He was such a handsome boy.

The only drawback to Killarney was the fact that we had to go to chapel every Sunday morning. Valentine and his family were devout Catholics. Everyone would congregate and wait until Valentine and his party appeared. The first Sunday was a nightmare. The chapel was full and I was seated in the pew behind Valentine where he sat with his head bowed, a large prayer book clutched in his hand, deeply engrossed in his sacred scriptures. Years later, Mummy told me that his specially bound prayer book was pornography. Although deeply religious, Valentine knew all the prayers and psalms and, having to spend so much time in church, he had found this a great way of getting through the morning ritual. Also it appealed to his sense of humour. I found all the kneeling and the heat inside the chapel dreadfully claustrophobic. There was that awful feeling of suffocation again, the ringing in my ears, and finally gasping for breath.

Too embarrassed to interrupt a church service by climbing over everyone, I passed out ungracefully, collapsing with a loud groan. Which of course ended up being a great deal more mortifying.

Back in London, I now spent a lot of time with Mummy and Valentine in their flat. I had a bedroom there as well. Valentine was not only famous for his daily column but had written the script for a hit movie, *The Young Mr Pitt*, starring Robert Donat. I saw the film six times I loved it so much. Now he was working on another film script and Mummy was painting an enormous scene of the battle of Waterloo, also for a film, as one of their great friends was the film-maker Arthur Rank. The horses and figures were life-size and the canvas took up one whole wall of the sitting room. She had convinced me to help her fill in the background but I never had her patience and I used to get very restless and bored.

I remember one evening in June, Valentine had gone to his club and Mummy, to please Caryll and me, had left her painting and taken us to a film at Leicester Square and then to dinner at the Savoy. We must have come back about midnight. As we drew up outside the flat, chaos reigned. It was very difficult to see what was going on because of the blackout but heavy objects and clothing were being hurled out of the window and we could hear Valentine screaming with rage. Caryll, deciding that discretion was the better part of valour and not wanting to involve himself in such a fracas, hastily disappeared back to Lees Place. I followed Mummy as she rushed upstairs. Chairs and tables had been thrown everywhere and were lying in pieces. Valentine was in the sitting room like an enraged elephant. He screamed, "You whore!" and as we entered the room, hurled the chair that was in his hand at my mother.

In all my years, I had never heard anyone raise his or her voice to my mother, let alone insult her. I turned to look at her with open-mouthed amazement. She had ducked from the chair and was now leaning against the wall, laughing. "I might be a whore," she declared, "but it seems to me that I am the one paying for your servicing!"

Valentine was screaming, "Who is he? I am going to kill that SOB. Who is the bastard that is fucking my pregnant wife? [The first I knew of a pregnancy.] I am not fathering someone else's bastard!"

By this time, he was sobbing and shouting and, while hurling abuse at Mummy, he was also kicking everything in sight. I started to make a quick exit to escape this horribly embarrassing situation. "Oh no you don't!" said Mama. "Give me the tickets."

In between her giggles, she managed to calm him down sufficiently by pointing out that if he kept this up he would have a massive coronary and the child would never see its father. I, thank goodness, still had the cinema tickets. She also asked me to call the restaurant at the Savoy and get hold of the maître d'hôtel. She then made Valentine, who knew him well, ask who had been at her table. As I finally managed to make my escape, I could hear Valentine sobbing and Mummy still giggling and telling him that she loved him.

I remember another instance of Valentine's rage. Because of his enormous stomach, he was unable to do up his shoes or dress himself; this was always taken care of by his very nice cockney valet, Welch. One evening Valentine and my mother had been invited to an official dinner at which the Churchills were going to be present. Like my mother, Valentine loved his bath and also, as with my mother, the bathwater had to be scented. On this particular evening I think they were probably making love before going out as they were in the bedroom for ages and nobody wanted to disturb them. (Valentine and my mother had another trait in common; they were both always late.)

When Valentine finally emerged to go to his own room, he

remained so long in his bath that, miracle of miracles, Mummy was ready before him. Anyhow they were now so late and Valentine was getting so worked up that everything was taking twice as long. It wasn't the right waistcoat, it wasn't the right tie, and poor Welch was running around. With Mummy helping, they finally got him dressed. Then he had to have his shoes, which were laced with big bows, put on. But with all the fidgeting and the rage, Welch couldn't get them tied correctly. By this time Valentine was screaming at Welch, "You bloody idiot. I'm employing a fucking blind man!" At which he kicked out, and Welch went flying, hitting his head on the corner of the wardrobe.

Mummy was furious with Valentine. There was nothing my mother liked better, though, than playing nurse to the sick, so soon her bedroom became a dispensary and everyone was rushing round with swabs, cotton wool, ointments and pain pills ministering to Welch. I did finally think it was time somebody reminded my mother that they were supposed to have been at dinner at least an hour ago. "Oh my God! So we should, where is that dreadful Valentine? Darling do go and find him, and do be sweet to him. He will be feeling so guilty, and by now will be hating himself."

I found Valentine looking like a deflated elephant, downing the most enormous whisky. Or rather, I should say he had almost finished the bottle. He looked at me very sheepishly, "I am excessively fond of Welch, I did not mean to hurt him. Is your mother very cross with me?" He then poured the rest of the glass down his throat. I told him that he knew my mother was never really cross and that she and Welch were having a good laugh over what they were calling The Valentine Pantomime. I said, "I don't think you need worry too much but please make my mother leave. You are so late that I am sure Winston and Mrs. Churchill won't forgive either of you."

Valentine by this time had become my most treasured friend. I had always found that my mother's generation were hopeless with the young. I realised that I was ugly, tongue-tied and painfully shy but they behaved as if I were a creature from another planet. As I was of no interest to them, I was ignored. They talked over me and around me but never to me. Valentine, on the contrary, was marvellous with young people. Mummy kept sending me to him with messages and I realise now that she did it on purpose so that I would get to know him. I would knock and on being told to come in, would half-open the door and, peering round, would try and deliver my message and run. Not a bit of it. "Come in! Come in!" Valentine would roar. Usually he was lying in bed, writing. "You are just the person I need. Your mother tells me you love history. I am writing the life of Tolstoy; what do you think of this?" And he would start reading passages from his book. It never seemed to matter that I was tongue-tied. At the time, I knew nothing about Russian history but he bought me books, which I still have, so that we could discuss them together. "Come sit on my bed," he would say. "I'm perfectly decent. Your mother lectures me enough about behaving myself when you are around."

Mummy had warned me too. "Never go into Valentine's room until you have knocked and announced who you are. Otherwise you are more than likely to find him naked." To begin with, I dreaded being sent with messages, especially at the thought of the embarrassment if I should find him in a state of undress. But it was not long before I used to rush to his room and curl up on his bed to read my book while he wrote or screamed abuse at someone or other on the telephone. "Bloody bitch!" he would say having slammed the phone down. "Wants more money; women are never satisfied. Just remember, my girl, when you grow up. Never ask a man for anything and they will appreciate you all the more for it." I wasn't even 18, but he always behaved to me as the mood suited him, either a woman of his own age or a child to be patted on the head.

Due to his bad heart, Valentine was supposed, on his doctor's orders, to go for a walk every day. Mummy now decided that when I came back in the evenings, I should accompany Valentine to Hyde Park with the dogs, thereby ensuring that Valentine would get his exercise as well as her poodles. Valentine loathed having to move off his bed but Mummy would tease him. "Come darling, you have just had the most enormous lunch and drunk half my wine cellar and Pat has to take the dogs out. You know she is too young to go on her own." Valentine would reluctantly heave himself out of his armchair or off his bed and then there would be a great deal of fussing by Welch over what his lordship should be wearing to the park. We would proceed for what Valentine called "his bloody constitutional!"

"The trouble with your mother being a beautiful woman," he would complain, "is that she invariably gets her own way. Not only does she hide all the food and starve me to death but she has now got it into her head that I have to be exercised into my grave."

After a great deal of complaining along these lines, I think he really enjoyed himself once he got going. We almost never finished our walk without somebody recognising him and asking for his autograph or people coming up and wanting to have a few words with him. Some days, Valentine would entertain me with hilarious anecdotes from his life or that of his friends. Other times we would talk about the books he had given me to read or he would recite poetry as I listened, entranced. Or he would turn Hyde Park into St Petersburg, and I would be lost in another world of beautiful women, of sleigh rides on the lakes and of palaces in the snow. He was the first person of my mother's entourage, apart from my immediate family, to treat me as an individual. As a result I adored him.

CHAPTER

17

At this stage of my teenage career, I was a filthy mess. My mother's perfection was difficult to live up to and in my teens, I rebelled for a while. She dressed perfectly and so I dressed like a whore. She was fanatical about cleanliness, so I became dirty. When the high-water marks on my arms became very pronounced, my mother did vaguely suggest that I should have a bath but mostly she never criticised. If the situations had been reversed, I used to say later, I would have given me a good hiding. The thing is that I wanted to be beautiful too and so I tried to compete. It was a disaster. While my mother wore Joy, I drenched myself in cheap scent. I was convinced that apart from my figure, the only asset I had was my eyes. In despair at being so stupid, and the ugly duckling in a beautiful family, I decided they would show up much better if my hair was dark. What's more, Mummy was fair and thus, given my reasoning so far, I would have to be dark. Therefore my hair went unwashed. Mummy, very worried by my fragile self-confidence, had obviously told everyone not to remark on her dirty daughter. It was Valentine who finally managed to get me to wash my hair. In his own subtle way, he kept telling me how much men loved blondes. On several occasions he said teasingly, "What a pity you are not fair-haired like the rest of your family."

Finally one night I washed my greasy hair, which I used to do up in elaborate rolls – the fashion at the time. I pinned my now shiny clean hair in paper rollers and the next day, abashed and shy, went to Valentine's room. I did not know what his reaction would be as now my hair was washed I had to let it hang loose. Without the grease to bind, it wouldn't stick into the rolls no matter how many pins I put in.

Valentine was about to appear for lunch. "Welch," he called delightedly, "come and look at what we have got here. A Botticelli angel."

I think part of Valentine's enormous charm was that he genuinely loved and was interested in the people close to him and under that terrifying exterior of cold cynicism and at times cruel and biting wit he was a man who knew how to love and give of himself. Mummy always said that he was generous to a fault and loved giving the most extravagant presents. Even if he had no money, he would find out what someone wanted and then go to any lengths to give it to them.

There was a celebrated photographer at the time called Harlip. Valentine suggested that my mother arrange for me to go to the studio and have a series of portraits done. For this I realised I would finally have to get myself into a bath. Valentine, like my mother, was fanatical about cleanliness and it gradually occurred to me that my parent was not carrying cleanliness to an excess with her scented baths and toiletries. And that that is what men expected of women. Now fearful that my much-admired new stepfather would notice how un-soignée his stepdaughter was, I went to the other extreme. After Furness, who disliked me so much, it was marvellous to have someone who took an interest not only in what I did but also in what I thought. Now I spent every spare moment in a bath and borrowed my mother's scents and sprayed myself from head to toe.

I remember one evening when the family had gone out to dinner. I was sitting with Maureen reading my book while she was ironing my mother's heavily laced silk underwear. She was always laughing and joking and she said to me, "Gosh, Miss Pat, you do smell nice." Maureen continued, "I like looking after her ladyship's clothes, I get all the fragrance of perfume as I iron." Maureen then told me that her friend who was lady's maid to the Duchess of Windsor was watching her iron one day and said how lucky she was to work for a lady who was so clean. "You should see the Duchess's underpants. They always have such dirty stains, you'd think she would be ashamed to give them to me."

Rory was now visiting again. Apparently, he had spent the first few months of his army training peeling potatoes and doing all the menial jobs in the army mess. Being such a wonderfully spoilt individual, it was very hard to picture him performing his humble G.I. tasks and his stories were hilarious. He had also fallen in love with a Princess Jorjadze, in fact an American girl, the daughter of a wealthy Cincinnati businessman, who had married first a Russian grand-duke and then a Georgian prince. This liaison did not stop Rory from leaving his spud-peeling one afternoon to go and seduce one of his officers' wives. As the story goes, the officer came back unexpectedly and Rory spent most of the afternoon locked in her cupboard. As Rory was very tall and the cupboard not very large, he had an agonising few hours.

Rory was staying at Lees Place and Mummy was busy writing to General Eisenhower, the American forces commander-in-chief, whom she knew, saying that she considered it a dreadful oversight on the part of the United States Army not to have made her son an officer and would he please do something about it. She proudly showed Rory that she was about to take a hand in his promotion. He was absolutely horrified and tore up the letter. So my very grand, fastidious brother never rose higher than sergeant. Later on, when Caryll became an officer in the Grenadier Guards, Caryll insisted that Rory salute him.

Like Valentine, Rory had a great many famous and terrifying friends, so my life at Lees Place was spent in hiding too. Every time the front door bell rang I fled. At least Mummy and Valentine never got up in the morning, while Rory would descend for breakfast at 8am. So throughout the day when he was in residence and I was at home I would disappear to the safety of the Grosvenor Square flat. I remember on one occasion, they were all going to a dinner and Rory insisted that I must go too. I was so horror-struck that I felt sick all day. Thank goodness Caryll was there and promised to stay with me. He also made me a little list of *sujets de conversation* in case anyone spoke to me. Unfortunately at dinner, he was not placed next to me and I got panicky. Valentine, realising my anguish, directed his entire conversation across the table to my two dinner companions, so that he had the table in fits of laughter for the rest of the evening. I spent the time twisting my bits of conversational papers around in my lap but I did not have to use them.

Valentine's sharp wit is illustrated by a tale told to me by a great friend, Sheila Southey. At a party in London, a woman commented to him, "Lord Castlerosse, if that stomach was on a woman I would say she was pregnant."

"Madam," came the W. C. Fieldsian riposte. "Half an hour ago it was, and she is!"

That year, 1943, we all had had another wonderful summer holiday in Ireland and I celebrated my 18th birthday on the shores of the lake. Valentine arranged a magnificent picnic. Apart from Averil, it was just family, for he knew that was how I wanted it. On my plate as we sat down was a beautifully wrapped present from my mother and another from Valentine. Mummy gave me a ruby eternity ring and Valentine, a big gold charm bracelet. I often look at them; they bring back such memories of Mummy and Valentine and that lovely soft smell of summertime June. Caryll and I went back on the ferry to England and Mummy stayed with Valentine. Without Miss Unger's premonitions to warn me, I did not look back. I was never to see Valentine or Killarney again.

Mummy was very anxious for Rory to see Ireland for he had not yet been to Killarney. Managing to get leave at the end of summer, he went over to join them. At the beginning of September he and my mother came back to Lees Place as she had an appointment with the gynaecologist. I remember after her visit to the doctor, her coming home to tell us that everything was still fine. I think they were a bit worried because of her age and Valentine, fussing so much, insisted that she had to have regular check-ups.

A couple of days after my mother's return from Ireland, Collins called me at the Embassy. "Miss Pat, you better come home." I wanted to know what was wrong but he just kept saying, "Her ladyship is terribly upset."

My mother had just heard that Valentine had been found dead on the floor beside his bed. She had been speaking to him on the telephone only minutes before; he would phone her daily to find out how the child was progressing and to make sure she was taking enough care of herself. He also wanted her to leave England and stay in Ireland away from the bombs. He told her that he had just been picking flowers in the garden to give as a present to his hostess as he was going out to lunch, and that he had phoned that morning and invited friends, the Knowles, to stay the next day. He had come in from the garden as he was starting to get a pain in his chest. Mummy told him to put the phone down and get help and that she would come back on the late ferry. She was trying to get hold of his doctor in Ireland when she got the news of his death.

It was a bitter blow to my mother, who once more had lost a husband and her security.

In George Malcolm Thomson's biography *Lord Castlerosse: His Life and Times*, he writes of the funeral, where 7000 people watched the cortege pass on the way to St Mary's Cathedral at Killarney: "Those who mourned Valentine on that autumn day in 1943 were aware, too, that something more than bravura performance had finished. The era in which such a rich and grotesque personality as he could emerge to flout, scandalize and animate social life – that, too, was passing. The future, it seemed, would be less garish and more grey."

My mother loved men and the companionship and security they gave her, all of which Valentine had provided. Furness had given her a wonderful life and they had many interests in common, but he had kept her as secluded as possible because he was so possessive of her. With Valentine, it was the opposite. Not only was he intensely proud of her but he took delight in flaunting her beauty in front of his many friends. Theirs was a highly social life, which she seemed to enjoy, mainly I think for Valentine's sake, for although she loved people she was shy of strangers. Certainly, she was always happiest with animals, the young and the insecure. Mummy loved the flamboyant man she had married mainly because of his many insecurities. He loved her beauty and gentleness; she admired his brilliant brain and mordant wit. He treated her like a precious child, she teased him unmercifully, and they were always laughing. Also, I recognise looking back, this was a time in her life when, with Thelma Furness's case and insinuations hanging over her head, she particularly needed Valentine's love and support and powers of the press.

Years after, long after Valentine's death, I asked my mother why she had never been unfaithful to Valentine. She was painting at the time and had a parrot perched on her shoulder. She looked at me over her spectacles: "Darling, we weren't married long enough for me to get bored. Also, Valentine had the most terrible inferiority complex." She laughed and said, "Just like you did, except Valentine's lasted a lifetime. Between his mother who never loved him and Doris who was forever unfaithful, he had absolutely no confidence in himself. He thought he was a monster of ugliness and was pathetically grateful for any affection. I married him for security and he married me for my money and yet in a funny way we loved each other.

"The doctors had warned me that he had a very bad heart and could die at any moment and that we were to try and avoid all sex. But it was one of the only pleasures left to him in life, so how could I ration him? I wanted to build his confidence in himself as a man once more, and I felt I was succeeding so the lover of my youth was not so very different from the lover of my old age. But all I succeeded in doing by ignoring the doctor's advice was adding the final nail to his coffin. For which I will never forgive myself."

I was devastated by Valentine's death; he had taken the place of the father who was only a dim memory. I refused to go to Ireland and I refused to believe he wouldn't come back. I couldn't bear the thought of seeing them lower his body into the grave. I did not want to recognise the finality of death. I retreated into my dream world where everything was perfect and we still went for our walks and we still discussed Tolstoy and the palaces of St Petersburg.

Mummy left for Killarney accompanied by the dowager Lady Kenmare. They were both dressed in unrelieved black with hats and veils covering their faces. As those two tall slender figures got into the car for the journey to the station, I felt as if my heart was being drawn from my body. I couldn't even cry. I could feel my mother's pain. For the first time in my life I realised that Mummy needed me. My mother was brought up in a strict school where you never showed fear, pain or grief. This was the first time I became aware that I was able to pick up another person's emotions. This gift in later years was to enable me to live with all my wonderful wild animals and for my lioness Tana to save my life. Now, in my selfishness, I understood I had let my mother down.

Seeing Mummy's black-clad figure following Valentine's mother and seeing the contrast between the loving personality of my mother and the ice-cold skeletal figure of the dowager made such an impression on me that I resolved as long as my mother needed me, I would never leave her again. I never did. Even my husbands had to live with my mother. It was only when Tana came into my life as a tiny lion cub that I left and went to live in Kenya but Rory had my mother firmly under control by then!

On their return from Ireland, the dowager Lady Kenmare haunted Lees Place. She was with Mummy every day. I could not understand how Mummy could bear having her around; she was like a sinister black crow. A few weeks after Mummy's return from that terrible trip to Ireland, she called us all together. We were in the sitting room, myself, Rory and Caryll. Mummy was standing by the fireplace, in her black dress and silver hair. She looked so beautiful and tragic, and she said, "You will have to make a decision that I find I cannot make. Lady Kenmare is adamant that I must not keep Valentine's child. Her reasons are that I am not a young woman, I have a grown-up family, and at my advanced age I do not need more children. That Valentine gambled away the Kenmare fortune, they are a very Catholic family, and as a Protestant, she feels I will never raise a child in the true Catholic faith. Further, she insists that it would be incredibly selfish of me to do Gerald [Valentine's brother] out of his rightful inheritance. On top of which she keeps assuring me that because of my age the child will probably be born an idiot."

"Lady Kenmare knows that I can afford to maintain Kenmare a great deal better than Gerald but when she asked me if I intended to make it my permanent home, I had to tell her that in all probability I would return to France after the war. It is now up to you to help me make the right decision."

I think my mother at the time was 51. This of course was not a consideration for her. I was thrilled with the idea of having a baby. Rory was adamant, however. I remember he said to her, "At your age, I think it is dreadful that you are even contemplating giving birth. If

Valentine were alive it would be a different matter but now it is just ridiculous."

Mummy always did whatever Rory told her so between Rory and the old dowager, she chose to have an abortion. Deciding we would never live in Ireland and implored by the dowager to restore the inheritance that Valentine had bequeathed to my mother, she agreed to give it back to the family. Tragically, the child was a boy, but this act of my mother's enabled Gerald to inherit not only the title but the estates and the lakes of Killarney as well. He never married. At his death, the estates and the title were no more and my mother was the last to bear the name of Kenmare.

CHAPTER

18

During this period I was working hard at the embassy during the day and every night was spent in nightclubs. Mummy had decided I was old enough not to require a chaperone any longer and that I did not need to be accompanied across Grosvenor Square by Nanny. I suppose she considered that I was old enough to have a bit of freedom. I remember, as if it were yesterday, the first time when I was allowed to go home on my own.

Mummy took me to Harrods to choose yet another present for being 18. Although she had given me lots of presents on my birthday, she wanted me to personally choose something that I would remember for a long time. Instead of making for the furs, I went off to the pet department and chose the most beautiful pale golden cocker spaniel puppy. She was about five months old and I called her Honey. Then to my great surprise, Mummy said she was meeting a friend at the Sportsman's Club for tea and that she could drop me at home unless I felt like walking the puppy back on my own. I couldn't believe it. I can remember her now laughing at my excitement. She was so beautiful, dressed in black, with layered ropes of pearls and emeralds twisted around her neck and hanging in cascades of colour to her waist.

I loved hugging and kissing her; she always smelt divine and she was a very affectionate mother. But now I gave her a rushed embrace, anxious to be gone in case she changed her mind. Arthur couldn't believe it when I proudly announced I would be walking home. I literally danced with joy at the thought of so much freedom. "Well," said Arthur, looking at my breast-hugging dress, "just you be careful, Miss. If you are not back within an hour I am coming to look for you."

The sense of freedom was extraordinary. It was the first time I can remember that I had been alone, except in bed. Since childhood, I had been surrounded by nannies, governesses and servants, unless I was with my mother or my brothers. The G.I.s all turned and whistled at me. I was in seventh heaven. These were my first steps as an adult and it certainly changed my life. From being a timid mouse I became wild and uncontrollable. I soon had boyfriends, and spent my entire evenings in nightclubs. The noisier the better!

Without governesses or nannies trailing after me, I went wild. Dancing to me was like a drug. I had no inhibitions on the dance floor. It was as if the music became an extension of myself. My shyness was forgotten and if I had a good partner, we would always end up by giving exhibition dances. The floor would clear and an admiring clapping crowd would surround us. I loved every moment of it. At last I could be the centre of attention and not have to compete with my incomparable family!

In London, my one great friend was Peggy Mathewson who worked in an American Red Cross canteen, the Victory Club, for the armed forces behind Marble Arch. Being close to Lees Place, it was easy for me to get to and I would spend a couple of hours working there in the evening, serving doughnuts and washing up. She was wonderful-looking: tall, blonde with brown eyes. Her first husband had been a pilot who had died in the Battle of Britain. When I met her, she was just about to marry a U.S. Air Force colonel, Christy Mathewson, a war hero with a chest full of medals. Christy was Christy Junior and his father had been a famous baseball player. Peggy's Christy looked like Clark Gable and had a marvellous personality. He was always laughing in spite of the fact that he had lost a leg when his plane had been shot down. He was on a bombing raid at the time and had just managed to make it back to the English coast. Now he had fallen in love with Peggy who was 24. It was all very romantic.

I was maid of honour at their wedding, which was held in a registry office, and through Peggy I met lots of glamorous air force officers. A few nights spent on the town and they were gone, mostly never to return, so many were killed. Life was frenetic, nobody knew whether they would be alive on the morrow and nobody seemed to care. It was one wild party after another. The English men had never really appealed to me but I had always had a love of Americans, mainly through my avid reading of the Zane Grey books. They were good-looking, danced well, had no hang-ups, and if I was shy and had not much to say, it didn't seem to matter. I liked their accent too.

In fact, my first kiss, very soon after being given my freedom from Nanny's care, was with an American G.I. He had picked me up on the way to the embassy and had walked me across the square. That evening, he was waiting for me when I had finished work. We went with the dogs to Hyde Park and as we sat on a bench he kissed me. It wasn't a particularly great sensation and it was not what I had imagined. When he stuck his tongue in my mouth, I seemed to be struggling for air. There was a feeling of suffocation and I promptly fainted. Needless to say I never saw him again.

For days I kept looking at myself in the mirror with great delight and wondering if I was pregnant. Not really wanting to ask Mummy, I took my problem to Maureen who finally decided it was time that I knew a few of the facts of life. Thank goodness she did as it was a great help when I started my serious dating.

It was a strange and heady time. In the war, you met so many people and the men were always all about to go back into battle. The Americans would fall in love just like that because they were desperate for comfort and away from home. They'd be back from the front, and they drank a lot. I would be in a cinema or at a restaurant and they'd come across to me to tell me how beautiful I was and so I would go dancing with them or go out with them. We would go to the Rainbow Corner services club in Piccadilly or to nightclubs like the Coconut Grove or The 400. Meanwhile, the bombing would be going on overhead. There was the feeling that death was just around the corner and that made the soldiers very randy. I probably looked a bit of a tart too, with my flared dancing skirts and long red nails. I can remember having to escape at least three different generals and I would have to come up with all sorts of excuses to rescue myself from these predicaments.

One of my first experiences of semi-rape, which did seem to happen fairly frequently after that, was with Rory's cousin George Tiffany. He was a colonel in the United States Air Force, stationed there having served in World War I, and he was visiting London. Mummy wanted some things taken around to him as she was going away for the weekend. She asked me to be delivery boy and go to Claridges on the way back from the embassy.

The front desk called to announce my arrival and George, instead of coming down, asked for me to be shown up to his suite. I had never met him and wondered if he was anything like his terrifying mother. He was not a huge and hideous figure as I had been imagining on the way up. He was tall like Aunt Nanny but not fat and although there was a certain resemblance, he did not have her bulldog face and drooping eyes. George invited me to have a drink with him. There was an open bottle of Dom Perignon in an ice bucket. Explaining that I did not drink he gave me a Coke. He said, "I never imagined I would be entertaining such a magnificent-looking girl. I thought one of your mother's footmen would deliver the parcel, I had heard that Enid never lets you out of her sight. I can now understand why."

I sat for what seemed like hours like a frightened rabbit while he drank his champagne and talked about the war. After all, he was an old man. I suppose he was in his late forties and I had been brought up to be polite. By the time he had finished his bottle of champagne he started getting amorous, telling me how beautiful I was, that it was a *coup de foudre*, that he had fallen in love with me. All the while he was kissing me passionately. We were sitting on the sofa and before long he was on top of me. Painfully shy as I was in those days, to be rude to an older man was not in my vocabulary. He was busy trying to get my corset belt off, which was a practical impossibility, and in the ensuing struggle once again I could feel my ears ringing and this feeling of suffocation. I think I said, "Please, George, let me up, I am going to faint." At least he was a gentleman. I must have looked very white and I was gasping for air. He took ice out of the champagne bucket and rubbed it on my forehead, repeating, "I am sorry, I am so sorry."

By now I had recovered but was sopping wet through his ministration of the ice water. When he escorted me through the front door of Claridges, I must have looked a mess. I was devastated. I thought all the porters were looking at me, and I was almost crying with embarrassment. Having delivered me back to Lees Place, he again begged forgiveness and implored me to go out with him for his remaining few days in London.

Again I was too nervous to say no, although I dreaded the thought of seeing more of him. That night he called around at Lees Place and took me out to the Embassy nightclub. During the next few days, he would pick me up at the American embassy, take me out to lunch and then in the evenings would meet me at Lees Place and have a drink in the sitting room while I bathed and changed. Being very rich, he would take me to the smartest places. Always to whatever film I wanted, to dinners at the Savoy or the Ritz. I think wherever it was fashionable he took me. Apart from telling me that he was madly in love and always holding and kissing my hand, he never again tried to make love to me.

On his last night, he asked me to marry him. I did not know how to get out of this so I said, "I will have to ask Mummy." All the way home, I kept praying she would be out in case she said yes. Although we waited for what seemed ages Mummy didn't appear so, kissing me goodbye, he left me with a studio portrait that he had had taken of himself so that I could "look at it and remember a man who loves you". He also said, "I will be writing to my mother, and to yours, and will try and get a transfer to England."

That was not to happen, for George died soon after. He must have written to Aunt Nanny the night he left me, though. After the war Aunt Nanny, who had disliked me so intensely on our journey across the States, was now determined that I go and stay with her. She told my mother that George had written saying that he wanted her to get to know me and that after the war he was hoping to bring me to the States.

She persuaded Mummy to bring me over. There, Aunt Nanny told me that the last two letters she had received from him were mostly about him telling her that I was not the child she disliked but the most wonderful girl he had ever met and quite the most beautiful. He said in one, "She is so good, so kind and so incredibly gentle and I want you to love her as much as I do." Before my return to Europe, she showed me that letter. It was the last he ever wrote to her. George Tiffany was the first person, besides my mother, to tell me I was beautiful. I did realise at the time that he probably hadn't seen a female face for ages.

It is amazing how circumstances change one's life. If I hadn't had my brief encounter with George, I would never have been invited by Aunt Nanny to America. I would never have gone to the Bahamas, and I would never have met my first great love, Richard Murphy, or my second husband, Aymon de Roussy de Sales.

Caryll had finished at Eton and was now at the Royal Military College at Mons Barracks in Aldershot, which is where the Officers Cadet Training Unit for the infantry was trained. At 17, he and another friend from Eton had gone to the Guards Depot at Caterham in September, 1944, for their initial training and from there to Mons. It all sounded very gruelling. To Mummy's intense pride, he won the medal of honour for being one of the most outstanding cadets of the year. He became a young lieutenant in the Grenadier Guards and was eventually stationed at Chelsea Barracks. After the war, because Caryll had access to the Furness Rolls Royce when most of his fellow officers had bicycles, his commanding officer would bark at him, "Closet! [Caryll was to inherit the title of Lord Waterpark] Make yourself useful!" He would be told to collect Princess Margaret in his Rolls for a cocktail function at the barracks. The two princesses, says Caryll, were lovely to look at and Princess Margaret was always full of fun.

The relief of this long long war being over was exhilarating. I still remember the excitement of V.E. Day. When the news came through, all the church bells started ringing, wonderfully exciting, joyous peals that vibrated through the streets of London. Everyone came out and there was laughing, kissing and dancing in the streets. Sir Winston and Lady Churchill asked Mummy to their celebrations at 10 Downing Street. All over London, bonfires were being lit and I went with all my friends to Berkeley Square. They were just building a huge bonfire when we arrived and one of the bystanders came up with the idea that to make the evening perfect someone should ride through the fire. As nobody seemed to be volunteering, I did and was promptly handed a bicycle.

Caryll and I had spent hours as children practising trick-riding. I now found it no great problem to leap through the flames. Once they had finished building me a ramp, it was only a matter of gathering enough momentum to lift the bicycle off the ramp and sail over in fine style, making sure to meet the downward ramp. I suffered no burns and it was wild and wonderful.

Gradually, my section of the embassy started closing down. I still used to walk across the square every morning with my dogs, my poodles having been joined by Honey, the beautiful cocker spaniel from Harrods. Mummy and I still used to go to Battersea Lost Dogs Home on rescue missions too and then the dogs would be driven down to Wales for Lane to look after. By this time, Lane must have had 40 or 50 dogs in her keeping. So many of them had been rescued from bombed-out buildings in which their owners had been killed. It was a tradition my mother started, of saving dogs, which to this day I have continued. Even now I have 35 dogs, all rescued and of various shapes and sizes.

One day, crossing the garden square, I had let the dogs off the lead as usual. On arriving opposite the entrance to the embassy, I was looking for Honey to put her lead back on so we could cross over when I heard the most terrible squeal of brakes and a dog screaming. It was my lovely Honey lying in the road. A despatch rider on a motorbike had run her over. He helped me find a taxi and I rushed her off to the vet. The doctor wanted to put her down. I begged him to try and save her. I was so distraught that he assured me he would do what he could but he held out very little hope. All that day, in between dictation and typing, I would rush to the loo and getting down on my knees would implore God and Daddy to save my Honey. That evening the vet called me up and said, "It is like a miracle but it looks as if she will be all right." It was another instance of one of my life's miracles and the way my prayers were answered.

The embassy, when they finally closed my wing down, offered me a job either in Washington or with the U.S. Air Force at France's Orly field. Mummy said she thought that Washington was too far from home. It was arranged that I would go and stay with Aunt Mimi in Paris and take the job with the air force.

CHAPTER

19

I thoroughly enjoyed working at Orly and living with Aunt Mimi, who had been married to my father's brother, Harry Cavendish. Her real name was Elise. She ran a very eclectic household. Amongst her friends were film stars, singers and circus trainers, and the Russian Prince Felix Yussoupov was a frequent visitor. I never ceased to be amazed at the thought that this elderly gentleman who wore make-up, rouged his cheeks and dyed his hair was the man who was involved in the plot to put the bearded and long-haired monk Rasputin to death because of his influence on the last tsar of Russia's wife. The mystic was poisoned, shot and finally drowned in the Neva river under ice. On reading my history of the Russian court in its heyday, I discovered it was common practice amongst the courtiers to wear magnificent costumes and to make extensive use of make-up and it was not a statement of homosexuality. At this time Paris was full of penniless aristocratic refugees who had fled the Russian Revolution almost 30 years before. A lot of the men had had to find jobs as taxi drivers or as nightclub commissionaires.

Aunt Mimi's flat was a rendezvous for these wonderful characters who congregated in her large sitting room. The music would flow through the open french windows because nearly all Russian noblewomen and men were talented musicians. It had been part of their upbringing as had the French language, which was extensively spoken at the Russian court. As I sat in Aunt Mimi's small garden, I could hear the muted sound of their voices and picture the champagne being poured into fluted glasses. In this beautiful Paris apartment, surrounded by luxury, for a space of time they were back in their beloved Russia.

Mimi was herself a great eccentric. Her first marriage had ended in disaster, she told me. She had unfortunately fallen madly in love with her stepson and he with her. She proudly showed me where he had burned his initials on her stomach. Then she married Uncle Harry but they were divorced in 1919. Uncle Harry, as far as I can gather, led a very eventful life having volunteered to serve with the South African Light Horse in the Boer War, made a scientific expedition to Patagonia, and been a Fellow of the Royal Geographical Society for 50 years. He explored Africa and the plains of America, hunting buffalo with Buffalo Bill Cody, and then in later life convinced himself he was Jesus Christ. Dressed in flowing robes and a beard he walked around Paris in sandals. The only thing he left out of this charade was the staff. I never saw him but apparently he was tall and, according to Mimi, marvellous looking. Uncle Harry left Mimi for another Frenchwoman, bought a house in Paris, which Mimi said was a brothel – after careful consideration he had decided that brothel-keeping was the way to make money – and he and his new wife took up residence on the top floor. I could not quite see how Jesus Christ and brothel-keeping were compatible but I suppose he was crazy enough to reconcile the two.

Uncle Harry was Daddy's older brother, later Lord Waterpark. He died without issue and so Caryll inherited the title, but if any member of the family has inherited Uncle Harry's cuckoo-ness, it is me.

Mimi told me the first time Uncle Harry was unfaithful to her, a van-load of yellow roses arrived on her doorstep. She had once told him that, in France, yellow roses were a symbol of infidelity. Mimi in her youth had been a concert pianist. Her lovely ground-floor flat was always echoing to the sound of music. She would sit for hours at her grand piano playing the classics or Strauss waltzes or even the latest music hall hits. She loved her music and had many friends amongst the great artists of that time.

Aunt Mimi's flat had a huge pale beige and white sitting room that always seemed to be full of light. The beautiful filtered sun from the garden came in through the french windows, lighting up a row of large crystal chandeliers. It was a room of beautiful music and the soft air of Paris in the spring. At that time there was hardly any traffic and the avenue was full of trees, as was Mimi's garden. Trees and yellow roses, the story of my life, said Aunt Mimi. I can still see her as she played, intent on the keyboard. She either wore black or grey; it was a uniform of mourning. She never wore any other clothes, they were all identical, and cut with a low V-neck over small breasts just covered by a white fichu. Grey with white fichu or black with white fichu. Grey stockings and buttoned-over shoes in grey, or black stockings with buttoned-over shoes in black. Her mourning was for the stepson of her first husband and the great love of her life. She was small and vivacious, slightly pigeon-toed. She never walked but trotted around the flat. Her short grey hair was parted in the middle in the style of the twenties, and she had beautiful skin stretched in a tight face-lift and huge blue eyes. She was very quick in all her movements, as if she were in a perpetual hurry, her beautiful hands gesticulating as she tried to make some point. I adored her; she was wonderful to me and my dogs when we took up residence in her immaculate apartment, treating us as if we had always lived there. At her death, she left Rory in her will a large portrait of herself painted in the 1920s. At the time I felt rather hurt, as Rory had never seemed that attached to her but who in the world could resist his incredible charm? Obviously not Aunt Mimi. Anyhow I have her portrait on my wall in South Africa now. Rory was not interested in keeping it for himself and offered it to me.

Her sitting room had many tables with photographs of herself and the famous – artists, musicians and friends. One of her guests at the time was singing at the Paris Opera House. With Mimi accompanying on the piano, he would practise every morning, wonderful arias from all the great operas. On the high notes, his beautiful powerful voice would even stir the prisms hanging from the huge crystal chandelier over the piano. I used to be entranced watching them rattle, dance and click as they came together in the light from the open window. The other thing he would practise was trying to seduce me. He would try and clasp me to his large chest and slip his equally big hands down the front of my dress. As I was heavily padded to simulate a film-star bosom, this was something I had to avoid at all cost. I soon made sure I was never alone in the same room. He kept telling me I had a very good singing voice but even that was a pretext to hold me in an embrace while he tried to get me to sing a duet.

I slept in a small room off Aunt Mimi's. She used to leave the communicating door open as she often used to come in and share a midnight coffee with me and discuss the day's events. I used to leave for my job with the air force at Orly long before she awoke in the morning. The colonel, the captain, or one of the NCOs would come and collect me in an open jeep. The first time I went to Aunt Mimi's room and found her asleep, I got a terrible fright. Her face had been tightened with surgery to such an extent that she couldn't close her eyelids. Mimi was lying still, and with her eyes half-open and unfocused. I thought she was dead.

In spite of Aunt Mimi's open door, Josephine Baker's accompanist invaded my room one night. He was a Spanish guitarist and also one of Josephine Baker's lovers. This did not prevent him from descending on me. He was very good-looking but he stank of garlic; I had a great struggle getting rid of him without waking the whole household while also trying to be tactful and not hurt his feelings.

Another frequent visitor was Edith Piaf and her boxer lover. She always seemed to be dressed in the same black velvet short evening dress which had sweaty armpits. I was so used to the immaculate toilette of my mother that these habits and the breath reeking of garlic everywhere were real killers. Obviously a woman of great passion, she could not keep her hands off her lover. Even at the dinner table, she would be feeding him from her spoon and giving open-mouthed kisses in which they exchanged bits of food. I used to watch with fascination. I could only imagine what was happening under the tablecloth by the expressions on their faces.

My favourite visitor was the wild animal trainer from the circus. An Indian, he used to come and stay accompanied by his two tigers on harnesses. They would sleep with him in the guest bedroom curled up on his bed like magnificent cats. He just adored them and told me that although he was getting old and wanted to retire, he loved them so much that he couldn't leave them. Poor man. I wonder how it all ended up. He was tied to the circus as long as the tigers lived. The circus owned them and refused to sell them to him. He said many of the trainers were very cruel and he would die if his beloved animals were tortured.

I had a great time at Orly. I worked for several officers, and took the testimony on two court-martials. One man I felt so sorry for. He had not committed any great offence and through my contacts I was able to get the case taken off the records so it never came to court.

One of the officers in particular, a colonel, had a very developed libido. I finally made arrangements with a sergeant that whenever I banged my chair on the floor, he would have to find an excuse to come in. The offices were housed in a huge and very temporary tin-like barracks that were not very well sound-proofed. My desk was in an outer office where I worked with some of the NCOs. At the beginning, I found it very difficult to ward off this man's attentions without making a scene. I only had to bend over the desk with some papers and he would try and rub this object over my behind or I would find it poking me in the ribs. His favourite trick was handing me papers in which he had tried to disguise his appendage. I would take the papers and find I was in possession of a pulsating penis. I do not know whether he found me irresistible or whether he was just so proud of this huge offering that he wanted some notice taken of it. If he did, he certainly got no satisfaction from me. Finally he gave up and I suppose took it around Orly looking for a more appreciative audience.

There was a very nice captain who loved dancing and he would take me out most nights. He would call for me in his open jeep, his two large Alsatians occupying the back seats, and I would load up my poodles and off we would go. We always took the dogs with us to the various nightclubs. On our first night out, we tied the dogs' leads to the chair legs only to find that halfway through the dance, the Alsatians had dragged the chairs onto the dance floor and had come to join us. He never made a pass at me. I obviously did not interest him physically but we had a wonderful time together.

There was another funny incident during my stay at Mimi's. She came into my bathroom one evening as I was getting ready for bed. I had divested myself of all my false bosoms, having graduated from cotton wool padding to rubber falsies, and was standing with a towel around my waist, cleaning my teeth. Before I could hide myself, Mimi grabbed me by the arms saying, "I don't believe this. You have the most perfect breasts. We have all been feeling so sorry for you. Please, you must come and show everybody."

I would have rather died than parade semi-nude. I had been brought up never to expose myself. I was clutching everything in sight to hide myself from her enthusiasm. "You should show them, you should show them," she cried, dancing a jig around me. Much to her disappointment I rushed off to bed. But I could see the next day that she had spread the news as her guests were all eyeing me with undisguised curiosity. Unconvinced by Mimi, I had already got my false breasts firmly in place. I only disposed of these rubber appendages finally a couple of months later when I went waterskiing in the south of France. The force of the water as I came up on my skis dislodged them and to my horrified embarrassment, two large pink rubber breasts went floating out the harbour on their way to the sea. I thought, "To hell with it. I'll never be Lana Turner so I better make the best of what I have got!"

CHAPTER

20

I remained at Orly for about six months before deciding to join my family in the south of France. Rory was anxious to start the restoration of La Fiorentina. During the war, the villa had been used as a German headquarters. Being right on the sea they had built underground blockhouses and numerous gun emplacements. When they left, they blew them all up, so parts of La Fiorentina went up with them. Rory professed to be delighted, saying it saved him the trouble of pulling down all the dark and depressing architecture.

Not only were parts of the house a ruin, but the gardens were just mounds of rubble where the guns and blockhouses had been. This seemed to please Rory even more. I can still hear him saying, "Mummy, the gardens were hideous. I am going to build you the most spectacular house and the most beautiful gardens in the South of France. In a few years, a Palladian palace will rise from the ashes." Which is what he proceeded to do. I remember, years later, him saying that Vicomte Charles de Noailles had the only other perfect garden, at his villa in Grasse, "and he was one of the world's great gardeners".

As we kept stumbling over the mounds of concrete I could see my beloved mother wasn't totally convinced by Rory's enthusiasm, especially as at one point, the ground crumbled under her feet and she went sliding down a hole into the blockhouse below. How she did not get seriously hurt, I do not know.

Rory wanted to be near Fiorentina so that he could supervise every inch of the rebuilding. He also planned to redo Le Clos. Therefore, Mummy rented La Leopolda, a magnificent villa which had belonged to King Leopold II of Belgium. La Leopolda was beautifully situated, overlooking the sea and Cap St Hospice, so from this height we could just see the villas of La Fiorentina and Le Clos at the end of our point. It also looked across the bay to Monte Carlo. At least it meant freedom for the dogs, that I would have endless waterskiing and I would be back with my adored family.

La Leopolda sat above the Moyenne Corniche, overlooking the magnificent bay of Beaulieu. It had terraced Italianate gardens, water features and fountains set either side of a long and winding drive that ended at magnificent gold-topped wrought iron gates and a gate house. (After Mummy, the Fiat magnate Gianni Agnelli bought La Leopolda and it was later purchased by one of the world's richest men, the banker Edmond J. Safra. It was while Safra was at La Leopolda in 1988 that he was told of the vendetta against him to ruin his reputation and his banks. That, and the paranoia it induced in Safra, resulted in his death when his flat in Monte Carlo went up in flames after an arson attack and he hid in the bathroom.)

La Leopolda had wide, shallow steps leading up to the colonnaded front entrance. From there, one passed into a large marble hall with endless statues on pedestals. I still remember one night, when we had moved to Fiorentina, we went back to La Leopolda for dinner with the Agnellis. Gianni, with his wonderful Roman looks and dressed all in black, was standing on the steps. With the columns lit up behind him, he looked exactly like a magnificent pagan god, with his patrician features and the short curly hair so beloved of the Romans. It was an unforgettable sight. Zeus descended from Parnassus.

I used to love the front drive of La Leopolda. I could practise all my circus stunts on the bicycle on my way to the village. I would fly past the shadows cast by the tall poplars and into the sun, with the calm blue sea of the Mediterranean spread below me. I'd hear the crisp sound of the pebbles being churned up beneath my wheels and the air would be warm with the scent of mimosa and orange blossom. The beautiful setting and the speed of my descent made it all come alive.

In the morning I would be sent off to collect the mail because my mother was worried that the long climb up the hill to La Leopolda was too hard on the elderly postman. She kept saying that his lungs were suffering. I wasn't surprised given the number of Gaulois he smoked by the time he reached the top. He would cough for about half an hour. So this became my job. Rory used to take the chauffeur off early in the morning, impatient to get to his beloved buildings at Fiorentina, and my mother never arose until lunchtime. I would collect the post and visit the pâtissier. He would always be standing in his shop, wearing the inevitable blue striped apron and with the wonderful smell of croissants and brioches issuing from the shelves of freshly baked bread. He was a great dog lover. "*Eh Mademoiselle! Vos chiens, qu'est qu'ils veulent aujourd'hui?*" he would ask in his thick Basque accent. My well-fed dogs would look at him pathetically as if they were dying of starvation.

"*J'ai gardé un petit morceau pour eux.*"

Then out from his pocket would come what looked like half his dinner in thick greaseproof paper, the meat cut into strips, which he would then feed to each dog as he patted and spoke to them. "*Et tu es beau, tu sais!*" he kept telling them while they hammed it up.

On leaving the admirable pâtissier and followed by the dreadful hounds I would head for the harbour. There I would install them in the boat and go out on the beautiful waters of the Mediterranean for my early morning waterski. Mummy had by this time bought a speedboat and employed an old sailor, Jean, to look after it.

This is how we found him.

One night we had been dining at Le Corsaire, a marvellous fish restaurant in the harbour of Villefranche. This old medieval port with washed pink houses and narrow cobblestoned streets climbing up the hill under archways was one of Rory's favourite places and the restaurant was famous for its *soupe de poisson* and its lobster Corsaire, which would arrive proudly borne by a waiter in a large silver dish, still aflame from the brandy. The tables were on the quayside under large white umbrellas, with checked tablecloths, white napkins, silver cutlery and floral decorations to match the tablecloths. It was like a film set. The harbour was built below the Moyenne Corniche, with Cap Ferrat rising out of the sea immediately to the left and on the far side was Cap d'Antibes. At night, it was always thrumming with activity, full of the fishing boats, either leaving or coming, the chug-chug of their outboard motors echoing in the still night air. Invariably there was a naval warship, usually American. Sailors and officers in starched white uniforms would be ferried backwards and forwards in pristine white boats with awnings flapping in the breeze. Sitting at the table we would watch all the activity as the boats drew into the harbour unloading their passengers. The black mountains, the white boats, the white uniforms, would be lit up as if by a thousand candles as the lights from the village flickered and danced on the still dark waters of the Mediterranean.

We would dine in Villefranche at least twice a week and it was during one of these evenings that an old sailor approached our table looking for work. He had been wounded in the war, had no money to buy a boat, and there was no employment. He spoke with a strong Provençal accent and Mummy, on being told his sad tale, said to Rory, "He has got a very sweet face; we cannot leave him without work. I have got a marvellous idea. Caryll is coming tomorrow and will want to go waterskiing. Caryll can go to Nice and find himself a speedboat and I will employ the sailor to look after it."

A few years later, when we were living at La Fiorentina, Caryll was taking this same magnificent boat to Monte Carlo, as a friend, Diana Abdy, the eldest daughter of the Earl of Bradford and the wife of Sir Robert Abdy, wanted to go shopping. Caryll had arranged for the car to meet them at the port of Monaco. Soon after leaving the harbour of St Jean, and as Caryll opened the throttle of those twin high-powered engines, the whole boat blew up. Jean had not cleaned the bilges properly and petrol was floating on top of the bilge water. When it blew up, Caryll and Diana were blown clear but Caryll saw that Jean was caught in the wreckage, which by this time was a burning inferno. Caryll swam back and managed to disentangle Jean but in doing so got badly burnt and was caught by the propeller, which sliced down his arm. At least Jean's life was saved, although he also was burnt badly.

I was in the garden at the time but I knew it was our boat because of the roar of the powerful engines. I heard the explosion and saw a pall of black smoke. I ran to the garage, desperate, and for once there was no spare car. The chauffeur had gone to Monte Carlo, Mummy and Rory had taken one of the others, Caryll had left his Buick at the port of St Jean and mine was being serviced in the garage at Beaulieu. I was in tears running round in despair. What had happened to my beloved brother? I grabbed the only remaining transport, a bicycle, and pedalled furiously to the harbour.

A flotilla of boats had gone to their rescue and by the time I got there, Caryll was coming ashore, blood pouring from his arm, his whole upper body just red flesh from the burns. His eyes were almost shut and even his eyelashes were burnt. He was unrecognisable. I was convinced he was going to die, like the pilot on the beach of Le Touquet.

Of course when he was better I used to tease him about his heroics. I said, "You will go to any lengths to give your poor mother a fright." He had been driving a jeep in Germany when they hit a land mine. I repeated the old adage, "Never two without three, what are you thinking of doing for a hat-trick?"

A few years later, farming in Kenya, he would almost kill himself getting blown up by a stick of dynamite.

As for the boat, soon afterwards my mother presented Caryll with a surprise, a replacement. She had bought it with the proceeds from a big gambling win the night before at the casino.

So that was my morning. In the afternoons, I would take my car up to the Haute Corniche and see how fast I could take the corners. At that time, there were no tourists and the coastal roads and villages were fairly deserted. Sometimes I would park and climb to the top of the ridge, sitting amongst the scrub from which arose the wonderful scent of herbs and look across the bay to Menton. I would watch a pair of eagles, nesting on the rocky outcrops, swooping down to land, their feet and wings acting as brakes. Below me, the medieval walled villages that had repelled raiders through the centuries looked like Benozzo Gozzoli paintings.

CHAPTER

21

At this stage of my life I didn't know my elder brother that well. He was 14 years older than myself and because of Furness he had only been allowed infrequent visits to Burrough Court. Then came the war and he had spent part of that in the United States. It was only when we were all living in London that I got to know him better, and of course at that time I had never had the joy of travelling with him. All I knew was that during my youth he had been held up as a paragon.

Rory loved the south of France and didn't like England, particularly after the war, when it was so drab and cold and everything good was in short supply. Mummy provided Fiorentina for him and for his brilliant and sophisticated friends. By the time he had finished rebuilding and decorating the villa to his idea of perfection, it had become a monument to his exquisite taste. No expense was ever spared and it became one of the most famous houses in Europe. In his book *The Golden Riviera* published by Weidenfeld and Nicholson in 1975, Rory writes of Fiorentina that it "had been a poor pastiche of a Florentine villa and after several false starts, we finally decided that it should be rebuilt in the Palladian style."

I love the way Rory says "we" as if our beloved mother had some say in the matter. He would discuss plans with her for hours but it was certainly not her prerogative to disagree with any of his ideas. As far as Mummy was concerned, if her adored son wanted to build the Cheops pyramid she would have been just as enthusiastic. As it was, money flowed out in all directions.

At the casino in Monte Carlo one night, Rory had obviously run out of money so he went up to Mama and said, "Give me 5000." Mummy, in the middle of a hand, was a bit slow to oblige. All her life, she used to go around with her special handbag in which she would carry as much as £10,000 in cash. Rory, who was never known for his patience, said, "Hurry up, darling. I can't wait around all night." Mummy duly stopped playing to hand out the necessary cash. After Rory left, a lady at the same table said, "Lady Furness, he might be one of the most beautiful young men I have ever seen and obviously he must be terrific in bed, but I have never heard a gigolo so rude and demanding. I would tell him to take a hike if I were you."

Mummy and Rory used to laugh over that for years.

She loved Rory so much that when she was with him, she was like an anxious child trying to please, worrying that she would not live up to the pedestal he had placed her on. She was in awe of his friends, although I don't think anybody else except myself saw that. She lacked academic education and some of Rory's friends made her realise that she could not compete with them on that level. She developed a series of ruses to protect herself, like coming down to lunch late so that everyone else would almost be finished their meal. Rory really only liked people who he thought had a brain, who were intellectuals or artists or had substance. Mummy's friends were very different; the hunting, shooting and fishing set from Leicestershire for instance, or army friends. Caryll remembers Mummy asking Rory, in a slightly terrified voice, if she could have so and so to stay. And of course, Rory would always say "No!" They were well below the salt in his opinion.

In the privately published book, *Remembering Rory*, written by our friend Anne Cox Chambers (who later became the American ambassador to Belgium during the Jimmy Carter administration) the gardening writer Peter Coats is quoted. He says that Rory became a good friend of his: "[But] at first, I found him over-critical and rather conceited, and there were some people who went on thinking so. He was certainly particular of his friends: one was rather proud of being one of the chosen. He worshipped his mother, one of the great beauties of the day, the much-married Enid, Countess of Kenmare. Between them, Rory and his mother created, in the south of France, out of a large villa much damaged by the Germans in the war, a Palladian palace of great beauty, filled with marvellous possessions. Rory was a great collector of rather special things, like Ingrès drawings. Many he bought and many he must have inherited from this much-loved and admired mother. After she died, he raised a carved marble memorial stone to her in his Provençal garden, amid rocks, cyclamen and olive trees. I cannot remember the exact inscription but it ran something like this: 'To the memory of Enid, Countess of Kenmare – one of the most beautiful women of her time.' It was an act of devotion, though an unusual thing to do, according to most Anglo-Saxons. But, as I already said, Rory was devoted to a chosen few."

Rory had dictated to Mummy what I should be taught and had told her it was not necessary for a girl to go to school. Not surprisingly, I too was in awe of this demigod when he, my mother, his latest girlfriend and I came to make a trip through Italy from our base in the south of France. He kept saying, "My beloved sister, I despair of you. All these beautiful houses, the frescoes, the paintings, the gardens and you remain huddled in the car reading one of those dreadful love stories. You are never going to broaden your mind if you continue like this!"

He dominated our lives, but in the nicest possible manner. We travelled everywhere with him, to one wonderful country after another, as he did his research for his books. He taught us to love visual beauty and through his eyes we saw the clarity of colour and light, the soft scent of flowers, earth and smoke. We met the people of the countries we visited, from peasants to princes. We stopped to admire the flora and fauna, the smallest shell on a beach. Everything held a beauty for Rory. Travelling with him was like treasure hunting. His quick and discerning eye would transform for me an oleleshwa branch into a Rodin sculpture, so lovingly would he admire its gnarled and twisted shape. A moth would become one of the jewels of the Peacock Throne. In *Remembering Rory*, the jeweller Kenneth

Jay Lane writes: "He invented, I think, aesthetic order! He must have a Japanese ancestor somewhere way back." And the poet Stephen Spender wrote that he was an amateur in the best sense of an old-fashioned word, that "he did all he did simply out of the love of doing it and not for gain."

The visit he made to Tutankhamen's tomb in 1922 as a small child, when my father had been posted to Egypt, had a profound effect on him. Lord Carnarvon, who organised the visit, had made the discovery with archaeologist Howard Carter. Rory remembers that Mr Carter was very impressed by his seriousness and so was perfectly happy to reveal the tomb to an eight-year-old. Rory wrote a piece about it for the American magazine *Architectural Digest*, which was published in 1985, the year he died: "I remember vividly the footprint of a sandal in the dust, left there, Mr Carter told me, by a high priest who had stepped forward to print a seal on a plaster wall behind which lay the sarcophagus." Rory always said that it was this visit that started his passion for beautiful objects. After that, his idea of pleasure as a tiny child was to go every afternoon to the museum after his Egyptian school. Accompanied by either my mother or his Nanny, he would spend hours entranced by the mummies, the jewels and the sarcophagi.

Rory was not only my beloved brother but an historian and author of several books: *The Golden Haze – with Captain Cook in the South Pacific*; *Australia: History and Horizons*; and *The Golden Riviera*; as well as *Time of the Mango Flowers*, on India, and *Equator Farm*, on Kenya, and there was also a book on shells. He published *Viceroyalties of the West: the Spanish Empire in Latin America* and, having studied architecture in Munich, he put together *Shadows From India: An Architectural Album*. He became well known for his interior design and for being an innovator, was a botanist and landscape artist and a well-known photographer. To all of these, he brought his particular sensibility.

Rory loved the feel and texture of fabric, of objects. I can still see him running his hands lovingly over the curve of a statue or the contours of a pot or surrounded by yards of material as he felt the quality of the silks, satins or cottons. He would also stand, his eyes half-closed, lost in another world as he examined paintings, objets d'art, colour schemes or even *"le placement des objets"*. Whatever he bought or chose had to be perfect. He was fanatical about scale, always complaining about walking into rooms and finding that people had got their proportions all wrong. The lights or the paintings were hung too high or were too small for the scale of the room. Or the colours were wrong, the volume was wrong. He had the most discerning eye and it would depress him to walk into an ugly house. He would get quieter and quieter and start fiddling with the signet ring on his little finger, a sure sign that he would be shortly making some excuse in order to leave.

At 6ft 3in, of wonderful build and with sapphire blue eyes, Rory had always had many girlfriends although, surprisingly given his aesthetic sense, none of the ones I can remember were beautiful. In fact, he seemed to prefer older women and larger ones at that. They were all very intelligent though and well read. That's what seemed to matter to him. When he was in his early 40s, he had a last long love affair with a woman married to a close friend of ours. She was voluptuous, clever and again, not particularly good-looking. In fact, I thought she was hideously ugly, a *jolie-laide*, and she was a lot older than Rory. One night, going up to bed, Rory confided in me that he didn't think he could sleep with her one more time. After that, he fell in love with a man called Yves. I don't think my mother was happy about Rory's changing tastes in the sexes, but she loved him so much that, in the end, anything he wanted to do was accepted by her.

Rory carried his dislike of anything ugly to such a degree that, many years later during one of his yearly visits to South Africa to visit me, he heard that there was a very pretty fishing village up the coast called Arniston. It was a three-hour drive and at the time he was not feeling well. It was the beginning of his AIDS, which in those days people did not know much about and we had no concept that his poor health was due to this deadly disease. On this occasion, Rory planned to stay the night at Arniston as there was a new hotel with a very good reputation. It had been a large house in the village and overlooked the beach. On the way we stopped and had lunch at a charming little restaurant in a beautiful Victorian village, and there he was told of another very pretty village and church in one of the valleys which was worth looking at. So we went and Rory was enchanted. We didn't arrive in Arniston until about 4 o'clock. As we drove down the hill into the village, Rory looked at all the cottages on the beach to which glass fronts and ugly red brick verandahs had been added. "Where is the village of Arniston, with the fishermen's cottages?" asked my brother. I explained that according to the signs this was it. "Not possible, it is a hideous suburban windswept excrescence, and if this is it I am not getting out of the car."

His boyfriend Gilbert and I went into the charming country hotel to ask for directions. We were in fact in the middle of Arniston. I went back to Rory and told him.

"Darling, cancel the room. I refuse to stay here. I want to go home," he commanded. Knowing my brother it was no use arguing but I was desperate for a cup of tea before facing a three-hour drive back. "No, absolutely not," he decreed. "I refuse to sit in the car while you and Gilbert eat your way through tea. You have got to get me out of this hideously depressing place."

So we cancelled the bookings. I looked longingly at the tea and scones as I fled past the hotel verandah where it was being served. I dared not keep my impatient brother waiting any longer. I could see him imperiously beckoning me to get a move on as he leant out of the window of the car blowing the horn.

During my life with Rory I had got used to his idiosyncrasies. In India, he could stand next to a corpse, which he never noticed, and remain entranced by a temple. Once, walking the streets and surrounded by the colour and smell of India, of dust and spice, we found ourselves near the *ghats* where bodies were burnt. A vulture flying overhead dropped its burden at my feet, a human thigh bone still with its dark and blackened flesh. The other vultures, determined not to be deprived of their feast, alighted almost on top of me, quarrelling fiercely over their human carrion. I pointed this out to Rory who was busy photographing the beauty of a little house crumbling with age but painted peacock blue and emerald green. "What nonsense," he said and continued his love affair with the Indian street.

Equally, Rory could depart in haste from a palace because the modern decor was so hideous.

Seeing the world through his eyes though was a life of continual enchantment. Looking back, I realise how incredibly privileged I was to spend so many years travelling in his wake as he and Mummy, following the sun, did the grand tours of Italy, Greece, Egypt, Ceylon and India. While Mummy bought jewellery, Rory would buy paintings, furniture, books, materials and statues. We always travelled by ship so as to accommodate the mountains of luggage and the unbelievable collection of objets d'art they amassed between them.

In the early days of our travels, Rory used to nearly kill me with embarrassment. As soon as he saw a really beautiful villa or even a farmhouse, Rory just had to go and look. I would try to hide under the dashboard so nobody could see me. Rory would serenely get out and go and ring the front doorbell. I was always expecting him to be thrown out by irate owners, but he never was. By the time the handsome, impeccably dressed Rory had explained, exuding charm, the reason for his appearing on their doorstep, he and Mummy would be greeted like visiting deities, the red carpet rolled out and the royal tour given. I had always implored Rory not to include me in these impromptu visits. Embarrassed and hoping nobody would notice me and associate me with this dreadful family, I would remain hiding in the car. Sometimes I would be there for hours stifling in the hot sun, trying to read a book while lying down on the seat, hoping I was hidden from view.

Later on, and in the different exotic countries of the world, I got used to these excursions into other people's territories and would enter in his wake and sometimes meet the most enchanting people. I particularly remember an old English woman living in a crumbled Victorian ruin in Mysore in southern India. She had obviously been beautiful and the faded pictures of her husband and child were everywhere. They had died during the outbreak of the Spanish flu that swept the world after World War I. She took us to their graves, the tears running down her cheeks as she laid fresh flowers on the tombstones. She visited them every morning and evening, laying little bunches of flowers carefully selected from her garden. She insisted that we walk back to the house for tea. Everything was laid out on white starched linen tablecloths, a heavy silver tea service, a large silver bowl filled with cabbage roses and lavender, and hovering around the table, her old and faithful retainers with their white uniforms, blue sashes, and turbans. In the background were the wonderful fretwork balconies and columns of her two-storeyed colonial mansion through which tropical palms were already entwined and from which the paintwork was peeling. The avid jungle had taken over what had once been an immaculate English garden and convolvulus and lantana smothered the roses.

We sat in this Indian sunset, amongst the smell of lush tropical vegetation and decaying leaves, with the sun casting a pink glow over the table and its occupants. The magpies and the mynahs were settling into the trees for the night, voicing their displeasure at some jungle inhabitant that had upset their evening nesting pattern. The monkeys had come down to help themselves to the scones and cakes displayed on the table, totally unfazed by the fact that we were still sitting there. The motley pack of dogs at her feet remained unmoved by the jungle's inhabitants even though they had now been joined by a mongoose, which was eating the crumbs cast off by the monkeys only yards from the dogs' noses. I realised this was a nightly ritual and we were privileged to have been able to share it with her. I often wonder what happened to this little oasis when this remarkable and very old lady went to join her loved ones in the graves of the church that was also crumbling. What happened to her devoted servants and dogs?

Ten years after Rory's death, his great friend, the interior designer David Hicks sent me a copy of a magazine published in Asia in which four pages were devoted to beautiful photographs of life in India. All of them were Rory's and one was of this lovely Victorian ruin.

CHAPTER

22

During our stay at La Leopolda, Rory had been decorating the Clos so that we could live there until the rebuilding of La Fiorentina was completed. Le Clos, with its green shutters and pink-washed walls, surrounded by olive trees and trellised grape vines, was to be our home for the next few years.

The house was built on the high ground of the Cap. The back of the garden rose in terraces as far as the road which led to a small chapel. At the front of the chapel was a giant statue of the Virgin. Larger than the chapel, it surveyed the bay. The story went that sailors caught in a violent storm had vowed to the Virgin that if their lives were saved they would build her a statue. Carrying out their promise, they built this towering and beautifully painted monument out of the remains of their wrecked ship. People never seemed to use the chapel though, and so the paint gradually faded and peeled off this touching example of gratitude from the seamen. Nevertheless, the Virgin still looked as serene as the Statue of Liberty as she guided the ships below into safe anchorage.

A very high wall and cypress trees separated the back of the Clos from the chapel. On each terrace below the wall fruit trees with white-painted trunks, rose out of a sea of white petunias. These in turn were bordered in squares of blue and mauve lavender. In spring, with the pink and white fruit blossoms, the white petunias and blue lavender all gently rippling in the sea breeze, it was like a Tchaikovsky ballet and the scent that permeated the air and filled the rooms of the Clos was almost overpowering.

By the time Rory had finished Le Clos itself, the top two floors consisted of six bedrooms and ensuite bathrooms and the ground floor was the dining room, a library and a large sitting room. The walls were painted the palest of pale olive green. I watched him pick an olive leaf and, turning the back of the leaf over, he got the painters to match the colour. The sofas were large and opulent, covered in off-white, thick textured cotton with matching cushions. The chairs were large and Louis XV. Stripped to a pale olive grey, they were also covered in heavy cotton but in the lightest of lemon yellows.

Rory was, I believe, the first person to conceive the idea of the modern-day tablescapes. Large tables were covered in thick layers of material that flowed to the floor and on them he would place his flower arrangements and his precious collected pieces. He would go to the Nice market and buy tuberoses, carnations, lilies, and roses, all in the palest of pinks, whites, creams and yellows. He would cut off the stems and arrange large bowls of massed flowers. The rooms all had french windows open to the sunlight, which used to filter through the leaves of the olive trees and dance on the Aubusson carpets. The scent of the flowers would drift through a house bathed in a glow of warm Mediterranean sunshine. One of the sitting room walls had Louis XV wood panelling to frame Rory's collection of beautiful leather-bound books, many of which were first editions of the Belgian botanical artist Pierre Redouté and the 16th-century Italian architect Andrea Palladio. There was a secret panel in the carving and on pressing one of the rosettes, a door would swing open, leading into a library where other first editions lay opened and displayed on easels, their pages changed each day. Not nearly as large as the sitting room, the library walls were also panelled and housed the rest of his famous collection of books.

The french windows in front of the house opened onto a terrace, to the right of which was what we termed the Long Walk. It took us towards the point through the gardens of the Clos into those of La Fiorentina. The path to the left led through banks of roses and lavender to the servants' quarters. This was a fisherman's cottage of the same colour as the Clos and built during the same period. The paved terrace in front of Le Clos was on the same level as the house. Steps led off it on either side down to the terraced gardens below. It was covered by an enormous and very old grapevine and looked directly onto the calm blue waters of the Mediterranean. It was on this terrace where most of the life of Le Clos took place.

Rory had arranged the first part of the terrace like an extension of the sitting room, with the same coloured large sofas and armchairs. Instead of the tablescapes, there were big pots with lemon trees. They were purely for decoration. Beautifully pruned, they always seemed to have an abundance of bright yellow fruit and the trunks were painted white with lime. Rory said it was against ants but I think it was for decoration as afterwards, in the orangerie, he did the same thing. The effect, as with all the things that Rory did, was quite beautiful. The fruit was seldom allowed to be picked, only those few that spoilt the symmetrical effect.

The second half of the terrace was the dining area. Rory had the table which sat 12 people specially built out of olive wood with a thick glass top. The oval-backed Louis XV chairs perfectly matched the pale grey wood of the table and again, were covered with the palest of pale lemon yellow cotton. All our meals were served on the terrace. Breakfast in the morning with coffee and croissants, and then gourmet lunches and beautiful candle-lit dinners. The candles were in large Biot glass containers; the grapevine and gardens below were lit with carefully concealed uplighters casting beautiful light and shadow onto the leaves of the orange trees below and the olive trees and trellis above.

At the end of the terrace, the pergola for the vines formed an arch that framed the bay like a Renoir tableau. The mountains rose out of the Mediterranean, stretching all the way to Menton. There was usually a large yacht moored in the bay of Beaulieu, sometimes Aristotle Onassis's. At night, the fishing boats were lit by lanterns in the stern and the lights would dance on the still waters of the dark

Mediterranean. In the distance we could hear the fishermen greet each other in passing in their soft patois.

When Caryll was at Le Clos, we spent most of the days on waterskis. We now had our own little harbour built in the rocks below. Caryll was perfecting all his acrobatics and would spend hours coming out of the water backwards before doing his twists and turns. Or he would practise his slalom before discarding his skis altogether to go barefoot. This entailed a large amount of time spent falling into the water while the speedboat circled around to pick him up so he could start all over again. I found this endlessly boring as I sat on the rocks with my dogs waiting for my turn.

There was an enormous amount of entertaining done at Le Clos, which continued when we moved to Fiorentina much later – lunches, dinners, balls and wonderful parties. (When I was doing the housekeeping at Fiorentina, we once served 3000 meals in one week.) Rory loved to serve little grilled crayfish which had been freshly caught at St Jean. Then there would be *oeufs à la tripe*, a chicken main dish, pudding and cheese. One Good Friday we had a huge lunch party and, to everyone's horror, Rory quite forgot and served beef. Another of our favourite guests, Sallyanne Vivian, now Wilson, who was just 17 at the time, remembers watching worriedly as the white-gloved footmen came down flights of stairs holding silver platters piled high with balls of ice-cream.

Amongst the visitors were the Shah of Iran's sisters. I remember that Princess Ashraf, who was his twin, had enormous charm and having studied history I admired the Shah so much for what he had done for his country, bringing it out of the middle ages, emancipating women and transforming Iran for the 20th century. A frequent visitor at the time was Prince Pierre de Polignac who had been married to Princess Charlotte, the daughter of Louis II, prince of Monaco. Another of Mummy's lovers, he was very good looking and had enormous charm. His son, Prince Rainier, came over one day though, and while he was nearer my age, I do not think he addressed one word to me. I was obviously not attractive or interesting enough to warrant his attention. Later he started dating the American actress Grace Kelly who was not only lovely to look at but very natural. I remember one day when she was by then Princess Grace, she arrived on her bicycle dressed in white shorts and top. She had come unaccompanied, complaining about the roads and the bad traffic and how it was much quicker to come on her bike.

In the early days of Le Clos when I was very shy and young, I could come down to lunch and dinner and nobody would speak to me. I once remember counting five days when I descended from my studies to eat meals with the guests, and for five consecutive meals not one word was addressed to me. The Mitford sisters were regular guests but none of them, including Nancy, ever paid any attention to me. I could have been a chair for all they noticed. Unity Mitford had been a special friend of Rory's before the war and the two had got to know each other when they both spent time in Germany in the early 1930s studying at the end of their schooling. Upper-class English families often sent their children to be "finished" in Germany, to stay with upper-class German families while they studied, which may explain why many of the English aristocracy underestimated Hitler in the approach to World War II.

I found all Rory's guests quite terrifying and was delighted that they chose to ignore me. They had discovered that if they did try and bring me into the conversation, I would be monosyllabic and blush with embarrassment. Therefore, it was not worth the effort.

At this time I had a history professor who Rory had employed to teach me the classics. A retired Oxford Don, he used to be collected by the chauffeur and for four hours every morning we would study Greek, Roman and Egyptian history. This also included classical mythology. I was given so much homework that I hardly had time to come out of my room. Thrilled at my progess, he then started me on medieval history as well. He was nothing if not thorough and every month we had to do a résumé of the tasks he had set.

I had no other life at that time and he had no other pupil. I became fascinated by his ability to bring these long dead figures to life. So caught up was I that one day, immersed in my book, I walked down to Fiorentina's swimming pool which was, I think, the first infinity-edge pool designed. There were seven shallow grassed steps leading down to this pool, lined by 20 foot tall cypress trees, and halfway down was a set of Falconnet sphinxes facing each other. One bore the head of Madame de Pompadour and the other the head of Madame du Barry.

Rory had just completed the pool ahead of the main house and above Fiorentina's harbour, and there he was sitting with all his guests. I was in another world, noticing nothing and transported in my imagination to the shores of Egypt where the Pharaoh was racing across the desert in his chariot, the pyramids resplendent in gold leaf, shining against the deep blue Egyptian sky. I could feel the chariot sway beneath my feet, the hot desert air rush past my face. I was far away in a foreign land. Fully clothed, I walked down the stepped avenue and straight into the pool. To this day I can remember the shock of the cold water and the astonished faces of the guests. To compound my woes and to my intense embarrassment, I had forgotten about the newly built fountain spraying its water into the pool and the lily pond behind it. In my haste to depart the scene, I scrambled out of the pool to find myself now floundering around in the pond like a buffalo in its wallow, the dogs all yapping delightedly around my legs. It was no wonder I had the reputation of being slightly retarded!

I remember one night though when the English writer and critic Cyril Connolly was one of the guests. He asked me dine with him at Beaulieu. I could not refuse at the time as to do so would have been the ultimate in bad manners but later I rushed up to Rory's room and begged him to get me out of this appalling situation. "Pat, don't be ridiculous," said Rory. "Cyril is very bright and will amuse you and he thinks you are very lovely." Horror of horrors, neither Mummy nor Rory could understand my terror.

It was the most dreadful evening. He took me to La Reserve at Beaulieu, the famous restaurant and hotel on the coast. We dined outside under the palm trees. Like all Englishmen in those days, he had no idea how to dress for these hot Mediterranean summer nights. He did not have a very good figure, was on the plump side and wore dreadful baggy grey trousers and a grey and white crumpled short-sleeved shirt in a horrid leaf design with a cravat around his neck. He was sweaty and had body odour, that of a hot and unwashed Englishman. He kept on dancing with me and pressing me close to his smelly body.

I realised later that there was very little else he could do except dance with me. All through dinner, whenever he tried to get me into conversation, I was totally unco-operative and would answer yes or no or giggle stupidly and then blush with mortification. He tried to kiss me on the way home and that was a nightmare from which I thought I would never be able to extricate myself. Holding my breath so I wouldn't smell him, and with my mouth firmly closed, I offered passive resistance before scrambling out of the car. Needless to say, for the rest of his stay he did not ask me out again.

Other visitors who came every summer were Donald Bloomingdale of the New York department store family and his friends. There was a very funny incident with Aunt Nanny, although at the time it was far from funny but typical of my aunt. I had taken her out somewhere and we were late for lunch. Donald had been placed on Mummy's right and the empty chair next to him had been kept for Aunt Nanny. With a great deal of huffing and puffing from hurrying up the steps she lowered herself like a battleship into her seat and was introduced to Donald. "Bloomingdale, Bloomingdale," said Aunt Nanny with a snort of disgust. "Oh! Pots and pans!" And turning her chair so as to present her back, she didn't address another word to him. It was not the most successful lunch party that Mummy ever presided at!

Another friend of ours was the decorator Brindsley Black. He was very good looking, a man about town and what you'd call "of independent means". He told me a story from one of his dinners at Le Clos while he was staying with us. The actress Claudette Colbert, who was one of Rory's girlfriends, had decided to give an Hawaiian dinner party and the guests had to dress accordingly. Brindsley, who was a very young man at the time, wanted to make some contribution to the evening and ordered a beautiful lei for Claudette. He nervously presented this famous film star with his offering. Claudette immediately embraced him, saying, "Thank you darling, that is the best 'lay' I have had for some time." Everyone thought it a huge joke and teased Rory unmercifully.

Peter Quennell, the biographer, journalist and critic who wrote literary histories and was a founder-editor of *History Today*; Charles and Joan Ponsonby Moore (Charles was the son of my mother's great friends, Kathleen and Henry Ponsonby, Earl of Drogheda); and the Abdys, Sir Robert and his wife, Lady Diana, were frequent guests. The one I liked though was the Argentine painter Leonor Fini as she somehow was not as frightening. She came, again with two lovers in tow: I don't know how she managed to keep them both so enslaved. She had a passion for cats and said that I reminded her of one because of my eyes. Again, she did lots of sketches and paintings using me as a model. Leonor, of course, I had known during the war when she stayed at Fiorentina and did the portrait of my mother which I have to this day hanging above my mantlepiece in South Africa. My mother must have placed it with all Willy Maugham's own collection of Impressionist art from La Mauresque, which she successfully kept hidden during the war after he had been evacuated. Sadly, my own romantic portrait of me by Leonor didn't join the hidden paintings.

The other guest that I always liked was Claudette Colbert. I think it was because she always came with her dogs and so we were able to communicate about our love of animals.

CHAPTER

23

There were two great villas on the Côte d'Azur, La Fiorentina and La Garoupe at Cap d'Antibes. The latter belonged to the Normans, Sir Henry Norman and the Hon. Florence McLaren. La Fiorentina however had the advantage of occupying the point of Cap St Hospice. Even the name of the house conjures beauty.

Under the genius of my brother, La Fiorentina began to rise like a phoenix from the ashes of the war and the depredations of the retreating German army. In his book *The Golden Riviera* he describes the renovations he carried out. He was meticulous. He had got in touch with an architect from Nice, a Monsieur Henri Delmotte who Somerset Maugham had used when he had remodeled his own villa at Cap Ferrat, La Mauresque. Fiorentina had some of the same problems as La Mauresque in that it needed extensive stripping and re-working. The roof had to be lifted two feet, and the twin-towered entrance had to go. A loggia that had robbed the drawing room of light was pulled down so that now five great windows could open onto the terrace. For some reason the downstairs rooms had ceilings that were far too high, but the bedrooms above had low ceilings. In the drawing room downstairs, there was a dreadful ceiling, "gold-starred and coffered, cast in plaster, which hung from chains attached to the rafters" as Rory put it. That also went, as did a fake medieval fireplace.

Listing all of this now, I agree with Rory when he wrote that our mother was to be applauded in ever seeing the possibilities in Fiorentina. It had been built for the Countess de Beauchamp just after the outbreak of war in 1914 and she had then sold it to a man who had made his fortune in South Africa before dying. Of course what was spectacular about Fiorentina was its location on the point, with gardens going right down to the Mediterranean and stone pines at the very end, which was left wild. The building itself though was really not very good.

Having decided to ditch the original Florentine pastiche for the classic and pure lines of a Palladian villa, Rory headed for Italy with Mummy and me in tow. It was the first of several trips, for he had a list of Palladian houses he wished to see. As he wrote in his Riviera memoirs, he marked a circle on the map – Venice, Treviso, Vicenza and Padua, and so we set off exploring. Between Rory and Alvilde Chaplin, the girlfriend of his who accompanied us on some of these trips, not only did we do a tour of houses and gardens but they seemed to have lists of very grand friends with whom we stayed when we were not in hotels. As far as I was concerned, the friends were as terrifying as their palazzos.

Rory travelled with Diane his greyhound, Mummy with her poodles, pug and Tikki the hyrax, and I with my poodles. It was left to Lane and me to keep the animals out of everybody's sight, except for Rory who was allowed to lord it around with Diane. As far as Rory was concerned Diane went with him everywhere. When she eventually died, Rory built a monument to her in the garden of La Fiorentina and she was buried at the end of the point of Cap St Hospice.

It was still not long after the war and so the beautiful towns and villages of Italy were practically deserted. There were few tourists, so Rory was able to admire the wonderful towns of Naples, Venice, Florence, Verona, Padua and Siena at leisure. In fact, there was not a village or a town that had flourished during the quattrocento or cinquecento that we did not visit. We walked through every little cobbled street and every cloister, sat in every square drinking cappuccino while Rory photographed and photographed or drew sketches. There was not a museum, not a fresco, not a statue nor painting that we did not examine at length or did not return to visit again. Rory and Alvilde were lost in another world and tireless in their pursuit of the incredible treasures of the Renaissance.

Italy, not only architecturally but culturally, was the country that had given birth to so many of the greatest artists the world had ever seen or would ever see. Having studied my history, I could feel the magic of this incredible country and the beauty of its landscapes. The world we saw then had not come into the modern era. The women in their long skirts and scarved head-dresses still worked the fields; the heavily laden donkey carts were still the main source of transport for all the peasant farmers. The cypress trees planted by the early Romans to provide shade for the marching legions still lined the roads. As we drove along I could picture the plumed horses pulling their chariots, the Roman soldiers and the sun glinting off their heavy breastplates as they came down the winding hills onto the long straight avenues.

The villages still clung to the hills, cart-horses still plodding solemnly up and down the vineyards. Customs had not changed since medieval days. The churches were still the focus of village life and the sound of the church bells calling the faithful to prayer echoed across the small fields and the dusty country roads that wound around the hillsides and stretched out across the plains below.

The warm breeze coming through open windows still brought the smell of crushed grass, cow manure and herbs. The only thing that looked modern was the large number of bicycles that were in every city, town and village and which, as far as one could see, were ridden by people with no idea of the rules of the road.

Nor for that matter did my beloved mother, who was invariably in the wrong gear and on the wrong side of the road. As she insisted on driving, it was a miracle that we survived. I had to sit beside her because otherwise I was carsick. As she didn't use the rear view mirror either, I had to keep telling her, "Mummy, do slow down, Andrew is miles behind and is bound to get lost." Andrew was the chauffeur who always followed in Mummy's cloud of dust, bringing Lane and our dogs. Except of course for Diane who always sat in the back between

Alvilde and Rory. Alvilde was too infatuated to complain about this cavalier treatment.

Rory had first met Alvilde at a very smart dinner held by Lady Emerald Cunard, a very old American lady who was a great friend of his, and who surrounded herself with the intelligentsia and gave innumerable parties courtesy of her shipping fortune. At the time, Alvilde was a music critic for one of the British broadsheet newspapers and, although she was married – first to Viscount Chaplin and then to the diarist James Lees-Milne – Rory was so excited by her that we all knew a close relationship was imminent. Alvilde became a part of Rory's life and their relationship lasted for several years.

Alvilde bought herself the most lovely little house near Menton so she could be near Rory. It was all on terraces overlooking the sea. On our frequent visits there, one had to leave the car in the village square and walk down little cobbled streets until one arrived at her door. Being Alvilde, she had made a wonderful terraced garden and like every thing she did, it was enchanting. Her second husband, James Lees-Milne, helped establish the National Trust in Britain and Alvilde later produced several coffee-table books on English gardens and houses. I had always hoped Rory would marry Alvilde as she would have made him a marvellous wife, and her daughter Clarissa Chaplin was my best friend. But that of course was not to be.

Outside Vicenza, Rory finally found the answer to his problems and here I will paraphrase his writing, for I am sure he would not have minded. It was the 16th-century architect Andrea Palladio's Villa Rotunda and he decided to copy its facade for the front of Fiorentina. Once he and Delmotte had decided on that course, the rest followed. The villa, with its facing of stucco, was washed a pale buff to contrast with Rory's favourite silvery olive-green. Inside, in the first hall, he chose the colours of ice-cream, pistachio green and dirty pink to marbleize the walls, and a ceiling painted blue with puffy white clouds to look like the sky. It was something you saw in many Mediterranean countries. The second hallway was *trompe l'oeil* with a theme of architectural drawings, which looked as if they had been done on vellum and then tacked to the walls. It had been painted by Martin Battersby and very cheekily, he had even included one of Rory's own letters about the restoration (which mortified my perfectionist brother as it contained mistakes in grammar). On the ceiling were "the elevations of a dome drawn on a sheet of folded paper in sepia". For the dining room, Rory had found a late 18th-century Piedmontese fresco, which had been taken from its original wall and backed onto canvas before spending the war in a warehouse in London. The fresco even escaped a direct bomb during the blitz. Rory hired experts from Pisa to apply the fresco to the walls of Fiorentina's dining room and wrote that it made him nervous to watch them as they snipped away with large scissors at this beautiful piece of work of which he wrote, "The painter is unknown but he must have specialised in rural landscapes and for our room had made a study of rocks and trees with here and there, views of distant castles. Clipped hedges framed the doors, while birds flit from wall to wall, in company with a hawk that dominates the ceiling which, of course, is the sky."

CHAPTER

24

Now that the rebuilding of La Fiorentina was almost completed, Rory was planning with Mummy, Caryll and me a trip to Egypt and then several months in Australia while the finishing touches were being undertaken. This wonderful travel was to be taken under the aegis of Thomas Cook again. Through them, Mummy had arranged to rent the Memnon, a magnificent houseboat later used for the Agatha Christie film *Death on the Nile*. Cook's were also arranging a camel caravan to take us camping near the Pyramids and then to the Fayum, an oasis just south of Cairo where there were some interesting ruins Rory wanted to see.

In Egypt, the four of us were to be accompanied by Averil Knowles, our beautiful Irish friend with whom Caryll was still enchanted, and a friend of Rory's, Hilda Lezard. We stayed at Lees Place while all the papers were being arranged. I now had to get a visa, for the others had all received theirs. For this, I had to go to the Egyptian consulate with my photographs to get my visa stamped. The Consul General was doing it for me as it had to be processed quickly. When I went in to see him, my passport was lying open on his desk.

I sat down opposite and he asked me a few questions. Then he said, "All right, you can take your passport, but I would also like you to take this."

There was now an object lying in the middle of my open passport. Not used to penises being produced ad lib I did not realise what I was staring at. As it started twitching, I finally understood to my horrified amazement what I was being asked to handle. Shades of Orly, where I had learned my lessons in available penises. Needless to say, I grabbed my passport trying to avoid even the slightest contact and fled. I wondered to myself in horror if Egypt was going to be a veritable forest of male organs. Is that why my mother loved it so much? I need not have worried. I did not see another one, Egyptian or otherwise.

Our first days in Cairo were spent at the Mena Palace Hotel near the pyramids. The hotel was an Arabian fantasy with tiled marble halls, columns and fountains. Amongst the conventionally dressed Egyptians and their very soignée elegant wives, there would be groups of Arabs in full regalia followed by their harem of heavily disguised and veiled women. They were like black crows, with only their hennaed feet and hands showing, and numerous gold and silver ankle bracelets jingled as they walked. They wore yashmaks so only their thickly kohled eyes and tattoo marks showed. Some of the women had a veil worn over the entire face; I always wondered how they could see to walk. They all wore strings of necklaces, mostly blue to ward off the evil eye, so I was told. They walked behind the men in little groups like mourners at a feast. I was fascinated to think that women could accept living like that but realised they had no other option and had lived under total male domination for centuries.

Thomas Cook had given us a wonderful guide, Bakry Ahmed-Abd-El Razzah, who was to escort us around Egypt for the next two months. In town, most Egyptian men wore a red fez, even the rich businessmen who had opted for the European style of Savile Row suits. They still kept the old traditional style of costume on leaving the city though: white baggy cotton trousers tied around the waist, a loose white shirt and waistcoat (and, depending on the wealth of the man, the waistcoat would be heavily embroidered). Over all went the principal garment, the jellaba, a long-sleeved, loose cotton caftan. The rich wore theirs of heavy cotton and again richly embroidered. Finally there would be either a fez or a *lebda*, a brown felt skullcap around which they wound lengths of white cloth to form a turban. The *fellahin* wore simple white thin cotton jellabas and the labourers seen toiling in their fields along the banks of the Nile wore just white loincloths and turbans. The women wore the usual style of Arab dress but mostly without being heavily veiled: at least one could see their faces. Bakry always wore striped cotton jellabas and a fez. Like a magician, he would conjure up camels, cars, donkeys or aeroplanes with equal aplomb. Nothing was beyond his capabilities. He was the Cook's representative in Egypt and he certainly was the jewel in their crown.

Taken by car to the pyramids on the day after our arrival, Bakry had all our camels waiting. On his recommendation, we were taught the correct way to ride them and their keepers were to remain with us for the rest of our trip. I was introduced to my camel whose name was Telephone. By the time I left Egypt I had grown immensely attached to this ugly creature, even though he spent half his day kneeling in the sand digesting his food, regurgitating and belching. If one was unlucky enough to be facing him at the time, the smell was nauseating.

They were racing camels, we were told, and therefore of much higher caste than the ordinary working camel. Accordingly, they were magnificently turned out. Their bridles and reins were highly decorated with coloured tapestry work and even the framework of their basket-like saddles sat on layers of Persian cloth from which hung enormous beautifully decorated tassels that swayed elegantly to the movement of their walk. This rocking motion that took time to get used to was the reason I am sure that they were given the name of "ships of the desert". Being such a bad sailor, I certainly felt queasy for the first few days.

We were taught to sit side-saddle with our ankles crossed, and to give directions by kicking the camels on the neck with our heel. Finally mounted, we set off for the pyramids and the Sphinx. We spent a few days at the Mena House Hotel as there was so much to see. We climbed to the top, or almost to the top of the pyramids because the enormously large blocks of yellow quarry stone made climbing extremely difficult. Looking down, I could see our camel train patiently waiting way below, like toys, lying or standing on the desert floor.

One memorable evening we went out at night. There was a full moon and we rode around the pyramids and the Sphinx. We were on our camels; there was no one else, only the distant lights of Cairo. The night sky was a deep indigo blue with a million stars sitting above our heads. For a few moments, a shooting star sped across the firmament before disappearing behind the pyramid of Cheops. The only sounds were the camels' grunts and the sand sliding from under their feet as we silently rode past these ancient tombs.

A few nights later we camped about a mile from the pyramids. It was the start of our journey to the Fayum. Our tents were the height of luxury, the walls lined with hanging tapestries and with Persian carpets on the floor. A separate section at the back held the canvas bath, toilet and washbasin with flaps that could be lowered to give one privacy. There was an entrance to the front of the tent that came out on poles. The canvas sides were lowered, leaving the front section open like a hallway to the main tent and that's where I used to sit during the heat of the day. On our journey across the desert we used to stop at noon during the intense heat and continue at four in the afternoon.

In the early morning, the pack camels would lie patiently chewing their cud while all the enormous tents were being packed and folded up to be placed on panniers that were fitted on wooden basketwork frames over the camels' humps. From these hung thick leather thongs for strapping on the paraphernalia of tents, crates of food, drinks, luggage and so on. It was a wonderful sight when the full camel train was on its way. I had always imagined the desert to be flat but it is very misleading because it is all hills of sand. To see the outline of the camels against the horizon, the lead camels being ridden and the pack camels being led as they plod their way sedately across the Sahara, is a never-to-be-forgotten memory. I would be lost in dreams of *Lawrence of Arabia* as I sat on my beloved Telephone, photographing this unforgettable journey across the yellow sands of Africa.

Once fully loaded, the slow pack camels would start off ahead, led by their keepers in flowing white robes and turbans. The mess tent where we could eat our breakfast after the caravan had left and one other large tent that would be used for the noon stop, with folding canvas beds and chairs and a toilet tent, remained behind. These tents would then accompany us on three camels which, being lightly packed, were also ridden.

During our first night, camped near the pyramids, Caryll and Averil had taken their camels and gone off, so they said, to take one last look at the pyramids but I think they had other things in mind. As they had not returned by midnight, Mummy considered sending a search party thinking that, being unfamiliar with the desert, they had got very lost. Every sand hill looks like another; to the untrained eye there are no landmarks and if there is a slight breeze tracks are soon covered up.

I almost did the same thing a few days later. Desperate to spend a penny, I took Telephone behind the nearest sandhill and to my horror, once I was mounted again and went to the top of the dune, there was no caravan in sight. I thought I could either wander round until they came to look for me or I could trust Telephone to find his friends. Which, within 15 minutes he duly did, although at the time I was convinced he was heading in the wrong direction.

Our first day's journey took eight hours. We left early in the morning, soon after sunrise to avoid the heat: five hours' ride in the morning and three in the late afternoon and into evening. When I climbed off the saddle at midday on the first day, I thought I would never be able to get up again. The movement of a camel is entirely different to that of a horse and takes a great deal of getting used to. Also, the heat towards midday was intense. I felt so sorry for Telephone that I made him sit with his head in the pavilioned entrance to the tent while I sat near him reading a book. Everyone else had gone to lie inside.

Needless to say, a couple of hours later Rory came out wanting to know what the dreadful smell was. Unhappily, Telephone not only was busy regurgitating but had made a large poo that was collecting a thousand flies. None of the occupants of the tent were too happy with Telephone or me, except Mummy who thought it was totally acceptable as long as the animal was content, which he quite obviously was.

For the rest of the trip Telephone and I were banned from the tents during the midday stops. Preferring to have my camel happy and in some shade, I commandeered the loo tent as soon as everyone had made use of it before going for their afternoon siesta. Then, using the loo as a chair, I would happily read while Telephone, with his head in the shade, gurgled and belched and pooed in peace. Rather unhygienic perhaps and the smell at times was quite dreadful!

After the long day in the saddle, when I climbed into my canvas bath on the first night, I stuck to the bottom because I had opened such a large blister on my backside. For the first few days, in spite of all the dressing, salves and cotton wool padding, camel riding was jolly painful, but by the time we arrived at the oasis, I was dedicated and could ride all day without a twinge.

During our journey across the desert, we had a slight contretemps with a horned viper. We had stopped and climbed off the camels so that Rory could admire and photograph a desert flower. Suddenly, coming towards us at 90 miles an hour was a snake. The leader of the caravan had a shotgun, which he produced out of his saddle bag and fired two shots, both of which missed. The viper was almost upon us when Caryll, seizing the shotgun, fired the last bullet in the barrel and killed it instantaneously. He always had been a brilliant shot and was forever practising at various targets. I suppose it was the result of his very English upbringing!

The next contretemps was on arriving at the Fayum. Mummy was a serious Coca-Cola addict and the camel train had run out of this commodity, not having catered for the quantity to be consumed. Mummy, on finding that this oasis had only three bottles – and these only appeared after a search party had raided every little shop in the bazaar – organised to have a plane fly out crates of Coke before we could continue our journey.

I arrived back at Cairo, by now a confirmed camel addict. We spent the next few days at the wonderfully glamorous Shepherds Hotel, a famous relic of the British Empire and redolent of the novels of Somerset Maugham, except it was in Africa. Like the Raffles in Singapore, the Mandarin in Hong Kong and the Taj Mahal in Bombay, these buildings held all the mystique of the East while embracing one with the luxury and comfort of the then modern world. Modern hotels of today are plastic imitations of the great hotels of the past and totally devoid of glamour.

I was now in floods of tears at having to leave my beloved Telephone and begged Mummy to let me take him back to the south of France. For once she was very firm and assured me that it would be totally the wrong environment for a desert camel. I knew she was right and was slightly comforted when she gave a massive donation to keep the camels of our caravan in the greatest of comfort for the rest of their lives.

The Memnon, our houseboat, was very luxurious, like an Edwardian country house transplanted to the Nile, as Rory once wrote. Our bedrooms were all on the lower deck and their large glass windows gave unlimited views of the banks of the Nile as we slowly made our way down to the first cataract. There were enormous beds, massed with cushions in all the exotic colours of the East, oranges, blacks and reds. There were Persian carpets on the wooden floors, and each bedroom had an ensuite bathroom. When I first entered my cabin, I fantasised that it looked like the inside of a Turkish harem. Not that I have ever been in one.

The main deck and the upper deck had wooden railings all the way around, with white canvas awnings that were looped back during the day and lowered if the sun got too hot. There was an enormous amount of staff, again all in their white jellabas and red fezzes. The Memnon, a veritable floating palace, was to be our home for the next month.

In the evening, as the sun was setting, it would draw up to the banks of the Nile and anchor for the night. Soon a swarm of villagers would arrive to watch this amazing sight. I believe we were the first of the cruise ships to go down the Nile so soon after the war. There were no tourists; we had the beautiful fertile valley of the Nile to ourselves. All the incredible tombs and monuments built for the pharaohs, their wives and ministers thousands of years before were deserted and standing in splendid isolation with only the encroaching desert gradually smothering them in a sandy embrace. We were the only paddle-steamer on the Nile. It would be a long time before the thriving industry of today made these large ships a common sight. Therefore, wherever we went, crowds of curious villagers would surround us. As we chugged slowly down the yellow waters of the Nile, the only other movement on the river was from the beautiful *dhows* that floated by, plying their trade from Cairo to all the outlying villages. The larger ones, I was told, came from Arabia across the Red Sea. There were lots of fishing vessels and the fishermen, very dark in white loincloths and turbans, stood dragging in their nets. The bright green and tree-lined fertile banks of the Nile showed off endless strings of heavily laden camels that would, with great dignity and a supercilious look of superiority, plod their way up and down the roads lining the banks. There were also heavily laden little white and grey donkeys, their owners invariably sitting on their hindquarters, kicking and plying a whip to make them go faster.

Every now and again villages built just above water level would appear. The houses were built of clay bricks, the same colour as the sand and the water that lapped the ground floor. They seemed to have very little ventilation, just small windows set high on the plain walls. Sometimes we would stop and, going ashore, pay a visit to the headman. Rory wanted to experience at first hand the workings of village life. Wherever we stopped we were always met and escorted ashore by the village policemen who would beat off with a stick any of the converging crowd who infringed on our space.

Our group was always offered sweet cups of tea which, out of politeness, had to be drunk. The floors in these houses were of baked earth, swept clean by the women with brooms made from the leaves of the rushes. Each village had its well with a poor ox or donkey tied to a yoke. It had to keep plodding around and around under the hot sun bringing the water to the surface. Every inch of the fertile soil lining both the banks was cultivated, the *fellahin* diligently toiling away from sunrise to sunset. Where the cultivated land stopped, so did the desert start. There was no gradual lead off.

At one stage, Rory decided he wanted to swim and so the Memnon was taken out to the middle of the Nile where the water flowed strongly. Rory, having taken the precaution to cover his private member with two french letters in case one leaked, climbed overboard. He was very worried that he might get bilharzia. Bilharzia, the curse of African rivers and lakes, comes from a snail that lives in the stagnant waters and reeds. It's a parasite that eventually kills affected humans. Rory would either have had to sit or stand on the banks or in a pool of water to have been at risk but he was taking no chances. Even so, I do not think he enjoyed his swim very much. The

A young Antony Armstrong-Jones took this portrait of Pat.
Later, one of her baboons happily wee-ed over it.

George Tiffany, left, fell in love with Pat. After World War II, Pat stayed with George's mother, ferocious Aunt Nanny, at her Boston mansion, above.

In Nassau, Pat became engaged to the poet Richard Murphy, left, the son of the Governor of the Bahamas, Sir William, here with his wife Lady Murphy.

A fastidious Rory Cameron enlisted in the United States Army and
found himself peeling potatoes.

Back at Fiorentina in the late 1940s, Rory Cameron restored the fabulous villa, dreaming up an infinity-edge pool, right, to overlook the Mediterranean.

Fiorentina, above and below, was the largest of four houses the family owned on the peninsula of Cap St Hospice, right.

Rory's renovation was inspired by Andrea Palladio's Villa Rotunda.

So many guests dined at Fiorentina at lunch and dinner it looked more like a restaurant, above.

Rory's intimate library and the grassy steps leading to the pool.

An 18th-century fresco adorned the dining room. Above, one of the Falconnet sphinxes from the pool steps.

Enid declared: never be ill, never be afraid, never be jealous.

An aerial view of Fiorentina shows its size and private harbour. Pat spent her days with her animals and history tutor.

Famous stars like Fred Astaire, above with an unknown guest, visited regularly.

Left, Enid's good friend Kathleen Drogheda, and above, Enid and Tikki with Rod Coupe, a regular who once had to rescue Lena Horne from nerves.

Rory was able to enchant both men and women with his charm and sense of style.

Above, Averil Knowles visited from Ireland, and another regular was Alvilde Chaplin, right, who later married James Lees-Milne. Pat secretly hoped Alvilde would marry her beloved Rory.

Writer Peter Quennell, top right, delighted Pat but "Spider Monkey", who he later married, was another matter. Above, Clarissa Chaplin was also a frequent guest.

Top, Pat and Rory prepare for one of Rory's tours, watched by Princess Chavchavadze, left.
Above, visitors from Kenya, Lee Harragin and his wife Petal, right.

Fiorentina's original cloistered garden, left, and the loggia which looked over the bay and was used for luncheons.

Pat found one New York adventure with "Spider Monkey" more than enough.

SWIM STAR TO WED COUNTESS' DAUGHTER

Frank O'Neill, Australian champion freestyle swimmer and record-holder, last night, at the North Sydney Olympic Pool, announced his engagement to the Hon. Patricia Cavendish, daughter of the Countess of Kenmare.

The marriage is to take place abroad later in the year. O'Neill and his fiancee will leave for Africa on Wednesday.

The Australian press made much of the social differences between Frank O'Neill and Pat, who married at the British consulate in Nice in September, 1950.

Pat, always terrified of commitment, insisted on a small, private, business-like wedding.

Any man in Pat's life had to embrace her family, home and animals, as her first husband Frank O'Neill, below, found.

Swimmer O'Neill was a champion. Right, Frank and Pat's home near Manly, Sydney.

Pat met her second husband, Comte Aymon de Roussy de Sales, in Nassau.
Above left and right, on a fateful trip to Kenya.

waters of the Nile were very muddy and dried buffalo shit swirling by kept latching onto his arms. Not Rory's idea of bliss.

Like Mummy, he was a cleanliness fanatic. One evening, as the sun was setting on the Nile, we were sitting on the upper deck of the houseboat with Hilda Lezard, one of my mother's great friends as well as Rory's. (Her second husband, Julian Lezard, had been an officer noted for his very good war record but he had a dubious reputation. He was commonly known as "Lizzie" Lezard because he was an absolute sex maniac. He was always producing his oversized penis while everyone was concentrating on their hand of bridge. He would announce "full house" and everything went on display. Hilda tired of him and he was later sent out to Kenya where, on arriving and discovering the country drowning in rain and his car sliding all over the road, he declared to a friend – according to James Fox in his book *White Mischief* – that he'd rather be a shit in London than a pioneer in Kenya.)

I sometimes used to wonder if Hilda was Rory's girlfriend as she used to spend so much time with us. Rory never seemed to worry whether his women were older than him, so long as they were intelligent, amusing and "*bien soignée*".

Hilda was intelligent and amusing but immaculate she was not. The camels we could see were silhouetted against a pale lemon sky and the evening star, which seems always to shine so brightly above the desert, was like something from a biblical painting of the three wise men. Hilda was remarking on the extraordinary beauty of desert sunsets but, as we turned to look at her, to our horror coming out of her hennaed hair was a foreign visitor, a louse no less. As we watched in fascination, it sprinted back into her hair, obviously to join its mates. I realised then that Hilda was not Rory's latest love, only an amusing companion. Hilda and her lice became a family joke for the rest of the voyage. Mummy, being her great friend, was nominated to tell her. We all watched with fascination as Mummy and her lady's maid disappeared into Hilda's cabin later that evening with bottles of disinfectant and shampoo.

Hilda created another disturbance during our voyage down the Nile. We were moored to the bank as we had gone to visit one of the temples. During these stops along the Nile, we not only had the head of the police waiting to escort us but donkey boys with their donkeys all saddled and waiting for us to ride. We had come back after another hot excursion into the desert and we had all retired to our cabins for a cold bath and change of clothes. Suddenly there was an uproar on the river bank where the usual crowd of curious villagers had collected. All the jellabas were raised and an absolute pyramid of penises were being tossed about in a whirlwind of delight. Caryll went ashore to see what had caused this commotion and came back to inform us that Hilda was doing a striptease in her cabin for the titillation of the herdsmen. Mummy, with her rather Victorian upbringing, where naked bodies were never displayed except I suppose to husbands and lovers, was not at all amused.

Our trip down the Nile took us to the Valley of the Kings. We must have chosen the hottest day in Egypt's history. Bakry had arranged a fleet of cars, not donkeys this time. They were old Model T Fords. On one, the steering wheel was jammed, so it was always circling off to the left. The others were not much better. None of the brakes seemed to be working properly but then again, with poor maintenance, lunatic drivers and the excessive heat, I am surprised any of them had survived. In clouds of thick and suffocating dust and intolerable heat, we finally arrived at our destination south of the valley Deir el-Bahari. The mortuary temple of Queen Hatshepsut, built at the foot of the Theban Mountains, rose starkly out of the desert, and enclosed one in a furnace of heat and flies. Queen Hatshepsut, of the great 18th Dynasty of the New Kingdom, was the wife (and half-sister) of Tuthmosis II. She took power after his death and her temple was an unforgettable sight. We were driven practically up to the great ramp. Rory said that the sight of the fleet of Model T Fords was a desecration of the grandeur of the temples and sent them back to wait at a little village we had passed on the way in. I did at the time think he was carrying things to excess and dreaded the thought of the return walk over the scorching sand.

Almost next to the temple of the queen was the temple of Mentuhotep II. They stood side by side, the queen having made a replica of the king's temple, which had been built during the Middle Kingdom over 500 years earlier. It was the juxtaposition of these two wonderful mausoleums that made such an impact.

On our long walk back to the village, the heat rose in waves. Even my eyeballs were burning and I wondered how our escort of police in their uniforms could look so unaffected. On arriving at the village we all rushed for the nearest shade. The tavern keeper put at our disposal bare wooden tables and we lay down, prostrate with heat and exhaustion. He also supplied some very welcome fans that enabled us to keep away the persistent flies and to get a bit of circulating air as the shade was only marginally less hot than the sun. The invariable baksheesh boys arrived only to be chased away by our police escort. Their outstretched hands and big sorrowful eyes made one feel eternally guilty. Mummy always came well prepared; wherever she went, she always carried two handbags for just such occasions. By the time we had gathered the courage to enter the stifling interior of the cars, she had given enough to the villagers and baksheesh boys to last them for the rest of their lives, or so it would seem by the amount of bowing and benediction they bestowed on her. It was as if a queen had arisen from one of their temples.

We were to meet our ship at Port Said. Hilda and Averil were going to fly home and we were continuing on to Australia so that my mother could meet up once more with her beloved family, her mother, brothers and sisters. There was one big hiccup though. Mummy was running a very high temperature and the doctor at Luxor diagnosed it as dengue fever and said that she was not to travel. Mummy was not to be put off. Her only worry was that they would not allow her on our ship, the Orion, if they knew she was so ill. A plane was chartered to get her, and us, to Port Said. How she managed to survive the customs shed, which was baking under its tin roof, and to finally get up the gangplank, I do not know. Caryll and Rory tried to help unobtrusively but she was looking too dreadful and was almost delirious. Nevertheless, she was determined to get on board.

CHAPTER

25

I was only three when I first visited Australia and on that voyage my mother spent a great part of the day on the upper deck by the large canvas swimming pool where she was surrounded by devoted swains. I must have heard my nanny gossiping to know such a thing. The only other thing I remember from that early visit was sitting on a beach making sand castles with my nanny in her starched white aprons. Suddenly we saw a man with blood pouring from his leg. He had been savaged by a shark but luckily had been dragged from the water. In my mind, I am convinced he had had his leg torn off. At any rate, I was hurried away with the echo of his terrible screams fading in the distance. Obviously I was a bit of a ghoul as I clearly remember my bitter disappointment at not being able to watch!

Now, with the war over, Mummy was anxious to see her family again on home ground. She rented a house in Bellevue Hill in Sydney, near the home of one of my uncles, and from there we did a lot of travelling. The Northern Territory was beautiful with its ghost gums, dry sandy riverbeds, and bright red soil. Alice Springs, then a small country town with little Victorian houses, verandahs and green tin roofs, was hot and dry and full of Aborigines. Rory was fascinated as usual. He even ate a witchety grub and generously offered me one too, a large fat slug with a black head, I almost threw up. I thought the Aborigines were wonderful artists and Rory collected quite a few of their paintings including watercolours in the European style by Albert Namatjira. Very perceptively, my brother later wrote in his book, *My Travel's History* published in 1950 that, "Surely they would be truer to themselves and more interesting for us if they revived their old tribal totemic signs, limited themselves to painting on rock with their red and yellow ochres, and drew their intricate geometrical patterns on squares and rounds of bark."

Meanwhile, I was entranced by the herds of wild horses. While we were in the Northern Territory it was the time of the annual cattle round-up. There were cattle and horses in all directions and I felt very emotional at the sight of the manes and tails flying as the horses galloped across the horizon, the dry red earth churned up behind them and covering any stragglers in a haze of dust.

We met Tony Chisholm, who had a station of 600 square miles. According to Tony this was relatively small compared to some others. They worked on three acres to a head of cattle and the annual round-up took forever. Tony, a most glamorous young man, took my cousin Judy Lindeman and myself on a few days camping, with packhorses and sleeping bags, while he and his men rounded up stragglers. It was all dry riverbeds, ghost gums, horses, kookaburras, flocks of galahs, campfires and, of course, kangaroos. It was another version of all my dreams of cowboys and the Wild West. On our return to Sydney we met up once again with the Lindeman family and there was a general exodus to Booti Booti at Forster on the NSW central coastline where Mummy's younger brother Uncle Stan had a house. He, Mummy and Uncle Grant were passionate fishermen. Booti Booti consisted of miles and miles of deserted beaches and great rolling surf. I had just got out of the water, when turning around I saw Caryll coming in on a breaker and in the clear water saw a shark only about 50 yards away.

While in Alice Springs, I had rescued some puppies that I called – blithely, and for that matter I don't remember anyone else at the time questioning it either – Gin and Abo. The house in Sydney had a large garden and these playful black and tan babies were soon house-trained. I took them everywhere with me, but from Forster, we were leaving for the Great Barrier Reef and Lindeman Island. Rory was collecting shells for a book he was writing. I left Abo and Gin with Uncle Stan who was going to take them back to his farm. It was arranged that after the cruise I would then go and stay with him and his daughter Judy for a while when Mummy and Rory went on to New Zealand and Caryll left for his first serious trip to Kenya where he had planned to eventually settle and farm.

Mummy rented a cruiser to take us around the Barrier Reef, to the various islands and in particular Lindeman Island. The owner of the boat that took us to the Barrier Reef was a retired bank manager. I hope he had been better at figures than he was at sailing because we ended up shipwrecked on a deserted island. As we approached the Barrier Reef, the sea seemed to be alive with enormous snakes. We had been followed by sharks a great deal of the way, so this was quite a change. We were in, I suppose, uncharted waters because there were continual lookouts for coral heads like huge mushroom heads that would suddenly appear close to the surface of the sea.

We visited quite a few of the coral islands and there were lovely beaches and shells everywhere. At low tide we all used to go walking on the coral in special shoes collecting specimens for Rory. At one stage I picked up a clam-like spiny shell but felt a bit squeamish at being touched by the inhabitant, so I kept it turned on its side. As I approached one of the sailors, he gave a gasp of horror. It was deadly poisonous. He had once seen somebody who had been stung by one and he said even the morphine wasn't strong enough to relieve his agony.

As we walked near the edge of the reef we were followed by sharks, which would cruise slowly around, their fins cutting through the water. A sinister sight although the reef itself was a mass of incredible colours and wonderful fish.

After several days, the boat began to smell too dreadful with the odour of dead sea creatures permeating everything and everywhere. There was no escape from it but Rory as usual was impervious. He was enchanted by his incredible collection of shells and the remarkable colours and shapes. Those shells soon got us into trouble.

On the way home, the Captain anchored off some deserted atoll for Rory to collect some more specimens but he didn't make allowances for the dramatic fall in tide. On our return we found the ship not only beached but with a small hole in its side. We camped out that night with a swarm of mosquitoes for company. Thank goodness the Captain had at least had the forethought to bring the necessary equipment to carry out repairs. He and his sailors worked through the night to get the ship seaworthy so that we could get out on the incoming tide. Apparently there was something like a 15-foot rise and fall.

Life on my uncle's farm, Farley, at Merriwa in the Hunter Valley was an eye-opener to country living in Australia in that era. Firstly, I was greeted by the news that Abo and Gin were dead. In spite of my cousin Judy telling him not to, my uncle had shoved them into the boot of his car. By the end of the long journey over dusty roads they had suffocated. I couldn't forgive him. Judy was a very attractive girl in her early twenties with the Lindeman red hair. I soon discovered that she did all the work on the farm. Like me, she loved animals and was always looking after the lambs and calves and turning them into pets. I helped as much as I could with the sheep, as they were all worked by horseback. Spending the days on a horse was my idea of heaven. In the evening I would ride into Merriwa town to collect the mail. Coming home, as it was getting dark, took a bit of getting used to as my horse would shy at every bush and I would imagine bushwhackers hiding in the shadows. While I did the long ride to Merriwa, Judy would be doing all the cooking. Uncle Stan would spend most of his time in the house with a woman friend of his. Large as she was, by the time I got home she would invariably be sitting in his lap, drinking sundowners, while Judy was slaving away at the household chores on top of having worked hard all day on the farm.

I had a room just off the feed store, and rats were regular visitors. I used to feed them on the sly in a far corner of the room hoping they would not run across the bed and wake me. I didn't tell anyone in case they got poisoned and I began to recognise them individually, gave them names and grew very fond of them.

I went to a country dance at Merriwa. Mistakenly, I wore a very beautiful Dior dress with a green and white striped top that fitted tightly over every curve and large V-shaped inserts below the hips, from which fell layers of white tulle. Wonderful for dancing, but I hadn't been to an Australian outback party before. I soon realised my mistake. Half the evening we never saw the men. They stood around a bar eyeing the women as if they were a foreign species. Then, full of liquor, they descended like uncouth savages. As I was a stranger, maybe they had taken a bet as to who was going to get me. I even got my beautiful dress torn in the ensuing scuffle. Having managed to extricate myself from the smelly horde I sat out the rest of the evening, glued to Uncle Stan and his girlfriend. Another time I went to ride in a country rodeo. On the way home I was given a lift by one of the local farmers and to my horror, a dog started crossing the dirt road. In spite of my screams, he went out of his way to run over it. "Stop making such a fuss. It's only filthy vermin," he said. I was so distraught that I made him stop and, having assured myself that the dog was dead and not still screaming with pain, refused to get back in the car. Instead, I walked the long distance home to the farm.

I realised that Australia was at that time not very animal conscious. Kangaroos and wild horses were shot, cockatoos were being poisoned and dogs, unless they were working for their living, were not appreciated. I thought it a very hard country. It is amazing how it has now changed, but then nobody had dogs or seemed interested in animals. One day, in what seemed a fairly bad area in the suburbs, I found fields full of horses. There were even children's ponies. When I enquired why they were there, I was told they were for the butcher. When Mummy got back from New Zealand, I took her there as she said she would buy them. But we were too late. It haunted me for weeks.

I went and stayed with my beloved Uncle Grant in Sydney. He was the eldest Lindeman and was very tall and good looking, with reddish hair. He was also a good artist and when he and my mother were together they were always sitting at their easels painting. Uncle Grant was a skin specialist in Macquarie Street (Australia's equivalent to Harley Street) and had a lovely house on Rose Bay with a garden going down to the water. I spent very happy days with him and his charming wife Anne.

There was one thing that used to amaze me about Australian life in the city. The pubs shut at 6pm and, as you drove past at closing time, there would be crowds of drunks who had been turned outside the doors littering the pavement as they finished their bottles of beer.

CHAPTER

26

During this time Aunt Nanny had been constantly writing and calling my mother begging her to bring me to the States. The thought of going to stay with her was quite terrifying. After giving it a lot of thought though, my fascination with America and everything American finally outweighed any other horrors. But I did keep wondering how was it possible that Aunt Nanny now had such a tremendous desire to see me when on our last journey across America she had loathed me. It was obviously because of her son George's letters.

Mummy and I went back to London and booked on the Queen Elizabeth, along with my dogs and two lady's maids. But before sailing to New York, we had a few weeks in London and again I had a romantic adventure, all without meaning for it to happen.

At that time I had a great friend, but not a boyfriend, called Adrian Foley. He was a brilliant concert pianist, very tall and thin with, although he was only 28, a receding hairline and glasses. He seemed a great deal older than his age. He did not worry at all about my shyness; in fact, being short-sighted he thought I was attractive and very frivolous. The fact that I had a passion for dancing and had no appreciation for classical music disturbed him immensely and he and his mother busily set about trying to reform me. Lady Foley, before her marriage, had also been a concert pianist and Adrian was her obsession. I remember her telling me that she still used to brush his hair and worry about his bath. She obviously wanted him as a child who would remain with her and not grow up. It was a fantasy world in which she lived and it centred on this genius who was her son. At the time I thought it very odd.

Lady Foley, for some reason, was determined that I marry her beloved Adrian. I suppose it was because, although we were great friends, I was not physically involved with him and he certainly was not in love with me. Therefore I didn't pose any great threat to Lady Foley and the devil you know is better than the devil you don't know. Also, even though she was a rich woman, it's possible that the thought of my potential fortune being acquired one day for her adored son might have had something to do with it. Lady Foley even took me into the bedroom of her suite at Claridges to show me all her jewellery. She had carefully laid it out on her bed. It was extensive and obviously expensive!

"Darling, if you marry Adrian all this will be yours when I die," she said to me. It was a very embarrassing moment; I could not very well tell a doting mother that neither Adrian nor I had any intention of getting married. So, blushing and stuttering some inanity about her lovely son and beautiful jewellery, I did my best to make a hasty exit without committing myself. To make matters worse, a few days later we were lunching at Claridges and Adrian had invited a great friend of his, Guy, Marquis de Cramayel, who had just arrived from Switzerland. Guy, in truly continental fashion, paid no attention to anyone else. I was bowled over by his looks. He was tall, fair, and as it turned out, shared my birth date. Unlike my mother, who as a rule seemed to prefer ugly – or what I considered ugly men – I love men to be glamorous.

From the moment we met and until I left for America two weeks later, Guy hardly left my side. The night before I sailed, he arrived with a gold charm bracelet on which hung the words "I love you" and, although he was officially engaged to a girl in Switzerland, he talked in a vague sort of way about wanting to marry me. Lady Foley must have known that Guy was rather attracted to me as a few days before I left she called me aside and said, "Pat darling. I hope you realise that to marry an English lord is far superior to marrying a foreign duke. Overseas titles are a dime a dozen; everyone is either a count, a duke or a prince. You really must not get carried away by his looks and his title and all the attention he is showering on you. Guy is about to get married and a big wedding is planned in Geneva. You must put a stop to all this folly."

Lady Foley need not have worried. I left on the Queen Elizabeth and never saw Guy again.

Aunt Nanny, wanting to make sure of our arrival, came over to meet us and travel back on the Queen Elizabeth. About the second night out, we were having dinner and there were two gentlemen dining on their own at a nearby table. They had been staring at my mother all evening. Finally, when the band started playing, one came over and asked my mother to dance. Mummy was about to rise and go with him when Aunt Nanny, in a voice of ice said, "Sit down, Enid, and behave yourself". Turning to the gentleman with a look that would kill, she said, "You have no right to insult my sister-in-law by treating her like a tart. I will lodge a complaint with the Captain on your insulting behaviour."

I couldn't get over my excitement as the Queen Elizabeth was about to dock in New York harbour. We sailed past the Statue of Liberty and there again was the amazing sight of the skyscrapers. I know of no sight like it, or the impact it makes on visitors. My dreams had come true again; I was once more in America, this country for which I had conceived such a passion.

Aunt Nanny took us to the St Regis Hotel. She had a penthouse apartment on top of the Cameron Building, on the corner of 34th and Madison, but I could understand why she had no particular desire to put up this whole travelling circus. Mummy stayed about three weeks, mainly to spend some time with my godfather, the financier Bernie Baruch. One day, Mummy had gone off somewhere and left me reading a book in his library, which was a small room off his office. I noticed that he had several paintings and statues of buffaloes, cowboys and bucking broncos, all the things I loved. It also turned out that he was a great admirer of Zane Grey and his library had all the books. He gave me one that I had not read. We were discussing the merits of these western adventures when he turned to me and, taking my hand, said, "Pat, I want you to promise me something. You seem a sensible girl. You are my goddaughter and your mother adores you. I want you to promise me you will always look after her." He then went on to say, "I first met Enid when she was about your age, she was the most beautiful girl I have ever seen and she is still the loveliest woman I have ever known." He continued, "I do not know whether Enid told you but I wanted very much to marry her but she always said I was too old for her. I have loved her all my life." As he said, she had never grown up and when he was no longer around to advise her, he worried greatly about what would become of his adored child – my mother.

At the time I just thought he was suffering from senile dementia and I was horribly embarrassed. I didn't understand what on earth he was talking about. But gradually, as the years went by and my mother got younger as I got older, I also saw and understood the tremendously vulnerable side to her character that Bernie had always known about. Towards the end of her life, she kept saying to me, "Darling, living with you is just like being with a governess." I kept the fortune hunters at bay, refused to allow her behind the wheel of a car, and generally tried to prevent her breaking her neck in some hazardous undertaking.

When I asked Mother why she had refused to marry Baruch, she said, "He was not much good in bed and he was very mean." She asked me if he had ever given me a present and I said, "Yes, a Zane Grey novel." She laughed and said that was typical.

Mummy eventually went back to our home in France, and I moved in with Aunt Nanny. One afternoon I was sunbathing in her garden while reading when I looked up from the pages of my novel and realised I couldn't see my dogs anywhere. To my horror, both grey poodles had squeezed through the iron railings and were walking quite happily on the thin ledge on the outside edge of the penthouse's parapet. Not wanting to frighten them, I kept gently trying to call them back as I crawled towards the edge. The cars down below were miniature and

I felt sick at the thought that if I made a false move, they would lose their concentration and fall to their deaths. Happily they did neither, but it took me weeks to recover from that nightmare scenario and I used to dream of their tumbling bodies. Afterwards, I was still able to climb the pyramids of Mexico and Egypt and the heights didn't disturb me at all. But several years later, while rock-climbing with a boyfriend, I suddenly looked down and it was if I were back on that ledge and I could see the dogs' falling bodies. I froze and my friend had a terrible time getting me down.

Aunt Nanny took me to stay with her friend Grace Vanderbilt, the doyenne of the Vanderbilt family, who had a house on the corner of Fifth Avenue and 86th Street at number 1048 on Fifth. I remember that I had only one winter coat and not only had it been lengthened but a couple of holes in it had been darned by one of my mother's lady's maids. Mummy had lectured me at the time about my lack of interest in how I dressed and the way I let my dogs chew everything. As it wasn't long after the war, I didn't have much in the way of any other clothing either. I had outgrown most of what I had, although Mummy's lady's maids had tried to take me in hand before I left home for the States, gathering up my dresses, coats and skirts. They had worked hard getting me ready by lengthening the garments and beautifully darning the holes where my dogs, silver foxes or Mummy's monkey had torn them. The result though was not quite what Mrs Vanderbilt's snobbish staff were used to.

To my embarrassment, one of her maids insisted on taking my things to iron and I could see her look of sneering scorn at this dreadful young overseas visitor without a diamond in sight who was only fit for the servants' hall and patently out of place amongst society. Obviously Mrs Vanderbilt must have been tipped off. The next day I was marched off by Aunt Nanny to Saks and outfitted. I couldn't escape as she sat like a black bulldog in the dressing room while I squirmed in and out of dresses and coats until she was satisfied.

I was never interested in dressing up and was quite happy with what I had and of course, during the war clothes were impossible to come by. I had always resisted going with my mother to the top fashion houses that she so loved. If she wasn't wearing Molyneux, she loved Chanel, Balenciaga and Hartnell. But all that time wasted with numerous fittings and fussing over accessories drove me demented. From having been rather plump as an early teenager, I was now tall at 5ft 10in and thin, and the only things I was really interested in wearing were skin-tight evening dresses with flared skirts cut on the bias so they swirled out on the dance floor and these my beloved Maureen secretly made me. My mother did not at all approve of my wearing "cheap flashy clothes" as she called them.

I had £100 a month pocket money, which in those days was a large sum of money for a young girl, but I seemed to manage to get through it quite easily with all the parties I paid for. Most of my friends were not exactly affluent and I was always buying them things they wanted. I knew that whatever I felt I needed I could have, for as far as my mother was concerned whatever her children required they got. Money was never an object and nor was it something I thought about. I had everything that I loved: my mother, my brothers, my dogs and horses, and dancing. Spending money on clothes or jewellery was simply not one of my interests or ambitions. Looking back, I often laugh to myself at the stories that must have circulated in the Vanderbilt servants' hall.

One night, there was a very grand dinner for eight people, all old and grey-haired and in full dinner dress. As usual I was suffering from being young and uninteresting. After dinner, we retired to a drawing room where Mrs Vanderbilt was sitting on a sofa. She was a very good-looking old lady with her silver hair and long evening dress, also silver, while Aunt Nanny, dressed as usual in black, was sitting on a chair near her. In my fantasy world, Mrs Vanderbilt looked like the old fairy queen in her glitter, and Aunt Nanny, with the folds of flesh on her face and drooping eyes, the wicked witch. At some stage of the evening Aunt Nanny, who as usual had been holding forth, paused for breath. Mrs Vanderbilt took the opportunity to start rising from her chair, saying, "It is getting late and if you will all excuse me, I am retiring to bed." Aunt Nanny immediately grabbed Mrs Vanderbilt's walking stick, which she had just picked up to help her to rise and, rapping her across the knees said, "Grace, sit down at once. I have not finished my story and you are being excessively rude." Mrs Vanderbilt subsided to her sofa like a pricked balloon and Aunt Nanny continued with her tale. I am sure she dragged it out so as to make Mrs Vanderbilt wait even longer.

Later on the way to bed Aunt Nanny said, "I have never heard of such nonsense. I would have thought Grace would have learned better manners by now... so nouveau riche."

Aunt Nanny was the first person I had come across who was the epitome of the word snob. She took enormous pride in the Camerons' Scottish clan beginnings. After emigrating to the Americas in 1773, various ancestors had made their fortune in Canada and then the United States and the family had at one time owned 87,000 acres in the oil and gas fields of Alberta as well as the shipping line. I became immensely fond of her but she had three serious failings. Her snobbishness, her anti-Semitism, and her uncontrollable temper. If my mother was a bad driver, Aunt Nanny was a great deal worse. She was always having fights with irate taxi drivers. Horns would be blowing as Aunt Nanny drove up and over the middle line. Meanwhile, she would have her head turned to me instead of looking at the road so she could keep talking. In a rage at the noise, she would wind down the window and scream, "You filthy Jew, how dare you blow your horn at me!" I would cringe with shame in the front seat, hoping I would not be noticed. "Pat," she would demand, "what on earth are you doing on the floor?"

"Looking for my handkerchief," I would reply, having a few excuses up my sleeve after my Italian travels with Mummy and Rory.

Aunt Nanny, wanting to show me as much of America as she could and knowing my passion for the country and its people, took me to stay first at her house in Boston. There I was given the job of walking the dogs, her two dachshunds, and my poodles. She had a lovely red brick Georgian mansion with columns, and the whole area was like a big 18th-century country village. I would take the dogs out early and there the whole of Boston would be, promenading their pooches from the very large to the very small and all immensely smart.

The Americans were so friendly and the various proud owners would greet me as if we had known each other for ages. As soon as I opened my mouth and they heard my English accent, they could not do enough for me. I was being invited to every house with dogs in the whole of that Boston area. Aunt Nanny would say, "Pat, what are you up to? I am getting calls from everyone in the neighbourhood asking us around for tea." When I explained, she said, "That is disgraceful.

You must never talk to strangers. It will get you in terrible trouble." I think she was very rude to the various callers as after that I would get strange looks and none of the pleasant greetings.

There was one very amusing incident in all of this, although at the time I was totally mortified. I was sitting at dinner next to a rather good-looking young man in his thirties who, being American and polite, was not ignoring me but struggling hard to get me to talk. Halfway through dinner he suddenly said, "I am not asking you to stop, but do you do that to everyone who sits next to you? Or is it that you find me particularly attractive? Anyhow it is very exciting, please continue." I was dumbfounded. I did not know what he was talking about. I must have looked like a fish in a tank as I stared at him in open-mouthed astonishment. It turned out that one of the dogs lying unseen under the table had got up and put his head in this man's crotch. He had obviously spilt some dinner in his lap and the dog was determined to make the most of this blessing. I was still looking at him in amazement when the dog emerged from under the table and, nothing loath, continued to try and extract the last crumb. The young man, puce in the face, realised his mistake and started apologising. I was still being slow and had not caught on to what was happening and thought him quite mad. It was only later, when I had time to think things over, that I realised he had been under the impression that it was my hand that was caressing his private parts under the tablecloth and not the dog looking for scraps.

Aunt Nanny seemed to have hundreds of friends and I couldn't get over the amount of alcohol consumed by these elderly ladies. Aunt Nanny had taught me the secret of dry martinis – pure gin and a squeeze of vermouth, don't forget the frosting – and my job was to see to the mixing while the maids served them. As I was far younger than everyone else, I used to watch in amazement as the women downed cocktail after cocktail. The men were even worse. I tried one of the martinis once and it practically put me under the table. Mummy, being a teetotaller, hated alcohol in any form and I think I developed her dislike.

From Boston, Aunt Nanny took me to her favourite place, her house in Charleston, South Carolina. It was near the Battery I think. While there, I got my first American driving licence. I remember being thrilled and feeling as if having a U.S. licence made me more a part of America. Aunt Nanny was very good like this and lent me her Buick. Now I was able to do all her shopping, and became her chauffeur, thank goodness. The insults to the taxi drivers now ceased but without them to vent her anti-Jewish feelings on she found another outlet.

Aunt Nanny's house had a lovely big hallway and staircase leading up to an inside balcony onto which the bedrooms opened. I was downstairs when the front door bell rang and so, seeing two strangers in uniform, I kept out of sight. It was the naval commander, based in Charleston, and his aide. Aunt Nanny had wonderful black maids, all in starched, pinstriped uniforms and white mobcaps and aprons. The commander had given his calling card to one of them and it had been taken up to Aunt Nanny on a silver platter.

The next thing, I saw Aunt Nanny come to the head of the balcony and, looking down over the railings, say, "Commander, you are Jewish. I do not receive Jews." And, turning her back, she retreated to her bedroom. I can to this day feel how my heart went into thudding overdrive as if I had been the one to receive this dreadful insult. I could not believe it. Also, I was not very clear as to what being Jewish meant. It wasn't a factor that had come into my life except in the Bible, and surely Jesus was Jewish?

Later I ventured to ask her what being Jewish meant and why it was so awful. Amongst a long explanation, I think it all boiled down to the fact that my mother was to blame. Explaining that she adored my mother but that her being Australian meant she had no sense of class, Aunt Nanny said that unfortunately my mother had an eclectic taste in her friends. "Dreadful," said Aunt Nanny. "One never knew with Enid who one was going to meet. I cannot see how Duke put up with it for so many years. Can you imagine, after my beloved brother died of cancer, her very first lover was that dreadful Jew, Bernard Baruch? Thank God she had enough sense not to marry him." Aunt Nanny said she was ashamed to be seen in their company. "As if I could condone such a flagrant flaunting of a lover and a Jew, she being such a young widow. Totally disgraceful." What Aunt Nanny did not mention and what my mother told me was that her niece had married a young man with the surname of Mayer, who had Jewish ancestry.

That niece had had a lovely daughter called Mary, after her mother.

She had a wonderful bubbly personality and, again to Aunt Nanny's horror, she had just married someone my aunt described as a rodeo cowboy. In fact, they owned racehorses and a farm in Tucson, Arizona. The young couple came to spend a couple of nights at her house in Charleston. They were very attractive and I liked them enormously. But with Aunt Nanny peace did not reign for long. I do not remember what Mary did but she was laughing at something and Aunt Nanny, in one of her towering rages, smacked her across the face, saying, "Don't you ever do that again in this house." Quite a shock. I was not used to such displays in public. Even Miss Unger would have considered this the ultimate in bad manners.

I found out after that Aunt Nanny had even lost her temper with my brother Rory whom she adored and she had once swiped him, something I cannot imagine. Once I saw her hurling an inkpot at her lawyer's head. I think I must have been the only one who escaped this kind of treatment as she certainly never raised her hand to me and I cannot recall, except on that first trip across America, my aunt ever being really angry with me. Annoyed yes, but never enraged. I think I was so subservient that I always did my utmost not to put a foot wrong.

The only time she was annoyed with me was over some great friends of hers who owned a wonderful plantation house with famous azalea gardens. The husband was breathtakingly good looking and knowing my love of horses he used to take me riding. He never made a pass at me and behaved with great decorum but Aunt Nanny soon put a stop to these early morning outings. Accusing me of trying to seduce him by cavorting around on a horse, she claimed, "It is disgraceful behaviour on your part." It had never occurred to me that I was doing anything wrong and I certainly hadn't flirted with him. After that I used to hide whenever I saw him and his wife coming.

The next time I got into trouble was also over a horse. I went to Texas to stay with my great friend from my war days in London, Peggy Mathewson. She and Christy had a very pretty ranch near the town of Helotes, close to San Antonio, and I was in seventh heaven. Come night-time, they used to take me to all the squaredances. In the daytime I rode all over the ranch. I soon got used to the western saddle, though at first it felt like being strapped in, with its high back and pommel and long stirrups. I was used to English saddles and fairly short stirrups. Again, everywhere I went, people would stop me. In drug stores, they would pay for my Cokes. Even in restaurants strangers would insist on paying my bill. I was stopped by a traffic cop for speeding, but once he heard my accent and we got to talk, he said, "Follow me." Then he escorted me back to the ranch through San Antonio with his sirens blowing. I felt like the queen of England.

Returning to the Mathewsons' one day, I found two horses tethered to a tree at the side of the road. I was very worried about them as there wasn't much shade, and no water; I couldn't imagine why they had been left there. A few hours later, I went back to check and they were still there. Asking Peggy's help I took them water buckets and feed and waited with them for the rest of the day. At nightfall, they still hadn't been collected.

Peggy then found out that they were waiting to be picked up by a trailer; they were going to the butcher because they were supposedly unmanageable. I immediately bought them and with Peggy's permission took them back to her ranch. As usual, I could not wait to get my legs across a so-called mean horse. I don't remember who the owners of these horses were but unmanageable they were not. Apart from a few bucks that wouldn't have unseated a child, they were models of good behavior.

Somehow news got around that I could ride and, through a contact of Peggy's, I was offered a job in a film that was about to be made. I was to double in the riding scenes for the star. I thought that was a great idea. It never came to pass though, because I had to leave Texas in a hurry.

The Mathewsons had neighbours who had lovely quarterhorses and the owner would take me riding most days. I had been riding with him one morning and that night everyone was going to a party at one of the ranches. Towards the end of this party, his wife got hysterical and started hitting him over the head with her stiletto heels. The last I saw of him, he was being pursued by this screaming harridan.

The next day the police came to interview me because his wife had shot him in bed the night before. As I had been riding with him in the morning, I was one of the last people to see him alive. It turned out that he had a secret girlfriend and his wife had found out.

Peggy called up Aunt Nanny who immediately summoned me back in case I should be called upon as a witness which, in my aunt's eyes, would have been an appalling breach. I was very sad to be leaving the ranch. Peggy had gone out of her way to give me a wonderful time and has remained a great friend over the years.

Aunt Nanny had now arranged for a tour of Mexico, the Yucatan, and Guatemala so that I could see as much of the continent of North America as possible. Our ultimate destination was a house she had rented on Cable Beach at Nassau. She had a great many friends there and was a regular visitor.

Mexico was an eye-opener. It was 1948 and these Latin gentlemen were not used to seeing tall blondes walking their streets in rather revealing summer cottons. I had quite a few pretty dresses from the south of France that, unlike my English winter clothes, had not had to be altered or repaired. In those days, as I soon learned, unmarried girls never went around anywhere unless heavily chaperoned. My first experience of this was on arriving in Mexico City. Planes were not well pressurised and as we were coming into land, I thought my ear was going to explode. It was agony, especially as I had a cold.

I was taken to an ear, nose and throat specialist recommended by the hotel. He was a very good-looking man and as I was ushered into his rooms he looked up from his desk. I thought he was going to have a seizure; he looked at me in pure astonishment then, rushing from behind his desk like a madman, said, "You must get out of here, you must get out. Where is my nurse? You cannot stay in here on your own with me. Where is your *dueña*?" He was running around like a lunatic, calling for someone. The receptionist arrived and took me back to the waiting room. She was in fits of giggles. In broken English she explained that the doctor thought that I would compromise his career if I remained alone with him. Even his own nurse, he felt, was not sufficient guarantee. He insisted on calling up the hotel to demand my *dueña*'s presence and on being told I was with my aunt, would not look at my ear until Aunt Nanny had duly arrived and anchored herself like a battleship in his surgery. To examine my ear, he had to sit close and position my head with his hands. I could feel them shaking, he was in such a state.

The next day, while I was waiting for Aunt Nanny, I ventured forth onto the streets to look at the shops. It was like an avalanche. Excited young men appeared from everywhere, giggling, laughing, and trying to touch my blonde hair. I had to return to the hotel.

Aunt Nanny took me to the pyramids and I climbed to the top with a guide while she waited below. As soon as we were out of sight, he was on his knees kissing my hand, saying I was a goddess; we were halfway up the pyramid, not the best location for declaring undying passion. It was all highly embarrassing; he was so pathetic and I did not want to be too rude and embarrass him. It spoilt my first visit to Popocatépetl. I went back next day without telling Aunt Nanny the reason why and arranged with the hotel to let us have an old guide. Aunt Nanny couldn't understand why we had to go back to visit the pyramids but was delighted that they had had such a profound effect on me.

We then left for Acapulco and stayed in a hotel overlooking the immensely high cliffs from which the death-defying divers plunge into the sea at high tide. The cliffs were either side of a narrow inlet where the sea rushed in. Aunt Nanny and I had inter-connecting rooms, which is what she always asked for when we were travelling. After dinner we sat on the terrace for a while and then went upstairs to bed. I washed my hair in my bathroom but broke the shampoo bottle. I decided to leave it and clear away the mess in the morning. I still had a bit of a cold and wanted to get my hair dry before sleeping so I read a book for a while and then turned off the light.

It was just after that, near midnight, when I heard my bathroom window opening. I sat up in bed wondering what was happening and then heard the crunch of broken glass as an intruder stood on the shampoo bottle. There was only the moonlight coming into the room. It was a warm night and I had not drawn the curtains. I was considering the best way to tackle the thief without waking Aunt Nanny when a dark shadow appeared at my bedside. It was the assistant manager who, kneeling beside my bed and declaring his love, seized my hand and started kissing up my arm. I realised I was in a difficult position. Terrified Aunt Nanny would hear something and come to see what I was up to, I explained that my aunt might wake at any moment. One could hear her snores through the open doorway.

I promised him that if he would just go, I would meet him outside as soon as I could put a few clothes on. Begging me not to be too long, he let himself out, obviously deciding discretion was the better part of valour. I hastily rose and locked all the doors and windows including Aunt Nanny's. I never told her about the visitation, but for the next two days of our stay I stuck to her like glue. She couldn't understand why I didn't even want to go swimming.

Indeed, she kept saying, "It is no use my taking you all this way if you insist on either staying in the car, or bottled up in your room reading those dreadful novels." Still, she rather got the point of why I didn't want to walk around when at one stage she asked the driver to stop so that we could walk to a sidewalk cafe where she had decided she wanted a cup of coffee. Once more, a lot of excited males converged on me. At first Aunt Nanny did not realise what was happening but, as we sat down, they all stood around and stared. Aunt Nanny couldn't make out what they were up to as they were talking in Spanish. I had taken Spanish at my secretarial college so I got the general gist of the conversation. On the way back to the car, the men got so bad with their attentions that I had to walk as close to her as I could. Once again, they were trying to touch my hair and brush my body. Aunt Nanny, suddenly realising what all the fuss was about, let out a bellow of rage. Wielding the black umbrella she carried to protect her from the sun, she hit out at all and sundry. She must have been dreadfully hot as she still wore mourning for George. Although I disliked having my hair touched by a lot of hands that weren't exactly clean, I did rather enjoy the sensation I was causing and being thought beautiful. I used to chuckle to myself. I had to fly half the way around the world and come to Mexico to be the focus of attention for a change.

My memories of Guatemala, apart from the magnificence of the lake, include the beautiful Indians in their wonderful colours of reds and oranges and the simple white churches perched on the hills where all the devout would collect to light their candles. They would come with their donkeys and llamas, panniers laden with produce, and spread their offerings on the ground of the church square in an informal market. Having knelt in adoration of Jesus Christ and the Virgin and lovingly placed hundreds of candles and little posies of flowers at the feet of the statues, they would then sell their produce outside the church to all the other devotees who would be winding their way up the hills, answering the call of the church bells.

The lovely hotel in which we stayed was a colonial Spanish haçienda, with verandahs leading into the gardens on the edge of a lake. Each verandah had birds in cages swinging from the ceiling. I couldn't bear it; the cages were tiny little bamboo prisons crammed with brightly coloured little singing birds. The night before we left, I was determined to do something about it. Afraid to go to sleep in case I did not wake in time, I read until dawn and then, as the sun rose, I went around to all the verandahs. Standing on chairs, I collected all the cages and let the birds loose on the lawn. What I had not realised was that the birds had been cooped up for so long that now they could not fly. I was trying to shoo them up into the air when to my horror, a gardener arrived and started collecting them again and putting them all back in their prisons. There was nothing I could do. He wouldn't accept money to let them free and obviously considered me quite daft. He said, "They are only birds. There are so many of them and if you let these go, they will get others. The visitors like them because they are pretty and they sing. They are always dying but we replace them."

We spent a few more days in Boston, before leaving for Nassau.

CHAPTER

27

The house on Cable Beach in Nassau was surrounded by a wall over which tumbled a mass of bougainvillaea and hibiscus. A two-storey house, it had magnificent views of the sea and was right on the sand. There were lovely deserted white beaches with palms and the sea was a glorious blue, so clear that in parts one could see the coral reefs and the brightly coloured fish.

Aunt Nanny seemed to know everyone on the island, so we were continually entertaining or being entertained. There were also quite a lot of young men around and I spent my life in nightclubs with the wonderful calypso music. There was a particular dance called the limbo in which you had to keep in rhythm to the music while trying to get under a pole. Every time you were successful they would lower the pole until it was only inches from the floor. This of course became a passion for me. Being very fit and with all my training in the gym as a young girl, I soon became an expert limbo dancer. Soon my friends were having bets on me against the tourists. That was a snip but against the Bahamian professionals it was another story. I could get as low as they could, with the back of my head only an inch off the floor, but being a girl and they were men, my bosom (no longer padded) used to tip the pole, much to everyone's amusement. The Bahamian men were marvellous dancers and we always seemed to end up giving exhibition dances to an enthusiastic audience.

In those days, Nassau was a beautiful unspoilt island with almost nobody on the beaches. Casuarina trees lined the roads making that unforgettable sad sighing whisper as the breeze off the sea stirred them into mournful life.

The town was enchanting with its colourful houses and brightly painted tin roofs nestling under the palm trees. Swarms of Bahamian children played on the verandahs, while grandmother in her rocking chair, often smoking a clay pipe, would keep one eye on her knitting or needlework and the other on the naked black babies. Time had no meaning in this sleepy, hot climate. The fishermen in their large straw hats would congregate by the harbour selling their fish, abalone and conch shells. They would sit strumming their guitars while they waited for customers. In fact, the whole island rocked to the sound of calypso music. The islanders would stroll down the streets arm in arm, playing their guitars. Everyone played music.

Dominating it all was the old fort with its gun emplacements and Government House. Below was the harbour, filled with magnificent yachts belonging to international celebrities, all vying for a place in the sun after so many years of the austerity of war.

Being with Aunt Nanny was very different from travelling with Mummy and Rory. She insisted we write our names down at Government House; Mummy and Rory never wrote their names down anywhere. She also made me wear my best summer dress and wanted me to wear a hat and gloves. Thank goodness I didn't own these items, apparently so necessary to pay a visit to the king's representative. "You cannot run around like a tomboy forever," said my annoyed Aunt Nanny. "I do not know what dear Enid was thinking of when she chose your clothes. Quite reprehensible!"

At least I didn't get a slap for not conforming to her exalted ideas of etiquette. Indeed, I hoped she would leave me behind. I had no desire to go to Government House or to lower her standards of what was acceptable. Aunt Nanny dressed in her best black clothes and now she added her hat with the veil and black gloves. I crept along in her wake, hatless and gloveless. Government House was a lovely old colonial mansion, typical of countless Government Houses, all romantically conceived and situated and built at the time of the British Empire through India, Africa, Ceylon and the West Indies, to suit tropical climates.

I was 23 and this was my first visit to such a place. The previous Governor had been the ex-king of England, Edward the VIII, then the Duke of Windsor after his abdication and marriage to Wallis Simpson. He had been sent here as the British Representative, Governor of the Bahamas. Obviously England had wanted him as far away as possible. Now, having entered Government House, I was fascinated to think this had been the home of a man who had given up his throne for the love of a woman. While Aunt Nanny was signing her name in the visitors' book, I tried to picture them and thought how many times they must have used this room where I was now standing. As I looked up, I saw the most beautiful, elegant young man walking by, his arms full of papers. He was very tall and had all the dark brooding beauty of a Byronic character. He was so perfect for this exotic setting that for a moment I thought he was part of my imagination. He smiled at me then disappeared through one of the open doors.

As a result of this visit and the signing of our names, we were invited to a garden party. It took place in the beautiful tropical setting of palm trees, waterfalls and fishponds and we were met by none other than the new hero of my dreams, Richard Murphy. This young man with the jet-black hair and the merry eyes I now learned was acting as aide-de-camp to his father, the Governor of the Bahamas. He introduced us to Sir William and Lady Murphy and various other guests, and then after a few minutes' conversation left to oversee the welcoming of other arrivals. Footmen appeared with iced drinks and snacks on silver trays and while I sipped my Coca-Cola I watched Richard out of the corner of my eye. I was very nervous that hawk-eyed Aunt Nanny might notice my distraction, or that Richard himself might realise that I was fascinated by him. There was no other man in that crowd of visitors who could even compare to him in looks. I kept telling myself that it was only in books that you could really fall in love at first sight. I remembered how cross I had been with myself because Guy de Lesseps had haunted my dreams since I was 14. Now I was letting another man do the same, just because again he happened to fulfil my fantasies of a romantic hero. On leaving Government House, Richard came to escort us to the car and say goodbye. I went home with Aunt Nanny fully expecting not to see him again but the following day Aunt Nanny received a telephone call from Richard asking us to a dinner party for the boxer Gene Tunney.

A few nights later, at the small dinner, I had the great honour of sitting between the boxer and Richard. It was astonishing to think that here was the heavyweight champion of the world and he was also a devotee of Shakespeare and loved to quote him. It was a fascinating evening. Not only was I sitting next to Richard, who I now realised must be finding me attractive or he would not be inviting us to all the Government House functions, but I was listening to Tunney and Richard discussing Shakespeare. Richard I now learned was an Oxford scholar and a poet. (He later became one of Ireland's most distinguished poets.)

At this time, apart from being wildly attracted to Richard, I didn't really know him. We were seeing a lot of each other but only at official functions. He would spend as much time as he could by my side but he was always having to interrupt our conversations to carry out his official duties. I finally got a telephone call from him, asking if he could come by after dinner and take me for a drive, as they were having an early night at Government House.

He arrived in one of the official cars and we drove along the coast before he turned off on a sand track leading to the beach. Having parked the car, he turned to me saying, "I have been longing for days to kiss you. I cannot wait any longer." I could see him clearly, the moon was so bright. The palm leaves were brushing the open windows of the car and the calm water of the Caribbean lay just below us, shining in the moonlight. Then I was in his arms being kissed. It was so beautiful, particularly as he never tried to carry things further and I did not have to fight off groping hands. We saw each other almost every day after that, and whenever Richard could borrow one of the cars, we would go for our moonlight drives.

Then for no reason that I could understand, for we had not quarrelled and nothing else had changed, I suddenly stopped hearing from him or seeing him. There were no more telephone calls inviting me to Government house or moonlight drives; nothing but silence.

Weeks went by. I thought sadly to myself, well, Richard meets so many lovely girls, and with his wonderful looks and brilliant mind he has found someone else more interesting and more intelligent. I had never telephoned a man in my life; in my day, it was considered *pas du tout comme il faut*. Nice, well-behaved girls did not go chasing after men, no matter how well they knew them. For days, I sat by the telephone, not wanting to leave the house in case Richard called. I had to keep trying to find excuses for not going out so that Aunt Nanny would not guess what was happening. Finally, I forced myself to realise that my beautiful romance had come to an end and I started going out again. Not that there was any other young man who I found remotely attractive, but I did love dancing.

Life in the Caribbean went back to normal. I was once more swimming, waterskiing and dancing but there were no more romantic evenings. Then one day, when I had just come back from the beach and was getting dressed, one of the maids came to tell me that Mrs Tiffany wanted to see me in the sitting room. Such a strange summons. I wondered if I had done something to annoy her. With great trepidation I went downstairs, and on opening the door I saw these two formidable ladies sitting on the sofa – my aunt and Lady Murphy. Aunt Nanny said, "Pat, come and sit down. Lady Murphy wishes to speak to you about Richard." My heart sank. I thought something dreadful must have happened; they were both looking at me with such serious expressions.

Lady Murphy fixed me with a baleful stare which made me feel like a fish wriggling on the end of a line. I held my breath waiting to hear what sin I had committed. There was a dreadful silence while they both stared at me. Then Lady Murphy said, "My son Richard is very much in love with you. I do not know how you feel about him but I would like to know what your answer would be if he were to ask you to marry him."

There was another silence as they both continued to look at me. "If your answer is to be no," continued Lady Murphy as I was trying to recover from the shock, "I will have to see what can be done for my son who, being a poet, is very romantic and I worry what a negative answer might do to his health. Ever since he met you, he has been most distracted and not his usual self."

Aunt Nanny glared at me and said, "Pat, Lady Murphy has spoken to you. What is going to be your answer? Don't just sit there in silence. Are you going to marry him?"

Instead of the gates of Hell opening up in front of me, these two old ladies were offering me a gateway to Heaven. I couldn't believe it. "Yes," I said, addressing Lady Murphy.

"Does that yes mean you will marry my son? If it does I will see that Richard comes and proposes properly as his father proposed to me, on his knees and offering me flowers," she declared. I almost broke into hysterical giggles at the thought. Pure Georgette Heyer, another of my favourite novelists. Fortunately Richard spared me this further embarrassment and, although he looked exactly like one of Heyer's romantic heroes when he came to see me, he did not indulge in these 19th-century fantasies. He asked me to marry him between kisses in the back of a Government House car on our deserted beach road.

We were given a large engagement party at the casino. In those days the casino was the focal point for glamorous evenings out. Apart from the gaming rooms, it had a very good restaurant and also a nightclub. It was much more sedate than all the calypso joints that I usually frequented. The dinner party was very formal and I had on a long, pale blue, tight-fitting dress. It was excessively hot in the restaurant and a few minutes before the royal toast was about to be drunk, I realised I was about to throw one of my fainting fits. I could imagine the scene if I, the Governor's daughter-in-law designate, passed out while the glasses were all being raised to His Majesty the King. My ears were ringing and as usual I felt as if I were about to suffocate. I had to get to the ladies' room and I remember scrambling from the table. Outside the dining room, there was a large entrance hall with columns. The door to the ladies was in sight but all I can remember is clutching a column as all went black. Still clinging to it, I slowly sank to the floor. In the distance I could hear a woman's voice saying, "How disgusting. She is drunk."

Someone helped me to the ladies' and after running cold water on my face and wrists and standing under a fan, I was sufficiently recovered to return, clutching some smelling salts the attendant had given me. I was just in time for the toast. I never discovered if anyone was conscious of the disgraceful performance the new daughter-in-law-to-be had put up, and certainly the subject was never mentioned. I prayed that nobody in the lobby, seeing a supposedly drunken girl, had associated me with the new member of Government House.

On Lady Murphy's invitation I moved into Government House with my two dogs. I had a beautiful room overlooking the garden. There was an enormous amount of entertaining. There were lunches, dinners, cocktails and garden parties, for all the visiting VIPs had to be entertained. As a result, I met a lot of very interesting people. I remember one particular occasion when another boxer, Joe Louis, arrived. Richard came to get me and said, "Do you know anything about boxing?"

I said, "Unfortunately I don't."

"Somehow I didn't think you would," he replied, "but you have to come and help." I should have known by the look in Richard's eye that he was up to something.

Joe Louis was in one of the reception rooms. He was an enormous man with a bunch of equally large bodyguards. They looked like a phalanx of Hannibal's elephants. I was introduced to them all and then, with a feeble excuse, Richard skipped out of the room leaving me of all people to entertain them. I of course was tongue-tied and felt a complete ass. Joe Louis was very nice but he was no Gene Tunney and his bodyguards were wandering around the room as if they were going to find assassins behind every chair. I felt so sorry for this famous boxer coming to Government House only to be entertained by a mute. Thank goodness Lady Murphy appeared and took over the non-existent conversation. Feeling more like Ophelia let loose in Elsinore, I went in search of my treacherous Hamlet!

Government House was nothing if not eventful, especially with Hamlet in control. At one of my first dinners at Government House as Richard's fiancée I had, before coming down, been very careful to shut the dogs in my room. My very spoilt grey poodles were not used to this cavalier treatment. After all, they had been halfway around the world, and accompanied me to lunches, dinners, and nightclubs as well as waterskiing and swimming. They had even been pictured in *National Geographic*, being rowed by me in the Caribbean. Now that we had arrived at Government House they were being continually shut up.

We had almost finished dinner and it had been difficult to say the least. On this occasion, the guests were rather pompous and boring and Richard had obviously primed the poor unfortunate man who sat next to me to stick to the topics of horses and dogs if he wanted to get me to talk. I think Richard had deliberately chosen someone who knew nothing about either subject. The poor man laboured away but he must have thought Richard had had a *crise de folie* when he had proposed marriage to me. The beautiful Richard, who was sitting on the other side of me, was chatting away to some female old enough to be his mother. She was practically swooning at having the undivided attention of this genius.

Finally I resorted to pinching him to get him to rescue me from my predicament. His reply was to grab my pinching hand and hold it under the table in a pseudo lover-like fashion. Not being left-handed, I was now unable to continue shovelling food down my throat, a ploy which I had figured out long ago was the one way I could be excused from conversing.

Richard had very beautiful hands but I could not believe the strength in those long tapering fingers. Finally he released me and with some excuse left the dining room. He arrived back just before the guests stood for the royal toast. To my horror, this time there was suddenly an unholy uproar to be heard coming down the passage. My dreadful over-indulged dogs had been let loose. I could have disappeared under the table with mortification. They erupted into the dining room like baying hounds after a fox. His Excellency the Governor of the Bahamas had just risen with his glass outstretched, as had all the guests, for the time-honoured toast of loyal subjects around the world: to Their Majesties, the King and Queen. At which there were supposed to be a few moments of silence to celebrate this awesome event. Not at this Government House dinner party. Protocol had gone by the board. I watched with dismay as drops of red port from Sir Edward Murphy's glass dripped onto the white linen tablecloth. He valiantly tried to steady himself and remain standing while the dogs, in their mad rush to get to me, collided into the back of his legs almost bringing him to his knees.

Lady Murphy, with true British sangfroid, rose to her feet suggesting that all the ladies might like to retire while the gentlemen drank their port. With abject apologies for this dreadful contretemps, I disappeared with the over-excited dogs to my bedroom. That wasn't the end of the horror. I arrived in my room only to find that the dogs, not content with disrupting dinner, had busily wrecked a Government House sofa. A beautiful 18th-century silken-covered settee was now in shreds. My dogs had taken a leaf out of another family dog's book. Diane, Rory's much-beloved greyhound, had once chewed up a sofa at the Gritti Palace Hotel in Venice. I had a sleepless night knowing I would have to face Lady Murphy in the morning. She was wonderful and shrugged off the disgraceful conduct of her daughter-in-law-to-be and her impossible dogs. She even accompanied me as I went shopping to try and replace the irreplaceable. Nassau, as I was soon to discover, did not have the facilities of a London or New York.

Richard thought it was a huge joke, and admitted that he had let the dogs out on purpose to liven up an excessively po-faced dinner. He said I should have thanked him for letting the dogs out when he did. Otherwise they might have eaten all the bedroom furniture.

Being engaged to Richard Murphy was wonderfully romantic. Every morning on my breakfast tray there would be one exquisite rose and the most beautiful poem. He had obviously spent part of the night composing verses that expressed in the most perfect way his love for me.

When his duties as A.D.C. to his father allowed him a few hours off, he would take me to the Government House beach cottage. A large bungalow, built on the edge of a deserted beach in a grove of palm trees, it was a romantic setting for the first overtures into sexual intimacy that we had not been able to share in the back of the car. I was now passionately in love. Being such a solitary young girl, I had built up my dream hero during my youth, never separating fantasy from reality. I had lived in a world of my own creation where I was beautiful and loved by a young man who, up until now, had been Guy de Lesseps. Now, my dream world had become a reality. Richard, although not fair like Guy, was tall and dark, a poet with the looks of a medieval prince and who wrote about me as if I were a princess.

During my time at Government House Lady Murphy had arranged a large fete to raise money for one of the charities; everyone was very busy as they were expecting huge crowds of people to turn up. Elizabeth, Richard's sister, was painting a caravan in which there was going to be a gypsy fortune-teller. She was doing a wonderfully artistic arrangement of banana trees against a bright blue background. For several days I spent my time aimlessly wandering around with my dogs trying not to get in anyone's way. A little before the official opening, I saw Lady Murphy advancing towards me. "Pat, I have had a wonderful idea," she said, having decided that her future daughter-in-law left a lot to be desired when it came to usefulness. "You are going to be a mermaid and sit in the middle of the pond. The children will love that. We can have a big sign saying 'Throw a coin in the water and make a wish'."

There was no gainsaying Lady Murphy when she made up her mind. Although a small woman, she was the force behind the throne and ruled Government House and all in it with a rod of iron. In no time at all I was taken up to her room, where she and her maid took measurements for a fish tail. Lady Murphy was determined the mermaid had to look authentic. She then set about combing Nassau for an additional hairpiece as she insisted I had to have long blonde tresses hanging to my waist plus a hand mirror and a three-pronged comb.

The day before the party, I came across the gypsy fortune-teller climbing into her wagon. I was walking by with my dogs when she said to me, "Come inside, I have got a lot to tell you." It was my first encounter with a psychic and I was rather nervous of what I might hear. Producing a crystal ball which she made me hold, she then asked me to place it on the table. Going into a trance, she started talking, "You will have many offers of marriage but it is not marriage you are looking for. Animals, not men will dominate your life. I see you always with wild animals. You are a child of the jungle and you will live your life accordingly." She told me so many things. "Your first husband will come from a far country, beginning with 'A', maybe Australia." She continued, "You will get a proposal of marriage from a man with half a crown, and at the time you will be wearing a blue scarf. But he is not for you." Years later I got a proposal of marriage from a German princeling; I had just washed my hair and it was pinned up in a blue hair net. She also told me, "Never ever go in a red car. Rather walk through mud or you will have a fatal accident."

I never forgot this. When I got back to Le Clos, poor Caryll had just been given a lovely new bright red Buick convertible for his 21st birthday. I made him have it resprayed green and he complained bitterly it was never the same again. To cap everything, I took it into my head I would not ever go with him in a red aeroplane. The psychic's words often made life difficult.

When it finally appeared, the mermaid tail was a work of art. Made of fishnet, it was covered in pretty sky-blue and white scales and there was a large padded fork, also painted in blue and white. On the day of the fete, I wore a small blue two-piece and was sewn into my tail. Armed with my mirror and comb, I had to be carried out to the island in the middle of the fishpond while a big buffet lunch was being served at about 2 o'clock in the afternoon.

By 8 o'clock that night I was still sitting in the fishpond. My beloved but complex and moody Hamlet had decided I needed teaching a lesson for some misdemeanour I had committed towards him. Night had fallen and I could see the Government House party settling down for dinner. There was no rescue in sight and I was immobilised because of my tail, exhausted from sitting for so many hours. My muscles had even gone into spasms. On top of which it wasn't only coins that had been thrown into the pond. Horrid little boys had come by and, thinking it a huge joke, had pelted the mermaid with pebbles when nobody was looking. I had visions of having to spend the rest of the night incarcerated in the pond. Finally, Richard's conscience got the better of him and I was rescued from my penitentiary.

My days at Government House were drawing to a close. Mummy was in New York and flying down to Nassau to collect me and take me back to the south of France. When she arrived, wedding plans were discussed and a tentative date was set for later on that year, 1949, an early September wedding in London.

For our last night at Government House, Lady Murphy gave a dinner party. Richard, knowing that my mother's famous décolletage would be shown to its best advantage in one of her beautiful evening dresses, had the footmen put the big mirrored top on the mahogany dining table. I didn't know this at the time but 50 years later Richard told me that he had done it on purpose as he wanted to see his father's reaction to such a magnificent exposure when it was duly reflected in the glass. My mother always wore her couture gowns so they just covered her nipples. As she used to say, "If you have attributes, show them. Be sure to leave something to the imagination – but not all." She often used to wink at me across the table as whoever was sitting next to her was clearly bedazzled by what was almost on display.

Richard not only dazzled his father but I think himself as well. He was certainly being immensely solicitous in pouring Mummy drinks of Coca-Cola and that could easily have been left to the footmen. I laughed to myself as I watched the admiring homo-not-so-sapiens congregating around my beautiful mother.

Mummy and I arrived back at Le Clos, having sailed on the Ile de France from New York to France. Lady Murphy and Mummy then got busy by telephone trying to arrange the wedding to get a date settled. My mother was about to go to Australia again but my family could not leave until I was finally disposed of! The month of September seemed to be rushing towards me. Plans were going ahead and now I began to panic. Richard was everything that any girl in her right mind would die for. But for me, who was never in her right mind, the actual commitment of marriage was a nightmare. This would happen to me for the rest of my life and it is why I have always refused to marry in a church. The gypsy fortune-teller was quite correct. Exactly like a wild animal, I have needed to feel free and marriage, in my mind, symbolised a loss of freedom.

A month before the wedding, I wrote to Richard and broke off my engagement. Mummy had friends staying at the Clos who were going to Nassau and I sent the letter with them. I enclosed the engagement ring and was in despair at giving Richard up. But equally, I could not marry him.

It was a very sad and emotional moment for me when I had to say goodbye to my beautiful Hamlet and he was terribly shocked and at first, very angry. He apologised and then came to see me in London to try and persuade me to change my mind but he couldn't budge me. When he left, I did not realise at the time that I would not see him again for half a century, only to find that he was just as beautiful and just as romantic. By then he had become recognised for his poetry and had been professor of Anglo-Irish Literature and Drama at University

College in Dublin. He was staying with the Irish Ambassador to South Africa when he called me up at my home. I recognised his voice immediately. I couldn't believe that I was really speaking to Richard again after all these years. I drove over to collect him as he was going to spend a couple of days with me. The ambassador was away and he had the house to himself.

As we were driving out of the ambassador's house, the electronic gates took a long time to open and Richard turned to me and said, "Would it not be wonderful if the gates refused to open and I could keep you here with me forever?" He also told me that at various times he had found himself following me around the world, visiting Cap Ferrat and also Kenya hoping he would find me, but I had been away. He gave me a copy of a book of his poetry, and inscribed it, "For Pat, with love rekindled after 48 years, from Richard... remembering Joe Louis and Gene Tunney and the mermaid forsaken in the pond at Government House in Nassau." For the few days of his visit, I was in love again.

CHAPTER

28

In October 1949, having said goodbye to Richard, I joined Mummy on another voyage to Australia, this time on the Orcades. Caryll was coming with us as far as Port Said and from there he would go on to Kenya again, having already spent time there farming. On board our ship this time were quite a few sportsmen including Frank O'Neill, the Australian swimming star. He had gone to the Olympics the year before in London. He hadn't been selected for the team but he hoped, by being there, he might still be included. That wasn't to be, but having paid for his own fare he spent the next year travelling and swimming by invitation throughout England and Europe. Now he was travelling home with a group of about 10 of his sporting friends.

Mummy and I had both been very ill from seasickness but we finally dressed and descended for dinner. In those days, one always wore beautiful evening clothes and shipboard life was very glamorous and smart.

Frank O'Neill says his first sight of me is a memory that will stay with him for the rest of his life. He and his friends were already seated in the dining room when he looked up and saw us coming down the curving staircase. Mummy was in her glittering diamonds, with Caryll beside her. He said I was slightly behind them, wearing a white evening dress, and according to him I was "breathtaking". He thought we were the most striking people he'd ever seen in his life. He could not take his eyes off me for the rest of the evening.

It was at the swimming pool the next day that we met up. I had been standing watching him swim lap after lap and was told by one of the stewards who was serving the noonday broth that he was a famous champion swimmer, and that was why everyone allowed him the pool so that he could get his exercise. I was lying sunbathing when he emerged from the pool. That was the first time I saw him properly. He stood at the top of the steps, water dripping from him. Frank had a magnificent figure with a very developed chest and slim hips, and the most indecent bathing suit of very thin material in navy blue that clung like a second skin. As I found out afterwards, all the swimmers wore the same suit, a very thin light cotton to offer the least water resistance. As he looked up, he saw me watching him. I knew he was going to come over so I closed my eyes and continued my sunbathing. I heard a deck chair being pulled up next to mine and a voice with an Australian accent saying, "Do you mind if I join you? I noticed you in the dining room last night." Laughing, he said, "I had a bet with one of my friends that I would get you to have dinner with me tonight. Will you help me win my bet?" He was full of charm and very easy to talk to. So of course I had dinner with him and we danced all evening.

By the end of the voyage, we were very serious about each other. We got on like a house on fire. He had a tremendous personality, was very outgoing and relaxed, and a great flirt. Mummy also adored him and had invited him to have dinner with us almost every night. He was, apart from being a great athlete, a wonderfully engaging person and funny. As I soon learned, he adored all women and loved his family. As a man he was one of the nicest I have ever met. I obviously must think that as I have been married to him twice and still have not changed my mind.

When we docked in Sydney, reporters swarmed on board. They wanted to know about my relationship with Frank but Mummy, being the widow of Castlerosse and a Lindeman, they were really more interested in her. One of the questions to my mother by a woman reporter was "and Lady Kenmare, how many times have you been married, and were they all millionaires?"

"Oh!" replied my mother with a straight face and in a bored tone of voice, "so many times I have forgotten. Of course they were millionaires, it would have been no point marrying them otherwise. Anyhow I killed them all, I needed their money and divorce is so messy!" I looked at my mother in absolute horror whereupon she started giggling. "My poor daughter has no sense of humour where her mother is concerned. I am always shocking her," she announced laughing.

She always had all the very laid-back Australian reporters eating out of her hand. She told them outrageous stories and was in her element, surrounded by good-looking men. Afterwards I gave her a long lecture on her outrageous behaviour. I told her it wasn't funny and they might have believed her terrible lies. I remember so well Mummy hugging me and saying, "You take life so seriously. They were obviously looking for some scandal to jazz up their stuffy old newspapers. I thought it would be fun to liven things up a bit and they all enjoyed themselves."

Then I met all Frank's charming family. His father, Tom, ran the baths at Manly and their family flat was over the swimming pool. Tom had also been a great athlete, a champion Army runner and boxer who had gone to Australia from England at the age of 15. Frank's mother was Australian by several generations and came from a farming family. His eldest sister taught swimming and was married and his younger sister also swam competitively and was known for her pioneer attempts with butterfly. They all adored Frank who was followed everywhere by a crowd of admirers. Frank's family knew he was a champion from an early age and so he wasn't allowed to do anything at home. All he had to do was train and swim. He wasn't even allowed to pick up a suitcase; instead, his best friend would carry his luggage. Everyone ran around after him. Not only was he swimming champion but also a very good surfer. He used to practise every day running along the bottom of the pool at Manly Baths so that he could get out beyond the waves quickly. His great friend Fitz first thought up the running as a way to entertain his friends and win bets. Then Frank developed the idea.

I soon discovered that he was not only a great swimmer but also very good at tennis, table tennis and rugby but had had to give these up to concentrate on swimming. Tennis and rugby use the wrong muscles and his father didn't like it when he surfed either. A swimmer, I learned, must have soft muscles, so he used to box under the eagle eye of Tom at the Manly baths and practise every day with punch-bags to develop the shoulder and arm muscles. He swam five miles a day and there was an hour a day of massage, water polo and water ballet. (He later swam in a large swimming extravaganza with Esther Williams, the swimming film star.) At the time, he held Australian titles in the 110 yards, 220 yards and the medley and all the clubs showed films of him swimming as he was supposed to be a perfect stylist. His nickname to the Australian public was "Swimmer O'Neill".

Our engagement was announced just after Frank had swum in the Empire Games in Auckland in early 1950.

There was such a lot of fuss in the Australian press about this swimmer who was also a dental mechanic marrying the daughter of a countess with millions at her disposal and a huge villa on the French Riviera. On one occasion I was walking near one of the harbours where there were wooden posts stretching into the sea, obviously the remains of an old pier. On the end post, I saw something bobbing up and down in the surf. After studying it for a while I realised it was a hooked seagull struggling on the end of a fishing line. I was wearing a very pretty cotton dress but taking off my shoes I plunged into the surf and swam out to rescue the seagull. It took some doing as I was being battered by enormous waves. I hooked my arm around one of the posts while I released the terrified bird. The next day the press had headlines, "Heiress plunges into surf to rescue a seagull".

I wasn't too fussed by any of this. The press had always been around Mummy and so they didn't really ruffle me. As for my different circumstances, I had done all that washing-up during the war at the canteens so it didn't seem very different to be with Frank's very normal family in the Manly flat and to do the washing-up there after the meals his mother cooked. Once the engagement had been announced though, we all left for Europe but this time with Frank as well. First of all, we went to Kenya on the way to visit Caryll and our friends there, and then to England and finally back to the south of France, to Cap

Ferrat. We were married in the British consulate in Nice on September 30, 1950, with a small lunch for 15 afterwards at Fiorentina. Once again, I had panicked at the thought of a church wedding. It was too official and binding. I could pretend to myself that the registry office was just a formality and not truly a marriage as such. In fact, to be truthful, I hadn't really wanted to marry Frank but my mother adored him and, she said, she'd had enough of my broken engagements by now.

Kathleen Drogheda, my mother's best friend and Furness's ex-mistress, and her lover the Albanian artist Chatine Charatsi, Hilda Lezard and Alvilde also came for the wedding celebrations and were staying at the Clos. Mummy had rented a huge yacht for our honeymoon to take us and the guests on a Mediterranean cruise.

We were supposed to leave from Le Clos to board the yacht, but again at the last moment I panicked and refused to go. Neither Mummy, Rory nor Caryll could get me to change my mind. I ended locking myself in my room, feeling as if all my days of freedom had come to an end. I felt claustrophobic. Mummy thought I was behaving very badly but she never got cross. I think she thought it was amusing. Finally it was decided that as the yacht was rented and therefore available, Mummy, Frank, the family and all the guests would go on the cruise, leaving me behind! Soon into the voyage, Frank changed his mind though and jumped overboard to swim the three or four miles back to join me at the Clos.

Of course it became a famous south of France story. Only the tale that went around was that I was on the yacht and Frank had decided to jump overboard to escape me. Supposedly I was so dreadful that Frank, suddenly realising what a horrible mistake he had made, felt that he would prefer to brave the ocean than spend another moment in my company!

Poor Frank. I really was the most unsatisfactory wife. Firstly I didn't want to go and live in Australia, although Frank later bought a lovely house on the seafront near Manly at Fairy Bower. I condescended to go a few times but hated it and missed my family too much. It was fine while I was furnishing the house but when that was finished there was nothing much to amuse me. Frank had rescued a sick penguin, which we used to feed. It lived in Frank's swimming pool at the house and would waddle between the pool and the kitchen for its fish. Gradually, as the bird's strength came back, he would waddle down the steps to the beach and take off for the day, only returning in the evening. Eventually he did not come back at all and I too felt it was time I returned to my family.

Frank came back with me to the Clos. He used to swim across the bay from Cap St Hospice to Beaulieu every day for exercise. As he had by now taught me to swim properly, I used often to put flippers on and accompany him. One time through my goggles I thought I saw a submarine but it turned out to be a huge whale I was almost swimming beside. It was very deep and cold in the middle of the bay and on several occasions there were naval ships anchored out there. Nearer to land, it was quite beautiful. One would swim over and look down on the shelving valleys of the underwater land mass. It was rather like the Barrier Reef, with exotic fish, mountains and valleys formed by the rock formations and all types of underwater ferns and plants waving in the slight movement of the Mediterranean.

Philippine de Rothschild and Clarissa Chaplin, Alvilde's daughter with Viscount Chaplin, were great friends of mine. Philippine used to play the guitar and sing. We would all sit by the pool on those lovely calm Mediterranean nights, looking over the bay to Monte Carlo, while Philippine would entertain us. Frank went to stay with Philippine's family at their Mouton Rothschild estate in the Medoc in France's southwest and came back in ecstasy over the wines. He also used to spend a lot of time with Alvilde and Clarissa at Menton. Everyone adored him. Mummy and Rory's friends were soon learning to swim, taking to the pool with Frank every day as coach.

All the swimming activity that Frank's presence caused used to amuse me. Women found Frank irresistible and so being married to him meant there were many funny incidents. In Australia he used to have a veritable harem following him around, like swimming groupies.

One time I was looking after my young niece Caroline and drove over to La Reserve at Beaulieu to pick up Frank who had swum across the bay as usual. When we got there, he was sitting at a table by the pool with a glamorous girl in a bikini practically sitting in his lap. I arrived with my niece and Frank got up, admittedly looking slightly embarrassed. He then introduced us but instead of announcing me as his wife, he called me Pat Cavendish. Laughing to myself, I sat and had coffee with them with the girl smooching him all over all the while. I kept thinking to myself, "if only she knew!" I decided I must leave them to it before it got too embarrassing. I did not see Frank again for at least three days.

Another enormously rich and rather well-known lady walked with me through the gardens of Le Clos saying, "Pat, I have got to talk to you. I am so in love with Frank. Will you not consider giving him a divorce so that we can get married?" I said, "Sure, I'll discuss it with Frank as basically it is up to him."

"God, no!" said Frank in horror when I mentioned her request. "It is nothing serious. How can she think so?"

Another memorable night, Mummy and Rory gave a ball in the gardens of Fiorentina. At one stage of the evening, my mother came to me and said, "Pat, you must do something about your husband. I have just come up the walk from the pool and Frank is in the bushes making love with some female and it is highly embarrassing. Darling you must go and stop him."

I said, "But Mummy, you always brought us up to never be jealous and you used to tell me that sex does not mean the same thing to a man as it does to most women."

"Yes," said my mother, "but don't you think that Frank is carrying things a bit far? Besides which my darling, he has chosen a place which is rather too public."

To this day, Frank protests that he was only talking to the woman concerned but it's true that sex, for him, was like his swimming – part of his life. I must say I understood that as he was very fit and as he had a rather uncooperative wife, what else was he to do? At least he was never underhanded about it. Possibly, if it had upset me, he would have tried to stop. I knew I was the only one he really loved and with all my mother's teaching that one should never be jealous... I was never jealous!

In fact, sex was what had won Frank his first world swimming record. He fell in love with one of the ladies competing in another event and she said she would only go to bed with him if he broke the record. So he did, and they did! He said to me that the effort nearly killed him, but all he could think about was the reward.

Which brings to mind another story. Years later during our second marriage I was in South Africa training racehorses when I got a call from an island off Australia. The operator put me through and it was Frank on the line. "Darling," he said, "you have got to get me out of here. I am with a very passionate lady but her husband is also here. Early in the morning as soon as he goes fishing, she climbs into my bed. I think he is beginning to suspect something. I am finding it very difficult to concentrate; I am sure he is going to come back early and surprise us one day. He has not got the best of reputations and will as sure as hell put the heavies onto me. Send me a telegram that I am urgently needed on the farm and you want me to fly home."

A few minutes later I got a call from the operator. "Are you really Mrs O'Neill, the wife of Swimmer O'Neill?" he asked. I said, "Yes, and I have just been talking to my husband." The operator confessed, "I have always been a fan of his so I listened in to your conversation. I cannot believe what I heard. Do you really not mind your husband having an affair with another woman? On top of which he is asking you to rescue him from his own folly. Don't you hate him for what he is doing to you?"

Feeling very much like my mother I said, "Of course not. He is a lovely person. As well as my husband, he is my best friend. I will do whatever I can for him."

"Well," he said, "I have heard everything now!"

I have often thought of that operator on some semi-deserted atoll. How stunned he must have been.

One of the funniest incidents happened in Australia. I had just come back to Frank's house, having done my early morning shopping while he had been out for a swimming practice. I was downstairs trying to unload the food plus some furniture I had bought when a very disheveled, half-dressed female leant over the banister and, obviously thinking I was the maid, said, "Do go away and stop making so much noise; we haven't finished yet."

Another one of his girlfriends said to me over lunch, I suppose trying to be catty, "You have very good teeth. Are they all your own?" I must say it was a laugh a minute being married to a famous athlete.

Funnily enough, having been faithful to him during the three years of our marriage, I was the one who broke it up. Frank came back to

Australia from France to prepare for the 1952 Helsinki Olympic Games. He had been made a member of the swimming team to compete in the 100m freestyle, 100m backstroke and the 200m freestyle relay. From that stage, everything started to fall apart. Frank felt it was time to settle in Australia permanently and he wanted to make a living there. I was feeling suffocated so I finally wrote to him in Australia and asked for a divorce. Being Catholic, he did not want this and I now know from his sister, Betty, that my letter came as a terrific shock to him. However, I knew that Frank could not live without women and so Mummy simply hired a firm of investigators. Typically, the first private eye who had been employed to get the necessary evidence on Frank was a female and she fell in love with him. After months of us waiting for the results of her work, she excused herself from the case.

There is an epilogue to this. I didn't see Frank again for 17 years. By then I was living with my mother in South Africa at Broadlands on her stud farm and I was quite miserable. Without my knowing, my mother wrote to Frank and then he wrote to me, saying he had read an article about me and decided to get in touch. What was amazing is that just prior to this I had been very worried about my mother's health, and a chemist friend of ours, Moishe Rome, had suggested that I take my mother to a famous faith healer, a Mrs van der Wat who was a Scotswoman married to a South African.

I waited in the car while Mummy went to see her. Mrs Van, as it turned out, was a medium as well as a faith healer and she started telling Mummy about me. She said, "You have a daughter and a white light shines between the two of you. She has a yellow dog with yellow eyes [this was Rogue, one of my rescued wild Bahamians] and I see a man coming towards her from a faraway country beginning with 'A', I think it is Australia, and they are explaining to me: it is like an old coat that becomes new." About six months later, Frank arrived from Australia at my invitation and Rory greeted him at the airport with, "Hello, old coat!"

We were married again in 1969, in a registry office in Nairobi (although not until Caryll had spent an exhausting couple of hours in a rowboat with me, persuading me not to bolt again). We have now been married this second time for 35 years.

CHAPTER

29

With Frank's departure to Australia and the effective end of our first marriage to each other, I went with my family to Paris. It was the early 1950s and by this time Rory had met Elizabeth Chavchavadze. We had all gone on a holiday to Venice, Mummy, Rory, Caryll, and myself a few years previously, and Rory had come back from a dinner enthusing over this fascinating and attractive woman he had met. It was Princess Chavchavadze who had been Elizabeth de Breteuil, the daughter of a prosperous American, and her first marriage had been to a French count. She had then married a Russian prince, George Chavchavadze, just before the war. Not only was he a composer and a brilliant concert pianist but one of the most amusing men I have ever met. He used to do a skit of a man going to the loo on Le Train Bleu and I would have to beg him to stop, my sides hurt so from laughing. Everything with George was hilarious and he was a great mimic as well.

Being Russian, he had only his title but no money. Elizabeth was very wealthy and had a house in Paris. When George practised there, passersby would gather outside on the pavement to listen to his playing. Sometimes there would be a singer as well. Elizabeth also owned a marvellous palazzo on the Grand Canal. We were all asked to a ball at her palace and I heard afterwards the entry of the Kenmare household created quite a stir and was the talking point of Venice for the next few days.

Elizabeth, who we called Cha Cha, was a very large voluptuous lady with auburn hair, who dressed beautifully and had large lovely eyes but was so myopic she always wore glasses. She was brilliantly clever and had wonderful taste and so appealed enormously to Rory. He became quite taken up with her – although it was Cha Cha who turned out to be his last female lover. George seemed to take the new living arrangements with Rory and his wife with a great deal of sangfroid. We were either staying with them in Venice or they were staying with us in the south of France. Her house in Paris was on the Rue Hamelin and before long Mummy had rented the top floor and Rory had taken it over and turned it into a large apartment, a kind of *pied-à-terre* for us, with four bedrooms, sitting room, a study for his precious books, dining room and a kitchen. At this time he acquired a wonderful cook and housekeeper called Eugenie who also remained with our family for years.

Of course with Rory's wonderful taste, the apartment became a magical place and we spent a lot of time there. During this time, we met up with Nora Auric and Guy de Lesseps. The dream lover of all my teenage years had once more come back into my life.

We were invited to Elizabeth's one night for dinner. The first thing I saw as we entered the sitting room was the tall, beautifully elegant figure of Guy de Lesseps standing by the fireplace and talking to one of the guests. The last time I had seen him had been on the staircase in Cannes. Now, seeing him again after all these years, the reality seemed even more heroic. He had the head and body of a classical Greek statue with his close-cropped, dark blond curly hair, his aquiline nose, beautiful sexy mouth and slumberous amber eyes. As if he knew I had entered the room he looked up. I could feel my heart dive and accelerate. I watched mesmerised as, leaving the very chic woman he had been talking to, he came across the room to me. He was very tall and as he bent over my hand to kiss it, he looked at me with amused eyes. *"Ma belle Patricia, pourquoi tu m'as fais attendre si longtemps?"*

I could feel myself blushing. Knowing women as well as he did, he was amused at my reaction to him. Guy spent the rest of the evening with me. He had himself placed next to me at dinner and flirted outrageously, enjoying my embarrassment at his excessive compliments. Afterwards he told me that it was such a refreshing change from the women who expected flattery as their due. Of course, I was much younger than those women. Guy was 39 at the time and I was now 26. He had been living with Nora Auric since he was 23 and she was 20 years older than him. Guy spent his time with her circle of friends and nowadays would have been known as a "toy boy" but that nomenclature was unknown in those days. He was famous for being the beautiful young lover of Nora Auric and the fact that he was descended from the famous Ferdinand de Lesseps seemed of no importance to French society. But with all my wonderful romantic memories of the Suez Canal and the enormous statue decorating the banks of the Gateway to Africa, he was a dream. It was as if as a 10-year-old child I had been brought so deep into Africa's embrace that it was never to let me go.

Now Guy was here beside me and even his voice was beautiful as he told me both in English and in French that I was *"une beauté"* and that he had never forgotten me since that memorable evening on the staircase. I could not believe that, with all the gorgeous, intelligent, and sophisticated women he met every day, the picture of a young teenage girl climbing the steps of the theatre in Cannes during wartime could have remained in his memory.

At one stage Nora came over and said, "I see Guy is embarrassing you with all his attention. Don't worry, he is passionate about women and you are a *nouveauté*."

Before I left, he asked me to meet him at a bistro on the Champs Elysées the following evening. I went home on a cloud; all I could think of was that I would be meeting Guy again and that he must find me attractive or he wouldn't bother to make a date. From then on, week after week, I used to meet him every day, sometimes for two or three hours, sometimes 15 minutes between his engagements. I knew he loved being with me but in all that time he never tried to carry our relationship beyond his outrageous flirting. One strange thing was that

Nora, as long as he was with me, did not seem to mind. I do not know what Guy had told her but she realised we had a lot in common. Cars and horses bored her. She also realised that I was not at all sophisticated and my family was always with me as chaperones. Having heard the story that Frank had leapt overboard rather than stay with me and that he had had to resort to numerous affairs to compensate for his dreadful marriage, she must have felt that I was a pretty safe distraction. Guy was a very good rally driver and loved fast cars and so did I; he loved riding and horses and so did I; he loved dancing, so did I.

One night, when Nora was at a concert, Guy and I were sitting in a bistro in Les Halles. About midnight, amongst the traffic I saw two magnificent percheron horses being led by a farmer. They had to stop at the red light just outside where we were sitting. Because of Furness and his famous percheron stud, I was thrilled to see these beautiful horses and so rushed out to talk to them and to their owner. To my horror, I learned that they were on their way to the abattoir. There and then I paid the owner double what the butcher would have paid. He then refused to take them back to his stable for safekeeping, so I had to get Guy to bargain with him. I stood in the Paris traffic holding those two horses for what seemed hours while Guy plied their owner with wine and more money to get him to agree to take them home for the night.

I didn't know anyone in France with a farm nearby who would take two carthorses so Guy spent the rest of the night calling his friends. They must have been amazed to be woken in the early hours of the morning to have two percherons thrust upon them.

The story soon got around. Nora was highly amused and was now convinced I was a total screwball who would hold no real interest for the very sophisticated Guy de Lesseps. Her one stricture to me was that if I was going out in the evening with him, I was not to let him drink too much. He is much too fond of his wine, she warned.

We then left for the south of France and a few weeks later Guy and Nora went to their house on the island of Porquerolles, off Provence. As Georges Auric was not there, Guy had to spend most of his time with Nora. They quite often came over to Fiorentina for lunch and whenever he had free time he would call up and I would drive over with my dogs and meet him on the beach. Even in those days without much traffic it was a fairly long drive over narrow winding roads. Often Guy would only have time for a quick swim and a few minutes' conversation sitting under the beach umbrella that I used to carry in the boot of the car. I was so besotted with him though that just those few minutes were precious and the long drive home was passed in euphoric memories of his passionate looks and the feel of his beautiful tanned body as he lay beside me on the beach.

Guy and Nora went off to Spain and I was in despair as weeks went by without my seeing him. The plan was to meet in Venice later in the season. We were again staying with Elizabeth in her palazzo on the Grande Canale when I got a call from Guy to say they would be arriving the following day. We agreed to meet in the Piazza San Marco. The sight of him walking towards us was unforgettable; he was dressed again in his favourite beige tight-fitting gaucho trousers and an open-necked coarse linen shirt. As he bent over to kiss my hand, I felt almost faint with emotion. He looked up and in a whisper said those magic words: *"Ma belle Patricia, que je t'aime."* He then drew up a chair and sat down beside me and in the general conversation, no more was said. He almost ignored me but under the table his leg touched mine. I tried to give him space but he wouldn't have it.

We were there together for three days visiting palazzos. Everyone had lots of friends in Venice so there were numerous lunches and dinners. We were never alone except on the last day when Guy called me up and said he had two hours while Nora was at the hairdresser. I was to meet him at Harry's Bar.

It was one of my favourite places. In those days, it was the one place in the world where if what one wanted to see was an amazing collection of glamorous people, there was nothing to compare with this bar. The Italians are a beautiful race and this was the meeting place of the *beau monde*. The Italian men there dressed superbly, their white shirts crisp against olive skins, black hair and dark brown eyes. They had white smiles and charming manners and the women were equally exotic. Harry's Bar also had my favourite croque-monsieur, a speciality of the house.

Guy was waiting for me outside the door when I arrived. Jokingly he said, "I could not let my belle Patricia go into Harry's bar unescorted. Those Italian men would never have let you out again." He was laughing and telling me about Spain and the beautiful women he had met and danced with, and the bullfight he had been to. Then reaching out and taking my hand he said, "All I could think of was my beautiful English girl and the horror she would have felt at what I was witnessing. I realised then that I loved you." Taking our clasped hands to his lips, he kissed my fingers and said, "I don't know yet what I am going to do about it but I realise that I cannot live without you."

I could not believe that Guy de Lesseps, the lover of my girlhood dreams, reputed to be the best-looking man in France, a man who could have any of the sensational women he met continually, was professing his love for me. I did, literally, pinch myself to make sure that this was reality and not something my overactive imagination had dreamed up.

In the days before the influx of tourists, if one was tall and fair and in a country like Spain, Mexico, Portugal, or Italy, men paid attention as I had already discovered in my travels with Aunt Nanny. I now noticed that men's heads had turned to look at me as I came into the bar and that one gentleman had hardly taken his eyes off me. Apart from being conscious of the fact, I took no further notice. I was too entranced by Guy and his declaration of love. I was enjoying my second helping of croque-monsieur, fingers of melted cheese between layers of crisp fried bread, when Guy suddenly seized the hand that was holding the croque-monsieur to my mouth and said, "Do you want to cause a riot in here? That bloody gigolo has never taken his eyes off you. You are lovely enough without having to simulate a sex act. Leave sexual innuendo to your mother. You don't have to copy her and if this is what you are so keen on, there is a hotel around the corner where we can go, and don't look at me like that, as if you don't know what I am talking about. Wipe your lips, they are covered in cheese." So saying, he dragged me to my feet. "We are getting out of here. *Tu n'es vraiment pas sortable* when you put on this sex kitten act."

We stood on the street arguing because now he wanted to drag me off to some seedy hotel and there was no way I was going to have my romantic dreams ruined by sordid lovemaking in a dirty bedroom. I tried to explain to him that I never flirted, that I had paid no attention or even looked at anyone else and that it was all total imagination on his part. He was much too angry to pay attention to me and in a way I was secretly delighted that he cared enough to be jealous. I never realised at the time that it was this excessive possessiveness of his that would finally ruin our relationship. The fact that I would not go with him to a hotel was now making him even angrier and I was too shy to explain that the first time we made love, I wanted it to be perfect.

Guy dropped me back at the palazzo in an absolute fury. They were leaving the next day for Paris. I wondered whether I would ever see him again. Having been so deliriously happy I was now in despair, wishing I had not been so stubborn. He had not even attempted to kiss me goodbye. I need not have worried. When we finally arrived back in Paris, I had hardly been in the apartment an hour before Guy called me up. I had not seen him for three weeks but I knew that if he still loved me our whole relationship would change.

Guy came to pick me up and we went to a nightclub in Montmartre for dinner. During the course of the evening I thought I would tell him a story that might explain my attitude to seedy hotels. I told him my story of how I had gone to a nightclub with George Chavchavadze and an ex-King and Queen. (Nothing, one would think, could be grander, even if the royal guests belonged to one of the smaller countries.) Later in the evening we had then gone to a very seedy place in a back street and had been shown into a dreadful room with mirrors and a large sofa bed. From the conversation, I then gathered we were going to see a live sex show. I was embarrassed and horrified. I kept thinking, "What will Mummy think if she ever finds out?" It was such a dreadful position to be in that I finally panicked and rushed out as the floor show arrived. There I was, standing in the street late at night trying to find a taxi to get me home, when they all appeared. Obviously they could not leave a young girl alone. I felt totally ridiculous having spoilt their evening and very guilty about being such a wimp, but there was no way in the world I could have sat and watched such an exhibition even if I was escorted by a prince, a king and a queen. When I told Mummy, she thought it was hilarious but agreed that I had done the right thing. I know she said something to George about taking her daughter to such a place because he apologised and said he hadn't realised that I was going to be so shocked.

My story rather missed the point with Guy though. I was trying to explain why I had been so adamant about not going with him to a hotel in Venice. The thought of booking into a third-rate hotel for a sex session was against everything that I had been brought up to expect from a man one loved. I was too shy speaking to Guy to introduce the word "sex" into our conversation though, so I tried in a roundabout way to convey how I felt. All he could seem to understand from this rather convoluted story was that I did not like cheap hotels and had a hang-up about sex. My one achievement was that he now wanted to go and beat up George. And he kept questioning me as to whether I would refuse to enter the doors of any hotels other than the Gritti Palace or the George V, and whether some man had put me off making love.

By the time we got into the car, the evening was ruined once more. As we pulled up outside the house in Rue Hamelin, Guy came around to help me out but I was already standing. I held out my hand to say goodnight. "No, chérie," he declared, "I am not accepting cold English handshakes from you any more. I have waited long enough." His first kiss was gentle as if he was exploring his options, but we were both soon out of control. We were almost making love on the bonnet of the car when Guy called a halt. Arranging my clothes, he laughingly said, "We would look great if the police came along and arrested us for indecent exposure. Your mother would never allow me to see you again."

He told me that he had intended taking me back to his hotel, but during the course of my conversation he realised that where he stayed was not grand enough. He lived very simply in a hotel in Montmartre. He told me that he did not require great luxury and preferred a simple existence; he could not live in the fast lane all the time. When I got to know him, I realised that he was not rich. He had enough for the life he liked to lead and as long as he had his cars and beautiful clothes he was happy. He really hated big functions, smart restaurants and famous nightclubs. He liked to eat in little bistros in Montmartre and Les Halles, preferred to walk barefoot and hated wearing ties. He only wanted to wear his beautifully cut trousers and open-necked shirts. Even for Nora it was a fulltime job to get him into anything else. I never tried, but then we never went to the places that he hated.

The following evening we did go to his hotel. I saw what he

meant. I had never seen anything quite so rundown, except in films. It never occurred to me that anyone could live in a place like that. He had a small room overlooking one of the busy streets of Montmartre. The noise and the fumes came in through the open windows but he was perfectly happy. He had his classical music continually playing from a huge collection of records, a table with all the road maps spread out and a three-quarter bed, not even a double. He had removed the bathroom to make a huge walk-in cupboard for all his clothes. As he said, there was a perfectly good bathroom and shower a few doors down.

Our first night together was unusual to say the least. He was an inexhaustible and very passionate lover. After several hours, I finally managed to get out of the door of his bedroom to go to the bathroom but, overcome with emotion, the heat and exhaustion I fainted in the corridor just outside his door. He must have heard me as I slid to the floor because he picked me up as I was just coming to and carried me to the bathroom. I would not let him in but he waited for me as he must have thought I was dying. He had called a doctor friend but I made him cancel that visit. I explained fainting was a frequent occurrence in my life when I was under emotional stress.

Then, very shamefacedly, he explained that Nora always arrived at 7.30am and we were already late. There was a mad rush to the car as he now had to get me home and be back at his hotel and in bed before she arrived. It was a good thing he was a rally driver as I don't think any journey through Paris has been undertaken at such speed. It also occurred to me that his sexual stamina must be quite extraordinary as he would now have to repeat that inexhaustible performance.

I lived with Guy in this way for about a year. In a sense, it was a beautiful time of my life. I was crazy about him and he was passionately in love with me, but as time went on this in itself became a problem. I spent my time being terrified Nora would find out. When he was out with Nora, no matter how late he came back, he would arrive, sound his horn beneath my window and then we would go back to his hotel. I could never get undressed properly as getting dressed again would take too long. In the evenings I used to have a bath and then get dressed in the minimal amount of clothes so that when he arrived I could throw a coat over myself and rush down to meet his car. I also had to look well enough dressed so if anybody saw me, it would seem that I was just hurrying down to a corner cafe.

It was certainly life on a knife-edge; I even took the trouble of ruffling up my own bedclothes and making pillows look like a sleeping form. I was worried that if I ever got back late in the morning Nora might find out, just by getting suspicious and checking on me. I knew that our housekeeper Eugenie would not wake me up if she thought I was in bed still asleep. Often we were able to spend the whole night together as Guy did not usually accompany Nora when she was out with her husband or entertaining friends at home. Guy was basically very antisocial, much preferring his simple lifestyle amongst his bohemian friends.

This suited me as I also hated the glitterati. I still had no conversation and was painfully shy unless people discussed horses, dogs, motorcars or history. These were not subjects of interest to most people I met.

Guy said I was a brilliant driver on the open road but not an expert in traffic. Every day with a stopwatch in hand, he used to get me to drive from Orly to the Arc de Triomphe. He taught me all the little tricks of driving safely at high speeds. I also kept two horses stabled at Fontainebleau and most days we would go for wonderful rides in the forest and afterwards would lunch at all sorts of charming little bistros. Life was idyllic, I was madly in love and we had many common interests. He was beautiful to look at, a superb lover and passionate about me. But this became our problem.

The fact that I displayed no jealous symptoms, and that I was now the one always in a panic in case Nora found out ended up driving Guy crazy. I never questioned him about what he was doing when he was not with me and showed only amusement when he openly flirted with other women.

"If you really loved me," he kept saying, "you would not be always worrying about Nora and making sure that I was always there for her. Why aren't you angry when I flirt with other women in front of you? You don't give a damn because you don't care enough."

He was also getting so possessive of me that it got to the stage that when we ate out, which was most days, I had to keep my eyes on the plate or look directly at him otherwise he would accuse me of flirting. It was no use trying to argue, he wouldn't listen. I was always terrified that he was going to punch some man who was looking at me or that he imagined was looking at me. He was getting very belligerent and would walk up to anyone he suspected of staring and try and get in a fight. I learned to walk around with my eyes glued to the floor or the table. I never could bear scenes. Even our rides were getting spoilt. We had often gone with friends but now he stopped all that, saying that I only wanted to go riding so that I could chat up one of the men. Dancing became a problem. Guy was an expert at the tangos, rumbas and sambas which were all the vogue. He hated the rock and roll that I also loved and said I just wanted to make an exhibition of myself. Of course, when we were on the dance floor, with Guy being so handsome and my beautiful clothes and figure, people looked at us as usual. I don't think he was used to many of his older women being expert dancers.

I was never inhibited on the dance floor; music and dancing were a passion I had had since I was a child and with all the lessons that my mother had seen to – private teachers, ballet classes and top ballroom and dancing schools – dancing was a natural part of my life. If I was with a good dancer, the bands used to love it and play up to it. All my other partners appreciated the adrenalin rush. Not Guy.

He would take me off the floor saying he was tired of having his evening ruined by my flaunting of my body in front of all the men. It got to the stage where he employed one of his friends from Les Halles, who was out of a job, to spy on me. Soon I could not leave the flat, even in the daytime and even accompanied by my family. In his mind it became an excuse to meet some other man. Finally, except when I was with him, I didn't move out of the flat. I couldn't even walk the dogs unless we were together.

Guy was used to being with Nora's friends who were older than him. I was the first woman he felt he could control. This was the first time he had had an affair with a young girl and he became so besotted it was lunatic. He made love now as if he were desperate to wear me out. He became not only inexhaustible but insatiable. I often used to wonder how he managed when Nora used to appear for her morning sessions. He would say to me, "I will make sure there is no passion left for anyone else." He began to not give a damn whether she found out or not. I was in a continual panic. In fact, there were some very close calls when on three occasions, Nora had called the flat early and Eugenie had told her I was still in bed asleep. My dark room and the pillows had worked. Every now and again Guy refused to go home after a night out; on one occasion, he insisted on going to the music shop where we often bought our records. It had private cubicles where one could sit and listen to the recordings of one's choice. Much to his fury I left him there. I said that Nora was going to call up and that I had to get home. Just as I walked in the door, the phone rang. I was able to say to Nora, that no, Guy was not at the flat and being very duplicitous, I also said to Eugenie so that Nora could hear her reply, "*Est-ce que le comte de Lesseps a téléphoné?*" Promising to pass on a message if by any chance he did call or came round, I was able to breathe once more.

Averil Knowles was staying with us at that time, so I asked her to go and talk some sense into Guy and to also tell him to call Nora. When I saw him later, he was even more furious, accusing me of being desperate to hand him over to Nora all the time. "Why did I not have the courage to say that I did not want him?" he raged. Why could you have not come back yourself, why did you have to send your friend Averil? And on and on. "Would you like to know something?" he went on. "I suggested to Averil that we make love in the cubicle while we listened to Mozart and she turned down the suggestion. So what do you think about that?" I said, "But, Guy, who you make love to or to how many is really no concern of mine. That is entirely your affair." Which of course upset him even more.

The only time he was not obsessive was when we were driving. I used to drive rallies with him and soon got to know all the roads, villages and mountain passes of Europe. I loved the speed. I loved the mental alertness, the controlled skids; it was like flying. I could understand Caryll's passion for his aircraft but I preferred to be on the ground. Even now, at almost 80, this passion for speed and fast cars has not left me.

Guy had helped me choose a big Citroën. It was a six cylinder, called the Big Six, and it was so fast and so good at holding the road with its front-wheel drive that gangsters used to use it for getaways.

The French police couldn't keep up with them so they took to driving the Big Six as well. Guy also had an extra carburettor fitted, so my car became even faster. I adored that car, it was like a friend, and it went with me around the world, finally ending up in Kenya, chauffeuring my beloved animals and my lioness around at vast speeds.

Guy was now leaving for Spain for a week and Mummy suggested I come with her to England. I had realised by now that I could not remain with him. It was worse than being married and I had to make an escape. Taking the coward's way out, I left the Citroën in the garage because I knew that Guy would believe that as long as the car was in Paris, I would return. I never told Guy that I was going back to England as I knew it might spark a showdown between Guy and Nora and there was no way I could spend the rest of my life with a man who was so jealous. I departed with Mummy to London and Lees Place.

Several years later, I met up with Guy when I was driving from London to Fiorentina. I stopped off in Paris. By this time Rory had made Mummy buy a house with a lovely garden in the Rue de l'Université. Rory's affair with Elizabeth was over but they remained great friends. As I drew up in front of their front door, there was a car behind me. It was Guy de Lesseps. We spent one wonderful, passionate night together and I left the next morning for Fiorentina. I never saw Guy again but he has always remained as one of my beautiful memories.

CHAPTER

30

Fiorentina had been finished to Rory's satisfaction at last, although when we first moved in there it was still covered in scaffolding. After so many years of renovating and rebuilding, Rory simply couldn't wait any longer to establish residence. The interior was complete, it was just the exterior facing that needed the final touches.

As for the three other houses on the point, Mummy lent Le Clos to her great friend the American socialite and philanthropist Rosita Winston for the summer months and La Florida was kept as a guest house for the overflow from Fiorentina. La Maison Blanche was rented on a permanent basis to Elvira de la Fuente and her girlfriend at the time. Elvira had a large birthmark just below her lower lip. I heard gossip that when Elvira had a hard night of passion, the lower lip would swell and the birthmark become very visible. I found it difficult not to stare; she wasn't an attractive lady at the best of times. She was a very good bridge player though, which is why my mother let her stay, and she was also a chain-smoker. Rory was determined to remove all these rabid bridge players elsewhere so they would not continue contaminating the pristine beauty of Fiorentina's sitting room with the smell of smoke and ashes all over the floor. He therefore built a pavilion in the forest, overlooking the sea. I can still see him opening all the shutters of the french windows flapping them back and forth saying, "I can't stand it any longer. The stink in here is unbearable."

It is this very pavilion where, according to south of France gossip and a horrible article in *Vanity Fair* by Dominick Dunne, Mummy is supposed to have left Furness to die during the war, locked out of the main house. The pavilion wasn't even built by Rory until after the war; Furness died during the war surrounded by nurses and doctors in the greatest comfort.

It was in this pavilion however that I first met Coco Chanel and was fascinated by how marvellous she looked; she was what the French called "*une jolie laide*" and was wearing a white corded suit with blue trimming, a blue blouse to match and rows of pearls to her waist.

Fiorentina was always open to guests. Again, in his book *The Golden Riviera*, Rory described our wonderful visitors' book and I will quote him at length. He wrote: "When we moved into the big house, we decided to keep a strict eye on the visitors' book: signatures and dates, no comments, only professionals would be encouraged to perform. There were the exceptions, Claudette Colbert for one. Not a painter, she nevertheless did a likeness of herself, substituting her head for that of one of the sphinxes guarding the walk down to the sea.

"The visitors' book starts off with a fine flourish, with [the British painter and designer] Graham Sutherland and on the opposite page, a gouache by the master, dated May 1947. Turning the pages brings back fond memories. One is reminded of incidents long since forgotten; the night, for instance, that Irving Penn the well-known photographer and his wife came to dinner. I was alone, it was spring and the garden was heady with jasmine and Fiorentina was looking its best, for houses, like people, have their good days. When the guests left, I escorted them to their car and turned to walk the dogs and was surprised when a few minutes later they drove back. I hardly knew them, and embarrassed at finding me there, they apologised, 'but we had to have one last look'.

"I find a page of George Auric's; he has written his initials, composing the letters with the opening bars of his ballet *Les Matelots*. [Author] Louise de Vilmorin's four-leafed clover appears quite often, and [novelist] Romain Gary has copied out a passage from his *Racines du Ciel*. Lesley Blanch, his wife at that period, was an even more frequent visitor, and from her I begged a paragraph or two from the *Sabres of Paradise*, an engrossing study of Shamyl [the 19th-century Muslim resistance leader against the Russians in the Caucasus].

"Somerset Maugham inscribed a page with worldly advice from his *Writer's Notebook* and Sacheverell Sitwell evokes the heat with the opening paragraph of *Southern Baroque Art* and how wonderfully evocative he can be. 'Six o'clock in the morning,' he writes, 'and already the heat of Naples was such that it required confidence to believe in any hours of darkness...'

"Freya Stark is another contributor on the occasions she would drive over when staying on the Italian Riviera. Small, compact, her feet barely reaching the ground when sitting down – coiffed in the latest Reboux hat from Paris, a large blob of a jewel on one finger, she is the last person in the world one would suspect of being an intrepid traveller.

"Of all the pages, the one that gives me the most pleasure is Peter Quennell's inscription copied from *Sign of the Fish*, what he is pleased to call an autobiographical fragment. The passage describes a flight of flamingos viewed from our point during a period of migration and begins: 'Up the Gulf of Beaulieu, arriving from Italy, came a column of slowly travelling birds – not in extended order as wild geese fly, when they travel at night above the Scottish lowlands, but linked one by one in a gently undulating chain like the floating tail of a vast celestial kite, the drifting streamer that might follow an archangel or a loose ribbon attached to the Chariot of Venus.'

"Quennell has copied out this passage indicating 'the gently undulating chain' by a dipping and rising script. It is a beautiful page, and opposite to it Gerald Van der Kemp, the curator-in-chief of Versailles, has done a sensitive study of shells in gouache – a pink strombus and half of a greyish-yellow clam.

"Cyril Connolly used also to be a frequent visitor in the days before we moved into the big house, and Cyril was another of those rare creatures able to weave a web of enchantment round the mundanities of everyday life. He would give a whole dissertation on the quality of a Charenton melon... the same for a particular wine, or the virtues of such and such a place for swimming. But he was at his best on the sensuous appeal of objects. He would touch them, hold them, and his passionate concern was such that it gave an added appeal to the object in question.

"Another page in the book is entirely taken up by Sir Frederick Mutesa's signature. It sprawls in secure English fashion proclaiming the hand of a gentleman. His Highness Mutesa II was the 37th Kabaka of Uganda [in fact, of Buganda, the main province of the country, which had a lot of power because of its history and influence] and had been almost exclusively educated by the British, with two years at Magdalene College, Cambridge, followed by an honorary commission in the Grenadier Guards. His stay at Fiorentina was a question of reciprocity. He had been our host at Kampala on Mengo, the royal hill [or palace headquarters]. The Kabaka, or King Freddie as he was affectionately termed by the press in London, was a young man of almost 30 when we visited him in the early 1950s [just before he was deposed by the British Governor on November 30, 1953, after a conflict over Uganda's future]. Slight, elegant and of medium height, he had a pleasant easy manner and a dry sense of humour, and had proved an excellent host; he delegated Prince Harry, his younger brother, to show us the royal tombs, and that same evening had driven us out to his hunting lodge situated about an hour out of town over a dusty road through acres of sugarcane. He told us that he would have liked to take us swimming, he had his own private lake, 'but you know, I asked the gamekeeper about the crocodiles and he answered that it was perfectly all right; that there was only one that he knew of. One too many for me!' laughed the Kabaka. He had a charming, soft-spoken voice, so soft at times that it was difficult to hear him. It was on taking our leave that we had invited him to Fiorentina, promising him, so we thought, a weekend of carefree bathing.

"It was full summer when he arrived with his suite consisting of his brother, a young sister, an aide and several attendants. We all trooped down to the pool. King Freddie was enjoying himself and was in very good form. The ramp of the diving board was about the height of a chair and if used as such, dominated the scene. Instinctively the Kabaka installed himself and held court, while the drinks were passed around. The young princess, in the meantime, had joined my brother and sister down by the sea. My brother dived in, to be followed promptly by the royal guest, her immersion taking the form of a wild jump. The sea was so clear that she didn't realise how deep it was. There ensued a terrible flaying of arms, followed by gasps and the Kabaka, had it not been for my brother, might have lost a possible heir. It appears she had never been swimming before and had been ashamed to admit it. 'You see,' the Kabaka laughed, 'your bathing is not much safer than mine.'

"One name that should have been in the visitors' book, only I never dared ask her to sign, was Greta Garbo's. I knew of the occasion when she had been staying with Grace Moore in Connecticut and Miss Moore, to pay her a compliment, had walked up to Garbo after dinner, before they all left for New York, and asked her to be the first to sign. Miss Moore was holding the book open, at the same time offering Garbo a pen. There was a terrible moment of silence and Garbo, in real consternation, like a trapped animal, had looked at the book and then up at her hostess and in almost a whisper said, 'Oh, no, Grace, I... can't.'

"Grace Moore, not known for concealing her reactions, was clearly astonished and vexed. Garbo burst into tears. The hesitation on Garbo's part was not affectation; she has a real phobia about signing her name. Is shy, in fact, about a great many things; refuses, for example, to discuss anything to do with her work and has never been known to pass an opinion on any of her own films, or what the press claims her to be, 'the most enchantingly mysterious woman of her time'. Had I not known about her before we met, I doubt very much whether I should have noticed anything so different about her, except, of course, for her extraordinary beauty. When down here in the south, Garbo always stayed with George Schlee, a Russian-born American. Schlee was her accepted *chevalier galant*; a pleasant, amusing man, older than Garbo and clever, one heard, on the stock market. I never saw Garbo without him, and it appears that with him she lost much of the timidity that at times turns her into a recluse.

"Garbo loved Fiorentina, felt relaxed there, and laughed a great deal, throwing her head back. It is difficult to describe the effect she had on one: apart from the extraordinary beauty, she wore an aura about her that, like royalty, makes one a little shy. She seldom refers to people by their Christian names, but with that wonderfully resonant voice of hers, with a slight accent, she makes one's surname sound like a caress. Slowly she pronounces it, teasing, with a slow smile."

These passages from *The Golden Riviera* make me so nostalgic now and bring back many memories of the glorious years. Amongst all the guests that came yearly I most enjoyed my Danish friend Eric Nielsen and loved his yearly visits to us. He was very, very fair, immaculately dressed and had a boyfriend who played the piano well. Like many of our regular guests, Eric had a little money of his own and he lived on that. He wrote in his will that he would like his ashes to be scattered off the point of Fiorentina and I understand that Gianni Agnelli complied with Eric's last request and took them out in his speedboat.

A procession of film stars like Fred Astaire, Frank Sinatra, Cary Grant and Marlene Dietrich would come to lunch or dinner. Some would be brought by friends; often they invited themselves, so much had they heard of Fiorentina. David Niven was there a lot. Other guests included John F. Kennedy, Jean Cocteau, Lady Diana Cooper and Irving Penn – which should give you an idea of just how eclectic the guest list was.

Roderick Coupe and his great friend Jimmy Douglas, a glamour boy from Paris whose father was some big wheel in the American air force, came every year to visit us at Le Clos and later at Fiorentina. In fact, the heiress Barbara Hutton thought Jimmy was so glamorous that she begged me to introduce her to him. I think as a result they had an affair, not that I think it lasted more than a few years, and Barbara gave me a most beautiful pink sapphire and diamond ring to celebrate the occasion. I was particularly fond of both Rod and Jimmy. Rod tells some amusing stories of his visits. One evening there was a really huge dinner, even grander and bigger than usual. At one table were Enid, Rory, society hostess Elsa Maxwell, the Duke of Sutherland, the diplomat and explorer Sir Bede Clifford and some others. At some point in the conversation, Elsa Maxwell, who was rather brash, made some derogatory comment about English titles. Something like "any bloke can be born". The Duke and Sir Bede, who was the youngest son of the Baron of Chudleigh, took great offence and rounded on her. Elsa Maxwell, who considered herself the doyenne of American society, was absolutely furious. She swept away from the table saying that Mr Onassis's car was awaiting her. She was last seen hitching a lift back to Monte Carlo!

Rod had another amusing Elsa Maxwell story. Elsa, who had never picked up a cheque in her life, gave a dinner with John Paul Getty seated at her right. At the time, he was one of the richest men in the world and also an ex-boyfriend of Mummy's who said that he was the meanest man she had ever met. During the time of their affair she would always have to pay for everything, even taxi fares. He was too mean to have a car and chauffeur because of the expense of maintaining the car and he had a notepad next to the telephone so that he could keep account of every call. When the bill for the dinner arrived, Elsa pushed it in front of Getty, who immediately pushed it back, saying that it was not his dinner. After a lot of to-ing and fro-ing, Enid said very sweetly that she would pay the bill which, with an immense sigh of relief, was quickly shoved in front of her.

Another of Rod's stories that he relayed to me was this one: "Jimmy Douglas had been in Milan and he was there at the time that some very rare mushrooms had become available at one place in Milan. He brought them as a present to Fiorentina knowing how much this gourmet treat would please Rory. Rory was delighted and said that he would save them for Saturday, that they were having a big lunch and they would make a very nice first course. He said he knew exactly how they should be prepared, raw with a vinaigrette sauce. At his table were no less than three duchesses. I sat at the children's table, although I was in my mid-thirties. One of the young people turned to me and said, 'Are they supposed to be like this?'

"I looked and to my horror saw that the mushrooms were covered in fine white worms! I glanced around only to see all the adult guests eating and being very complimentary about the delicious mushrooms. In particular, the beautiful Margaret, Duchess of Argyll, was saying to Rory that they were the best she had ever eaten.

"So I gave up. I don't suppose it would have harmed anyone."

Rod also reminded me of the time he was sent to collect Lena Horne, the very glamorous American singer. Says Rod, "I was asked to go and meet her at the Negresco Hotel where she was staying in Nice. She was absolutely beautiful and I was a great fan of hers. So we drove back to Fiorentina and she asked me if we could stop at the Reserve Hotel and have a drink.

"She said, 'I am very frightened of meeting the formidable, beautiful Lady Kenmare and I really need something to give me courage.'

"So we had a lovely cocktail there and she was very lively about all these jazz subjects that I was interested in. When we arrived at the house, Enid captured her and took her off to sit at her table. Lena Horne was soon surrounded by Prince and Princess Liechtenstein, Prince Pierre de Polignac and Prince and Princess Chavchavadze, all of whom were paying her court. I could see that she and Enid were getting on famously, and the beautiful Lena Horne had overcome her fright and had settled peacefully among half the minor royalty of Europe."

CHAPTER

31

Now that we had moved into Fiorentina, Rory convinced Mummy to sell Lees Place, the house in London. Not content with this, he also made her sell the house in Wales. I was in despair as now I had nowhere to keep my beloved horses and had to give them away. Certainly I could not keep them at Fiorentina. Mummy brought Miss Lane and all the dogs over to France. Lane was not much happier than I about this move and was always grumbling to Mummy, "Just because Master Rory does not like the country does not mean that we all have to sit around looking at the sea, and my Lady, you did so love the fishing."

For most of mother's day, if she was not with her friends playing bridge she would remain in her room painting. Rory did not allow her to paint her large canvasses at Fiorentina though because he said it made a mess. I could see his point as she did have the most enormous and exquisite bedroom overlooking the Mediterranean. There he allowed her to do only her small watercolours and oils. Mummy did all her painting at night. Rory had forbidden her any more lovers and so my beloved mother now had a lot of hours to spare for her art.

(Although my brother Caryll swears she used to still smuggle in the occasional lover and I certainly helped her with some of her escapades.) In the morning, her painting table would be removed by the footmen, not to be seen again until the following night. Rory was rigid in his attempts to keep her and her artistic abilities under control. Amazingly, he succeeded.

Meanwhile, for the first time in my life I was without horses; all I had was waterskiing, which was a poor substitute. Thank goodness every year we had started visiting Caryll, since he had moved to Kenya, and I was able to go riding there but that wasn't enough to keep me really happy. I think for this reason I never liked the south of France. It was not my lifestyle and I had very few real friends. Caryll had married a beautiful French girl called Danièle Guirche but they used only to come over to France for a few summer months. The rest of the time I had to pretend I wasn't the village idiot for the benefit of the rest of the guests who thronged Fiorentina. As I hardly ever opened my mouth, for the most part, thank goodness, I was ignored.

One of Rory's greatest friends was Peter Quennell who used to come and stay every year with his girlfriend, and later wife, to whom he had given the nickname Spider Monkey. She was over six foot, very slim, with enormously long legs and young enough to be his daughter but of course she was very sophisticated. Rory also found her charming. I could not quite see the fascination she held for all these men, especially as one evening in New York she had gone nightclubbing with a friend and myself. At 3am, when we were going home, she refused to give her address and we had to drive endlessly around the city while she kept laughing and kicking up her legs which, much to my annoyance, I had to keep dodging. She kept saying, "I am not feeling tired. I like driving around looking at the city lights." I can't remember how we finally managed to get rid of her. She thought it was funny but I certainly did not.

The dining room at Fiorentina always had various tables of eight or four on which to seat the guests. Peter had been with us for about a week when he ended up having lunch at my mother's table. Mummy, being very shy like myself, although a great deal better at not showing it, would invariably be late for every meal so her table would start eating long before she appeared. Peter rose to greet Mummy when she made her grand entrance surrounded by her dogs and cheetah and dressed in one of the latest Dior or Lanvin creations, with ropes of pearls and diamonds around her neck. My heart used to glow with pride as I watched the reactions of the roomful of guests to the impact of her extraordinary beauty. It didn't matter how many times they had seen her before. On greeting Peter this time, my mother said, "Peter, how wonderful to see you, you must come and stay." Peter, very taken aback, replied, "Enid darling, I have already been at Fiorentina a week. Am I so insignificant that you have not noticed my presence?"

Staying at Fiorentina one summer was Godfrey Winn, at the time possibly the best known society columnist on Fleet Street. He was chubby, balding and not at all good looking, had been a frequent visitor to Burrough Court and was an ardent bridge player. People pandered to him like mad because of his column.

On one occasion we were all down by the pool. As well as Godfrey, who was lying on one of the sunbathers reading a book, there were other house guests. Some young people who I had been out with the night before arrived. I did not know all their names, although some were minor royalty, and I had invited them for a swim and waterski. One of the footmen, Jean, offered the drinks around and then I took them down to our harbour where the speedboat was waiting. At the time I had not thought to introduce them to Godfrey or to any of the other guests for that matter. I thought no more about this until I went up for lunch and one of the footmen came to tell me that my mother wanted to see me.

"Darling, Godfrey has been to see me in a terrible state," Mummy began. "He tells me that you were extremely rude to him, ignored him, refused to introduce him to your friends and behaved in the most insulting fashion. I had to calm him down, otherwise he was off to pack his bags and leave. Please, darling, go and apologise to him."

I found Godfrey who was puce in the face when I approached.

"Apologise? Apologise! Do you know who I am? I am GODFREY WINN! I am world famous, much better known than those princelings and dukes you were panting after. Your poor mother does not realise what a little bitch she has for a daughter, I never want to speak to you again."

He continued that if I was going to sit at her table at lunch, he was going to another one.

I said to Mummy, "Don't worry. I will go and sit at one of the other tables."

There were five tables of eight in the dining room this day, so seating was not a problem and I asked Eric Nielsen if he would take my place. But worse was to follow. That night we all went to dinner in Monte Carlo. I usually sat near my mother. On this occasion I was sitting opposite her but quite far away as it was a large table. Godfrey waited for the table to be silent which happened when the *beignet de pommes* arrived in a sauce flambé, and then he started. His opening gambit was, "Enid darling, I have been thinking you have such magnificent jewellery. Where do you keep it? I hope it is locked in a safe. With a daughter like Pat around there is no telling what would happen if you ever let her have the key."

An absolute hush fell over the table. Mummy behaved as if this was a perfectly normal conversation. "Are you meaning that Pat might try and steal it?" she asked. My mother started laughing, "Godfrey, if you only knew. I would be only too delighted if she showed any interest. In fact, I would give her the lot. I am always in despair. She has no time for clothes or jewellery. All she cares about are her horses, dogs and her car."

In fact, Mummy took her jewellery so much for granted she always kept it in her tissue boxes. And she was quite right about my interest in fashion. If she was lucky, Mummy would get me to the end of season fashion shows in Paris where I would buy at a discount the clothes the models had shown. At least then I didn't have to go for lots of fittings.

Eric came to me afterwards to say he was horrified by Godfrey's behaviour and that my mother should ask him to leave. A few days later, I was sitting on the wall of the harbour surrounded by my dogs and waiting to go waterskiing, when Eric arrived with a friend. "Pat," he said, "I want to introduce you to Art Buchwald, he is staying for lunch and would very much like to talk to you."

I did not have a clue at that stage that Mr Buchwald was a widely syndicated American journalist and columnist, then with *The New York Herald Tribune* in Paris, and he soon started questioning me about the Godfrey Winn saga. He was a charming man. Making himself comfortable, he came and sat beside me on the jetty and soon had me in fits of laughter. He saw the funny side of the pompous and conceited Mr Winn. The next week, the Art Buchwald column appeared and it made for hilarious reading. It said something to the effect that if one wanted to get onto the guest list of the elite of the south of France, there was only one requisite – to be a good bridge player. It was quite permissible to be rude, bad-tempered and insult the daughter of the house in front of all your friends, but so long as you play bridge all is forgiven and you are a welcome guest. He put it in such a funny way but Godfrey, much to my delight, was livid.

I finally decided that I was not going to let him get away with all his insults and I knew the perfect way to do it. Willie Maugham was having a birthday party. Not that I was invited, but Mummy, Rory and most of the house guests including Godfrey were going. Willie Maugham often came to Fiorentina but it was Alan Searle, his secretary and companion, who came over most days. I waited until Alan appeared and then in the course of conversation told him that Godfrey, when he first came, had informed everybody at a lunch party how, when he, Godfrey, was younger, he had been so good looking that Willie had fallen for him in a big way and chased him all over London.

I knew that Somerset Maugham, who stuttered a great deal, was a very private man who would not like to know that his homosexuality had been a matter for discussion. That Godfrey had bragged to all and sundry that Willie had pursued him would in particular make Godfrey *persona non grata*. The axe was soon to fall. A few days later, Alan called Hamish Erskine who at that time was in charge of Fiorentina and Mummy's other estates. Hamish was given the list of names of the guests invited to the birthday party, but it specifically excluded Godfrey Winn. Hamish imparted this information to Godfrey as tactfully as he could and Godfrey, making urgent business the excuse for his early departure, left Fiorentina, never to return. Needless to say that was to my great delight.

Alan was supposedly Willie's secretary but he was also the boyfriend. He himself was not that discreet. At the time there was a famous doctor who had a clinic in Switzerland and it was said that his treatment made the elderly young again. I don't exactly remember the details but the treatment meant lying in bed while the patient was dosed with pig blood or goat blood or something. The rich and famous went in droves. Alan and Willie went and Alan afterwards told Rory that he just prayed they never had to go back. He was sure Willie had been infused with goat blood because ever since he, Alan, had been pursued from bedpost to bedpost by a rampant Willie and he was getting quite exhausted.

There was another little contretemps between myself and one of Mummy's guests over introductions, and this was with an American high society hostess Mrs Elsie Woodward who I remember as tall, grey-haired and very distinguished looking. Another great friend of my mother, she used to come and stay fairly frequently. Winston and Lady Churchill had just arrived and he had been helped up the front steps by Rajabo and Mahommet, the butler and footman. Mummy, of course, was late as usual and I was in a nervous tizz at being the only member of the family present to welcome these prestigious guests. At this stage, Mrs Woodward arrived on the scene and I had to make the introductions. In my nervous state and with the disaster of Godfrey Winn fresh in my mind, I panicked and for the life of me could not remember Mrs Woodward's name. I knew it had something to do with trees and introduced her as Mrs Treewood. I could see that yet again I had made a dreadful gaffe and that she was not amused. Mrs Woodward corrected my mistake but I felt as big as a worm.

As far as I remember, it was around the time of this visit that her daughter-in-law, Ann, shot her son. At the time, the death and the circumstances were front-page news for weeks because the Woodwards were such a well-known family in New York. The story given at the trial was that the son had gotten up during the night, unbeknown to his wife, and gone outside. When he came back into the room again his wife thought he was an intruder and shot him. I must say old Mrs Woodward stuck by her daughter-in-law, at least publicly, throughout and we all knew how she adored her son. I remember Mummy being so upset that her friend had suffered such a terrible loss and saying to me, "I cannot bear to think how I would feel if it was either Rory or Caryll. It is a tragedy from which no mother would ever recover."

There were so many famous visitors but the one who fascinated me was Prince Aly Khan. Women went crazy over him. I never thought he was that attractive, not that he ever made a pass at me, but I used to hear these lovesick women discussing his prowess in bed. It is amazing, if one keeps quiet and is totally insignificant, how much one hears. One of his greatest assets, according to them, was that he could make love all night: he used to keep ice cubes beside the bed to cool his ardour and keep going longer. To this day I cannot quite conceive what he did with the cubes. It leaves one's imagination open to all sorts of possibilities. He had another hang-up, which was horrid. He liked all his women to smell *au naturel* and remain unshaven. I used to watch with horror all these beauties becoming *unsoignée*, going without make-up and gradually losing all their glamour. Having reduced them to the mundane, he would move onto the next one and repeat the process. Even the beautiful actress Rita Hayworth, who he married, succumbed to the process.

Apart from Greta Garbo who used to mimic Rory perfectly, pacing the garden, pretending to make sure the plants were placed exactly so, the most beautiful guest at Fiorentina was Pamela Churchill. She had been married to Winston's son Randolph, and was later to marry the agent and producer Leland Hayward and then the multi-millionaire, diplomat and statesman Averell Harriman. In fact, my brother Caryll remembers that as a very young woman, Pamela was rather fat and plain and a friend once insisted that he ask her to dance because no-one else would. After the war, Caryll used to take her to Maxim's in Paris so she could be amongst all the South American millionaires. But she really had a brain, he says, and that made all the difference. By the time I knew her, she was well-known for her liaisons with powerful and rich men. She reminded me very much of my mother with her lace and satin nightdresses and peignoirs and she used to float around her room like a nymph rising from the sea. The first time I saw her arriving at Fiorentina, it was by speedboat just as the sun was setting. She and her lover Gianni Agnelli were standing in the stern, outlined against the sunset. It was an unforgettable sight; they were both godlike in their magnificent beauty. I believe she also used to make use of ice cubes for her male lovers but I understand they were inserted. Maybe the Aly Khan had been one of her boyfriends and taught her his little tricks.

I suppose one of the most famous of all Mummy's friends was the

Duke of Windsor. I remember my brother Rory complaining one night after they had come back from dinner with the Windsors. Rory, who prided himself on his beautiful tailoring, always dressed immaculately. Both he and my mother only patronised the best; even the shoes had to be hand-made. The night they had gone to the Windsors, Rory was wearing the very latest fashion in ties, slightly wider than the conventional post-war model. The Duke had taken him aside and said, "Rory, that tie is not the thing. Come with me and I will let you have one of mine." Windsor took Rory upstairs and then he and his valet brought out a selection of ties. Choosing one, he said to Rory, "Stand before the mirror and I will show you how to do it properly." The Duke proceeded to tie Rory's tie for him in the fashion named after him, the Windsor Knot.

On another occasion when the Windsors came to Fiorentina, they were escorted by Jimmy Donahue with whom the duchess was having an affair. Donahue was the cousin of Barbara Hutton, the Woolworth's heiress and he too had inherited some of the Woolworth fortune. Mummy was very disapproving of this liaison. I remember her telling me that she had been most upset a few nights before when they had all been dining in a restaurant. Their party consisted of several tables and all through dinner the duchess had been sending little *billets-doux* – or rather my mother presumed they were little love notes – to Jimmy who was at another table. Mummy went on to say that almost before dinner was over the duchess had summoned the car and sent the duke home, saying that she wanted to go onto a nightclub and she knew how much he disliked them. Mummy could not believe the duke could accept being dumped in such an unceremonious fashion. "After all," said my mother, "David has given up his throne for love of her. The least she could have done was to behave herself."

Mummy had known Windsor for many years and, although I do not think he had been one of her lovers, she liked him very much. It was not long after this that they came to Fiorentina with Jimmy. After lunch, everyone was sitting on the terrace talking when the duchess said, "I just want to take Jimmy and show him the marvellous view from your point." The duke sat around reminiscing, saying, "When I was monarch..." while everyone knew the duchess was having it off with Jimmy in one of the upstairs guest rooms. Mummy told me that the duchess was famous for her expertise in fellatio: rumour had it that she had had lessons in China on this particular art. She was a very masculine woman; there was nothing soft or feminine about her, and I personally did not think she was at all good looking. She had a presence. I suppose that was the best one could say about her.

I think though of all the world-famous women that came to Fiorentina, I liked Barbara Hutton the best. Her grandfather had started the American chain-store Woolworth's and after his death and later his wife's, she inherited millions from the Woolworth estate, thereby becoming one of the richest people in the world. She was 11 at the time.

She was wonderful with me and was the most generous person with her money. I used to get fabulous presents. On my 21st birthday, she gave me a dinner for myself and all my friends and all our guests at the Chateau de Madrid. A caviare dinner no less, as she knew that it was my favourite dish. Another thing that remained in my memory was Barbara saying to me one day: "I think it is so marvellous the wonderful relationship you have with your mother. You are so lucky to be so much loved. It is something that I never had in my childhood." She also went on to say that when she went to visit her grandmother as a child, the old lady used to get so over-excited that she would start playing with herself and Barbara would have to be rushed out of the room by her governess. Suffering a broken heart, Barbara's own mother had committed suicide in front of her at her suite at the Plaza Hotel when Barbara was only four. The suicide was hushed up and recorded as death from chronic ear disease.

I remember her telling my mother that of all her husbands, Cary Grant was the only one who never took money from her. In fact, he cabled her when she announced she was marrying the Dominican polo-playing playboy, Porfirio Rubirosa, trying to persuade her not to do it. Rubirosa also wanted Barbara to marry him on Dominican territory at the Dominican consulate in New York, and Barbara's friends were concerned he would get his hands on her entire fortune – by Dominican law – if/when there was a divorce. A generous pre-nuptial avoided that and the wedding went ahead in front of the Dominican Consul General.

At the time Rubirosa married Barbara, he was having a passionate affair with another famous beauty, Zsa Zsa Gabor. Mostly he was known for the size of his appendage. The marriage to Barbara did not last more than a few weeks and he returned to his latest lover. Thank goodness, owing to her friends and relatives, he did so without acquiring all her money.

On another occasion, Mummy and Barbara flew to the Far East and when they landed at Singapore, Barbara invited the Captain of the plane to lunch. By the time lunch was over, she had bought him his own airline. She said to Mummy, "He was so nice and gave us such a good flight, I would like to give him something in exchange."

I know she often used to stay at the George V while in Paris, and because she liked the voice of the telephone operator she sent her a mink coat. Barbara was like that, unbelievably generous.

Mummy's friends were much less frightening to me than Rory's. They tended to be from the English set. Margaret, Duchess of Argyll, was the original Mrs Sweeney who the composer Cole Porter cited in his rhythmic paean to such icons, *You're The Top*. She was quite lovely to look at and always very nice to me. The Mosleys, Sir Oswald and Diana, also came quite often. She was another of the beautiful Mitfords and I adored her. On one or two occasions the Mosleys brought the novelist Ian Fleming to lunch. I used to look at him and wonder how that insignificant exterior could hide such a vivid imagination. I was intrigued at the thought that maybe he pictured himself as the dashing James Bond. The author Louise de Vilmorin who is supposed to have been a great femme fatale was another guest, and one of Rory's lovers, but as far as I was concerned she didn't have the warmth to go with her enormous – I thought superficial – charm.

One of Rory's greatest English friends was Lady Kitty Lambton who was a wonderful and eccentric old lady. She was the daughter of the Duke of St Albans and had married twice, the second time to Major-General Sir William Lambton, son of the Earl of Durham. Rory used to visit her every week as she had one of the most famous gardens in the south of France. On the Moyenne Corniche above the peninsula Cap Martin, the garden went down on terraces almost to the sea. I often used to accompany Rory. On her terrace outside the house, she had what seemed like millions of pot plants that she and an equally dotty gardener would bend over and lovingly water, talk to and at the same time caress as gently as if they were adored and beautiful children. I would watch this activity with amazement and feel quite ashamed of the way Rory used to accept little cuttings as if he were being given the Taj Mahal. His gratitude, I felt, was far too excessive for such dirty little offerings, which used to be carefully placed in a white plastic bag and then rushed to the car. Lady Kitty's brother, the Duke of St Albans, also seemed to view this charade with some amusement when he was there. "Darling sister," Rory would say to me. "You have no soul. You have no eye for beauty. You have no feeling for anything that does not bark or neigh. I am doing my best to educate you but I see that I am wasting my time!"

Then there was someone who was one of my great friends as well as Rory's, David Hicks. The first time I met him, I had come into the sitting room where he and Rory were standing discussing the painting that occupied almost the entire end wall. It was by Jean-Baptiste Oudry, considered one of the greatest painters of wildlife of the 18th century and it was a magnificent life-size portrait of a heron standing on the edge of a marsh. David was dressed in white trousers and a pink open-necked shirt and with his blond hair and blue eyes he was quite breathtakingly beautiful. At that time, only a few years after the war, nobody dressed in bright colours. I think it was David who started the fashion for lovely pastel shades and open shirts. Open shirts, if worn at all, were worn with cravats by British men; they certainly didn't wear them exposing a lot of tanned chest as did David.

I soon found he had a wonderful sense of humour and I would be reduced to tears laughing at his outrageous character sketches and puckish remarks. In just a few short sentences, he could annihilate some unfortunate, boring or pedantic guest. At that time he was just starting as a decorator and Rory had an enormous influence on his designs.

One day, while he was courting Pamela Mountbatten, Lord Mountbatten's daughter, he sat me down on the sofa at Fiorentina and said, "Pat I have got to talk to you. I need some advice. You know I am very much in love with Pamela and I admire her above everyone but I have had affairs with men. Am I being fair to her in asking her to marry me? I would hate to do anything that would hurt her in any way and I can hardly sleep at night worrying about my past and how it could affect her. How would you feel if you were in her position?" I told him that it would not worry me as, I said, "My brother whom I adore is homosexual and he has had very successful and lasting affairs with women. Most of my best men friends are also homosexual. I cannot see that it should affect your life together."

We all went to the wedding in Hampshire at Romsey Abbey and I think the Hicks's marriage was very successful. He always adored Pamela and I often used to go and visit them at their beautiful house and wonderful garden on the edge of Oxfordshire and I kept all his letters, which were always full of news and the latest gossip.

I loved listening to Pamela's sister Patricia tell fascinating stories of her time in India, with her father when he was Viceroy of India, later Governor-General. I particularly enjoyed the story of how, when she was one of the aides-de-camp to her father, they used to keep bicycles to get around on because the corridors of Government House were so vast.

CHAPTER

32

Mummy and I, looking for the sun, used to go and spend one or two months of each winter at a house on the beach she had bought in Nassau, the same one where I had stayed with Aunt Nanny. (After one visit Rory never went again; it was not his scene.) It was on one of these visits that I met Aymon de Roussy de Sales. Mummy, Clarissa Chaplin and I had gone to Nassau for the winter. Clarissa was a lovely girl, several years younger than myself, very dark and glamorous. By the time we had spent the days soaking up the sun on our beach she looked like an Hawaiian islander, especially in the evening when we went nightclubbing. She would often pick a hibiscus from the garden and wear it behind her ear.

The first time I saw Aymon, Clarissa and I were in a nightclub with two rather dull escorts. I noticed a most gorgeous young man come onto the dance floor with a girl who had her dachshund with her. This man duly obliged and, picking up the small dog, placed it on his shoulder. Looking at him reminded me of the *coup de foudre* I had felt the first time I saw Guy de Lesseps. I could not take my eyes off him. Later on, when Clarissa and I went to the ladies' room, she said to me,

"Did you see that beautiful young man dancing with the puppy on his shoulder? What a pity we can't meet someone like that."

The following evening, Clarissa was going to a cocktail party. They were my idea of hell as one stood around having to talk, not something I was good at, and drinking was another of my dislikes. I invariably found that if one remained sober, by the end of the evening everyone else seemed to be half-seas under and not making much sense. I hated seeing middle-aged women behaving in a ridiculous fashion. Anyhow, this time I let Clarissa convince me and as we walked into the sitting room, which opened onto the beach, the first person I saw was the young man of the nightclub.

He was dressed all in white, white trousers and open white cotton shirt, looking even more beautiful and again with his girlfriend and her dachshund. I was talking to Pitt Oakes who was madly in love with me. I liked him, he was a great friend, but he drank excessively at the time and he got so jealous that when I went out with other men he used to follow me from nightclub to nightclub. I never ever allowed him to even kiss me as I could not bear the smell of his alcoholic breath. I liked him enormously though and felt that having had a father, Sir Harry Oakes, murdered in the horrific fashion in which he was, was enough to send anyone off the rails. Sir Harry had been bludgeoned, and then found dead in his bed in his Nassau mansion during the war, on July 8, 1943. His body had been set alight.

Sir Harry's son-in-law, Count Alfred de Marigny, was one of the chief suspects but the murder remained unsolved and there was always the question that the two detectives the then Governor of the Bahamas, the Duke of Windsor, had summoned from America had planted a glass with De Marigny's fingerprints near the scene of the crime. Certainly, there were people on the island who had no intention of the real criminals being found. I was told that an American female newspaper reporter who was following the case and had supposedly come upon some evidence was later found murdered, drowned in a well. One theory was that Oakes, the Duke of Windsor and another man, Harold Christie, had been involved in a money-smuggling operation and that something went badly wrong between the three of them.

Pitt's sister, Nancy Oakes, had been married to de Marigny and had always stood by him. Pitt once told me he knew who had killed his father but said he would rather I did not know, although I did try and persuade him. Pitt always told me that if anybody got too close to the truth they always ended up dead.

As I was talking to Pitt and a few friends, I felt a frisson of awareness. Before I even turned, I knew that the young man I had noticed in the nightclub had come to join us. I had gone back to calling myself by my maiden name and as I turned he said, "Patricia Cavendish, I am Aymon de Roussy de Sales. I have been told that you are not only the best limbo dancer but the best swimmer and waterskier on the island. I had to meet this paragon and watching you tonight I have decided you are also the most beautiful."

I realised that I had met another Guy de Lesseps, a practised seducer of women. Nothing mattered. He was so devastating that I was once more in the throes of a passionate love. I laughingly told him that I might easily be the best limbo dancer because at home we had a gymnasium and a gym instructor and one rarely saw women dancing the limbo. As for swimming, I had been married to an Olympian and, wearing flippers, would accompany him on his five-mile swims. Waterskiing, I said, I am not the best. I know a few other girls who are just as good if not better, but again I am lucky to be able to waterski almost every day of my life plus I was taught by the best, my brother.

(It was just as well I had that expert tuition for it was in Nassau that I had a horrible experience. I was on a mono-ski going from Nassau to one of the islands and was halfway across when I realised that I was being followed by a shark. There was nothing I could do. Nor could my driver. If he had stopped, I would probably have been eaten by the time he got around to picking me up. The choice was between turn back or go on, the devil and the deep blue sea. I decided to continue but for the next half hour I could feel my heart beating and I kept worrying that I might have one of my fainting fits. I did not practise any more slaloms on the way across. Instead, I felt like a granny I was skiing so sedately and I would have given anything for the security of a second ski.)

During the course of the party Aymon said to me, "I am going to take my date home. Will you wait for me? I want to spend the rest of the evening with you."

Clarissa could not believe my luck. "Why didn't he pick me?" she kept saying. Laughingly I said, "He probably prefers blondes."

Aymon was staying in one of the island hotels that belonged to friends of his. It had been their private house and was an exquisite two-storeyed building with columns and fretwork balconies, one of the colonial houses for which Nassau was so famous. Aymon's friends, the present owners, were a young couple and were as glamorous as their hotel. They ran it beautifully and it became one of my favourite places on the island. In the evenings, they had wonderful late-night fish and lobster barbecues on the terrace. A calypso band played and sang all the glorious island songs against a backdrop of towering tropical trees and the sound of running water from the fountains. The hotel had a large garden and the scent of frangipani and cyclamen permeated the soft tropical night air.

As Aymon and I walked up the steps to the terrace, he bent down and picked some camellias growing in large pots lining the stairs and, placing them behind my ears, said, "Now, with your long hair and suntan you look like a blonde islander."

Later when we made love, the scent from the crushed camellias and the Joy which, like my mother I used to liberally spray on my bed linen, rose from my pillow. It was a heady passionate perfume and if I close my eyes now, I can still smell it and remember that incredible night. Aymon was everything one could wish for in a man. He was not only beautiful to look at but passionate, romantic and the most perfect of lovers. He told me that for him it was love at first sight. He could not take his eyes off me and he knew then, without even having spoken to me, that I was the girl he wanted to marry.

The next morning he moved into Mummy's house on Cable Beach. There were no more long early morning swims or long hours on waterskis. If the decision had been left to Aymon, we would never have got out of bed at all. He used to say, "I want you in touching distance." In those heady early months, we could never get enough of each other.

Aymon had a lot of friends on the island and most of them had yachts and as Aymon loved sailing, he, Clarissa, my dogs and I spent quite a lot of time on boats. I used to row the dogs ashore to do their business and so we had to go from island to island. One time, the yacht we were on came to a stop during the night. Aymon decided to go up on deck and see what was happening. He came back saying,

"It's a good thing they didn't see me as it looks very much as if the Captain and crew are gun running."

Nassau was quite a violent place in those early days. On one of our visits, Clarissa and I had been walking along a beach and had seen a man in a green bathing suit, his body trapped by the rocks, being eaten by sharks. We rushed to the nearest police station. Apparently he had been murdered and his body dumped in the sea. Aymon also told me that all the nightclubs that I liked so much were a great source of illegal drugs and that under the surface, my beautiful, peaceful, sunny island was a well-known haven for drug and gun smugglers.

We had another adventure with one of Clarissa's friends who had a plane. Ted had been a bomber pilot during the war on the American flying fortresses but when we went to the airport to pick up his plane, I was amazed that he did no pre-flight tests. I was used to my meticulous brother, Caryll, who would spend ages draining petrol from the tanks, checking engines, brakes and so on. But Ted just taxi-ed down the runway and took off. I thought to myself that he must know what he was doing, he was the one who had been a bomber captain, not me. We were already well out to sea and I was sitting in the co-pilot's seat. I kept looking at his instrument panel and in spite of what I was telling myself, it still looked to me as if his petrol tank was showing just about empty. Finally I couldn't bear the strain any longer and said, "Ted, I am not used to this plane but isn't your petrol tank reading empty?"

"Oh my God!" said Ted. "So it is. I forgot to check the bloody thing."

We banked steeply and headed for home. He had a reserve tank but even so, we only just made it. It was quite a tense flight. The engine started spluttering as we circled to land.

Another time we rented one of the island schooners with friends of Clarissa. I think we were off Eleuthera when we got a hurricane warning. Panic reigned. The idea was to lift anchor and sail to a safe harbour but as luck would have it, the crew hadn't attached the anchor correctly and when the rope was winched up, there was no anchor. The captain, quite naturally, could not leave without it so he sent the crew overboard to retrieve it. The Caribbean waters are so clear the anchor could be seen lying innocently amongst the fish. The procedure took so long though we were able to watch the storm approaching. All the other yachts had long departed and we were still flapping around even though where we were was very sheltered. The wind by now was hurricane force, the sea was mountainous and the sky black. The palm trees were bent double with the sand spiralling along the beaches. With our anchor now retrieved, we were running before the wind. I had shut my dogs in the cabin and was worrying about whether I would be able to get to them in time if the boat went down. Nevertheless, it was fascinating to watch the tornado approach. Unless it changed direction, the spiral was obviously going to miss us by miles. Our yacht would come out of the huge waves, shudder and then plunge once again into the trough. The water on either side looked to be mast-high. We were all securely fastened to prevent us being swept overboard and Aymon had his arm around me. I could see he was enjoying every moment. "Anyhow, darling," he said, "if we sink at least we will be together and you have given me the most wonderful months of my life. I love you. I cannot live without you. If we make it back to Nassau will you marry me?"

I could hardly hear him above the screaming of the wind. He was laughing as he bent to kiss me. I knew also that I wanted to spend the rest of my life with this wonderful man. Lost in a passionate embrace, I forgot the mountainous seas, the screaming hurricane, the danger. In the middle of a tornado I had received a proposal of marriage from a man I knew I loved more than life.

There was one complication. I had not seen Frank for a few years but I still had not managed to get a divorce. Mummy called her lawyers at Theodore Goddard, and they advised us to establish a residence in Florida and get a quick divorce there. Mummy arranged to buy a cottage on the edge of a lake. We left Nassau and I became a resident of Ocala where I think we had to remain for a month to establish residence. I remember the humidity and the heat. I also remember going to the bird park at Ocala and being distressed to see all the parrots suffering, their beaks wide open gasping for air. I've never forgotten it and as a result all these years later, I now have overhead sprays for my parrots which they can sit under during the long hot summer days.

Having achieved my divorce, Mummy took us on a trip to Mexico while her New York flat was prepared for Aymon and myself. We got married in a registry office in New York. I hadn't realised until we had to arrange all the necessary forms that Aymon was eight years younger than myself. He was amazingly mature for his age. He told me that he had been seduced by one of his mother's friends at the age of 14 and from then on he had never looked back. One of his girlfriends, Pamela Moore, had even written a book about him called *Chocolates for Breakfast*.

I had the greatest difficulty in getting Aymon to invite his mother to the wedding. He had no great filial feelings, which was something I could not understand. But he said that as a child, he had always been given anything he wanted. His mother never took the trouble to say no to him or be strict with him in any way. When he learned that life did not just dole out gifts every time he screamed, he became very resentful. Aymon's theory was that she did not love him enough to take the trouble to say no. Instead, she preferred to take the easy way out. The result was that he had no respect for her. Aymon's father, Comte Raoul de Roussy de Sales, had been sent to Washington by the French government just before the war but when France fell to the Germans, he was without a job. He remained in America, Aymon's mother being American, and Aymon was brought up in New York.

His father was now dead and Aymon was Comte Aymon de Roussy de Sales, a descendant of the patron saint of journalists, St Francis de Sales, a nobleman who had given up his vast wealth to the poor and spent the rest of his life living and caring for them.

Mummy went back to France and Aymon and I now settled down in New York. I had never really lived in a city for a long time except during the war in London. I had my dogs but there were no horses, no waterskiing, no real driving. I had a car but there was no exhilaration of speed. The limits were so severe on all the roads that I practically fell asleep from boredom. Our apartment was on the 17th floor but had no garage. In New York at this time you had to rush down at the crack of dawn and change your parked car from one side of the street to the other or it got impounded.

I had spent a few months in New York the year before when Mummy had been working on the large screens that Rory would not let her do at Fiorentina because of the mess. With Mummy then about to join Rory on a trip to the northern countries to study the architecture of Norway, Denmark and Finland, I remained behind in the Manhattan flat to finish off all the backgrounds of these enormous canvases. I could not bear the furniture in the rented flat and so I put it in storage and went out and had a marvellous time refurnishing. The flat had large rooms and so I made it very modern to suit the glorious architecture of New York.

I used to walk the streets entranced with the city's beauty. I made all my friends go for walks with the dogs and me. We would look up at the ever-changing winter skyline, with the snow falling, the Christmas trees and the lights shining through the clouds from the top of the Empire State Building. It looked like a fairy palace emerging from its beautiful blanket of swirling mist. New Yorkers are so busy rushing from one place to another they never look at their city. It is magic.

I was enraptured, but after a few months of any city, I get claustrophobic and long for the open country. By this time, I had also spent a great deal of money just refurnishing and paying the rent. I realised that I would have to cool it as I would soon be penniless and I didn't want to bother Mummy to send more.

Then an American friend who I had known in France, Gordon Wholey, came to the rescue. He gave me a job in his travel firm. Gordon had no idea what he was letting himself in for nor, for that matter, did I. Having been a very successful secretary at the American Embassy I thought working at a travel agency would be a piece of cake. One thing became patently obvious; I was totally uneducated when it came to mathematics. Rory had considered it an unnecessary subject for his sister to learn because, said he, there was nothing beautiful in mathematics. Apart from the very basics, I could hardly add or even subtract but now I was supposed to do both, as well as percentages. I was horrified. No matter how much time Gordon spent in trying to show me the movement of that horrible little dot, I just could not get it through my thick brain. The more he explained it, the more my mind became a quivering blank. Much to my humiliation, it was decided that all the tickets I wrote out would then be passed on to someone else so they could do the financial aspect. I soon realised that I was becoming a burden to the efficient running of the firm.

Possibly an even bigger burden were my dogs. They of course had to go to work with me. I couldn't leave my beautiful Bahamian wild dogs shut up all day. Gordon's office soon became a glorified kennel. I used to tie the five dogs to the desk but the office was only so big and there was quite a large staff. Gordon Wholey's travel agency soon became an assault course of dogs darting out from my desk, people tripping over leads or being baled up by irate Bahamian wolves. Mayhem reigned supreme.

Gordon did politely suggest I might prefer to work from home and I realised I could not strain our friendship any further. I suggested we remain friends and that I resign. I could see him visibly breathe a great sigh of relief.

I had another great friend who came to the rescue. This was David Chimay who ran a large model agency. David and one of his models, a beautiful Swedish girl called Sophia, came up with the idea that on her next modelling assignment she would use my dogs. Soon I was living off the proceeds of my big amber-eyed wild dogs who were featuring alongside all the beautiful models in the streets of New York. David also used my sitting room with Mummy's screens for backgrounds. So now, without having to worry about mathematics and percentages, I was doing very well. My dogs and I would also go and stay most weekends with David at his lovely country home.

Having had the time to finish all the backgrounds on Mummy's screens, I then wanted to get back to my real home, Fiorentina. Flying the dogs back was going to present a problem. I didn't want them to have the trauma of flying on their own in the hold. I called up a friend of Caryll's who was the managing director of Pan Am. I suggested that he put me on a cargo plane going to France, which would mean I could sit with my dogs in the hold. He said that was not a great idea but he would see what else he could do and let me know.

I cannot say enough for Pan Am. They organised the luggage section behind the first class compartment in such a way that it would accommodate my huge dog kennels and I could visit them during the trip. About an hour before landing though, one of the stewardesses came to me and said, "One of your dogs has escaped and the passengers are too frightened to pass him to get to the toilet." I could see their point as he was sitting on guard, snarling at anyone who dared approach. A very nice gentleman gave up his seat so that I could now put Smokey next to me, and he sat in a luxury first class seat for the rest of the voyage.

Smokey, Bandit, Billy the Kid, Annie Oakley and Rogue went with me around the world, to Nassau, the States, the south of France, Kenya and finally South Africa where they all lived to be well over 20.

This time, as a newly married woman, my stay in New York with Aymon meant spending most weekends with friends, nightclubs every night, and the rest of the time making love. I remember at one lunch party, Aymon was sitting next to a young, very attractive American girl. As she was leaving she said to me, "Countess, I just have to tell you that your husband is the most beautiful man I have ever seen. Not only is he magnificent to look at but he has all that French charm. You are such a lucky woman." I thought to myself, dear heavens, I must be looking old. Not only is she addressing me by my title, but she is referring to me as a woman and not a girl. I obviously look like an old harridan with a beautiful toy boy husband.

The following winter, Aymon and I went to stay with Caryll and his wife Danièle at their farm in Kenya. I still had my passion for Africa and Mummy and I loved to visit. One day after lunch Mummy wanted to go to Nairobi to get her hair done and do some shopping so Caryll flew her and myself to the city while Aymon and the others decided to stay on the farm. We were supposed to be gone for a couple of hours but Mummy, as usual, took so long that by the time she was ready, the clouds had come down and Caryll decided that with night falling, it would be too risky to fly. In those days there were none of the sophisticated aids there are today for light aircraft. We stayed the night in the Muthaiga Club and it was the first time I had been away from Aymon since our meeting in Nassau.

When we got back to the farm, Aymon was not his usual self and accused me of having left him behind on purpose. I didn't know why he was behaving so strangely and it took quite a while before he became once more the Aymon I knew. We were at Fiorentina one day much later when Rory said to me that he had something to tell me. "Did you know," he said, "that while you were in Kenya, Aymon was unfaithful to you? Apparently, you spent a night in Nairobi. According to Aymon he had gone to bed when the door opened and a figure appeared and climbed into bed with him. Aymon does not know whether he should tell you but he feels so guilty and has asked advice on what he should do. He is very worried that if he tells you it might ruin your marriage."

I spoke to Aymon about it and he said that he was feeling so guilt-stricken that no matter how much in love he was with me he still had not been able to control his own libido when this night visitor had come onto him so strongly. I assured him that he was totally forgiven and that on the night in question, I had gone to a nightclub with Caryll and one of his Italian farming friends had almost raped me on the dance floor he was so pushy with his attentions.

I thought this story might comfort Aymon a bit. Not at all. He was beside himself with fury at the thought of another man's erection being pressed against my stomach.

In a way, this episode did affect our marriage as Aymon could not forgive himself.

After a few months, he wanted to return to New York to be with his friends again, but there was no way I was going with him. It would have meant leaving Mummy and by this stage I had had a very bad health scare: an ectopic pregnancy that had left me exhausted, scared, sad and upset. Instead of returning to New York, I went with Rory and my mother to stay with Barbara Hutton in Tangiers. Barbara lived in a lovely old palace in the Kasbah that looked like a fort. Tangiers itself was wonderful. The old *souk*, the marketplace, consisted of tiny cobbled streets with heavily laden donkeys and camels jostling the pedestrians aside. As in the Egyptian bazaars, the *souk* was filled with the wonderful smells of spices and an incredible variety of goods on display spilling out of the little shops into the streets. There was hardly room to move but we loved the exotic ever-changing scenes laid out like a feast before our eyes. For me, it was the wonder and mystery of Africa again.

Mummy, of course, always created a stir. She was never parted from her beloved Tikki the hyrax, which sat perched on her shoulder like a huge furry guinea pig. I was now given the job of finding fresh food daily for the horrible, spoilt animal. I would sneak out at six in the morning searching the suburban villas for rose petals and bamboo shoots. Barbara's very smart chauffeur would drive me to the affluent area of Tangiers where climbing roses, bamboos and fig trees were abundant and could be accessed through the iron perimeter fences.

I used to sneak down the street feeling like a thief and, looking around to make sure there were no guards watching, I would grab handfuls of the various offerings and then, exhausted from the fear of being caught, would return to the safety of Barbara's castle. I don't know what her chauffeur thought of these early morning sorties but he was invariably polite and would see to my comfort, collecting my basket of ill-gotten gains as he handed me back into the car.

Mummy and I had our rooms in one of the towers with a winding narrow stone staircase. Barbara had been very upset one evening after dinner as one of the guests had burnt a large hole in her priceless Persian carpet. Since my illness, I now slept with my door open so that I had easy access to Mummy. It must have been about one o'clock in the morning when my dogs woke me up and I saw my mother in her floating blue negligee descending the staircase. I thought I had better go and see what she was doing as the household was in deep sleep and I hadn't noticed any possible lovers. I found my mother trying to drag the burnt carpet up the stairs. As I went to her aid, she explained that she felt the least she could do was repair it for poor Barbara before she woke up. As well as her paints, Mummy used to carry a basket of cottons and wools in every conceivable colour so that if she could not paint she could do her needlework. Mummy worked on the carpet until daybreak and when I returned from my morning raid on the gardens for Tikki, I helped her put the carpet back in place. I must say the effort was worthwhile. Barbara was thrilled. Everyone looked but nobody could tell where the hole had been. Mummy was nothing if not a perfectionist. I was so proud of her, my heart was bursting and I was almost reduced to tears. For once, it was not the fact that she was beautiful nor that she was the mother of Rory the genius that had made her the centre of attention; it was her own skills.

Soon after our return to La Fiorentina from Tangiers, I received a "Dear Jane" letter from Aymon asking for a divorce. He had met someone while on a trip to Mexico. Quite naturally, I replied that he must go ahead with his romantic plans and I would not try and stop him, although the letter had come as quite a blow.

Winter arrived and Mummy and I were on our way to Nassau again. Rory as usual was staying away, in New York. As Mummy and I were going to spend one night there on our way through, I asked Aymon's aunt, with whom I got on well, if I could stay with her but she refused saying that I was now Aymon's ex-wife and that he might not like it. I was very hurt as she had frequently visited Fiorentina and I didn't think Aymon and I were enemies. Then Aymon called me. He had been most upset at his aunt's refusal to let me stay and asked me out. We went to a movie and soon after the lights went out, he leant over and took my hand, held and kissed it as if once more I was his precious possession. Later we had dinner in a little restaurant where he was his usual adoring self. He put his arm around me so he could bring me closer while he nuzzled my cheek and neck, my arms and hands. I was getting rather embarrassed as I felt everyone was watching this show of sexual attention. We finally ended up in my hotel bedroom where we spent the whole night making love. I had to get dressed early to meet Mummy at the airport to catch our flight to Nassau. When I bent down to kiss Aymon a last goodbye and he awoke to the realisation that I was leaving, he begged me not to go and to stay with him. My last sight of Aymon is him naked and lying on the floor holding my ankle as I opened the door, pleading with me not to go. "I love you, my darling," he protested. "Don't do this to me. Please stay."

I left for the airport. I never saw Aymon again, although many years later he sent me some of the wildlife paintings he had done, and he asked me to remarry him. I have always kept my lovely memories of this man to whom I was married for a few wonderful years. My divorce from Aymon was meant to be though. If I had stayed with him, not only would the marriage have not lasted, I would never have had the opportunity to lead my wonderful life in Africa with my beloved children, the wild animals.

CHAPTER

33

My life now was to change dramatically. I was to begin what has always felt like the real life for which I had been born. My family too was changing.

On our return from Tangiers, Mummy decided to take me to her doctor in London, Dr Goldman, as I was still complaining of terrible pains, like glass shards, in my throat every time I swallowed. A year earlier, I had come close to death because of the ectopic pregnancy. During that frightening time, I almost bled to death and both lungs collapsed. I had been extremely lucky though. Aymon and I had been staying together at a friend's house in London. I had gone to bed early because I had suddenly felt the most appalling pain in my stomach. I had a dreadful night, with the most searing pain like knives and my stomach getting larger and larger, but I hadn't wanted to disturb anyone or to complain. Early the next morning, a medical student friend of my host's assured us I was suffering from appendicitis. He said he would come back later to see how I was. Thank heavens I thought about it after he had gone and insisted on seeing our family doctor, Dr Goldman. He came at once and immediately demanded an ambulance. In hospital, I had the best obstetrician in England called in to look after me. I was lucky to be alive, Dr Goldman said later. However, a tube had had to be inserted to re-inflate my lungs and it must have nicked my windpipe. Ever since, I had been exhausted and stressed by the constant pain in my throat. I knew Dr Goldman would be the only person to tell me what was wrong.

Having now done a thorough examination plus X-rays, he told me that all he could find was a slight abrasion of the trachea. But it had healed perfectly, he said. "It will never cause you any problems. You are an extremely healthy young lady. If my other patients were as physically fit as yourself I would have to close up my practice."

I went back to Claridges with Mummy feeling like a different girl. I knew Dr Goldman would never lie to me and if he said I was in perfect health then it meant I was. I had a dreamless night and the next morning I could swallow without any pain.

Having this time been too frightened to contemplate our yearly visit to Kenya because it was so far away from expert medical help, I was now longing to see my brother Caryll on his farm. But first we had the whole summer in the south of France ahead of us to get through; Mummy never moved to hotter climates until winter in Europe approached. She always followed the sun and I always followed her.

At home, Mummy never got out of bed before midday now. Whenever I suspected she was not well, I would summon a doctor so that he would arrive before she got up. This would infuriate her but as she ignored her health I had to be particularly careful. I had on several occasions saved her from being seriously ill. Mummy had practically died on me in Egypt, Mexico and the south of France with the high fevers she had contracted. She had also developed osteo-arthritis and the first signs were starting to appear. Mummy, who was tall and stood very straight, was showing signs of stooping. It was so slight at first that the difference was hardly perceptible. Rory would admonish her, "Mummy, you are not standing straight. Do stop carrying that hyrax around. You are starting to hunch your shoulders."

Mummy not only had arthritis but I was beginning to worry about her health generally. There was a fragility about her that had not been there previously and it occurred to me that my mother, who had always seemed ageless, could die. I would go to her room last thing at night to make sure she was all right. One night I was sure she had died and I was bending over to ascertain whether she was still breathing, when she woke up and said, "Darling, what on earth is the matter?" I burst into tears and said that I thought for a moment she had been dead. I remember so well her embracing me and the feeling of warmth, of silk and of scent and her laughing and saying, "Oh, my darling! If I look that old I had better go and get another face-lift."

I watched as Mummy started spending more and more of her time in her room, surrounded by her dogs, cheetah, hyrax, mongoose and parrots, intent on her painting. I would spend hours just lying on the floor of her room with my book; I felt that she might in some way need my company. I gradually took over the running of Fiorentina and paying the bills. I knew the handling of money, which she had never done, was beyond her. Never having been taught arithmetic I was a poor choice as her replacement but at least I was methodical, which Mummy never was, and I was filled with youthful enthusiasm to shift the burden of running such a large establishment off her shoulders. I kept meticulous books. There were always lunches, dinners, balls and dances and a house full of guests. With the marvellously competent staff at my disposal it was not a difficult job and at least if things went wrong, I was there to blame. Rory demanded perfection in everything. He was the most immaculate and fastidious of men and so spoilt that if he saw a speck of dust on furniture at home, he would create a scene. But if I was ever at a loss, I could go to him for advice.

I even took over the role of chauffeur, as Mummy's would invariably leave. She would make them sit in the back seat while she drove herself. Having no fear and being oblivious to the rules of the road, she would terrify them with her recklessness. I, however, refused to be placed in the back or let her behind the wheel. I would even drive her to the casino at night, myself in full evening dress too, accompany her inside and then go back to sleep in the car until she was ready to leave.

It was definitely life in the fast lane and also a life where people fed on gossip, intrigue and innuendo. Rory who had none of this weakness for tittle-tattle and who, like Mummy, only saw the world through rose-coloured glasses, was surrounded by the rich, the famous and the intellectually brilliant. But the hangers-on and the gossip-mongers were like crows at a feast.

Mummy once had to come back very quickly in the early 1950s from New York. Her friend Donald Bloomingdale, the same one Aunt Nanny had snubbed at lunch at Le Clos, had died from an overdose of some drug. Mummy had been staying with him and was one of the last people to see him alive as they had all dined together that night. All that Mummy told me when she got back was that her friend Rosita Winston had come around when the news broke saying, "Enid, you must leave. If there is an inquiry into his death you must not be here and get involved in anything so sordid." Mummy said Rosita was marvellous and made all the arrangements to get her on a plane back to the south of France.

She was not well when she arrived though. I think it had all come as a tremendous shock. Mummy had been very fond of Donald and she was a sensitive person who really never showed her true feelings, instead always keeping an outward facade of complete tranquillity. I think this was due to her very strict Victorian upbringing where emotions were unladylike and pain was a subject you never ever mentioned. Unless you knew her well, most people saw only the rather cold and beautiful facade and never glimpsed the extraordinarily loving person beneath.

One of Mummy's last lovers towards the end of the 1950s was an Austrian called Tony who used to get around on a little bicycle with an engine that you had to wind up. Mummy used me as her front. We all knew she loved golf and so she bought herself a little cottage near the golf course at Eze. Then she bought the most hideous furniture because she knew that meant Rory wouldn't visit. I used to have to go away with Mummy on weekends to this golf cottage but it was really so she could have time with the dreadful Tony. I would sleep in the second bedroom and spend the weekend being bored to death. Tony was, like so many of her friends and lovers, a very good bridge player but he wasn't a pleasant person. He drank so much Mummy eventually had to send him to a clinic for his alcoholism.

It was only slowly that I was realising that Mummy, for all her beauty and glamour and attentive lovers and ex-lovers, was in fact vulnerable and insecure in an alien world. All my life I had felt an urge to protect my mother from the people who surrounded her and who understood her so little. I did not fit into their cut-throat world. I was able to sit day after day on the rocks overlooking the gleaming Mediterranean surrounded by my dogs and watch the world of the glitterati and the cruelty they displayed to each other. While they played, I wove dreams of a new life in Kenya where my brother already was, with its mystery, its vast stretches of uninhabited mountains, of hills and lakes, where the animals peopled the universe and the people lived with nature.

Mummy and I finally left on our trip to Kenya to visit Caryll. I drove away from Cap St Hospice. With these regular visits during the 1950s to the continent of my dreams, I was taking the first step in leaving France and my life in Europe for good but I didn't know it. I could not foresee that by the end of that decade the rest of my life would be spent in Africa with only occasional visits to Rory at our beautiful house Fiorentina. My carefree travels around the world with my mother and my adored Rory were almost over. My life, surrounded by vast wealth and incredible luxury, was to become but a distant memory. The future was to bring incredible changes and Africa was to be the most magical experience of my life. It would also be the most tragic.

ACT TWO

CHAPTER

34

When Caryll and I were little, my mother created a magical world for us out of her travel stories and we couldn't wait to inhabit it. At bedtime, she would tell us of her adventures in Africa. We could picture the long line of porters, the dugout canoes, the campfires, the wild animals and the pygmy hunters of the Congo. I think this is where my passion started and it bloomed, for Caryll too, when we went on our first safari to Kenya as small children. Neither of us could ever forget what we had seen or experienced.

When I finally settled in Kenya in my thirties, the African continent changed me. The shy timid girl who once only came to life in a swinging skirt on a nightclub dance floor or in the arms of an admiring lover turned into a woman who knew how to outwit a crocodile, run a household in the remote wilds and who could fall head over heels in love with two of Africa's creatures: a hunter and a lion. For my whole life, I had loved animals and got to know them and their ways. I was more comfortable with them than humans. Now I had found an entire continent filled with animals.

Caryll was the first to move to Africa, in 1947. My mother's present to him after the war was an aeroplane; the next was his farm in Kenya. For his plane, he chose a Beechcraft Bonanza and then flew into Nice airport, arriving at Fiorentina filled with enthusiasm for the adventure ahead. Maps were spread all over the table as Caryll charted his course across Africa. I watched with amazement at his competence with sextants, rulers and protractor. It was all Greek to his uneducated sister; I'd never even learned the multiplication table!

The next day before leaving, Caryll came down to the pool for an early morning swim. He took the li-lo with him when he left, saying, "It might be of use if I have to ditch in the sea."

My mother had asked him to telephone from each overnight stop but after leaving Cairo, we had no news for three days. His plane was reported missing. Mummy was in despair, blaming herself for having given him such a lethal gift, and she organised a charter flight to take her out there to search for him. We were just about to leave on the plane when Caryll's call came through. He had been caught in the rolling clouds of a huge sandstorm. It was over the Sudan and, by law, single-engine planes had to be escorted by a larger plane over that country. Caryll was tucked behind a DC3 full of nuns going back to the Congo from Belgium. He says, as the sandstorm hit, he flew so close to the DC3 his wingtip was practically in its fuselage and he could see the nuns in their white habits crossing themselves and blessing him. By the time he got through the storm, his windscreen was sand-blasted and he had to land using his side-window. I should say that Caryll is one of the bravest men I know. He does things in the air that require enormous courage and a cool head and yet he is never stupid or reckless. That is the true meaning of the word "bravery".

The Beechcraft Bonanza was with him for years and took him all over Africa and Europe. Every year he would return to Cap Ferrat for summer and we would wait impatiently for his arrival. He would announce his presence in his usual dramatic fashion, buzzing Fiorentina, flying low over the rooftop and down the cypress alley to the sea.

Like many British and Europeans after World War II, Caryll wanted to test himself out in an exotic wild country which, being a crown colony, still had strong links to back home. He could be an adventurer and a pioneer who worked hard to clear his land, but he could also have a gin in a gentlemen's club, play polo, fly his plane around the countryside and be with other men and women who had been brought up like him. Kenya had a lot of very rich English people. Its beautiful fertile country, the climate and glamour attracted second sons of aristocratic families who wanted their own land, people who wanted a new start and others who just wanted the freshness and promise of a country that hadn't been ripped apart by war. Compared to Kenya, post-war Britain with its rationing and austerity seemed very dull.

When Caryll first arrived, he went to work for Bruce Mackenzie, a South African by birth, who had been seconded to the RAF durng the war and made a colonel at just 24. Later on, after Kenya got its independence, Bruce became the first Minister of Agriculture in Jomo Kenyatta's government. Years later, he was killed on his way back from a visit to Idi Amin, Uganda's despotic leader, blown up by a bomb planted on board his plane.

Bruce, a big man with sideburns and a military moustache, was a very good farmer. He specialised in cattle and took Caryll on as his assistant, the idea being that Caryll would learn the practical side of farming and when he felt proficient enough, Mummy would buy him a farm of his own. Towards the end of his year with Bruce, Mummy decided that the two of us must go to Kenya too as she hadn't seen her blue-eyed boy for months. She adored her children and hated being parted from us for any length of time.

On that occasion, we stayed with our friends Derek and Elisabeth Erskine, who had an enormous gothic house, Erskine Towers, at Riverside Drive in Nairobi. It was practically in the wilds and it was impossible to see any neighbours. Wildly eccentric and totally crazy, they were a marvellous family. Derek, very tall and dark, was proud to call himself a grocer and he had made himself very wealthy conducting that business. No safari went out without first going to Erskine and Duncan for provisions. He was also a prominent polo player in Kenya and a sports enthusiast. As founder and chairman of the Kenya Amateur Athletics Association, he was instrumental in seeing the country's untapped potential as a source of great runners. He always seemed to be dressed in breeches and boots and his voice could be heard all over the house, shouting for the various members of the family. His wife Elisabeth, very small, fair and delicate-looking, ruled her unruly household with an iron fist. She was a fervent Christian Scientist and their tracts would automatically appear with the breakfast settings and just as automatically be swept aside by Derek who would chuck them on the floor, roaring with laughter.

Petal, their daughter, was small and fair. She was so named, according to Derek, because in one of the scenes of a play he once saw in London, the male lead was nibbling at the ear of his co-star and saying, "What a pretty little petal." It suited her beautifully. She was divine looking, with enormous blue eyes and a wonderful smile, and she had an infectious gaiety, bubbling like champagne. She charmed us all and in turn was entranced by my brother, even though she was engaged to Lee Harragin, a young lawyer whose father, Walter Harragin, was the Attorney General and lead prosecutor at the time of Sir Henry John "Jock" Delves Broughton's trial in 1941 for the murder of the handsome Earl of Erroll.

Petal was a very good actress and had the lead in a play at the Nairobi Theatre. When Caryll was in town we seemed to end up going to watch her perform every night. Caryll would sit with his eyes glued to the stage but after the first few nights, my mother and I were beginning to wish he was friends with someone other than an actress. We could see endless evenings sitting in the front row would be our lot if we wished to keep him company. Eventually Petal married Lee and Caryll was usher at the wedding. All three remained the greatest of friends.

On my first morning at Erskine Towers, Petal's brother Francis asked me to help him exercise the polo ponies. Nairobi in those days was not the sprawling town it is today and we headed off towards the golf course. I wasn't paying much attention as I was busy admiring the marvellous scenery. The Ngong Hills were in the background and the trees through which we were riding were heavily entwined with exotic flowering creepers. Above my head, a pair of crowned hornbills objected in the most raucous terms to the intrusion of our ponies. I was gazing at them in some amusement when suddenly my horse reared and headed in the opposite direction. I glanced back to see what had caused this display of temperament. To my delight, I saw an enormous male lion disengaging himself from behind one of the uncompleted bunkers on what today is the Royal Nairobi Golf Club course.

During the day, we spent most of our time on the polo field watching Derek and Francis swearing at the ball. By the end of the first chukka, the onlookers were wreathed in a cloud of red dust. Then everyone would retire to the grand-sounding Nairobi Polo Club, a wooden *banda* with a *makuti* thatched roof, where the ice was always melted and tepid soft drinks or lukewarm tea and coffee were the only options. In spite of the drawbacks, the polo field was obviously the "in place" for the English and Indians. Abdul Gafour Sheik, affectionately known as Gabby and who had studied at the Harvard Business School, played on the Erskine team and was the only member of that side whose voice was never raised. In any case, it would have been hard to hear anything above Derek's consistent bellowing and the thundering hooves echoing like gunshots on the sun-baked earth. Afterwards, everybody would descend on the unfailingly hospitable Erskine household.

I remember one such evening when Elisabeth had just installed a dumb waiter between the kitchen and the upstairs dining room. It was not a particularly large hatchway and worked on a rope pulley. Elisabeth had gone to great lengths to instruct her cook on the use of this new contraption as that night there was to be a big polo dinner.

The first course had come and gone, the cold consommé had been cleared off the table. Then there was a long wait. Occasionally, over the hum of conversation, one could hear in the background the sound of a workman hammering away. Elisabeth was just about to send one of the waiters to see what was happening when, during a sudden lull in conversation, there came a frantic banging from the hatchway. I will never forget the scene when Elisabeth slid the door open. There was her cook, crouched in the dumb waiter like a contortionist, clutching an enormous silver dish containing a large leg of lamb. He had understood he was to accompany the meat and of course had got stuck in the hatch. How he had managed, in such a tiny space, to get both himself and the meat in there was a miracle of ingenuity!

Caryll had by now completed his stint with Bruce and, smelling more of cow than cologne, he went off with Bruce to buy his own dairy herd. His intention was to start farming north of Nairobi, somewhere in the rich Rift Valley, that amazing fault-line that runs through Kenya from north to south. The drive out of Nairobi towards the White Highlands was so beautiful, climbing up into the lush and fertile land that traditionally belonged to the Kikuyu. It is tropical rolling hill country at 7000ft going up to 9000ft and everything is a lush bright green. There is the emerald green of the coffee plantations and the contrasting yellow-green of the tea bushes. Massed everywhere are those typical trees of the Kenya highlands, giant crotons spreading their magnificent branches and dappling this tapestry of greens with deep patches of shade. On clear days, just before the sharp descent into the Rift Valley, you can see in the distance the snow-clad peaks of Kilimanjaro to the south and Mount Kenya to the north. An unforgettable sight. Each time I drove that way, I would stop and gaze with awe.

The steep road down into the Rift, built by Italian prisoners of war, follows old elephant trails. For a long time, it was the only proper road in the whole of the country. Spread out below in the valley is an amazing spectacle of volcanoes, plains and lakes. To the right are the Aberdares, to the left the Mau range and Loita hills. The valley is part of the Red Sea fault and it is easy to imagine how it must have looked as it rose from the sea in a vast spewing forth of volcanic ash so many millions of years ago. Now it is dominated by the extinct volcano Mount Longonot and stretching from it, the great lakes of Naivasha, Elementeita and Nakuru. The valley then teemed with game and the lakes were crimson with the dense flocks of flamingos standing on their shores.

My mother bought Caryll a magnificent piece of land, 12,000 acres in the beautiful Subukia Valley high in the eastern foothills of the Rift and bisected by the equator, for £25,000. He named it Equator Farm and built the most lovely African village-type farmhouse using local materials. Large round huts and square huts of brick covered in clay and with tall thatched roofs were joined together by passages. The outside walls were painted terracotta and most of the inner walls were painted Rory's favourite colour – the pale silvery green of the underside of an olive leaf.

The London decorating firm Colefax and Fowler was given the commission to furnish and decorate Caryll's entire house except for the pieces sent from our various homes in England and France. Years later, I heard that it was one of the most difficult commissions they had ever been given. All the four poster beds and all the wooden furniture had to be treated against white ant; all the light fittings had to have special wiring and plugs and almost everything had to be termite-proofed before being shipped out.

Caryll sent crates of furniture and objets d'art over by sea. Both Caryll and I made a habit of raiding the storage rooms under Fiorentina to furnish our houses in our adult years. They held lovely antique furniture and paintings, ruthlessly turfed out by Rory when he was busy re-doing one of the other houses. Furniture from Lees Place, flats in Paris and numerous houses in the south of France. As well, trunks of my mother's fabulous dresses were contained in these vast storerooms. Later, when Fiorentina was sold by Rory, what remained in the storerooms was left behind for the new owners. When I think of the magnificent pieces, even after our depredations, I could cry. Strangely it was the loss of a beautiful Japanese screen of peonies and birds of paradise and some enormous 18th-century Venetian glass chandeliers with velvet bows and tiers of candles that most upset me.

Caryll's land went from 6000 to 8000 feet, and the escarpment, itself heavily forested, rose to 10,000 feet. I remember very well on one occasion when Caryll, with Mummy, Rory, me and all the luggage on board, made three unsuccessful attempts to clear this escarpment. With the downdraught and a heavily overloaded plane, we didn't make it and had to go all the way around and down the valley. We only just made it to Nairobi for the B.O.A.C. flight to London.

The house had a garden with wonderful indigenous trees and views across the foothills. At the back were the forests and waterfalls, the water cascading over the rocks and falling thousands of feet into the valley below. Towards the top of his wheat and cattle farm, Caryll had cleared some of the trees and planted pyrethrum as a cash crop. It was a beautiful sight with its white flowers against the deep green of the forest. I used to ride up there every day to admire this African garden of Eden. The pyrethrum fields – a powerful herbicide is made from the flower-heads – were at about 7,000 feet and the views from the escarpment, as the dark forested hills gently flowed into the valley below, were breathtaking.

Leaving the clearings behind, I would enter the dense forest undergrowth, so thick in places that I would have to lie over the horse's neck and trust his instinct. We followed the buffalo and elephant trails as they leisurely traversed the steep slopes until eventually arriving at the top of the escarpment. From here, one overlooked the little village of Thomson's Falls. Sometimes on these rides I would come across elephant and even buffalo and very, very occasionally, I would catch sight of that beautiful shy antelope, the forest bongo.

Caryll had married Danièle, whom he had met on a blind date in Paris. She subsequently told me that when he arrived to pick her up, she looked over the staircase to see him standing in the marble hallway and decided he was so glamorous that he was going to be the man she would marry. Her father, Roger Guirche, a very rich industrialist, doted on his tall, blonde and beautiful daughter and at her instigation, after discovering that Caryll would be spending the summer holidays with us, he rented a house in Cap Ferrat. She and her sister used to waterski past Fiorentina every morning. Danièle was not only beautiful but had the most gorgeous figure as well. We would watch these lovely girls as we lay by the swimming pool. Before long, my brother had joined them and then there were three silhouettes skimming across the bay.

Danièle's wedding present from her father was a twin-engined Macchi as he was very concerned about his daughter being flown across the ocean in a single-engined aircraft. As it turned out this new Maachi, which Caryll started flying, had numerous engine failures. Monsieur Guirche's wedding gift turned out to be a potentially lethal acquisition.

CHAPTER

35

Caryll and Danièle soon started a family and had two little girls, Caroline and Juliet and later a son, Rory. We would go out to see them every year and it was during one of these visits, when we were staying with great friends of my mother's, Roy Whittet and his wife up on the Kinangop Plateau, in the White Highlands, that we saw the first signs of the troubles to come. These eventually had their own influence on how my life turned out.

The Whittets had a typical Kenya farmhouse with a magnificent garden. Kenya is a gardener's paradise; every imaginable plant and flower grows in the rich loam soil and gentle climate. The garden, as with so many others, had rich green kikuyu grass lawns, lovely trees and views that stretched to the horizon over lakes and plains. In the distance would always be the blue foothills and mountain ranges that make Kenya so unique. The English *memsahibs* in their cotton dresses and large-brimmed hats, with gloves and wicker baskets, would work away endlessly with the *shamba* boys, recreating the hedges and herbaceous borders that they had left behind in England.

In no time, the roses, hollyhocks and foxgloves would be

overflowing their beds and the exotic jasmine, hoya and petrea would spill their waves of colour and scent, competing with their delicate cousins. Water was never a problem. Great bamboo thickets would be mirrored in the translucent waters of ponds or miniature lakes with streams running through them. Lotus and waterlilies vied for a place and the carp were so tame they would feed from one's hand.

In this extraordinary land of Kenya, the air has its own perfume, a mixture of wood smoke, damp earth and honeysuckle. I remember sitting on the Whittets' verandah watching the sun setting; the sky bright red and outlining in black the towering hills and the lacy fretwork of the acacia trees. The sweet scent of jasmine lay heavy on the evening air and I can still hear Roy talking to Mummy as he sat with his sundowner in one hand and his pipe in the other, the typical English colonel with his sandy hair and military moustache.

Over the clink of ice rolling around in his glass, I heard him questioning the new attitudes of his staff and the surliness of the Africans in Fort Hall where he went for his shopping. Nobody at the time realised the significance of these idle remarks, but the build-up of resentment felt by the African towards the settler was the first rumblings of what was to become known as the Mau Mau rebellion.

Violence – of any kind – was far from everyone's mind as Roy Whittet's manservant arrived in his starched long white kanzu, red cummerbund and fez with its large black tassel almost swinging into his eye. He bent over Roy, announcing in the most English of accents, that, "Dinner is served."

We were enjoying the large freshly caught grilled trout when the well-ordered existence of colonial English life in the highlands was shattered by the trumpeting screams of an enraged elephant. Everyone left the table, dashing out to see what the noise was about. To my great delight and Mrs Whittet's total despair, we saw a huge herd of elephant charging through her immaculate garden and beyond. One of them had possibly been wounded by a poacher's arrow and it was a very agitated herd that was trampling down the fences and invading the beautifully mown lawn.

It was full moon and the massive shapes appeared out of the darkness, a bull bellowing his defiance, his trunk raised, as the cows and little calves lumbered by, the white of their tusks clearly visible in the moonlight. They came so close one could almost feel their fear and confusion. I was tempted to reach out from where we stood on the terrace to touch them and give comfort. The feeling was so strong I had to clasp my hands together to prevent such a foolhardy impulse.

Afterwards came the silence. Tikki, Mummy's tree hyrax, which had draped itself around her neck, broke the lull with his usual loud croak. This sound, like a rusty hinged door, was the prelude to a resumption of the usual sounds of nightfall, the shriek of the nightjars, the somnolent sound of cicadas, the croaking of the frogs.

The scene of primeval beauty might never have been, so quickly had this large herd arrived only to disappear into the deep shadows of the trees. It all seemed to have passed in a dream. This again was Kenya and the unexpected was one's constant companion. Only in the light of next day when I saw the destruction the elephants had left in their wake did I truly take in what I had been privileged to witness.

It was 1952 and we were back at Fiorentina when we heard that the Mau Mau rebellion against British and colonial rule had begun. A state of emergency was declared. The rebellion petered out four years later and by the time the emergency was officially over in 1960, 11,000 rebels were dead. It had killed less than 100 whites and that included 63 soldiers, and 2000 loyal Kikuyus, many of whom were tortured and buried alive. Even I, on one of my many journeys, had come across this gruesome sight. The victims would have been buried head-first in ant-bear holes and, although we would dig frantically, they had obviously suffocated long before we arrived on the scene. (Mau Mau, strictly speaking, was a schism in the Kikuyu tribe.)

Jomo Kenyatta was imprisoned, supposedly as the leader of Mau Mau, an allegation that he always denied. He admitted he was head of the Kenya African Union for African freedom but not Mau Mau. I, who knew Mr Kenyatta, had only the greatest of admiration for him and he later proved, as leader of Kenya 10 years after his imprisonment in the remote north in 1953, that he was a man of infinite compassion. I don't believe he could ever have been party to the bloody and dreadful oaths that were required of the loyal supporters of Mau Mau. The sight of poor disembowelled cats hanging on a doorstep and hamstrung cattle, which would have to be despatched with a bullet after one of their raids, was enough to sicken anyone, let alone their indiscriminate killing and torturing of men, women and children who either resisted or were suspected of not being sympathisers.

Derek and Elisabeth were great supporters of Kenyatta and gave a home to his children during his time in jail. Kenyatta's children were treated as honoured guests while the white settlers were either being killed or were out fighting the Mau Mau. Very soon, Derek's friendship with the imprisoned Kenyatta and his family had him practically ostracised.

Francis, small and fair like all the Erskine children, having been brought up with the Kikuyu, was fluent in their language. With one of his Kikuyu friends, he went off into the forests to join the pseudo-gangs which operated with the authorities and pretended to be Mau Mau so they could infiltrate or gather information. The pseudo-gangs were very successful. One famous account of Francis's activities was that when the time came for his gang to attack the settlers or the loyal Kikuyu (of which there were a vast number), Francis, dressed in old torn clothing tied with string, his face blackened and an old hat pulled low over his head, would suddenly spring to his feet and, producing a machine gun, mow the gang down. He saved the lives of many whites as well as Kikuyu.

Francis, like his father, was a dreamer. He loved the land of his birth, his friends were the Africans and he too was fighting for Kenya's independence from colonial domination. But Mau Mau to him was an anathema, destroying the principles of freedom of choice and he chose to oppose it the best way he knew how. The bravery that Francis and his friends displayed was quite exceptional. Even more remarkable was the fact that Francis was so fair, thereby increasing enormously his risk of discovery.

The Erskines were a truly remarkable family. That Derek and Elisabeth were great Kenyatta supporters and that their son was an arch Mau Mau hunter never fazed this wonderful family. During his numerous visits home, Francis would be greeted as if he had just returned from a holiday on the French Riviera.

I met Francis again towards the end of the worst of the Mau Mau and by then the work of pseudo-gangs like his had been brought under the strict military control of General Sir George Erskine, a distant relation of Derek's. From then on, Francis's activities were curtailed. Although thin, Francis was very strong and seemed to have taken on most of the mannerisms of a terrorist. I couldn't believe the change in him. He had always been wild but the handsome young man with the lovely blue eyes and vivacious Erskine charm had vanished. Francis, like all those who operate under cover of darkness, had bloodshot eyes that darted restlessly around the room, never focussing on anything. Instead, he was continually on the alert, searching for some unseen enemy. He was also decidedly jumpy as if the constrictions of being in a house were unbearable. Never sitting still for long, he would pace up and down like an animal on the prowl. Even his speech seemed to be affected and when he did speak, it was so fast that most of what he had to say was unintelligible. During this period I saw a couple of Mau Mau terrorists and they also had the same bloodshot wild eyes.

The next time we went out to Kenya, Caryll was busy hunting Mau Mau himself. He had command of the Subukia area as an assistant district commandant in the Kenya Police Reserve and was giving all his Africans the benefit of his Grenadier Guards training. At one stage, Caryll had been schooled in tropical warfare because of the war against Japan and the authorities thought that experience should now be put to use. As far as I could see his men were marched around endlessly in terribly smart formations. Caryll, a crack shot, was also instructing them in the use of rifles instead of *pangas* (machetes). Targets were put up all over the place and it was worth more than one's life to appear within gunshot range of the farm. Mummy and I would practically arrive with white flags flying from every window of the car whenever we gathered up sufficient courage to visit.

At dinner, the table would have guns decorating every place setting like Christmas crackers. Caryll would sit opposite the door with a Beretta sub-machine gun. Under his bed, he kept a box of 36 grenades. I think he secretly longed for something to happen. The Mau Mau's big ploy was to burst into a room behind the servants who had sworn their oath and take the owners by surprise. When Caryll and his men were not drilling, they were charging up and down the escarpment. The thick forest was a great hiding place for the gangs and on one occasion when we were there, they chased after fleeing Mau Mau three times in the one day. Each pursuit involved a climb of several thousand feet.

The Mau Mau would wear monkey furs and headgear made out of the colobus monkey, and their faces would be bearded. If they had guns, they were simple and not very effective, my brother remembers.

We were all highly amused when, months later, Caryll discovered that his vegetable garden on the edge of a forest belt had been one of the places the terrorist gangs had hidden in at night. It was just 15 yards from where Caryll, his family and friends had dinner. They had quite rightly felt that the safest place to be was in the middle of Lord Waterpark's arsenal. (Caryll had inherited the title in 1948 on the death of Daddy's elder brother, mad Uncle Harry.) During a thorough search of the garden, we came across a waxen effigy of Mummy made from a melted candle; it had pieces of her hair and even nail parings which must have been gathered by the household staff.

After independence, Derek Erskine received a knighthood and his friend Mr Kenyatta became President after having first served as prime minister. We were with the Erskines prior to this when Derek decided to dine at the Muthaiga Country Club which in spite of its reputation for hi-jinks and anything goes was still the bastion of colonial imperialism. He warned everyone that in all probability the die-hard section of the white community would walk out at his entrance and there was a possibility that all of us might be asked to leave. As it turned out no such drastic measures were taken. It's true though that a great many of his friends at the club disappeared on urgent business, thereby avoiding having to acknowledge him.

Our visits to Kenya were regular but fleeting during this period and we would probably have continued indefinitely in this *va et viens* way, but an event took place that was soon to change my life.

CHAPTER

36

During one of these visits to Kenya I had met a friend of Danièle's called Pierre d'Unienville. He was Mauritian, tall, fit and with a lot of superficial charm. I suppose his attentions soothed my battered ego after Aymon's departure. On this occasion I had gone ahead of Mummy as I was going to stay with Pierre at his house in Langata, on the southern outskirts of Nairobi and near Nairobi National Park. Pierre was a tour guide and also very conceited, forever looking at himself in the mirror. Like so many weak characters, he had a surface bravado. I think I can honestly say he was the only man I ever had an affair with for whom I had no admiration.

Pierre came to meet me at the airport. Tucked under his arm was a tiny little fluffy cat, its eyes not even open. As we walked to the car, he handed it to me and said, "Darling, this is a present for you." She had been found next to a dead lioness in the Tana River country to the east. The little lion cub was so small she fitted into the palm of my hand. Giving her the name of Tana, I took her home.

For the next seven years she would become the axis of my life, the object of so much of my love, the cause of so many tears. Until the day I die, she will be part of me. A lion is the symbol of courage, the emblem of England, the hero of tribal folklore. The early British explorers referred to them, not as a herd or a group but as a pride. My great golden lioness was my Africa. She was my constant companion for many years, sharing my days and my sleep at night. She saved my life, she made me part of her world. She shared with me the freedom of her life just as she readily accepted the restrictions of mine. Tana became the reason for my life in Africa and through her I became involved with all the animals of the wild.

Pierre had arranged for me to stay with him in a house he had rented. As usual, my dogs slept on the bed having come with me on the flight from Rome, and so did the minute lioness. I hardly slept that night, I was so worried that I might roll on her in my sleep. Kenya nights are cold and I had a leopardskin coat that my mother had given me when I was 21. In those days, there was no consciousness of the horror of furs. Although I would never wear it now, I still have that coat, still in wonderful condition after all these years. I look at it every day and it brings back such wonderful memories of Tana. It was this fur that I used as a rug at night-time and Tana was brought up on it.

It was almost dawn when I felt a little warm trickle. Her wee had come through the thick fur and onto me. Used to house-training all the dogs, I felt we must start the way we wished to continue. Rubbing her nose in it and administering a sharp slap to her backside, I took her out in the garden which was heavy with dew and cold on my bare feet. This of course continued for several days and nights and a great fuss was made of her when she condescended to piddle in the flower bed. It was not long before the penny dropped and from that day on, she never ever made a mess in the house again.

I soon realised I was now responsible for a very special being. At first she was more difficult to train than my puppies had been. Tana did not grasp the idea of following and kept going off at a tangent, but as she grew older, she started to consider herself one of the dogs. Then, like her canine companions, she would heel beautifully. By the time she was three months old she was already quite strong and Duke the Alsatian, whom she adored, would have to give her a sharp reminder as to who was boss. She was wonderfully affectionate; if I was lying in bed, she would drape herself over my chest and rub her little head under my chin.

When my mother came out to Kenya, I discussed the problem of Tana with her. What were we to do? The answer changed everything. Tana did not like Pierre and I felt he was too irresponsible to be in charge of any animal, let alone a lion cub. He just liked the glamour of being seen with her and accepting the admiration of his friends. I loved her too much to now abandon her to his tender mercies. My mother, being the angel she always was to her children, had the idea that I should stay in Kenya and bring up Tana myself.

We were soon house-hunting for my little lion. It had to be a very special place, far enough away from Nairobi but not too far away from the shops. Eventually we found just what we were looking for. It was a house on the Ololua Ridge at Karen, about half an hour's drive from Nairobi, called Ol Orion. It belonged to the widow of a settler, Jenny Homewood. Ol Orion was a typical Kenya bungalow, with a shingle roof, leaded diamond-paned windows, verandahs, lots of rooms and above all a wonderful garden. The 25-acre property bordered the Ngong Hills and nature reserve. There were only three other houses on the ridge and they were far away. In front, it was all Masai reserve – the Masai cattle-farmers being one of Kenya's most striking, proud and fierce tribes – and behind was thick indigenous forest going down to a stream.

Ol Orion was a dream come true. I fell in love with it as we entered the wonderful drive with its towering bougainvillaea hedges, at the top of which was an enormous datura tree in full bloom. The house was hidden behind the hedges but I can still remember the feeling of enchantment, as if I had walked into a fairytale and was about to awaken the sleeping princess. The mullioned windows glowed in the afternoon sun, great flat-topped acacias and wild olive trees spread their boughs over the immaculate lawns. The perimeter was a mass of colour from the herbaceous borders going down to a ha-ha and beyond was the wonderful deep blue of the Ngong hills. I was standing in an English garden with all of Africa spread before me. It was almost the same view that Karen Blixen so lovingly described in *Out of Africa* and the area, Karen, was named after her. With binoculars, one could see the grave of her lover, the hunter Denys Finch Hatton, on the lower ridges of the Ngongs. As Tana grew up, she would wander off there and lie up under its shadow.

Jenny Homewood was a marvellously gentle lady who became a great friend of my mother. After Mummy bought her home, she stayed on with us for a while. Her husband had died and she wanted to return to England but she loved this garden that she had worked on for so many years and created out of the bush. She had planted jacaranda in front of the natural forest and the bright blue against the dark green was breathtaking.

Mummy bought Ol Orion for £10,000 for myself and Tana and she spent her winters with us. She and Rory went through the basements at Fiorentina and sent out enough furniture for a five-bedroomed house. Once she returned to Karen, my beautiful mother spent hours of each day at the top of a ladder as she marbled the entire dining room, the walls as well as the table, in soft grey. The curtains were Colefax and Fowler, heavy glazed chintz of large pink cabbage roses and tied back with ornate sashes and big grey silk tassels. The chairs were Chinese Chippendale. At night with the lovely Sèvres china, the Cavendish silver and the centrepiece, a huge ornate silver bowl of roses and Queen Anne lace, it really looked too beautiful.

My mother would sit at the head of the table in very *décolleté* lace evening dresses, usually in shades of white, grey or pastel to complement the room. Sometimes she would combine both and wear a deep rose-red underdress, with either a white or grey lace top. Mummy invariably changed for dinner and if there was an attractive male guest, the décolletage would become daringly low. She had a marvellous neck and bosom and was never loath to show as much as was permissible. The Venetian chandelier, with its many-tiered crystal drops vied for attention, but eyes were continually drawn to this incredible beauty who would sit like a snow queen in her diamonds and laces amongst us mere mortals.

Ol Orion might have had five bedrooms but that never seemed enough. We added on two guest cottages, rondavels with thatched roofs, double bedrooms and bathrooms. Mummy's family also came out from Australia for visits and there were always guests, dinners and bridge during Mummy's stays. I also had my dogs and people, knowing how much I loved and cared about animals, soon started giving me other wildlife to look after. My household grew.

Pierre d'Unienville used to take out photographic safaris but after one or two I refused to go with him: like all vainglorious men he was foolhardy and although not a brave man he would take incredible risks through stupidity and ignorance. He was a rally driver and we planned the East African Safari Rally together, 3000 miles around east Africa and the toughest rally in the world they say. I did the reconnaissance, going around the circuit and marking the speed at which each corner could be taken when Pierre eventually drove it. He was fun, good-looking and drove superbly but I had no respect for him. When I found out, after we all moved into Ol Orion, that he was telling his friends that it was his house and that my mother and I were his guests, I had had enough. We remained friends and I used to see him from time to time but he ceased to be part of my life.

When Tana was about five months old, a film company arrived in Nairobi to make a film for which they required the services of a male lion. They had imported a big black-maned lion and his trainer from Hollywood. One day, I went to the New Stanley hotel for lunch, having parked Tana and the dogs under the shade of a tree. The first sight that greeted me as I walked into the lobby was a gentleman emerging from the lift, accompanied by an enormous lion in a harness and lead. Thrilled, I went over to talk to him and told him of my lioness cub. He had told his lion to sit which he was doing quite perfectly, only giving an enormous yawn now and again, as if totally bored. I noticed that he had no claws and asked the trainer about this. He explained that the claws on a lion can be lethal and that as a precaution he had had them removed. I later had the harness copied for Tana but of course I never had her de-clawed; she was always so perfectly behaved it wasn't necessary and even if it had been I would never have done so.

A few weeks had gone by when I received a telephone call from the lion trainer. He was in town and would like to come and see my cub. He spent most of the day with me and was fascinating about his job training wild animals for the films. I owe him a great debt for he was instrumental in helping me understand the nature of the wild animals that have since filled my life.

He was most impressed by Tana's gentle nature, for even at this early stage she had never spat or tried to claw in aggression. She had been brought up on my bed with the dogs as part of the family and was house-trained accordingly. He explained to me that a lion is a killer. "You are dealing with a deadly weapon and you must respect it as such," he said. "Remember, never look a wild animal in the eye. To do so is an incentive to fight. Eye contact in the animal kingdom is a challenge." (I have found this to be so true and have often seen Buster, my male baboon, enraged by eye contact when I've forgotten to warn my visiting friends.)

Then he gave me these rules. "Never let her bring her claws out, never let her become possessive of her food, never put yourself in an inferior position. You must always be the leader, the matriarch and always command respect. Remember, she must be punished for any infractions of the rules you have set. A lioness will give her recalcitrant offspring a swipe. Never hit twice as that is not punishment but an incentive to fight. All correction of animals must be administered at the time, not five minutes later. One of the most important things to remember is that animals, especially wild ones, are sensitive to human emotions. Aggressive and moody people should never have dealings with wild animals, though unfortunately they often do."

He also explained that animals, like humans, all have different characteristics and the handling they receive when they are young will set the pattern for their future. He said I was lucky that Tana had an exceptionally large head and was very wide between the eyes. Narrow heads and eyes set close denote a mean disposition in lion.

Armed with this invaluable advice, a lot of which I already knew from all my other dealings with our family's animals, I set about training Tana. The first thing I stopped was the romping around. Before his visit, I used to roll about on the floor, playing rather rough games with her. This now ceased and if she ever became too rough with the dogs, I would give her a smack and firmly say "No!" at the same time. As she grew older, she became so muscled that it was like smacking a ton of concrete so if I had no stick handy, I would hit her between the eyes with my balled-up fist. This invariably hurt me a great deal more than it did her. She was, in fact, so extraordinarily well-behaved that as she grew older she almost never put a foot wrong. Tana only had one hang-up; she liked killing chickens. I think it was all the clucking and the feathers flying that she enjoyed for she never ate them.

It was easy to tell when Tana had misbehaved as she would approach very sheepishly with her face all screwed up, anticipating her punishment. Invariably it was a chicken that had crossed her path. Then I would go on a hunt until I found the evidence. Picking up the carcass I would return and find Tana who by this time would be hiding from me. I would rub her face with the remains of the bird and give her a smack at the same time.

After Tana had been weaned from the bottle, her food consisted of about six kilograms of meat a day, cut into small chunks, but I always added two litres of milk to the beef and this mixture would be put in a large bowl. I fed her once a day with the dogs at 6.30am, doing it at that time because I had no intention of getting up half the night to let them out to make their poos. Tana had her lavatory just outside my bedroom window, in the herbaceous border which was soon flattened. Just like a cat, she would loosen the soil and then squat, with only her ears visible above the hollyhocks. Having finished, she would cover it up with soil. I became so used to the smell that I never noticed it but friends and visitors remarked, that on a hot day, my bedroom smelled like London Zoo.

To prevent Tana becoming possessive of her food, I always used to put my hand in her bowl while she ate. This became such a habit that if I ever forgot, she would wait, even allowing the dogs to take the food from her. On one occasion while I was feeding her, the telephone rang, so picking up her bowl I took it along the corridor with me. I put the bowl down by the telephone and stood with my foot in it, while chatting away. Suddenly, I felt my toe go into her mouth and before I could move her teeth had started to close. She realised at the same time as I did that a terrible mistake had occurred and let go, thank goodness. Instead of being minus a toe, there was only a large and rather bloody scratch. She had leapt away in horror when I shouted and I had to leave the telephone to pacify her, telling her what a darling girl she was and kissing her all over, while my toe left bloody tracks all over the floor.

Tana was such an extraordinarily affectionate animal. She would always stand leaning heavily against me or, rubbing her large body around my legs, she would place her enormous head under my chin and gaze adoringly at me. Taking whatever part of her I could reach into my arms, I would cover her face with kisses and she would purr with delight. She used to love lying on her back while I was reading, and with my bare feet I would stroke her stomach. She would lie for hours like this, her eyes closed in ecstasy. At night she shared my bed with the dogs and as she grew bigger she took up more than half the bed, her head on my pillow, her soft breath in my ear. She was my comfort, my friend and my companion. With her I shared my life and my secrets. She came to know my every mood and she also knew the depth of my love for her. As she matured, we shared an extraordinary degree of mental telepathy. I do not know how else to describe it; I did not even have to be in the same room with Tana and I could share her feelings. This amazing degree of communication is what one day saved my life.

When fully grown, Tana was on seven kilograms of meat a day in two litres of milk. With all this good food and calcium, she had developed into the most enormous lioness but she still retained her incredibly sweet nature. Unlike Joy Adamson's Elsa of *Born Free* fame who was always leaving Joy rather battle-scarred, Tana, apart from that one tooth mark on my toe, never again gave me so much as a scratch. Like the dogs, she followed me around and either sat beside my chair or under the table at mealtimes. I also taught her that when she came into a room and strangers were there, she was to lie down. I considered that visitors and guests would be less nervous if they saw a recumbent figure instead of a gigantic prowling lioness.

Just by Ol Orion's front porch was a large and beautiful Cape chestnut tree. In the long hot days of summer, Tana would jump into the tree, then lie astride the shingled roof under the shade of its branches. Even as a cub she had taken to tree climbing after following my chimp Joseph one day. After that, the roof became her favourite siesta area and it gave her an outstanding view of the countryside. It soon became a familiar sight to us all, this great lioness lying asleep on the roof, her tail hanging down and occasionally swishing as she dreamed away the long summer afternoons.

CHAPTER

37

Not long after I was given Tana, I also acquired Joseph, a baby chimpanzee, named after Joseph in the bible. He had been rescued from a village in what was then the Belgian Congo. The poor little mite had been tied to a tree by his waist and the rope marks had left open and bleeding wounds. He was half-starved and terrified, his cuts suppurating, and so bundling all the animals into the car, we went off to see my local doctor, William Boyle. It's been written that chimpanzees are only 1.6 per cent genetically removed from a human and these primates also have many of the human diseases, so I decided there would be nothing but the best for my little Joseph and Dr Boyle was the best. Not only was he a wonderful doctor, he was a great family friend. He was round-faced with grey hair for he must have been in his fifties then and spoke with a very English accent.

For Joseph's first visit to the surgery, I put him in a *kikapu*, a large basket with a lid, from which I was terrified he might escape. When the nurse eventually came to call me from the waiting room, I rushed into William's office, closing and locking the door behind me. William in his white coat rose from behind his immaculate desk and said, "Good

God, Pat. What are you about to unleash on me now? Whatever it is, I don't want it." He was eyeing with trepidation the basket which I had dumped on his desk, especially as it was starting to sway. I said, "I have brought you my baby", and I produced this almost hairless little creature covered in sores and dried blood.

Being blessed with very good health, it was seldom that I required William's services myself but Mummy was a patient of his for years. He always treated her with great tenderness, a side of his character he never displayed towards me. I received the lectures. During Joseph's infancy we had to pay William many visits and climbing the stairs to his surgery became a familiar occurrence. Joseph had to have all the childhood inoculations and he was forever getting temperatures and colds, so I was always in a panic. After his first visit in a basket, he used to climb the stairs sitting on my head. As he grew older, he would climb the stairs holding my hand and, like all well-behaved children, he would sit in the waiting room on my lap. He would fix his eyes on the surgery door where he knew there was a large glass bottle of jellybeans waiting on William's desk. Joseph came to associate visits to a doctor with this jar of untold delight. William would feed him jellybeans one at a time and Joseph's big mouth would pout. He would give his "OOH-OOH" of delight and then, holding out his arms like a child, would go to William and cling around his neck as he reached for more.

Poor little Joseph. It took me weeks to overcome his initial fear of the human race and in his terror he bit me every single day. It was usually on my right hand which became swollen and difficult to use. His bites, although they hardly broke the skin, caused deep bruising. I never scolded him for this as it was done in fright and I was determined to gain his confidence and trust. Of course, later on when he was completely adjusted to life at Ol Orion and had lost all his fear, I would give him a smack on his backside if he ever did anything I judged warranted it. In his case it was usually for crapping in the house and just as Tana would wrinkle up her face when she had done wrong, Joseph would come into the room with his hand over his bottom.

When Joseph did make a mess, he would rush to get a newspaper to pick it up. Of course he was not very successful and so instead of his poo being in one place, it would soon be scattered over the floor. To add to the mess, he would move on to stage two, which involved getting a cloth from the kitchen. With a look of great concentration on his face, he would diligently and happily rub away in ever-increasing circles. By the time he was bored with this, large areas would be spread with chimp crap. There was nothing I could do about it except watch in great amusement and rush to remove the carpet.

He was the most affectionate, brilliantly clever animal, totally human in his characteristics and understanding. Once he gave me his trust, he never bit again. He had nearly all his meals with me. Only in the evening would he eat in the kitchen as I put him to bed before it got dark. He used to drink out of the beautiful Sèvres china cups and was very careful of everything. One day as I was clearing up after a visit, having picked up some dirty glasses in the sitting room, I tripped over the edge of the carpet. One of the glasses fell from my hand but Joseph, who was walking beside me hanging onto my skirt, recovered it before it could hit the floor. He then handed it back to me. I was continually amazed by his intelligence. One could teach him almost everything. It was just that his powers of concentration were limited and like a child he would get bored quickly.

He adored people, especially children. He was a great show-off and always wanted to be the centre of attention. I could never leave him parked in a car without him waving his hands out of the window. Having succeeded in capturing the passing crowd, he would entertain them by standing on his head, doing somersaults or anything else he could possibly think of to keep them amused.

At the time I got Joseph, I employed a young man of 16 called Kimoyo to be full-time nanny and playmate to him. He could have been an African twin of Antony Armstrong-Jones, Princess Margaret's former husband, having the same shaped mouth and teeth and even the same height and build. We nicknamed him Tony Jones and he was marvellous with Joseph. It was common to see Kimoyo pedalling his bike with Joseph sitting on the seat holding him by his shorts. They used to go all over the place and down to the *dukas* at Karen with Joseph waving to passers-by.

When I first had him, I put him in a wooden cot beside my pillow at night so that I could sleep with one hand over him. I feel that one of the great measures in bonding with animals is to have them as close to one as possible at night. All animals, unless they are nocturnal, cling to their mothers through the hours of darkness and sleep. I am convinced this is the best time for them to build up their feeling of security and one can more easily convey then the love and protection that is necessary for a young and disorientated animal.

I couldn't have Joseph in the bed though in case Tana should lie on him. She was already quite large – eventually she weighed almost 400lbs. The closest I could get to her weight was on my bathroom scales. I would heave her front part on and weigh that, then the back half, and add the two together. It was never very successful, but it was a lot of fun and the dogs thought it was hilarious.

CHAPTER

38

Pierre had long ago departed with another girlfriend and life was wonderfully uncomplicated without any man around. The animals had become part of my family and I was much too busy with them to want the complications of another romance. Once again, I was perfectly happy and my mother and Rory spent a great deal of time with me.

I couldn't travel to France any more because of Tana and so they came to Karen instead. We would do our own little safaris. As long as one was prepared to drive long distances, there were marvellous lodges and tented camps to go to in the more popular areas. I had a Land Rover and we would fairly frequently go south to the Ngorongoro crater in what was then Tanganyika, now Tanzania. It was huge, and dense with game because it was like a lush green haven contained between high walls. Leopards, lion, wildebeest, zebras, gazelles, buffalo, baboons, monkeys, in fact almost every animal except giraffe. We would spend a night at Arusha on the way. I would bring along my animals and my mother invariably had Tikki plus her new acquisition, a mongoose she had rescued from the side of the road where it had been run over. Nursed back to health, it remained with her for years, eventually accompanying her here to where I now live in South Africa.

When my mother was at the racecourse, she would leave the mongoose on its collar and lead with the ladies' cloakroom attendant. The cloakroom lady came up to me once, unrecognisable now with age, and said that looking after Mummy's animal made her day. Very sweetly she said to me, "It used to make me feel so important."

On one of these safaris, I think at Manyara across the Tanganyikan border, a lioness jumped onto the roof of the Land Rover. She was probably after a bushbuck that I had rescued which was lying on the open front seat beside me while Mummy and Rory with their cameras were on the seat behind. As soon as the lioness landed, I skidded the car around a low hanging tree to brush her off before she could grab my poor wounded buck.

On another occasion, we were photographing a pride of lion when two of them ambled towards the car. The next thing they were using my front mudguard as a scratching post. So violently were they trying to get rid of their itch that before I could move away the whole thing was completely buckled and bent. Mummy and Rory were sanguine. Life with me was always going to be life with animals too.

A cheetah, Duma, had now been added to my menagerie at Ol Orion, fully grown and in appalling condition. She had been chained in someone's backyard and almost starved to death. When I found her, she was skin and bone and covered in sores. The fleas sat on her in clouds. The first day I went to feed her, she was so hungry for the food I was bringing that she swiped at my hand as well, opening it to the bone. As usual it was the right hand and required a visit to Dr Boyle. My hand was pouring blood so I wrapped it in a towel and drove myself off to town.

I was shown in fairly quickly as I was making a mess of the waiting room. William's language was choice as usual so I had to remind him that I was probably bleeding to death. "Possibly, but now that you are here, unlikely!" said my solicitous doctor. I was laughing so much from having to put up with his nonsense that I hardly noticed the stitches going in. The cheetah's claw marks are the only lasting scar I bear today from all those years with the many animals of Kenya.

I had quite a few more animal sessions with William. One was a Sykes' white-ruffed and chestnut-saddled monkey that someone had rescued. Now that I had a house of my own, I seemed somehow or other to have become a collecting point for unwanted or injured animals. It happened so gradually that I hardly realised how involved I had become. I wrapped the monkey in a baby blanket, fed it glucose water and put it on antibiotics to tide it over until I could get it to William in the morning. It was so ill during the night that I had to walk up and down my bedroom cradling it in my arms. It was the only thing that seemed to keep it quiet. The other animals watched this performance with sheer disgust. At about two in the morning, it started convulsing and during its last convulsion bit me through my thumb and died. I had to prise its jaw open to get my thumb out.

I covered the wound with that good old stand-by Mercurochrome and went to bed. Next morning, the thumb was very hot and swollen and my arm was aching. For once William was not his usual cheerful self. He was worried the monkey might have been rabid. I hadn't considered this possibility but the monkey had to be sent to the laboratory at Makerere College in Kampala for the brains to be analysed. William warned me not to be far away from a telephone until he had the results back. Looking at me over his glasses he said, "Pat, for once try and behave in a sensible fashion and do not go haring round the countryside until I know what caused the monkey's death. There is always the possibility that you also could be infected." I was lucky though. The monkey bite left me with a septic thumb but no dire disease.

Apart from Tana, Joseph and Duma, the cheetah, I had a baboon named Jason who had been rescued from a tree in Arusha, several vervet monkeys, two Sykes' monkeys and a very rare owl-faced monkey from the Congo. A bushbuck, two baby warthogs, two genet cats and two crowned cranes used to wander around the garden. Unfortunately one of the cranes was killed by Duma who, unlike Tana, was never very trustworthy with other animals. Her terrible upbringing meant that it took her a long time to adjust to life on the farm. As well as the wild animals, there were my five precious Bahamian wild dogs and also the two poodles Minou and Minette, Panya the Pug and Duke the Alsatian. Afterwards I rescued an

Alsatian bitch that I called Duchess. All the domestic animals were neutered including the various cats.

There were so many dogs that my mother decided to send out Miss Lane who was still with her. She was given her own cottage on the farm and saw to all the feeding and grooming. It was lovely having her, this familiar figure from my childhood. When she had first arrived at Burrough Court as assistant lady's maid, she had been a pretty young woman with large brown eyes and curly hair. She soon graduated to looking after all my mother's wild pets and canines. I remembered her walking the lanes of Leicestershire with packs of dogs because Furness did not like them going into the fields amongst the cattle and horses. Now she was grey and rather bent. A chain-smoker, she always had a cigarette in her mouth and my mother was always telling her off for it. Lane would just laugh and cough away. In Kenya, she would insist on still helping with my mother's clothes but as Mummy said, she would much prefer she did not. She would say, "Lane, you look like a dog, smell like a dog and have less sense. They at least don't smoke and put cigarette ash all over my clothes."

Lane was forever fussing over Mummy as if she were some recalcitrant child. She would bang open her door in the morning – nothing was ever done quietly while she was around – and I would hear her voice lecturing Mummy. "Look at you my lady, you haven't slept all night. If you go on like this, it will be the death of you and then where will we all be? Look at the mess, paint all over those good sheets. I have brought your breakfast, you must eat it this morning, not just pick at it." And my mother would reply, "I am likely to live a great deal longer than you and Miss Pat with all those bloody cigarettes you smoke and do mind the tray, you are dropping all that filthy ash on it."

"My lady," Lane would retort, "I am not listening to you when you use all those dreadful words."

Lane was very religious and highly disapproved of bad language, so my mother used to say something shocking every now and again, winking at me as she did and giggling when she saw Lane's face.

Joseph was now Mummy's constant companion. He used to paint with her and when she left to go back to Europe for the summer, he sat at my desk and used crayons to draw away. At one time, I had a suitcase full of his paintings, some of them with great splashes of colour and quite beautiful. When Mummy started to marble the dining room, he would lean over the back of her chair, his gorgeous little hairy arms clasped around her neck, his head cuddled up close to hers as he watched, fascinated by her efforts with the brushes and the cottonwool. Otherwise he would sit on the floor with large sheets of paper and his box of paints and crayons, scribbling away. Whenever he got bored he would disappear through the window and go and play with his bicycle or in the garden with his nanny Kimoyo.

He was so tame that the tiniest child could be entrusted to his care. They would go to the sandpit and play with buckets and spades or use the swing that I had made for my nieces. I used to love watching the happy and intent faces and the childish voices as they sang to him or took him to dance around one of the trees; my own beloved child amongst all these conventional east African children.

Tana, at these times, would have to be shut away as she loathed children and could not be trusted with them. I would lock her in the bedroom with the dogs. I am sure that like all the large cat family – Duma the cheetah was the same – she hated the quick movements and childish voices. It was difficult to explain to a group of children that in the presence of lion, they must not run, jump, scream or cry. Therefore, children as a rule were discouraged from coming to Ol Orion.

Chimpanzees on the other hand adore children. Joseph would happily spend all day playing and was never more content than when surrounded by screaming kids. My nieces, Caroline and Juliet, used to tell me that the highlight of their trips to see me was being able to play with Joseph. Caroline remembers being woken for early-morning tea; 6am chai was an essential part of life to all the white settlers. There would be the knock on the door and then the tray brought in by Kimoyo with Joseph hanging onto his kanzu. Joseph, as soon as he saw my two nieces, would leap onto their beds and give them hugs and kisses. Then their day would start with Joseph as their constant escort.

It was a beautiful sight, the two very blonde children and the hairy black chimp. By this time, Joseph's coat was silky and very shiny, a sure indication of a healthy and happy primate. He seemed to know that with my nieces he had to be very gentle. They never played rough games and I could leave them unsupervised knowing he would take care of them. All my family had the greatest confidence in him and Mummy, Caryll, Danièle and I could go to Karen, leaving the cook Mutete in charge and the children playing happily in the garden with Joseph and Kimoyo. The one fear Danièle had about her precious babies was snakes, but I assured her that Joseph was fully aware of the dangers and he would scream and alert everyone and drag the children away before they came to harm. Being a wild animal, he would notice things long before we, the domesticated variety, did.

He was such a loving extrovert child that as soon as he heard a car coming up the drive, he would rush to meet it and, climbing in through the window before the car had even come to a standstill, would put his arms round one's neck and smother one in kisses. Unsuspecting visitors used to be either horror-struck or delighted, depending on their love of animals.

Hilary Ruben, who writes children's stories of life in Kenya, said that when she went to one of Mummy's first lunch parties at Ol Orion, she was warned that my chimpanzee and a lioness were bound to be there. In two minds as to whether to accept the invitation, she was finally persuaded by her husband Monty who assured her that they would sit miles away from the animals. It was a buffet in the enclosed garden and they made sure to remain at the opposite end of the lawn to me. The animals remained down my side and she breathed a sigh of relief when it finally came time to leave. Having made a wide detour to avoid approaching me, they went to say goodbye to Mummy at the front door. Hilary, thinking she would be in the safety of her car in just a few seconds, was suddenly confronted by the chimpanzee who leapt into her arms to kiss her goodbye. She says it was one of the most horrible experiences of her life. Hilary later became one of my great friends and was in the end quite blasé about chimps and lions.

CHAPTER
——
39

On this occasion, my mother had been with me about six months and Rory, who had departed much earlier, was getting very impatient and wanted her back at Fiorentina. I used to dread her departures, not only because of my loss but for the chaos I knew it would entail. When travelling, Mummy always arranged for a wheelchair. She had a reason, because of what she had done to her back horseriding, but it was only when travelling that she used it as an excuse. Being in a wheelchair meant she could keep her animals Tikki and Minnie the mongoose well hidden. They were in a bag that she carried on her lap. She was also able to load herself with handbags, jewel boxes and a vanity case. Apart from this, there were her dogs and the pyramid of suitcases.

The panic would start with the rush to the airport as she was never on time. I would have to drive like a maniac so everyone's nerves would be frayed before we even arrived. Then we'd have to cope with the overweight baggage plus porters and all the dogs whose leads would invariably get entwined around legs as they pulled in every direction. In the middle of this maelstrom, my mother would sit calmly, her hand in the bag in which Tikki and Minnie were hidden.

The dreadful moment would come when it was time for Mummy to be wheeled through the "Passengers Only" gate. I would gaze at that lovely face trying to imprint it on my memory. Now the moment of parting had come I would be in despair that I could not go with her, and I would torture myself with what terrible thing might happen to her without me being there for her. I used to rush sobbing back to Tana at Ol Orion, burying my face in her neck, comforted by the familiar feel and strength of her. I felt that somehow she understood my unhappiness.

Everywhere I looked around my home I would be reminded of Mummy. Her scent clung to the rooms, her boxes of paint would not yet have been tidied away and the tapestry work would be lying there half-finished. Poor Joseph would visit all the rooms looking for her. I can still see him now, as he turned his depressed little face to look at me before opening the door to her bedroom.

Joseph had a whole collection of artists' materials that she had given him. These were put away at night as he would strew them around the house. Now he would collect them in the morning and take them to her room. I would go in to find him sitting on the bed, surrounded by his crayons and paper making wild drawings. When I came looking for him, he would leap into my arms and I would carry him through the house explaining that the rooms were empty and that my mother had gone. It would take him several days of searching the house for her and going to her bedroom, to wait on her bed, before he understood. He would haunt the dining room where she had been working on murals.

He had a teddy bear that he loved, which accompanied him everywhere. It was his security bear and he would tuck it under his thigh when he climbed trees. His other comfort was a little cotton baby blanket that he never wanted to be parted from. As he grew older, he did leave them behind from time to time, then race back from whatever he had been doing to take them with him on his next adventure.

After Mummy left, Joseph and I would cheer ourselves up by dancing. At this time the twist was all the rage in Africa and Caryll, who was also a marvellous dancer, had taught me in the night-spots of Nairobi. I had bought a collection of records but needed a partner at home so I taught Joseph to dance to Chubby Checker's *Let's Twist Again*. I remember a friend arriving during one of these twist sessions, when the music was so loud I didn't hear the door open. He said it was the funniest spectacle he had ever seen. An enormous lioness sprawled all over the sofa, myself gyrating furiously to the rhythm of Chubby Checker and a chimpanzee with his arms above his head shuffling to the music. He laughingly said, "I always thought you were a bit peculiar, now I know you are quite demented."

The animals loved driving and Mummy's pale yellow Buick stationwagon, my Citroën and the jeep were fitted out with mattresses instead of seats behind. As soon as they saw me heading for the car, there would be a mad rush to get in. Tana, by far the laziest at any other time, invariably got there first. Leaping in, she would establish herself on the mattress and everyone else had to settle for next best. The back seat would look like a carpet of lion and dog. Tana had grown up with this huge variety of animals and they had become the equivalent of her pride. I am sure this helped to keep her the very sweet-tempered animal she was and always remained.

I used to like taking Tana and other animals including Joseph in the car into Nairobi and we would go and do the shopping or make some social visits to the coffee bar at the Thorn Tree. A thorn tree had been planted outside the front door of the New Stanley Hotel and the pavement under it had become a famous meeting place. On several occasions the police in Nairobi had already asked me to kindly remove my car and not return to the city with my animals. One day I had parked near the Thorn Tree and was having a cup of coffee with friends, when I saw crowds running and police arriving on motorbikes. Thinking it might be some kind of riot, I went to have a look. My heart sank when I realised that the crowd were massed around my car. Of course it was Joseph at the bottom of all the trouble. He had wound the window down and was doing handsprings on top of the roof, much to everybody's delight, while Tana was standing on the back seat with her head out of the window, not at all happy with the vast crowd who were disturbing her afternoon nap.

Nairobi in those days was used to strange sights, but possibly this was a bit more extraordinary than most.

We also used to go down to the Karen *duka* for provisions, but by now the sight of my car there with its animals hardly raised an eyebrow. Joseph, of course, would wind down the windows and wave to the passers-by, refusing to be ignored until he had at least gathered a few wide-eyed *totos* to watch his handsprings and somersaults, all of which had been taught to him by Kimoyo. He was a real little ham and thoroughly enjoyed his outings, especially as I used to get him lollipops and sweets. Anything new, he would put into my mouth and, with great concentration, watch me take a bite before trying it out himself. If he decided he did not like the taste he would then very generously feed me with it. As I had usually chosen something I liked, this was no hardship and the fact that he had been sucking it himself so it was covered in chimpanzee spit never worried me. My brothers used to be horrified but as I explained to them, "Animal saliva is a great deal healthier than human. Think of all the diseases we catch from one another and how few from animals." Rory took this lesson to heart. My terribly immaculate brother developed a habit which horrified his friends. At Fiorentina, he would feed his numerous dogs the leavings on his plate. Then when they had finished licking it, he would calmly return it to the table.

Joseph had his favourite dogs and used to lean over the front seat of the car trying to dole out sweets only to those he preferred. Of course they all used to try and get in on the act and push and shove him for attention. He used to get so cross, puffing himself up, doing his little war dance and waving his arms at them. I loved watching him. I would say, "Joseph, give me the sweets", and he would come clutching his packet against his chest, then reluctantly hand them to me. I would give everyone a sweet and then return the rest to him. By this time, he would be jumping up and down going "OOH! OOH!", his mouth puckered up. He was so adorable and quite irresistible that I would have to pick him up and give him a hug and kiss.

The house at Karen was built like a shallow U. There was my room at the end of a pillared verandah, my bathroom, a guest room and small bathroom, then Mummy's large bathroom. The opposite wing housed the pantry and large kitchen. The front of the house consisted of Mummy's bedroom, the sitting room and the dining room. Then there were a further two bedrooms and a bathroom next to the garage.

At the back of the house were huge cages that I had had erected in the forest for all the sick and wounded monkeys that were now being brought to me so I could care for them. Once the monkeys were healed and established, I would release them but continue to feed them there so they always knew they had the security of a safe place if they needed it.

The indigenous forest covered a hill, at the bottom of which was a stream that flowed throughout the year and where I had planted lots of bamboo and all sorts of water-loving plants. It was a beautiful walk and Mummy, all the dogs, Tana, Joseph and I would often go down there for picnics.

A verandah ran around the inside of the house, opening onto a fenced-in garden and surrounded by a large hedge of blue plumbago that almost hid the wooden fence. The columns of the verandah were planted with pink climbing roses, their lovely heads hanging towards the morning sun. As the evening light faded they danced in the breeze from the river, entwined in the jasmine and honeysuckle. Around the house were elaborate flower beds, a profusion of colour, and hanging over all were the jacarandas, showering everything with a mass of blue confetti.

My bedroom was large with a mullioned window opposite my bed looking out onto the back garden and the indigenous forest beyond. There was another large diamond-leaded window to the right, which looked over the lawn to the jacaranda forest. I had no carpets on the floor but kept the parquet very highly polished so that it was easy to clean. The only furniture was a dressing table, sofa, chair and a large four-poster bed, which I had designed myself.

Buying a king-sized mattress and base, I had erected four large bamboo posts as uprights and used yacht varnish to lacquer them to a high gloss. I did the same with the cross-pieces, then draped it all with matching *kangas* which were cheap and easy to replace, and easy to wash and starch. The curtains at the windows, also ruffled and starched, were of the same material as on the bed. One always had to take into account that my monkeys would possibly use them as swings. The walls were whitewashed with a touch of blue in the paint and the whole effect although entirely practical was quite dramatic.

What was even more dramatic was Tana who had discovered at an early age that if she took a flying leap onto the bed from the doorway, it would take off across the room. To make cleaning easy I had put the bed onto castors. The sight of this enormous lioness tearing across the room on her bed became a daily entertainment. To keep her balance, Tana would swing her tail from side to side and keep to a half crouch. Often she would have a wastepaper basket on her head.

Her love of wastepaper baskets stemmed from her passion for footballs I think. I used to buy them for her when I realised that any other type of ball was too delicate. She could easily deflate rubber balls with her teeth and she loved watching the air hiss out. But then there was nothing left to throw for her. So from an early age she learned to put these flattened balls on her head, holding them in place with one paw and often rolling over and over with it, replacing it when it became dislodged.

She graduated to hardier footballs but as she grew older, they suffered the same fate. They never lasted for long. The sports shop even ran out and a whole new order had to come from England. I decided that as they were such expensive items to replace I would hide them away after our game of catch and not give her the time to destroy them. In frustration at not having a ball to put on her head, she started to use the wastepaper baskets.

Two large peach-coloured datura trees were planted outside Mummy's bedroom and sitting room windows. No scent is more evocative of tropical nights than the glorious, heavy, cloying perfume of the datura. I loved those trees and in the daytime I would watch the way my golden Tana would crouch, half-hidden by the branches of enormous golden bell-shaped flowers. Oh, Tana my love! How often I pretended not to see you crouched there as I walked by; your beautiful coat dappled by the sunlight, your glorious amber eyes filled with happiness as you prepared to leap out on me, the supposedly unsuspecting victim.

From her childhood, it had been one of our games and people who watched said it was the most extraordinary sight: this giant of a lioness suddenly appearing from behind a tree or a bush, springing with all four feet off the ground onto me, and departing just as rapidly. She was so incredibly controlled that she could hit me from behind with both front feet on my shoulders and her touch would be so light I would hardly know she had done so. I would then turn and chase her as she tore off into the undergrowth. It was our game of hide and seek.

This was her very favourite game but in all the years we played together she never once tripped me or bowled me over. I often used to wonder how it was possible for her, with all her strength, to have such precision that she could play with someone who was by comparison so weak? And how did she realise this?

Unfortunately on one occasion Tana's little game did get out of hand. My mother, who always wore very high heels even when visiting us in Africa, was walking along the verandah from her room on the way to the sitting room when Tana, who was crouched in the lavender bush behind a column, decided to play her game of tag. The floor was highly polished green tiles and Mummy was carrying her paints and brushes and, as always, had Tikki the hyrax on her shoulder. She had entirely forgotten about the bouncy Tana and so when my lioness went through her usual act, Mummy skidded in her heels on the slippery floor and hit her face against the wall. The result was that for weeks she had two black eyes and a swollen nose. Mummy, of course, made up the most incredible stories to account for her mishap. I had to keep writing letters overseas to assure everyone that she had not been attacked by Mau Mau, beaten up by an irate wife or escaped the jaws of a ravening lion.

CHAPTER

40

We often went to the coast with our friends, the Blocks, who were hoteliers. We stayed with them at their lovely beach house at Nyali in Mombasa, near the Nyali Beach Hotel, which they eventually bought too. Tubby and Aino Block were two of my greatest friends and I used to love being with them. Unbelievably hospitable, nothing was ever too much trouble; they had the greatest gift of making their guests feel as if they were part of their home. Cars, aeroplanes, servants and lovely houses, with the best food that I have ever eaten anywhere in the world, were all at one's disposal.

At one time, Tubby and his brother Jack owned practically all the hotels and safari lodges in Kenya, including the famous safari firm Ker & Downey, in which Jack was a partner, and Bunson's Travel Agency. In Nairobi, their hotels were The New Stanley and the lovely old Norfolk, the first proper hotel to be built in Kenya, the Nyali Beach at Mombasa, the Outspan at Nyeri, as well as the safari lodge Treetops. Prince Philip and Princess Elizabeth were at Treetops when they received the news of King George VI's death in 1952. It was there that the princess became Queen of England.

My favourite place of all was Tubby's house at Lake Naivasha. At one time they owned a major portion of the east side of the lake but Tubby (who was not the least tubby) sold most of it off and kept only enough land to grow his glorious flowers and vegetables for the export market.

Between the Blocks, who owned so much commercial real estate, and the Delameres who owned much of the land, Kenya had almost become, in the early settler days, the kingdom of these two great and famous pioneering families. Errol Trzebinski writes about Tubby's father Abraham Block in her book published in 1985, *The Kenya Pioneers* (William Heinemann). He had left Lithuania, she says, as a young man to escape the pogroms and persecution. He had gone with his sister Annie to England to stay with his uncle, a much respected rabbi in Leeds, before arriving in Cape Town. He then took various jobs to finance his trip north to Johannesburg. He enlisted in a Boer Commando Unit and was only 18 when in 1902, the Peace Treaty was signed between the British and the Boers. The following year, Abraham Block heard about the settlers in the East Africa Protectorate (which later became the colony of Kenya). Persuading five friends to join him they set sail for Mombasa, but not before he had worked hard to raise the passage, both for himself and his Basuto ponies. He also took a bag each of peas, linseed, beans and potatoes and his savings of £25. From this meagre beginning Abraham Block built an empire.

Meanwhile Hugh Cholmondeley Delamere, the third Baron Delamere, had also come out to settle in Kenya. Very rich, he had received an initial government grant of 100,000 acres in the Rift Valley for a cattle and sheep ranch, establishing himself first at Njoro with Equator Ranch (because part of it was on the equator) and then moving to Soysambu near Lake Elementeita. Lord Delamere was passionate about Kenya and it was he who led the revolt by the British settlers against the Colonial Office in the early 1920s when it seemed to be working against them with its plans for enfranchising the Indian immigrants. There were also question marks over the European claims on the highlands. The rebellious Delamere even went so far as to concoct a plan to capture the Governor of Kenya and keep him prisoner until the settlers' demands were met. The compromise eventually agreed on, after Delamere and others went to London in 1922 and then 1923, was that the Kenya highlands would virtually remain exclusively white in perpetuity. But the Duke of Devonshire, secretary of state for the colonies, also declared that the colony was to pursue African interests over those of other residents.

Jack and Tubby Block had immense charm and warmth, were good-looking in different ways, but had two things in common. They both dressed superbly and entertained like princes. Tubby's sons, Jeremy and Anthony, whom I watched grow up from little boys, inherited all their father's charm and business sense, as well as his generosity. Many years ago now, Jack Block had a tragic accident. We had had dinner with him and he was leaving the following day to go on a fishing trip to Chile. We later heard that Jeremy Block's Chilean wife Nana had been sitting on the bank, reading a book, while Jack was standing in the middle of the lake with his waders on, fly-fishing. When she looked up, the lake was deserted. At first, she thought Jack might have gone to another spot and went looking for him. It was only four days later that they found his body. His wife Doria arranged for his ashes to be scattered over Lake Naivasha.

Jack will always remain part of the country he loved and we his friends will remember him as a special person who added an extra dimension to our lives. We would often travel down to Mombasa with the Blocks in their plane, with me invariably being ill as we bumped around. I usually tried to persuade my mother to go by car. They were marvellous holidays though and I look back on them with nostalgia.

I would go into Mombasa with Aino to buy the fruit and fresh vegetables from the market early each day. I loved the colour; the fresh produce, the curries set out in a glorious array, the African women in wonderful flowered *kangas*, the Muslims concealed behind their flowing black *bui buis* and the Indians dressed in silk and cotton saris in all the colours of the rainbow. The noise and bustle, the filtered hot sunlight and the raucous calls of the crows made for a kaleidoscope of eastern splendour.

Returning in the heat to the magic of a cool swim in the lovely pool or a sortie into the sea after a brisk jog along the beach, Aino would then bargain with the local fishermen selling their early morning catch, suspended from poles carried across the men's shoulders. White sands, blue seas, coconut palms, flamboyant poinsettias and sweet-smelling frangipani, Mombasa and its coastline was truly a tropical paradise.

Tubby and Aino once lent me their house for a few days when I was on my way back from a safari. I had a young Tana with me at the time and the humidity was too much for her. She would spend her day in the room lying on my bed with the air-conditioner full on. The excessive humidity of daytime would cool towards evening, and then Tana would reluctantly venture out and slowly follow me down to the beach, complaining all the way. She had decided that she hated the sea. I spent hours getting her used to it until she finally realised what fun it was. Then she would endlessly chase after crabs and myself as I raced in and out of the shallow waves.

Joseph would watch all this from a coconut palm. Chimpanzees cannot swim and I never tried to get him into the water. What he liked was the return to the house when he would open the fresh water tap and splash himself while I rinsed the salt water off Tana and myself. He would do little war dances in the pool of water and clean his hands and face, throw the droplets into the air and try and catch them in his mouth. Then we would have great fun and games while I struggled to put his nappy on for the night. I was never very expert at it and he would wriggle so much and usually disappear up a tree just out of reach before I had half-finished. To complete my frustration, he would dangle the nappy above my head until I would finally get annoyed. Then he would reluctantly hand it to me. He loved it once it was on and would pat it as if it were a child and needed comforting until his eyes gradually closed in sleep.

Mummy and I also used to stay at the Blocks' Outspan Hotel, between the Aberdares and Mount Kenya, and the breakfasts there were a feast of all the traditional English foods. We would breakfast on the terrace overlooking the beautiful lawns and watch the early morning mists clear, gradually revealing the majestic splendour of Mount Kenya. The contrast between the wonderful English gardens, with their lawns, herbaceous borders and neatly clipped hedges and the backdrop of this great snow-capped mountain never ceased to thrill me. The undoubted magic that Kenya holds for people is the fact that it is such a land of contrasts. I know of no other country where, within a few hours of driving, one can be in the tropical rainforests with orchids in every tree and then, in the heat of the plains, with camels and sand.

CHAPTER
41

Life in this country I had chosen was endless days of happiness; I loved the sun, the air, the beautiful skies, the beauty of the landscape and the people. The days turned into years and time passed. Tana matured into a magnificent and enormous tawny lioness with the character of an angel. I would refer to her as *malaika* (angel) and Mutete the cook would take great pleasure in coming to me, all grins, and saying *"Malaika yake, alifanya kitu mbaya sana leo."* I would rush to see what the angel had been doing that was so bad, only to find another punctured football and a guilty-looking Tana holding it on top of her head.

Tana would often spend her days going off to the Ngong Hills to lie up under a bush. The first time she disappeared I was frantic but Mutete assured me that she had been seen going off to the reserve and was probably looking for a husband! He thought it was very funny but I was not at all amused. Assuring him that she was much too young for husbands, I took the jeep and went looking for her. I spent hours driving around blowing my horn, imagining all the horrors that might have befallen her. I was practically in tears before I saw her emerge from under a large bush, stretching and yawning. I had obviously interrupted a long siesta. Evening was upon us and she had walked far from the house. We were almost at the top of the hills and in places I could see over the escarpment. Like a well-trained chauffeur, I got out and opening the back door held it wide for her majesty to climb in.

This became an almost daily pattern. When she wasn't lying on the roof, she would be up on the Ngong Hills and each evening I would drive up to fetch her. This went on for several increasingly nerve-wracking months until I couldn't take the suspense any longer; often it would be ages before she would appear in answer to my frantic blasts of the horn. It was a large area of Africa and I would have no idea how far she might have travelled during the day. Another problem was that it is Masai country and I would have visions of her speared to death by a *moran*, a young warrior. To kill a lion was a symbol of their manhood.

I decided her best protection was to hire a Masai warrior to follow her to the hills and stay with her during the day. As is usual in Africa, word was sent out and the *moran* arrived from far and wide. A tall magnificent race, the Masai are of great physical beauty, both the men and the women. The warriors, all over six foot, are dyed head to foot with a paste made of red ochre and cow urine. Even their long plaited hair and *shuka*, a cloth draped over one shoulder and hanging loosely to their knees, their only form of clothing, was also stained the same dark earth red. With their plaits, beautiful teeth and fine features they were the glamour tribe of Kenya, more written about, more filmed and more romanticised than any other.

No decision is ever taken lightly by the Masai and the *baraza* (get-together). The question of who would accompany Tana took most of the day. I sat with her on the lawn under the shade of a giant mukuyu (an indigenous *Ficus capensis*) with the blue Ngong Hills in the background and in a circle, sitting or standing, were the red warriors. Fascinated by Tana they would go up to have a close look at her, then back away holding hands. Laughing and leaning on their spears they would share some joke about her. When at one stage she yawned and rolled over on her back with her feet in the air, they thought this was hilarious.

Finally a warrior was chosen. From his point of view they had conferred on him a great honour and I had promised him many cattle. Mutete had also arranged with the butcher for an ox to be cut up and the pieces of meat were cooked over the open embers.

As the sun set, blood red in the azure sky, the flat-topped acacias stood out in stark relief, black against the mauve of the towering hills, their outlines sharp against the light of the fast descending African night. The drums started and the warriors in ones and twos started their stiff-legged dance, the *ngoma*, rising high off the ground. An *ngoma* begins with a grunting chant while the *moran* move their heads and necks to the rhythm. Gradually, with stiff legs, they leap into the air, each jump getting higher and higher, so finally the whole column is leaping up and down on the spot. Higher and higher the tall red warriors go, holding themselves almost as rigid as the spears in their hands. Their long hair, in small red plaits, and their beaded necklaces swing as they leap. Their ear-lobes are almost detached from their ears, the holes in them are so enlarged by the weight of the leather and beadwork adorning them. As the decorations swing with the rhythm, it seems as if the entire ear might tear apart so heavy is the jewellery.

Soon I was surrounded by these leaping figures, black silhouettes against the flames. I could feel the vibrations pulse through the earth, the very heartbeat of Kenya.

The English settlers had a great respect and admiration for this magnificent tribe. Being nomadic and dependent on their vast herds of cattle, the Masai would follow the grazing and the only employment they would take usually was as stockmen. Therefore, most of the farmers used the Masai for their own cattle and dairy herds. Large territories of Kenya and parts of Tanganyika were Masai country and it never ceased to thrill me when I came across groups of these red warriors. With their fine features, they looked like wall paintings on the tombs of the ancient Egyptians.

They were also the despair of many of the district commissioners who could not get the Masai to understand that if they reduced their herds of cattle they would also reduce the problems they were having with soil erosion and over-grazing. Certainly in the drier areas, one could see these lean hump-backed cattle, all colours and sizes, spread across the country, intermingling with the herds of zebra, giraffe and buck and leaving devastation in their wake.

One could understand the Masai reasoning though. If they had a thousand cattle and there was a drought and they lost 500, they were still left with a sizeable herd. If they were reduced to 500, they could not afford to lose any. Their whole eco-system revolved around their cattle. The staple diet was meat, blood and milk and they would bleed the cattle by tying a thong tight around the neck and then, with the sharp tip of the spear, make a hole in the jugular. The blood would be drained into a gourd and the women would mix this together with the milk into a smooth mixture. Bride prices were paid with cattle and the size of your herd was the size of your wealth.

Tana, who long ago had retreated to the roof, chose this moment in the *ngoma* to reappear. This was all very far from her daily routine and she was not pleased. Standing in front of the porch, her ears pricked and her tail swishing gently from side to side, she was searching the night for me and, having found me amongst all the gyrating figures, she came towards me. I watched her, the slow measured walk of a lion, the power, the silence, the deadliness, every muscle and sinew showing beneath the sleek golden skin. As she approached so did the dancing stop. These warriors, their spears in hands, turned to watch their ancient enemy, the king of beasts. Uncertain as to her intent they regarded her with awe, even the drums had stopped. I could feel the night air suddenly chill my bare skin and I shivered as I reached out to place my hand on her head. I think only then did I realise that any movement on her part might be misjudged and she could end up with a hundred spears piercing her body.

Tana, ever sensitive to atmosphere, could feel the tension, the awe, the fear that her presence elicited. As she faced the hills, so did her head come up and her nostrils widen as she smelled the strange odours surrounding her. She let out a roar; it was her challenge. This was her territory. I was overwhelmed by my love for her and the possible danger I had placed her in. Praying for her continued obedience, I told her to sit. I could feel her reluctance but she had obeyed me for so many years she didn't dispute my authority now. As she lay at my feet, I could feel the tension diffuse and hear the pent-up breath released from a hundred throats.

The drums once more broke the silence, the dancers leapt to even

Tana the lioness became Pat's trusted companion and confidante.

Caryll studied farming after World War II and then moved to Kenya where he established a ranch, Equator Farm, above, in the Subukia Valley. For all the White Highlands glamour, it was hard work.

Danièle, Caryll's wife, left, was the daughter of a rich French industrialist from Paris.

370

Life in British Kenya combined settler farming with interiors by Colefax and Fowler and travel by private plane. Pat lived at Ol Orion near Nairobi and brought her beloved Citröen with her.

Tana copied Pat's chimpanzee Joseph and learned to climb Ol Orion's roof.

Pat's animals loved driving as much as she did. Enid kept a beautiful Buick, top, at Ol Orion and Tana was a frequent passenger. Tana as a cub with a friend's child, below. Caryll's children, right, with Joseph.

Photographer Bini Malcolm, left, became part of Pat's household in between assignments. She preferred to take pictures but could also, below with Pierre d'Unienville who first found Tana, become a glamorous model. The press adored photo-shoots like this while the Kenyans, top right, flocked to Tana.

Joseph the chimpanzee was a ham and could be relied on to entertain children. Visitors to Ol Orion, like Petal and Lee Harragin, above, had to be prepared for chimp cuddles all round. Left, Aino Block watches Tim Tom with her son. Below, Pat photographed at the Muthaiga Club in Nairobi.

Tikki, top, Joseph, back, and Jason, front, simply treated Pat as one of their own.

Tana had a very large head and eyes set wide, which mean good temper in a lion.

Some guests to Ol Orion were sanguine about Joseph's attentions, above, but another considered his hug "one of the most horrible experiences of her life".

Enid, with Tikki and Joseph, above right, bought Ol Orion for Pat.

Joseph had his own nanny, Kimoyo, above left, while Mutete, the chef at Ol Orion, also ran the household, organised Pat and kept her safe. Below, champion jockey Buster Parnell, a Beryl Markham favourite, on Lone Eagle.

Danièle, above centre, on safari with oil heiress Olga Deterding, above left. Left, aviatrix Beryl Markham grew up in Kenya and was taught to train horses by her father, an English settler. Below, Enid with Tubby Block.

A Stanley Lawrence Brown safari was like no other, writes Pat, of the business run from Langata by her big game hunter lover. He was immaculate and so were the safaris. Everything had a film star glamour to it.

Whichever animals made it to Pat and Enid's car in time came on safari.

Stan Lawrence Brown learned to hunt throughout Africa as a teenager.

Rich Americans brought their families on safari but gradually, under Pat's influence, Stan switched to photographic trips. Twice, sickened by indiscriminate shooting by clients, he closed down safaris.

Stan always wanted Pat to be with him but she couldn't bear the killing.

Stan, with Tim Tom and Masai above, said Pat turned safaris into zoos.

East Africa was made glamorous by films like *Hatari* and many stars, including William Holden, who co-owned the Mt Kenya Safari Club, became regulars. Safaris, below, looked like film sets and even Pat's friend, designer Enrique de Medina, far right, put himself into khaki.

With Stan, Pat travelled from Mt Kilimanjaro to the deserts of north Kenya.

greater heights, the flames from the bonfire crackled and spat large glowing embers of the aromatic cedarwood, leaving trails of fiery sparks to light the blackness of the night. I knelt to embrace *malaika*, my angel, my African lioness, for whom I felt such pride that I could feel the tears come to my eyes. I watched as one dropped slowly to land on her face as she looked up at me. It lay caught for a moment and then was gone. Was this prophetic? They were the first of the many tears I was to shed over the years and still do as I awake from my dreams of Tana, only to find there is no reality, just the shadow.

The Masai *moran* soon became part of our lives. He was known as Mkuki (the spear) because even when he was drinking his cups of tea in the kitchen, his weapon would be close to hand. He wouldn't arrive until midday as it was only in the afternoons that Tana would take off into the hills. On the days she decided to remain on the roof, he would stand guard in the garden; a tall motionless figure, one leg propped against a tree, his red figure dappled by the sunlight as he leant on the spear that was even taller than himself. The other familiar sight was seeing them heading off to the hills: a large lioness followed by her shepherd, the beads in his ears swinging against his neck as he covered the ground in a long loping stride which often had to be reduced to a crawl so as not to pass my lazy lioness.

If they were late coming home and I was busy in the garden, Mutete would come and say in Swahili, "It is time to collect your child." Mutete was the pivot around which the household revolved. From the Wakamba tribe, and of indeterminate age (though probably a lot younger then he looked), he was small and wiry and always dressed in khaki shorts and shirt, a white chef's hat given by some previous employer and a starched white apron that came to his knees. He spoke no English, nor did any of the men that we employed. In those days, all the Europeans including myself spoke kitchen or up-country Swahili with varying degrees of fluency.

Mutete was a chef par excellence. He would produce amazing recipes, and his vegetarian dishes were out of this world. He filled the house with his friends and fellow tribesmen and ruled them with a rod of iron. There was Mutete, a kitchen *toto* and three others in the house. Outside there were four *shambas* (or garden boys) and Kimoyo,

385

Joseph's nanny. Kimau, the head *shamba*, had no great experience but was eternally willing. He would happily plant flowers upside down as he did on one occasion when I left him unsupervised. But all of Mutete's friends were marvellous with me and wonderful with the animals and I blessed the day that the Blocks' cook had sent him to us. I had come to rely on Mutete for everything; always rather scatter-brained myself, he provided the rock on which I leant. He was the one who sent me into town with the orders, he arranged the meals and saw to the drinks. He ran the house and organised my life. He once told me that working for me had elevated the status of all the staff because of my association with Tana. They had come to be regarded with awe by their relations and therefore accorded great respect.

Mutete adored Tana and now made sure that her personal bodyguard was kept happy. I would find him stuffing Mkuki with helpings of half-cooked meat and endless cups of heavily sugared tea. The kitchen took on a totally different atmosphere. Joseph had also discovered the delights of tea and the new arrival never ceased to fascinate him. I would come into the kitchen to see Joseph standing on his chair examining the long red plaits or looking in Mkuki's scalp for *kunguni* (bugs). I have a horrible feeling that he would often find what he was looking for as he would pounce and squeeze them between his nails. What became highly embarrassing was when he discovered that Mkuki was, apart from his *shuka*, naked. Thereafter, he was continually pulling the cloth aside to examine his genitalia. They all thought it terribly funny and there would be gales of laughter from the kitchen. I couldn't very well ask him to wear pants but I told Mutete to smack Joseph's hand should he become too familiar. And I personally gave the kitchen a wide berth when Mkuki was around.

Tana and her faithful Masai follower continued to be a familiar sight heading off for the Ngong Hills. One day though, the peace of my afternoon was rudely disturbed. I was arranging roses in bowls around the house. Their fragrance was strong and sweetly scented the sitting room, the windows were open and outside I could hear the hum of bees as they gathered nectar from the honeysuckle in the bed below. Suddenly, Tana appeared on the scene. She hadn't even waited for me to open the door but had jumped through the window and, obviously disturbed, had come to sit beside me and then turned to face the

Ngong Hills. I didn't know what she could be watching so intently for, when Mkuki arrived on the scene. Very upset, he told me that on the way to her siesta area, they had come across a herd of buffalo. As soon as Tana saw them, she had turned tail and fled. Mkuki was most indignant. He announced that he would not look after Tana any longer. He was a *moran*, a warrior, and he refused to be seen in the company of a cowardly lion.

I looked at my beloved cowardly lion and, highly amused, tried to pacify Mkuki but he would have none of it. Gathering his spear and his dignity, he loped off down the drive. Once more I took up the burdensome duty as chauffeur to Tana until much later, through another friend, I found a Kipsigi warrior, who I hoped would not be so fussy about the moral fibre – or lack thereof – in his charge.

CHAPTER

42

My mother had a very casual attitude to the hiring of staff and if three people could be employed to do the job of one, so much the better. There was a whole block of staff houses in the forest and I used to love going to bed at night with the sound of the drums beating their monotonous tattoo. We always seemed to be adding staff quarters and guest cottages and I used to supervise the building. We would make them into rondavels, built of clay, with wooden poles and steep thatched roofs.

In the daytime life centred around the kitchen. It was full of light. Painted white and with the door to the garden open, it was shaded by a giant bombax tree, its clumps of pink flowers so bright against the blue sky, their colour only dimmed by the scarlet and mauve blooms of the tall bougainvillaea hedge that separated the kitchen wing from the house. The air hung heavy with the smell of Africa: the smoke from cedar wood fires, the damp red earth, the herbs that hung in bunches from the ceiling, the jasmine and honeysuckle that clung to the outside beams. The days would be full of sun, the sound of bees and the lovely bell-like call of the pheasant-like coucal. This was my African home.

At night, above the sound of Tana's heavy breathing, I would hear the drums and lie awake watching the moon as it rose above the forest. Often I would notice the beam of a torch flashing past my window. Idly imagining that it was one of the men on their way home after a late night. I would go to sleep, but soon I noticed that it was happening more and more frequently and I would lie there watching and wondering why whoever it was always came so near the house. One day I questioned Mutete about it and he said that he was worried about my being on my own in such a large house and that he would go around during the night to make sure I was all right.

I tried hard to reassure Mutete that with Tana and the dogs I was totally safe and that I had a hand alarm in my bedroom. It was a large green iron thing with a handle which, if turned, emitted a screech like the sound of the sirens during the Battle of Britain. It would have woken the dead, let alone the living.

Mutete was still not reassured and insisted on his nightly patrol. It was on one of these self-instituted night watchmen rounds that Mutete found some bandits stealing the cattle. With great bravery he rounded up all the boys and gave chase and recovered the herd. I only heard about it in the morning having slept soundly through the excitement. I had inherited the cattle from Mrs Homewood who had kept milking cows. As I didn't want to kill anything, I couldn't afford to let the herd increase and so didn't put the cows in calf. That meant we had to buy our milk and Tana consumed most as she would drink at least four litres a day.

The night after the cattle raid, as a reward for their bravery I gave the staff a big feast. The sounds of the *ngoma* went on for days.

My friends had been telling me that as I lived so near the forest I should have a security fence. I did not pay much attention but finally one good, close friend insisted and I decided to go ahead. At least it would enable Mutete to relax at night and not have to worry about me. I decided to enclose the open verandah, that ran from my room to the sitting room where the telephone was, with a steel wire mesh. I hired some *fundis* (builders) and soon they had almost completed the job and were working on the steel door. It was the middle of a hot day and I was bathing Joseph, a daily routine that he loved. Tana was lying on the roof under the shade of her tree and the workmen were busy just below her. I had just lifted Joseph out of the bath, and I still remember he was clutching his toothbrush, when suddenly I could feel Tana's rage.

Leaving Joseph, I flew down the corridor to find Tana on the roof about to spring on the men working below. Her ears were back and she was crouched ready to leap. I shouted at her and she backed off. I had never seen her like this, spitting with fury and her tail swishing with rage. I paid the workmen off and asked them to leave. I spoke to Mutete about it and we decided they must have teased her in some way. He added that it was very strange as she was so used to people. In his eyes, Tana could do no wrong and he suggested that maybe they were bad men and she was trying to tell us this. I did say, "Mutete, she doesn't have to kill them to make her point." He left the room, laughing and shaking his head. It was an incident soon forgotten and the security fence was never finished. I was loath to hire someone else in case we had a repeat performance.

About two weeks later, on a dark moonless night, I was woken by Tana leaping off my bed to go to the window overlooking the forest. She started padding up and down, her tail swishing and giving short grunts like a hunting lion. I sat up in bed watching her for a while and she gave me the feeling that something sinister was about to happen. Even the drums sounded evil. All around was the complete stillness of an African night with only the far away beat to break the silence.

Suddenly I realised what she was trying to convey and I knew we were about to be attacked by a gang. Going to the phone I called the Karen police. I knew I couldn't say, "Please can you come, a gang is about to arrive. My lioness told me." They would have thought me quite daft. So having total faith in Tana, I said simply, "Can you come; I think the Mau Mau have arrived on my farm." An *askari* answered me and said they had no transport: was there any way I could get to them? Putting my lion in the back of my car, I went off to the police station and collected all the *askaris*. On the way home the car bristled with armed African police who were nervous of getting too close to Tana. I had to keep reassuring them that she was as gentle as a kitten.

On arriving back at the farm, all was silent. I hadn't had the time to go to the men's quarters to wake them up as I had been in such a rush to get the police. There was no light, even the drums had stopped. It was utter stillness. My heart sank. I thought, "I have led them on a wild goose chase." The *askaris* in their dark blue jerseys and khaki shorts, rifles at the ready, converged on the house and were soon swallowed up by the darkness. I stayed by the Land Rover watching Tana who, ears pricked and very restless, was peering over towards the forest. It seemed like hours but it was possibly only minutes before the stillness was interrupted by the sound of battle. Running feet, shouts and soon a couple of shots rang out.

Tana was frantic, obviously longing to join the fray. In her desire to be allowed to get out she was rocking the car as she charged from one side to another. While I was trying to calm her, the *askaris* arrived with the first of the prisoners. Mutete had now appeared, with the rest of the staff, and the lights were on, immediately dispelling the sinister atmosphere but highlighting the confusion. My staff, armed with *pangas*, were running around looking for someone to carve up.

The leader of the gang was none other than one of the *fundis* who had been working on my security fence. Such was his hatred that on the way back to the police station, he suddenly lunged forward and tried to strangle me with his handcuffs. One of the policemen hit him over the head with his truncheon and I nearly drove off the road.

Afterwards, when I had time to think over the whole episode, what struck me was the fact that Tana lying asleep on the roof must have felt the evil intent emanating from this man. I learned later from the police that he was a killer and had escaped from Mathari, the hospital where they kept patients with psychiatric disorders. My lioness had wanted to kill him; I had such telepathic communication with her that I had felt her rage and been able to run out from the bathroom and save his life.

This whole episode was incredible enough but what was even more remarkable was the fact that Tana had once again picked up vibrations, this time at night over a vast distance and had sensed the danger of an impending attack. I worked out that the gang had come from the other side of the river, which was a fair distance from the house. Tana's waking me, my going to the phone and then to the police station and back must have taken at least an hour and it seemed that the attackers had only just arrived at Ol Orion at the same time as the police and me. How was it possible that Tana could pick up these vibrations so far ahead and over such a distance? To me, it is inexplicable, but the fact is that she did, otherwise I would possibly not be alive today.

There was a strange sequel to this story. Months later I was lying sunbathing on a deckchair in the garden when I felt an alien presence. Looking up, I saw three Africans standing, watching me. I immediately recognised one as the leader of the gang that had attacked me. Without a word being said, they stood for a few seconds more, then walked away. I had not at any time felt threatened by their presence. Nor did I ever see them again.

CHAPTER

43

I first met the big game hunter Stan Lawrence Brown at an auction. I had gone looking for china. Often, when settlers left the country, and many were leaving now because of the troubles and what might lie ahead, the most incredible pieces would come up for sale amongst their household goods. Sèvres, Compagnie des Indes, Meissen and Rockingham. I still have some lovely pieces collected from these unlikely outlets.

I was after a set of Sèvres plates that was coming up in a job lot and was sitting catalogue in hand on a wooden bench, when I became conscious of someone staring at me. It was a strange sexual awareness that is hard to define. I looked up and, over the heads of people, I saw him leaning against a column. A big man, very tanned, wearing a cream silk shirt and cream drill trousers. He had his safari hat under his arm and was lighting his pipe. He was dark and clean-shaven and with rugged good looks; Stan knew how to dominate a room. I was totally conscious of him and, as they say, we could have been the only two people there. It was all there in a glance. I looked away but in the periphery of my vision I was well aware of his movements. I knew he had gone over to sit on a bench to the side of where I was sitting.

I bought my plates and got up to leave as I had no further interest in the sale. As I waited for my receipt, he approached me. I had sensed he would. I could even feel my heart beat that much faster as he came up. Looking at me for a moment he said, "Aren't you Pat Cavendish, the girl with the lioness?" He had a beautiful warm voice with an undercurrent of amusement. He said, "I am Stan Lawrence Brown and we are practically neighbours. I have seen you in the distance many times." He was with his wife Ronnie to whom he then introduced to me. As my plates had now arrived he came with me to the car, placing them carefully on the seat. I thanked him and as I drove off I saw the pair of them getting into their open safari car.

Next morning, I went into Nairobi to get some pictures framed and on my return home, there was a Stan Lawrence Brown open safari car parked in the drive. I saw the gun racks and the men in the back talking to my houseboys. I was used to the jeeps and the Land Rovers, but this was a big International safari car and was obviously loaded for a hunting safari. Dark olive-green and with khaki-covered benches, it was designed for the bush and in its ugly way it had a film star glamour. As I looked at it, I could feel my heart accelerate with excitement. That vehicle would always have this effect on me, even through the years and the thousands of miles of African country that I would eventually travel in it. Somehow it personified Stan. He was always immaculate and he kept all his equipment the same way. With military precision and polish, the trucks and lorries would leave their base at Langata and go north, south, east or west, wherever their safaris took them. Sometimes they would remain out for six months at a time.

As I skirted the safari car and went through the opening of the bougainvillaea hedge, I saw Stan talking to Mutete on the porch. He was dressed in a beautifully tailored dark green, short-sleeved bush jacket and matching trousers. As I came up, he took off his safari hat and as we shook hands said, "Could I speak to you for a minute?"

Offering him a cup of tea, which was the invariable Kenya gesture of hospitality, we went inside. He said, "I would love to stay and have tea but I am picking up clients at the Thorn Tree and am late already." When I got to know him I realised that to be late was totally out of character. He asked to use my telephone so as to call them and on his return said to me, "I came here this morning because I have to see you. I am off to the Voi area for six weeks, we will be camping near there and I wondered if you would come down to Voi and meet me."

I think I was totally stunned by such a direct approach from a stranger. I replied that there was no question of my coming. He smiled and said, "I expected as much, but there was always the possibility and I have thought of nothing else since I saw you yesterday." He added, "I have been waiting for you all my life." Whether this was a phrase he had used before, I don't know, but I did realise that at this moment he meant it. I said, "I am not looking for a man, I have a wonderful life. I don't want to complicate it and if I did, it would not be with you. I have never had an affair with a married man and I certainly don't propose to start now." Stan then said to me, "The fact that I am a married man makes no difference to my life. I have been totally unfaithful to Ronnie for years."

His frankness amazed me. Here we were discussing a physical relationship and we were virtually strangers. I probably looked astounded. He gave me a half salute and smiled as he turned to the door, then he leant towards me. I thought he was going to kiss me but he picked up a lock of my long hair that was falling over my shoulder. I remembered noticing how fair it looked against his tanned skin and I could feel the slight pull against my scalp as he lifted it to his mouth. Looking up at me, he said, "I won't rest until I see this beautiful hair spread against my pillow", and with that he was gone.

I think I knew that he wouldn't leave it there. He wouldn't have been the man that he was if he had. From then on, his safari car became a familiar sight in my drive, parked there on the excuse that he needed spare parts for the trucks or to replenish the stores. I don't remember all the reasons he gave me or his clients but he would say, "Even if it is only to see you for an hour, it's worth the drive from Voi." At this stage, he didn't try to take the relationship any further and I began to relax and enjoy his company. He was a master storyteller and he had lived an incredible life.

Stan spoke to me of his youth. I think he had been born in Kenya but I never heard anything about his parents. At the age of 18 he became an ivory poacher. He and his gun-bearer would follow the elephant herds for months on end. For three years, he walked all over Tanganyika, Kenya and Uganda, even following them as far as the Sudan. During all this time he would never see another European. The country in those days was wild and the animal herds were vast, even the various tribes were few and widely spread. He learned to have an enormous respect for the animals he hunted. He told me of the amazing intelligence and the bravery of elephants. One day he came across a young elephant that had been badly wounded, possibly by lion. Unable to keep up with the herd, it eventually collapsed. Stan was about to go and put it out of its misery when two old females detached themselves from the rest and, coming up to the young elephant and placing themselves on either side, hoisted him to his feet and supported him between them until they reached the river close by. There they kept filling their trunks with water and showering him. While Stan watched, they remained near the river for three days. They kept watering him and breaking off choice bits of the trees on the riverbanks for him to eat. They never left him, but nursed him back to health. When he was strong enough, all three then slowly left in search of their herd.

Stan then joined the legendary J. A. Hunter, the greatest white hunter of all, in his opinion. He was certainly always his hero. Hunter, who made his home at Makindu, a big game centre under towering Mount Kilimanjaro, was a colleague and friend of Denys Finch Hatton and he also wrote several books about his life in Africa, including *Hunter's Tracks* and *Hunter* (Hamish Hamilton). In the former, published in 1957, he wrote: "I had an uncle, George Hunter, an eminent surgeon from Edinburgh, who came out to Makindu years ago to indulge in a big game hunting expedition for himself and try to get me to return to Scotland to carry on farming in the family tradition; but I would have none of it. Africa had cast its spell."

Stan told me stories of his many safaris and the close brushes with death... how, as the years went by, he began to hate the unnecessary killing of animals and finally only really enjoyed the safaris that were there for the trophies. He had one famous American couple who used to come out with him every year and they would spend as much as six months at a time on safari, often content to just get the one special trophy. Months would go by without a shot being fired. Year after year they came back and he had the greatest admiration for them and for their love and appreciation of life in the bushland.

He also told me of two other safaris where the people were only interested in slaughtering the game and shot at everything that moved. He said the wounded animals would be lying everywhere, so he aborted the safari each time, refused to continue and refunded their money.

Stan not only told me about the animals and the safaris, but also about the women. He never spared the details of his numerous love affairs. Mostly it was with women he took on safari, but even newlywed brides seemed somehow to end up in his tent for an hour or two while the husband slept. I suppose when you are in the bush and your life depends on your White Hunter, that man takes on a certain aura that women find irresistible. Also, so many of these men like Stan adored women, and hunting and sex seemed to fill their mind to the exclusion of all else. Stan loved the hunt; therefore he loved hunting women.

I would see a lot of Stan over the next few months and he would call me most days on his radio telephone. A fairly erratic contraption that looked like a wireless, there was usually a lot of static on the line, which went through a central exchange. One could only have one-way conversations. I found them quite difficult to adjust to and would never correctly get my "over" or "out" at the right time. I think during this period one of the reasons why Stan never tried to deepen the relationship was that he wanted to see me every spare minute he had and that meant my being able to come to his house. He knew that a more intimate association would prohibit my doing so. I think this was also why he was a great hunter; he had infinite patience and an uncanny knack of picking up emotions. During this stage I saw quite a bit of his wife Ronnie. I had no intention of letting Stan get any closer but I had come to rely on him being in my life. If there were problems I knew he would solve them and he gave me that feeling of security that I have always needed.

I was speaking the truth when I told Stan that I did not need a lover. I had never been promiscuous except for a brief period when I was very young and all the male attention had gone to my head. I had never gone in for drink or drugs – only chain-smoking, which I also eventually gave up. I don't think to this day I've even taken a sleeping tablet.

At various times, Pierre would still turn up with rescued animals. Duma the cheetah had been given to him, for instance, and he had brought it to me to take care of. There was also the owl-faced monkey from the Congo but he hated Pierre so much that I had to be careful to have him locked up whenever he visited. I didn't encourage Pierre but he would turn up at odd times and Stan found this hard to accept. Everything was brought to a head when Stan, Ronnie and I went to Lake Nakuru, north of Lake Naivasha, for the day. Some friends of his had a boat and we had a wonderful time out on the water with the fish eagles overhead and the banks a mass of crimson flamingo. Stan let the boat drift fairly close to the shore and we spent most of the afternoon watching these fabulous birds. Nakuru has colonies of both the lesser and greater flamingo. It is an amazing sight on a cloudless day. The lake and the shore merge to form an incandescent band so it looks as if there is a beach of cyclamen pink sand. The long-legged flamingo are so clearly silhouetted in the waters of the lake it is hard to tell where reflection begins and reality ends.

Afterwards we went to the clubhouse for a drink. Stan as usual knew everyone and soon friends of his had joined us. My heart sank as I caught sight of Pierre coming in as I knew that Stan would be furious if he came and talked to me. I turned my back and pretended not to see him. The next thing a familiar voice was saying. *"Cherie, qu'est-ce que tu fais ici?"* Pierre had drawn up a chair and had come to sit beside me. We were quite a party. I, as usual when nervous, was chain-smoking and drinking Coca-Cola and fundamentally not displeased that two such attractive men were giving me so much of their undivided attention even though I knew Pierre was only flirting with me to annoy Stan.

On the way home, I could feel Stan's displeasure at the way the evening had turned out. I concentrated on talking to Ronnie and telling her what a con artist Pierre was and how I much preferred my animals to human beings. I added that I had spent most of my life with my family and was really happier without a man to complicate one's existence. At the time I truly believed this and felt sure I could contain the attraction I felt for Stan. I stayed for dinner that night and I think it was Ronnie's suggestion that as it was so late, I should stay overnight and Stan, who was leaving on safari early, could drop me off in the morning. I called up Mutete, made the arrangements for the animals, and was shown to Stan's room at the other end of the house from Ronnie.

About midnight, the door opened and Stan came in. All he had on was a *kikoi* tied at his waist and before I was fully awake, he was in bed with me. He immediately started attacking me about Pierre, asking why I had lied to him when I had told him that I had broken up with him years ago. It was obvious to everyone, he said, that we were still lovers. Nothing I could say would pacify him and his argument was that if I was so available for Pierre, why was I still messing him around. I could see that he had got to the stage that he didn't give a damn that we were in his wife's house; he was determined to make love to me. Terrified of the consequences, I leapt out of bed and like a terrified virgin told him that unless he left the room immediately, I would scream the house down. This whole scene was conducted in whispers, which got louder by the minute. My last sight of Stan that night was him standing by the open door in his *kikoi*, so tanned that in the half light he looked like an Indian, and saying, "My God, you are a bitch." I heard the front door close and then there was silence once more.

I lay in the dark thinking of the dreadful scene that had just taken place and wondering whether I shouldn't get up and walk home. I hated the idea of remaining in a house where I wasn't welcome. The thought of the long walk in the dark filled me with apprehension but it almost seemed better than staying where I was. Working out that it would only take me a couple of hours and that dawn would soon be breaking, I was talking myself into departing when the door burst open and the lights were switched on. It was Ronnie, with her red hair and sallow complexion, wearing an old orange dressing gown. It was passing through my mind that the colours did nothing for her when she demanded, "Where is Stan?"

I was able to sit up in bed and say with perfect truth that I had no idea. My heart was racing; it was getting too much like a scene out of the worst melodrama. It was obvious he wasn't in the room so I told Ronnie that I had heard the front door slam, maybe he had gone outside. We ended up having a cup of tea and she told me how it was to be sharing a bed with him again. It was like being on a second honeymoon he was so passionate! I realised that Stan was a very virile man but I also thought to myself, if what she says is true, he has certainly carried it to extremes this night.

Stan drove me home early next morning and we hardly spoke on the way. I didn't even discuss Ronnie's visit with him. I kept thinking that instead of treating me like a leper, he should have been intensely grateful to me that we hadn't all ended up in a terrible confrontation.

When he climbed out of the safari car to say goodbye to me, he said, "I'm off for two months and possibly it is best if I don't see you again until I return." He bent to kiss me on the cheek saying, "Forgive me for last night." He turned to leave, and then came back saying, "I know I have no right but if what you tell me is true and you don't love Pierre, could you promise me not to see him while I am away?" Then he left and I didn't see him or hear from him again for the two months.

I went to meet him one evening when he drove up the roadway to Ol Orion, thrilled at the thought of seeing him again, but unsure of my welcome after all this time of silence. As he came towards me, he said that he only had a few minutes as he had left his clients at the hotel and finished, saying, "I didn't intend coming here tonight but my clients want to extend their safari and I cannot do so until I have spoken to you."

We were standing in the garden. I could barely see him in the dim reflection of the porch light but even today I can still hear his voice. He told me, "I have done everything to forget you but you have become an obsession, I want to be near you, to see you. I want to hear your voice and to watch you smile. You have ruined my safari. Every time I pick up a rifle, I think how you hate hunting, and at night I have a woman in my arms and I can only think of you. I am willing to accept life on your terms."

He added that he did not want to extend the safari he was on, that he had three weeks until his next booking and that he would take a safari to the Mara reserve by the Tanganyika border, a wonderful place to see wildlife and game, for those three weeks if I would go with him. I explained that my mother was arriving and I knew she would love to go, and there were also the animals and they would have to come too. I did not think he would agree to this too easily but he laughed and said, "If I have to play chauffeur to the whole of Barnum and Bailey and watch the Mara being turned into a circus act I will go but, my darling, can we leave in the middle of the night? If any of my friends see me I will never live it down and I would hate to be known as Noah."

I went back to his car with him. It was still full of safari equipment. His gun bearer and two other safari boys were busy drinking the tea that Mutete had provided. They were bundled up in khaki overcoats against the chill of night and they were so dark I could not see their faces, only hear their muted laughter. Stan said something to them I did not understand and there was more laughter. I felt shut off from this male society and wondered if I was the object of their merriment. I asked him what they all found so funny and he said that he had told them if they had never been to a zoo, they soon would be driving in one, and what do zoo keepers spend most of their time doing? Cleaning up the crap!

I can still see the darkness, the safari car, the guns, the Africans in the back with their overcoats and bare feet. I can smell the wood smoke and Stan leaning against his truck, laughing at the thought of his next safari.

CHAPTER

44

We left for the Mara a few days later, I with my animals and Mummy with hers. It was quite late in the morning, Mummy delaying departure as usual, so it was evening when we arrived on the banks of the Mara river and dinner was ready by the time the tents were erected. Mummy had wanted to have a picnic on the way and that had delayed things even more. We had the International and two five-ton lorries, all painted in the safari dark green with matching canvas coverings. They carried the equipment and because of Tana we had to carry an enormous amount of meat and so extra paraffin fridges had had to be loaded. I wasn't having anything extra killed to supply her food.

Parts of the Mara are like English parkland but instead of fat cows grazing there were herds of elephant. We could drive almost up to them at times. Other days we would go to the Loita Hills, their slopes covered in thick forests. We were so high that we were often in clouds which, when they lifted, gave us views across the whole of the Rift Valley. The trees would drip onto the ferns below and glades full of filtered sunlight would open up as we walked. Mummy would collect the wild orchids that hung from the branches overhead. It was a magic land, the days were full of adventure under a hot sun and the nights were cold. We would sit in front of a campfire, with the tented camp behind us and in the distance was the roar of lion or the mournful scream of the hyena.

Stan, as he had promised, never tried to take things further in our relationship but I was in love and seeing Africa in a golden haze. His hand would brush me and it was as if a thousand needles had touched my skin. While we were driving, I would sit in the middle of the front bench between Stan and my mother. I could feel the muscles of his thigh where it touched mine. I was playing with fire and I knew it but Mummy's presence was a barrier that I had erected and one I desperately wanted to maintain. How long he would have allowed me to go on with my games I don't know, but then Tana saved my life and that changed everything.

Mummy, myself and Stan had been camped on the Mara for a week or so. The large green luxurious tents were spread out under the shade of the fever trees, the most beautiful of all the trees of Africa, with their yellow trunks and wide spreading branches of small feathery leaves, such a pale green against the blue sky. Because these trees grow in wet and marshland conditions which favour the breeding of mosquitoes and because their tall spreading branches provide ideal campsite shade, the early pioneers whose tents would be pitched under them, were convinced that their fevers (malaria) were caused by them.

In the forests of fever trees, we could always see giraffe, with their long necks and their heads with those enormous and heavily lashed eyes peering at you from out of the branches. Motionless, these giant dappled pre-historic figures merged so well into their surroundings that often they were hard to pick up. With unblinking eyes, they would stare at you before turning and moving off. They were so graceful with their enormous loping stride, their long legs and incongruous body and neck topped by that small beautiful head. Giraffe have a natural elegance that reminds me of the Christian Dior models who used to parade for my mother.

Each evening, I would take Tana for a walk along the banks of the river on which we were camped, keeping a wary eye out for crocodile and hippo. Stan would be out shooting some poor Thompson gazelle or plains game for the African staff. I refused to go with him on these occasions and made him go as far away from camp as possible so there was no possibility of my even hearing the sound of a gun.

Mummy would sit outside the tent with her easel and watercolours and she often used to lecture me on my behaviour, saying, "Darling, you must realise that Stan is a hunter and you will never be able to change him and it is very wrong of you to even try." I would put my arms around her and in my arrogance tell her that I was not prepared to be all things to all men as she would always be. I didn't have Mummy's patience, I didn't rely on men and I had no great talent for anything. All I had inherited was her great love of animals and a passion for my family.

It was on one of these evenings when Stan had gone out shooting that Tana and I were following the magnificent Mara River which winds this way and that in the most erratic fashion, its steep banks rising from the muddy waters, almost sheer in some places. The river and its banks were a seething mass of hippo and I loved their roaring grunts, one long one followed by three or four short blasts. Like the giraffe, hippo have hardly altered in shape down through the centuries. I remember the great anthropologist and archaeologist Louis Leakey, showing me the skull of one in the Coryndon Museum in Nairobi, dating it some 20 million years old.

As I walked through the thick forest and lush green vegetation that lined the banks of the river, I watched with amusement as the mother and baby hippos charged about with a great deal of splashing in the river below. The setting sun was a large red disc, casting an orange glow over the river and countryside, and the hippo were bathed in its wonderful light. It was like stepping into another enthrallingly magic and mysterious world.

I was strolling along in a dream and Tana was pacing slowly somewhere behind. She always behaved as if my mad desire for walking was a habit to be discouraged and she would follow as if every step was a supreme effort. I would have to stop for her to catch up, whereupon she would usually flop down as if to say, "Enough is enough!" When I was on my own like this I very seldom went out of sight of the camp, but this evening I was lost in the beauty of my surroundings and I was also watching an eagle soaring above the plains beyond. Black against the crimson sky, it was sailing in the thermals, giant wings outstretched as it drifted on the vagaries of the evening currents. I saw it plummet to earth, then soar once more with legs outstretched, bearing its captured prey homewards. I followed its path and was almost up to its nest on the other side of a large swampy area when Tana charged, throwing me to the ground.

Suddenly I was lying on my back in the mud with Tana on top of me. Used to her games of hide and seek, I thought for a minute she had gone too far in her exuberance. I could feel the cold water seeping into my shirt and the smell of the mud as I lay there. Unable to move because of Tana's weight, I was about to shout at her when I realised her whole being was concentrated on a point somewhere beyond my head. My instinct and faith in her told me that she had done this for a reason and that I must remain as still as the lioness above me. Tana's weight had pressed me down into the mud and I had visions of lying there unable to move while I was buried alive in this foul-smelling viscous earth. All I could see was Tana's head and shoulder and I could feel her heartbeat through my chest, or was it my own heart I felt? I was conscious of the mud, the thud of the heart, the smell of lion and the sense of danger and of waiting. Slowly I turned my head and still Tana sat unmoving. Then I saw them, dark shapes in the tall swamp grass, a herd of buffalo. How many I could not see but I could hear the sucking noise as they moved in the mud. I could hear them munching and it seemed I could even hear them breathing. I had almost walked into a herd of one of the most deadly of animals.

Tana, probably astounded by my carelessness, had leapt to protect me as she would have done for an unruly cub. Maybe the herd got the scent of lion for they started moving off. I could hear the sound of the mud churning and smell the odour of excrement and urine that rose from the water. I could feel Tana relax on top of me but she still kept me pinned to the ground and I could picture the old bull probably standing guard over his herd as they departed.

Then I watched Tana turn and look in the direction from which we had come and I wondered what new danger was upon us. I slowly moved my head and saw Stan standing there, his rifle cocked ready to shoot but at what I could not see. For one dreadful moment I thought it was at me. Afterwards he told me that when he returned to camp and I was not in sight, he had decided to follow our tracks and having found us, he thought Tana had attacked me and that it was my lifeless body lying under her.

Tana now removed herself and I was able to sit up. As I did so, the filthy muddy water from my hair trickled down my face. Stan strode towards me and I could see him laughing at my predicament. I felt furious that he should look so immaculate while I was such a stinking mess. I wanted to sulk and not get up as he leant down to help me to my feet. I could even have pulled him down into the mud; he was laughing so hard that it would have been quite easy. Then it struck me how funny this whole situation was and there was the relief of knowing that I was safe and that once again Tana had saved my life. I started giggling and longed to tell Stan the story but as he pulled me into his arms, my laughter turned to tears. We stood in the filthy swamp, with the mud dripping off me, and I knew there was no other place I wanted to be.

I think I had always realised that one day we would become lovers, but now that I had lain so close to death and now I was in his arms, smelling of filth and covered in mud, I knew he was my security and a man I could love.

CHAPTER

45

Mummy never mentioned our changed relationship. I moved into Stan's tent for the rest of our time on the Mara and began a passionate affair that lasted for eight years. In many ways I spoiled the even tenor of his life. We were continually being forced to separate for months on end because of his business commitments and he didn't like that. For the first few years he would insist on my coming with him but this really did not work. He refused to see it but I found the whole situation uncomfortable with his clients and I couldn't accept the killing of animals.

My participation in his hunting safaris became more and more disastrous. One time, we were driving along and came across a large bull elephant. Leaving me in the car, Stan and the client went after it. I thought hard about what to do but finally couldn't bear it any longer. I loudly sounded the horn. That of course spoilt everything. The client was furious. Stan, when he recovered from the shock, thought it was very funny.

My animals were also a problem as I couldn't take them with me when he had his clients on safari. I could only take them when we went off on our own. I think the more problems I created for Stan though, the more he loved me. As the months turned into years, he began shifting his safaris onto his other hunters and he only took out his very special clients. This way he was able to spend more time with me. Taking his safari car and a lorry, we would go to all his favourite sites. These times together had the most profound effect on my life. Stan Lawrence Brown was one of the most famous of Kenya's elite band of white hunters. Seeing this land through his eyes showed me a country of miracles. He had a camp site he loved on the Mara. In the late fifties and sixties there weren't a million tourists as there are today. It was a wild and beautiful place, brimming with game.

On one occasion, going back to camp, we joined a migration of wildebeest, and drove for hours at walking pace, surrounded by thousands upon thousands of these antelope. Under a haze of dust, I could see a moving sea of brown stretching to the horizon. They were also packed solid around the car which, being open on all sides, allowed me to touch them if I leant out. Stan drove more and more slowly to enable the herd to pass but so enormous was it that dusk had arrived before we were clear.

It was late at night before we finally arrived back because we had travelled such a distance with the herd. It never seemed to worry Stan. He knew every bush and hill in east Africa as if he were in his own garden. He had camped in the hills, the forests and the plains since he was a boy and through the years had learned to love this beautiful land and respect the game that lived off it.

He taught me so much. His knowledge of game and their ways was infinite and each piece of dung told its story and each track was a tale. He was unmoved by the magnificence of the scenery. It was his country and he knew no other. My continual ecstasy over the various splendours he unveiled as we explored each bit of new territory never ceased to amuse him. He took me as far afield as Uganda and Tanganyika, to find areas new to me. After so many years of hunting, they were totally familiar to him.

It's probably not that surprising that Stan and I fell in love. Although he had made his life out of killing animals and I only wanted to save them, a hunter has to be almost psychic with animals. You have to know animals if you are to hunt them. As Stan would say to me, "You have to understand them, read them and understand your country."

Stan, knowing the habits of the wild, tried to teach me their ways and through his knowledge I came to see Africa with different eyes. He would take me into a herd of elephant and I would have no fear; we would follow hippo trails for hours at a time. Sometimes I would be up to my shoulders in muddy streams and on leaving the water he would show me how to get rid of the leeches with which we were covered, lighting a match under their tails. We would often walk 12 or 15 miles a day: through the forests of the highlands, through the great savannah lands of the plains where often the elephant grass was higher than my head, or over the deserts of the northern frontier.

Stan would lead the way. He always wore his wide-brimmed safari hat, green bush jacket and khaki drill trousers and tennis shoes. He said it was for easier walking and he insisted that I do the same except I wore khaki shirts and skirts and positively refused to wear a hat. He was a stickler for dress and I think would have refused to take anyone unless they conformed. For him, no garish colours. "I refuse to get charged just because some idiot looks like a Christmas cracker," he would say. I once dared to put on a pair of blue jeans in camp and he sent me back to get changed. His theory was that wild animals are the colour of their surroundings; therefore, if one wished to live amongst them, one had to emulate them.

We would walk for days and miles following elephant. He always carried a gun as did Ismael, his gunbearer, but they were never fired. He let me experience the excitement of the hunt without being the hunter. How marvellous to come right up under an enormous bull elephant after several days of following his trail and be able to stand silently watching him as he browsed on the trees in passing. Once we came upon a herd grazing on a field of white flowers. I sat entranced for hours as mothers with their babies walked through this dream garden, lifting great bunches of flowers in their trunks, looking like brides going to a wedding. For days I would close my eyes and recall the beauty of this scene.

Although he never spoke of it, I think in the years I spent with Stan his business must have suffered. Our relationship must also have affected the family as now he was hardly ever at home. When in

Nairobi, I never allowed him to spend the night at Ol Orion but because he was such a jealous man he was convinced that it was because I wanted to see someone else. He would turn up at odd hours of the day or night, if only for a few minutes, and on any excuse, because he didn't trust me. Having had so many affairs, he did not have any confidence in the fidelity of women, and the fact that I was never jealous of him – or had any desire for marriage – made him even more uncertain of me.

When Stan went on his long hunting safaris, which I started refusing to go on because I could not bear the killing, I would arrange to join him for a week or a few days. Stan hated going off and leaving me behind because he was so certain that I would find somebody else. Going to meet him kept him from chucking in his safaris altogether. I would take the International that Stan had given me – it was the same model as his own – and I would drive to meet him. This way I got to know all the roads of the east African countries and had some marvellous adventures while doing so.

Meanwhile, Stan would feel the frustrations of being confined to the safaris and worried about me being on my own. He had developed angina and these problems were not helping. Then he started taking out more and more photographic safaris so that I could be with him. This was all very well but the company relied on the hunting safaris for its real money. One day in Arusha we met up with one of his hunters in the bar of the hotel. The bar was crowded and Stan knew almost everybody there. During the course of the evening, one of the men laughingly said to me, "You must be the most expensive girl in east Africa. How can poor Stan afford you?" At first I didn't realise what he was talking about, but thinking it over I realised that I must be a disaster for Stan's business and that outfitting our luxurious safaris with cars, lorries, provisions and all the men must be costing a fortune. Certainly no expense was ever spared. In his business, Stan was a perfectionist and his safaris were Hollywood-style, everything was the best. Even the tyres of the safari cars were polished. It was only later, after I went to live further north-east with Tana at the game reserve at Meru, so many miles away from Nairobi, that Stan finally felt safe to go back to his old hunting safari lifestyle.

During our years together we never discussed marriage. He loved his wife and adored his children and as far as I was concerned, the idea of actually being married had always terrified me. I think that one of the reasons why very attractive men like my husbands Frank and Aymon who loved women, and the two men I had affairs with, Guy de Lesseps and Stan, loved me is because I never threatened their independence.

On one occasion, Stan and I had just come back from a trip. I had to spend a few days at Karen and had told Stan that I would meet him at the Thorn Tree when I had finished my shopping. The International with his safari boys and the animals was parked outside and we were sitting having coffee with some friends when his wife Ronnie arrived. I had not seen her for years and my heart sank at the sight of her approaching our table. Ignoring Stan, she picked up a saucer and threw it straight in my face, thank goodness just missing my eye but splitting open the skin over my cheekbone. Stan took me into John Kamali the chemist, for a patch-up.

It was all rather dramatic and embarrassing being in such a public place and I hate scenes. Stan then insisted on taking me to William Boyle to have the wound stitched because it was still bleeding profusely. "My! We do live dangerously. Serves you right," said William cheerfully. "She should have done it long ago!"

I had a black eye for a while but I couldn't really blame her. And in fact, I respected Stan's love for his family. He was a man who was totally indiscreet about his love affairs and I would be given the most intimate details about these various ladies. But Ronnie, he never discussed with me. She was the mother of his children, a good and faithful wife, and not only did he love her but he also had the utmost respect for her.

Stan, my animals and the country were like a woven tapestry of great beauty. They became an intrinsic part of my life and I loved them with a passion. Years later, I had to make the terrible decision to leave everything and everyone I loved and accompany my mother to South Africa. Only on the day that I told Stan did he beg me to marry him and stay with him in Kenya. He came with me to South Africa, our last journey together, but he had to return to Kenya and he refused to believe I wouldn't be coming back.

CHAPTER
46

In late 1960, Stan and I were in Tanganyika, and had come into Arusha for a few days as Stan had to see one of his hunters. I decided to borrow his International and went off to see a friend of mine, Suki Bisletti, who was nearby looking after the animals for a film they were making at the time. It was *Hatari*, which in Swahili means danger. Suki usually lived at a marvellous farm at Naivasha overlooking the lake and was passionate about wild animals. She had tame lion amongst which was Tana's full brother, her great pet Shaibu who had been rescued at the same time as Tana. There were also lovely leopard cubs that she had tamed.

Suki, like so many women in Kenya, was not only beautiful but striking. When she walked into a room, you were immediately conscious of a vibrant presence. Tall, with long blonde hair and a lovely figure, she stood out from those around her. Although young, she had had a tragic life and it was a testimony to the strength of her character that she had not only survived, but could still present such a gay and vivacious personality.

She had been living in Vietnam with her parents, still a very young married woman with a baby, when they were all taken prisoner by the Japanese. They were put in a prison camp where she and her mother were separated from her father. Thinking of her child, Suki had managed to grab some Entreviaform when the Japanese took them and had concealed it on herself. This medicine was particularly effective in cases of dysentery and she feels that it was because of this that they were able to survive when so many others died during the terrible three years of captivity.

I parked the car with my animals at the bottom of the drive of the house where Suki was staying as I didn't want to upset the animals that were in her care. As I walked towards the house, I saw a magnificent black-maned lion lying on the lawn. He was tied to a running lead suspended between two trees. It gave him ample freedom and he was separated from the house by a low hedge. Suki, looking as glamorous as ever, was on the verandah feeding some wild birds.

We were just sitting down to have tea – it was a custom that no matter what time of day one arrived tea was always on offer – when a Land Rover arrived and parked. It was another friend of mine Diana Hartley and she had just unloaded two cheetah that were to be used on the film set. Diana had come by our camp a few weeks before and we had gone for a walk with Tana. We somehow got onto the subject of death and she told me in detail how she had been staying with her parents during the Mau Mau uprising and was there when they were attacked. Her stepfather, Gray Leakey, was a great admirer of the Kikuyu, a blood brother, and spoke their language fluently. He considered them his friends and refused to believe that they would ever harm him or his family. All the same, when the Mau Mau gang arrived, her parents took the precaution of hiding Diana in the roof of their house, the access to which was a trapdoor. Then they went out unarmed to meet their friends. They were both killed.

Diana then married one of the Hartleys from the famous family of hunters in Kenya, and her husband, Lionel, died in a plane crash soon after, leaving her with two young children to bring up. She had almost killed one of them when a shotgun she kept in the back of the car went off when she was picking it up. She said to me and I will never forget it, "I have had such a violent life that I am more and more convinced that I will die a violent death. I seem to feel death all around me."

By the time we had returned to camp I was feeling quite chilled and watched the shadows with apprehension. Death was usually far from my thoughts but in the cold evening air that night, it seemed to be very close. She was a lovely person and full of life and, watching her laugh and joke with Stan later, I refused to believe that such a cloud could hang over anyone so young.

Now, when Diana climbed out of her Land Rover and came towards us, I remember noticing that she was wearing white, sling-back, open-toed sandals. In those days dress was very conventional in the bush. It was a matter of life or death to be dressed so as to merge into the surroundings. The garish colours you see today on the tours hadn't arrived on the Kenya scene. Diana was dressed in khaki but still, to wear sandals when safety around wild animals requires you to wear what allows for maximum agility at all times was, to say the least, unusual. Suki went to meet her and I heard Diana say, "I would just like to go and say hello to Yusef [the lion]. I know him well." She did add, "I don't really suppose I should as I must smell of cheetah and I have got the curse." She was laughing as she spoke.

Suki said she went with Diana to see the lion and on approaching him, Diana asked her, "How well do you know him?" Suki answered, "Hardly at all." Diana then said, "Maybe I shouldn't go nearer, I don't like the look in his eyes." At this stage she started to slowly back away. Suki said in retrospect that if Diana had jumped back immediately, she would have been all right. At that moment, the lion sprang, knocking Diana to the ground. Suki, with tremendous courage, started beating the lion over the head with the stick she was carrying and that succeeded in getting the lion off Diana.

I went to see what was happening. I heard Diana's voice saying quite quietly, "Please help me," and to my horror I saw her on the ground, one shoe off and lying to one side, and the lion sitting with both paws on her shoulders swishing his tail while Suki frantically tried to drag Diana away. At this moment, the men arrived and one tweaked the lion by his tail. As he twisted around, Suki managed to get Diana away. I think she was still conscious. Suki told me later that as the lion reared up, it had grabbed Diana by the throat and torn her jugular. I did not see any of this; only Diana like a rag doll lying crumpled at the lion's feet. I was now late and so Stan had come to find me. I told him of the horror of what I had just witnessed. "Come," he said, "we will go back to the camp. I will drive you home as I know you will want to be with Tana." One thing I found so amazing about Stan was his insight into nature. He was right. It was to my lioness I now needed to go for comfort.

Stan had organised for a portable wire cage that could be easily fitted into the back section of the International for when we travelled. This was for Tana who, as she grew older, began to show distinct signs of disliking children. In villages, they would crowd around the car and I didn't want to take any unnecessary risks.

It was in this section, with its floor covered in mattresses, that I now went to sit with her. When I had started out that afternoon, the sun had been hot. Now the chill of early evening had me shivering and I think the shock was beginning to take effect, even my teeth were starting to chatter as I buried my face in Tana's neck. I was so cold and I needed her warmth. It was a long drive home in an open car and putting my arms around her I lay as I had so often done, curled up against her back.

Tana could always sense my moods and she soon rolled over so that I was lying rather like a cub between her front legs, my head resting on her forearm. She draped the other over my shoulder while she nuzzled my face like a huge cat. Tana would always rub her head against me; it was one of her signs of affection.

Now as I lay with my face in her neck, I could sink into the sweet lion smell of her. My love for her was so intense that it was almost a physical pain and I knew that she also knew this. It was as if she and I were one being and her blood was flowing through my blood and the beat of her heart beneath my ear was my heart, and the soft sound of her breathing was my breath and her fur was soon wet with my tears.

The next day I learned that Diana was dead. She had died the violent death of which she had been so conscious, and of which she had spoken to me only a few weeks before.

CHAPTER

47

It was Tubby Block who, as one of the stewards of the East African Turf Club, first introduced my mother to racing in Kenya. He also re-introduced her to the aviatrix and horse trainer Beryl Markham whom she'd known when she was married to Furness. Thus began the Beryl saga which had such an impact on my own life.

Very tall and fair with marvellous blue eyes, Beryl had an aura of tranquillity about her although she was, in reality, anything but. She had a lovely soft voice, gentle serene face, perfect skin and teeth, a Botticelli angel so beautiful she was all soft shadows. She fascinated and intrigued anyone who came across her. Always in immaculate tailored trousers and loose shirt, her clouds of blonde hair would peep out from under her blue sunhats. In the presence of a lover or an attractive male, her tall willowy figure, usually very erect, would droop helplessly like a flower towards the sun and she would adopt a young girl's awkwardness.

Beryl had been taught by her father to train racehorses as a young girl and she had been Kenya's first professional woman pilot licensed to deliver passengers and mail, but she was the epitome of femininity. She had a way of opening her enormous eyes as if the lids were too heavy to support them and gazing at one with a childlike innocence and trust. Over the years I watched mesmerised, as we succumbed to her magic. She was a chameleon, adapting herself to the person she wanted to impress. She also had a totally ruthless side to her character. Once she had made up her mind on a course of action, nothing and no one was allowed to get in her way. It was this determination which in 1936 and in spite of all the terrible risks made her the first person to fly across the Atlantic alone from east to west. She was only 33. It was this quality that eventually also ended up taking my mother and me to South Africa with her, and it was this tenacity that made her Kenya's greatest horse trainer.

Tubby was a leading owner with some top horses in his string and Beryl trained for him. One Derby day, he had a horse running, and my mother accompanied him to the paddock. She was not allowed through though because she didn't have the necessary badge and so she turned to Tubby who had come to her rescue and asked, "What do I need to get into this bloody place?" Tubby replied, "A horse."

"Well," said my mother, "buy me one."

That is how she started her Kenya racing chapter with Beryl and she ended up with numerous top horses. Just a few years later she won the Derby with Lone Eagle, a horse owned in partnership by her and by Beryl's lover Jan Thrane. The horse was named after Beryl's hero, Charles Lindbergh, whose nickname was Lone Eagle and who had been the first man to fly the Atlantic.

Beryl had been abandoned at an early age by her mother who couldn't take the hardships of the primitive life the settlers in Kenya had to endure. Beryl was raised by her father, an English gentleman, Charles Clutterbuck and a housekeeper, Mrs Orchardson, and the Kipsigi tribesmen near Njoro in the White Highlands. According to my mother, she had never seen a pair of shoes until she was 17 and would run barefoot in the forests all day with the warriors on a hunt or ride vast distances to visit her friends. Warriors had no time for the weak or the sickly, they were left outside to die, and Beryl inherited this attitude. She was merciless in her scorn of frailty, either in man or beast. No concessions were made for age, illness or pain.

Beryl never had money yet she lived in comparative luxury. Her house, lent to her by Tubby, was beautifully run; she had a marvellous cook and a houseboy. Her extravagances were hairdressers, manicurists and tailors but she never wore dresses. Her car was an old blue Mercedes she had had for years, and she was always accompanied by her dogs, a boxer and two Alsatians who were almost totally disobedient but adored.

At the time I got to know her, she was in her early sixties although she looked half that age. There were stories about her legions of lovers and of wild parties but when I knew her, she seldom went out and seemed totally content with the love and companionship of Jan Thrane and Charles Norman, her present and past lovers. My mother told me that Beryl had a very masculine attitude to sex and had been on the fringes of the Happy Valley crowd for a time. The life there – captured later by the James Fox book and film *White Mischief* about the murder of Lord Erroll – was almost entirely devoted to sex and drugs. Drugs as far as Beryl was concerned were a perquisite of the weak and therefore they were taboo. The African attitude to sex was very casual though and Beryl, being a very beautiful wild girl who had been brought up almost exclusively in a tough male society, was promiscuous from an early age.

Indeed, as a result of her upbringing, she was totally amoral, not only sexually, but in her attitude to life. One could never afford to leave anything of value in her presence; a camera that could be sold, jewellery or money. As she once said to me, "If you are stupid enough to leave it lying around then I would be stupid not to avail myself of it."

On one occasion I had just been to the bank to cash wages for my staff, the equivalent of £50, a great deal of money in those days. Stupidly, I left my handbag in her sitting room and had only driven a short distance away before realising what I had done. Before turning back, I drove to the nearest telephone at Naivasha. I knew Beryl could not miss seeing my bag and I told her exactly how much was in it, as I felt that would be the only way of protecting the money until I could get there. I knew and she knew that there was nobody else in the house, but by the time I got back half an hour later the money was gone. When I pointed this out, she opened her eyes very wide and in the softest voice, said, "Oh sweetie! How very unfortunate! It must have been Timau. How very naughty of him."

We both knew that there was no question of it being anyone else.

Only a few weeks earlier she had nicked a very good camera of mine so I was more furious with myself than with her. I should have known better. The remarkable thing about Beryl was that I never thought less of her for it. She was so blatant about her dishonesty that one almost admired her for it. The fact that she had been raised almost entirely by the Kipsigis made one forgive her all her sins given she had inherited so many other outstanding qualities from them.

Maybe in a way, this added to the mystique surrounding her.

Mummy had known her before because she had been the girlfriend of Duke Furness's pilot, Tom Campbell Black, and used to visit Burrough Court. Mummy told me that when Beryl decided to have her nose remodelled, she had consulted her as to who was the best plastic surgeon, and accordingly had then booked in to my mother's own specialist, Sir Archibald McIndoe. Having done so and being short of cash at the time (the usual scenario with Beryl) she had sent the bills to Furness to pay. Beryl had decided too that she required a smart new wardrobe to suit the lifestyle she was leading and the large accounts – for Beryl hadn't stinted herself – were also sent to Furness's office for payment. Mummy thought it very funny but told me that Duke nearly had a seizure, he was so furious. Mummy managed to pacify him and saw to it that the bills got paid.

When we caught up with Beryl in Kenya at Tubby's, she was living in one of the manager's cottages on the Block estates. Tubby had offered her the use of one of his farms at Naivasha for her stables and gallops because she was training so many of his horses. Somehow she wangled a cottage for herself as well. It was a charming typical Kenyan house with a green tin roof and a large garden gently sloping down to Lake Naivasha which was thickly fringed with the magnificent tall fever trees, the yellow-barked acacia that are seen in most of the lake and river areas of Kenya.

The house was very comfortable and furnished in pale cool colours. Beryl had delicious food and a particularly memorable salad dressing made with crushed garlic, oil, vinegar, sugar, pepper and salt. She was a very informal easy hostess, leaving guests to their own devices, but she made use of whoever was staying to do the shopping (which included paying the bill), collect the mail or do any other of the various chores that bored her.

The gallops for the horses she trained consisted of black-larva soil beautifully maintained by Tubby's equipment, large harrows, tractors, and then a row of stableboys who used to walk behind the machinery, picking up any of the pieces of larva upturned or stray stones. Beryl had a meticulous eye for detail and no expense or effort was spared on the horses. All the time I knew her she was having rows with someone who she considered had failed her in this respect. Mostly it was directed at Tubby's manager who was expected to drop his other activities to concentrate on her. As he was doing her a favour in the first place, I felt she should have shown slightly more gratitude. Her other *bête noire* were the jockeys, except for Buster Parnell, who she adored and who could do no wrong.

The pair of them were a marvellous combination; he, good looking, intelligent and articulate and above all a superb rider. Buster later became champion jockey of Ireland. When he left Beryl to ride in Ireland, life on the farm became unbearable. Together they had won every classic in the country and Beryl, a perfectionist, was not prepared to accept second best. Admittedly, Buster was a hard act to follow and her frustration was soon in evidence with the appalling treatment she meted out to his successors. She would devise fiendish ploys to force them to resign. The fever trees surrounding the gallop were full of long thorns and when the devil was in Beryl, she would go out training particularly early, usually before the dawn had broken and the hippo were still lumbering around. Their great dark shadows would emerge out of the night to go splashing back into the lake, much to the terror of the horses who never got used to them.

It was a brave jockey who lasted with Beryl longer than a few weeks. Either he would be ripped because a frenzied horse who had been kept waiting too long galloped headlong into the thorn trees, or he would be unseated in the path of an enraged hippo. Beryl, a superb horsewoman would calmly ride up and, eyeing the unfortunate man, say, "If you can't control your horse, get down and I will put one of the syces [stableboys] on." Or, "If you can't ride, why did you become a jockey?" as the victim emerged dripping mud from out of a hippo pool. The final insult delivered in the sweetest voice would be, "Oh dear! I am afraid you will now have to walk back." She would then turn the string and head off into the dawn.

I could always tell Beryl's string. They had none of the lean ribbed appearance of most horses in Kenya. They were big, beautifully muscled-up and with a lovely bloom to them. One could have eaten off the floor of their stables so meticulously did Beryl keep everything. She fed them well and she worked them hard. Those early morning rides there were memorable for me. Where else in the world could one watch a beautiful string of thoroughbreds work, while dawn broke from behind the mountains of the Aberdares, colouring the lake in pastel shades, and the first cries of the fish eagles could be heard as they rose from their nests in the fever trees? All around would come the startled grunts of hippos disturbed from their grazing and charging back into the water, their massive bodies making great waves before submerging into the lake. The egrets and herons disturbed by their passage would rise in clouds out of the papyrus shrilling their alarm. Feathery fronds of these reeds rose like giant flowers, black against the pink waters of the lake in which the rising sun was so gloriously reflected.

Lake Naivasha, surrounded by its mountains and volcanoes, its fever trees and tropical vegetation, is a sanctuary for bird-life, from its eagles and pelicans to all types of lesser waterbirds, including the brilliant malachite kingfishers and lilac-breasted rollers. If the bird-life does not enchant one with its endless colours and variety, there is in addition a plethora of game to be seen on its banks. Reigning over this kingdom by the lake was Beryl and how well she managed to compete; she also was magnificent.

Although I was 30 years younger, she was one of my greatest friends. There was no sense of age difference. Just as with my mother, I often felt I was the elder and would strive to protect this fragile creature from the harsh realities of the world as did her entourage of admirers. I was the only woman friend in her close circle during this period of her life at Naivasha; Beryl had no time for the "weaker sex". I think her friendships with women during her life were few and far between; yet when a friendship evolved, she became very dependent on it. In her personal life she was rather disorganised and as she grew older, and when a lover was not always there to smooth the way, she turned to her few remaining women friends.

During the years I knew Beryl, I was continually being called up and asked with the greatest urgency to come down and sort out some problem or other for her, as if she were incapable of doing so for herself. Beryl would turn her back on anything unpleasant, either sweeping it under the carpet or waiting until one of us had solved the problem. Her personal bravery was phenomenal, she was totally and utterly fearless, but she was a moral coward. It used to amaze me to what lengths she would go rather than face up to someone.

All her scare tactics had failed to dislodge one jockey. He was a Scotsman with red hair and, although he must have loathed her, being stable jockey to Beryl Markham was the plum job in Kenya and he clung to it. The time had come when she couldn't bear him any longer and decided to dismiss him. I got a telephone call. "Sweetie, I desperately need your help," she cried. With Beryl, as soon as one received a call and she started with "sweetie pie" or, in extreme cases "darling", I knew that some unspeakable errand was being handed to me.

"Sweetie," she said, "you have to get rid of that dreadful little man." She followed up with a litany of his awful misdeeds. When I rather feebly pointed out to her that I did not employ him and so it would be difficult for me to fire him, she said, "But sweetie, your mother does own most of my horses."

There was one occasion when I did refuse to come to her aid. I was just about to leave on safari, and all the animals were in the International, when Mutete called me to the telephone. It was Beryl. "Darling, the most dreadful boring thing has happened to me," she announced. My mind was busy thinking: what now, what now? I uttered a few soothing noises down the telephone. It turned out that her son had arrived. She had not seen him for several years and he was determined to meet up with his mother again. His origins had always been a bit of a mystery, which Beryl had never attempted to clear up.

Beryl's second husband, whom she had married in Nairobi, had been Mansfield Markham, the wealthy second son of an English baronet but she had been having a passionate affair with Prince Henry, Duke of Gloucester, brother to the Prince of Wales and whom she had first met in England. Both princes visited Kenya in late 1928. The story goes that Queen Mary, terrified her besotted son would marry Beryl and cause an horrific scandal in royal circles, offered Beryl an allowance for life so long as she left Prince Henry alone. Certainly the only money Beryl ever had was an allowance from Buckingham Palace. Equally certain, it was not a very princely sum as Beryl was always short of money. Towards the end of her life when she did not have the horses to sustain her, she had to rely on the charity of her friends Tubby Block and his racing partner Aldo Soprani, who was rich from his coffee-growing interests, plus her allowance and finally, the donation of a house from the Nairobi Jockey Club on the racecourse grounds just to survive.

Beryl's son Gervase was naturally rumoured to be Prince Henry's although, unfortunately for the romantics, the dates for the affair and his birth don't match up. She wasn't a maternal woman, the child was sickly and so he was soon left with the Markham family in England. Beryl took off. Now to her horror, Gervase, grown-up, had arrived in Kenya and she wanted my help. He was coming down to Naivasha for the weekend.

I said hopefully, "Beryl, I think that is marvellous. You will probably find him charming and he must be good looking." Beryl replied, "Sweetie, are you out of your mind? I haven't seen him for years and I can't imagine why he wants to see me now; it is so boring of him and I am much too busy to be bothered. You must do something for me. I will spend one day with him then you will have to call me up and say that it is urgent that I come to Nairobi, as you have found a horse for your mother and I must have a look at him straight away otherwise the sale may fall through."

For once I was not prepared to help and I suggested she try Jan. The poor young man spent the weekend with his mother. I believe it was not a great success. They had nothing in common and he would have terrified Beryl who, in spite of her extraordinary life, was still shy and wary of strangers. She would have been horrified at the thought she might be expected to answer personal questions. She always steered clear of any talk of the past. That she had been an international celebrity, a great aviatrix, or that she had written with her third husband Raoul Schumacher the book *West With The Night*, which became an international bestseller, was not the Beryl I knew. If I should be so rude as to question her on anything she would say, "Sweetie, how do I know?" or "I can't remember."

The only bit of information that I gathered from her, was that she was the person Denys Finch Hatton had asked to go with him on the flight that ended in his fatal plane crash returning from Voi on May 14, 1931. Also from the way she spoke of him, I gathered that he had been one of the great loves of her life. Occasionally she spoke of Campbell Black, but that was only because I had known him so well when I was a child. Beryl did entice men and keep them enraptured.

When I first knew her, she had a very nice young boyfriend called Jorgen or Jan Thrane. He was there at the weekends when we went down to stay with her. And so was Charles Norman. The history as I heard it was that Charles Norman had been Beryl's boyfriend and Beryl, as usual suffering from a shortage of money had, in spite of Charles's wife, moved onto their farm. She lived at Charles's expense for several years – until a young farm manager, Jan, arrived from Denmark. He was almost 30 years younger than Beryl at the time and she fell in love. Beryl moved out of Charles's bed and into Jan's. That made life on the farm even more complicated. I suppose the only person vastly relieved by this turn of events was Doreen Norman, Charles's long-suffering wife.

There was a footnote to this several years later. Douglas Penwill, my friend and one-time district commissioner, was now chairman of the Muthaiga Country Club. He told us that as all the committee drank very heavily, if he wanted to get anything settled he would try and get the important subjects on the agenda passed during the first half hour of the meeting. On this occasion there was the matter of Beryl Markham to discuss.

A few days previously, Jan Thrane, who by now was trying to disentangle himself and end his affair with Beryl, had been entertaining a new girlfriend for dinner at the club. All the members were fascinated, knowing his connection to Beryl, and so they were covertly watching this new development. After dinner, Jan and his companion went to sit in the corner of the small lounge overlooking the car park and the imposing entrance to the club.

Suddenly the french windows to the lounge were flung open. In strode Beryl, still in riding breeches and boots and wielding an enormous hunting crop. To the guests' horror, she marched up to Jan and his new lady love, saying, "Get out, you bitch or I will kill you."

She then proceeded to thrash Jan Thrane who ran to the car park, all the while trying to shield his head and neck as best he could from the whip-wielding Beryl. As I understand it, the lady in question eventually married Jan.

I didn't realise it at the time, but this was the real reason I ended up in South Africa a few years later. Jan had to find some way of getting Beryl out of Kenya. Very cleverly, he and Charles Norman came up with a scheme involving my mother, getting her to provide the money for Beryl to set herself up there with a horse stud.

But meanwhile Douglas had to call a meeting to decide what was to be done about Beryl and the disgraceful scene she had created at the club. The obvious answer to the problem was to make her *persona non grata* and ban her. But as Douglas confessed, knowing Beryl he was too "cowardly" to make this decision on his own. He wanted to take the line of least resistance; he could imagine the scenes that would ensue as a result otherwise.

Douglas decided to start the meeting with a discussion regarding the toilet paper. There had been various requests by the lady members for the club to start using the new soft tissues. One gentleman when this subject came up for decision said, "I don't see anything wrong. In my day a handful of pebbles was considered more than adequate."

Douglas then waited until a few strong whiskies and sodas had been drunk before embarking on the sensitive subject of Beryl Markham. He said he looked around the room and realised most of the committee had been her lover at one stage or another and thought to himself that he couldn't see any of them brave enough to face an irate Beryl.

"Gentlemen," he said. "These are the options, or otherwise we take the line of least resistance and brush the whole episode under the carpet."

There was a deadly hush, a lot of swallowing of whisky but no voice raised in objection. Douglas breathed a huge sigh of relief and jumping to his feet said, "I understand from the silence, gentlemen, we forget the subject of Beryl Markham and continue with the other matters on the agenda."

CHAPTER

48

Stan was on one of his long safaris near Arusha in Tanganyika, when Olga Deterding came to stay. She was a great friend and, being the Shell oil heiress, one of the richest girls in the world. She was great fun but very scatty and I had just arrived back from Arusha, having left Olga at Ol Orion while I was away. I went to run myself a bath when Olga came in and said, "Pat, there is a naked woman in your garden with Duma on a lead." I thought she was hallucinating and didn't pay much attention but she insisted that I come to the dining room window which overlooked the entrance.

I couldn't believe my eyes. There was a safari car parked by the Datura tree and a woman, wearing a safari jacket, a bikini and not much else, was pretending to climb into the car while posing for a photograph. Furthermore, and what gave me a rush of blood to the head, was that she indeed had Duma on a lead. Spending so much time with animals, I am very even-tempered but my animals are my children and so a scene involving them with semi-naked strangers and photographers was more than I could stomach. In a furious rage, I charged out. Snatching Duma, I told them to clear off immediately and that unless they gave me all the film as well I would call the police. The photographer kept trying to tell me that we had met at the Thorn Tree and I had given him permission to come out and photograph the animals with a model. I couldn't remember having done so, but Tana had been photographed so much that it was possible that permission had been given. But certainly, if I had, there had been no mention of bare flesh.

Soon after, Stan was back in Nairobi for a couple of days and we were again having coffee at the Thorn Tree. Stan wanted me to go with him to Uganda for 10 days and he had come up to arrange to take on an extra hunter so he would have more freedom. We were waiting for the hunter to turn up and when he did he was accompanied by a girl who looked like a missionary. She had short cropped hair, loose-fitting clothes, heavy shoes and very wrinkled coarse stockings and carried a big canvas bag over her arm. I thought what a pity that a potentially beautiful girl could make herself look such a fright.

It turned out that she was working for the illustrious Black Star photo-journalism agency in New York, and that her husband John Moss who also worked for them had gone off to cover the war in the Belgian Congo. She was very upset as he had refused to let her go with him. I found her charming and I felt sorry to think of her sitting in a hotel awaiting his return. I suggested that she come and stay at Ol Orion instead.

I remember she looked at me oddly at the time but she agreed and moved in. I liked Bini enormously. She had been with me about a week when, over dinner she said to me, "You don't recognise me do you?" She revealed that she was the half-naked model that I had chased away and that her husband had been the photographer. I couldn't believe it! My little missionary had been a swan, albeit a risque one.

Highly intelligent and fun to be with, Bini stayed with me regularly after that. She got on well with all the animals and did a series of photographs of Tana. She had come from the Cape and, horrified by the apartheid laws of South Africa, had got a name for arguing with her law professors at university. She had married at 22 and she and her husband had gone to South America where, because of her fabulous figure, he had been able to use her as a photographic model. She had found this kind of life fun but ridiculous and felt her talents were being wasted. Being a brilliant photographer, she finally achieved her ambition to work on assignment for *National Geographic*, *Time* and *Life* magazines and had come to Kenya on another project. She now seemed to dress invariably in the worst possible dresses, never wore make-up and didn't bother about her hair. It was only if she was doing a modelling assignment that I would see her emerge from this chrysalis to look like a film star. Shoot over, she would go back to her missionary look.

Bini Malcolm as she is today having re-married, lived many years in the Arab countries and Persia and is now one of the world's authorities on Persian carpets.

She would often go off on various assignments for top publications, coming back to Ol Orion in between. On one occasion she was off for a few days and before leaving she asked if a friend could come and spend a night on his way through to South Africa. He was a friend from university days, on his way back from studying for an MBA in Switzerland. Neither of us being very practical, I think she forgot to mention the date of his arrival or if she did I didn't remember it.

I was in the garden one afternoon trying to prune the bougainvillaea with Kimau, the head *shamba*, on top of the hedge with a ladder and me underneath. I love gardens where flowers flow and mingle and I hate seeing soil so I always plant abundant ground cover. I also love trees with lots of creepers tumbling out of them. Having been raised in the immaculate and famous Italianate gardens of my brother, I needed the contrast and lots of clutter. Even so, I soon came to realise with my first efforts at gardening that a modicum of restraint was necessary. Rory, on one of his visits said, "Dear sister, if you like jungles you have achieved a miracle!" I told him not to be so facetious.

I was surrounded by branches when I saw Mutete sprinting across the lawn towards me, "*Memsahib, unaweza kuja mara moja, bwana mgeni alikufa kabisa nyumbani.*" What he was saying was that there was a dead *bwana* in the house and he had added the word *kabisa* which has several connotations but in this case meant "very". My heart dropped like a stone at the thought of the very dead *bwana*. He did not need to add that his beloved Tana must be the culprit.

I rushed to the sitting room and there, lying on the sofa, was a total stranger, as white as a sheet. I have ever since realised the accuracy of this expression. I immediately registered the fact that he was bald and there was a tiny scratch on his head and as he was wearing short sleeves I could see a slight scratch also on his arm. I could see no other damage. Mutete reluctantly informed me that it was a friend of *Memsahib* Bini but as she was away he had shown him into the sitting room. He was coming to look for me, when he heard a scream. He had rushed in to see Tana jumping out of the window.

Mutete and I carried the stranger to the guest room. I managed to get William on the telephone and asked him to come at once saying that I had a dead man in my guest room. I remember him saying, "I suppose it is your bloody lion? But what makes you think he is dead?" I told him the story and how we had carried him to the bedroom. "You idiot," he barked, "Tana probably broke his neck and if he had any chance of surviving you probably finished it." He asked me if I had taken his pulse. I said I had no idea how to do that. "Heaven preserve me from incompetents," said William. "Get a mirror, place it under his nose and mouth, watch for misting and put your finger on the vein running down the side of his throat. I will hold on and don't dare come back and tell me you don't know."

William, apart from being a great doctor, was so abrasive that it gave one confidence. I used to tease him and say that I hoped he used more of a bedside manner with his other patients or he would end his days penniless.

The mirror misted and there was a pulse. William said he would be right out so I left Mutete with the stranger and left the room, closing the door behind me. I was too scared he would die before William arrived and too cowardly to offer any further assistance.

I'll never forget William coming out of the guest room. He looked at me over his horn-rimmed spectacles and said, "Well my girlie, you have had a lucky escape this time. He is only suffering from shock. I told him, if any man was foolish enough to go anywhere near your farm, then he was asking for trouble. Including myself." Almost as William said this, Joseph appeared round the corner and seeing his friend of the sweets, leapt into his arms, going "OOOH! OOOH!" with delight. William said "Pat, get this filthy monkey off me."

I told him that Joseph wasn't a filthy monkey; he was a beautiful, sweet-smelling chimpanzee and I knew William adored him.

When Bini arrived back that night, I told her the story of her guest. After being shown into the sitting room, he had picked up the morning newspaper and was reading it when Tana came in through the front door. (She was able to open every door in the house.) Seeing a bald head, which was a novelty to her, and thinking that maybe it was a new type of football, she went to investigate. The stranger, feeling her hot breath on his head, had turned round to find an enormous lioness about to eat him. Screaming with fright, he threw up his arms and legs to protect himself. Tana thinking, "Goody! He wants to play", had jumped and landed on top of him As she weighed almost 400lbs, it wasn't surprising that he thought his end had come and he passed out in shock. Tana, who was strictly forbidden to play rough games, got such a fright when he collapsed that she escaped through the window.

Bini gave the poor man a lecture for being such a wet and he departed in a tremendous hurry, not wanting to accept even another few hours of Kenyan hospitality. He got himself all bandaged up and went around telling the story of the narrow escape from death he had had and the man-eating lion kept as a pet by Lady Kenmare's crazy daughter.

When I finally got through to Stan hours later, he thought it very funny and was delighted that Tana had seen off a male guest. My worry though was that a game warden might have been forced to shoot her had she actually killed someone. Stan, knowing that I was still upset by Tana's narrow shave, arrived that evening with detailed maps of his whereabouts. From then on, for each one of his safaris, he made sure I knew within a few miles the location of his camp. He also arranged for his mechanic to fit a compass on the International he had given me. When I had to move to Meru with Tana later on, that compass became one of my most precious possessions. Stan had driven a long way to spend that hour with me and to arrange all these details. Having done so he departed, driving back through the night to take his clients out at dawn.

CHAPTER

49

Stan did not particularly like spending time in Nairobi. As soon as his safaris were finished, he would refit the lorries and we would go off, often taking friends of mine along. We had one amazing adventure in Ngorongoro Crater when two guests, Genevieve Francois-Poncet, daughter of the former French ambassador to Germany before World War II, and a medical professor Jean-Paul Binet were with us. We had a lovely camp at Lake Manyara and from our tent, I would watch the spur-winged geese fly off in the light of dawn, skimming over the backs of the herds of elephants that had come down to drink. This day we had gone to Ngorongoro. Stan had just come off safari and all the guns were still in the gun racks, unloaded except for the one he kept ready for emergencies with just the one bullet.

It was evening when we came on a pride of lion and we stayed to watch them for a while. As we went to drive off, the back wheel of the International disappeared in an ant-bear hole. This was a continual hazard on safari but as the equipment to deal with the emergency was always carried in the truck or car, it was never a problem under normal circumstances. These were not normal circumstances though. We were in the middle of a pride of lion and in an open safari car. To get out and dig would be highly dangerous. We stayed for a while, hoping they would move off. Dusk was fast approaching when one of the safari boys who had his head through the hatch said "*kifaru*". Rhino. These huge animals almost invariably charge and we were sitting ducks.

Stan did not hesitate. He made the two guests go to the back of the International and take cover behind the spare wheels. I was sitting in front on the side of the lion. Handing me an empty rifle, he told me, "When a lion charges, his mouth will be open. Your one chance is to take the rifle and ram it as hard as you can down its throat. I am going to try and distract them while the men dig us out." Then he walked over to stand by the lion.

As a rule it did not take long to dig a vehicle out as the tools were ready but maybe because the men were nervous, it seemed now to be taking hours. I kept saying prayer after prayer. It was the first time in my life that I have been truly frightened. I was sure Stan would be killed and I didn't hold out much hope for the rest of us. My hands were sweating so much I could hardly hold the rifle. It felt like a ton weight. My heart was racing and my mouth had gone dry with fright.

Then, to my horror, I saw a lioness creep towards Stan. He watched her coming and slowly raised the gun to his shoulder. I saw him take out two of his heart pills and swallow them; he couldn't afford to have an angina attack with our lives at stake. With the gun aimed at the lioness, he stood motionless. The whole scene was frozen; the man, the gun and the lioness. I thought I was going to faint. She made a short charge then stopped, snarling with rage, her ears back, crouched, staring at Stan. I knew he only had the one bullet and the other lions were getting restless. I also realised that Stan would do everything possible not to shoot a lioness in front of me. She made two more charges, and with her last charge she ended almost at his feet, yet he never moved. I heard one of the men whisper to me "*iko tiari*". It's ready. I tried to tell Stan without raising my voice and distracting either him or the lioness. I watched him back slowly away with his gun still trained on her and I realised that that day I had witnessed the true meaning of the word courage. For Stan to be charged three times and for him to stand his ground without moving was an amazing feat. He had faced the lioness with such lack of fear that she had sensed his confidence. The fact that he remained so still disconcerted her. The lioness was the one that backed down in the end. I don't think our visitors from France ever realised the courage Stan had displayed, or how near to death we all undoubtedly were.

I asked Stan that night why he had not fired when the lioness charged. He said he knew he could drop the lioness but the rest of the pride would probably have attacked. "And there was only one bullet," he said, before adding with a laugh, "Also if I had killed her and survived you would never have forgiven me!"

I thought of the safari I had been on when I was first engaged to Frank in 1950, and with Mummy and her friends visiting Caryll in Kenya. We were in thick bush when we were charged by a female elephant. The first person to run past us was the white hunter. Thank goodness the elephant had a calf and so, having made her charge and scattered us in all directions, she returned to her child. Later, when I came to know elephant better, I realised that she must have been making a false charge to scare us away from the baby she was protecting.

Years after that, I was with Stan and Mummy's great friend Prince Ferdinand of Liechtenstein and one of Stan's trainee white hunters. A blind, our hiding-place, had been set up under a tree of thorn bushes and the leopard bait was on a large branch not far above us. Ferdinand wanted some good photographs. That morning Stan had had a particularly bad attack of angina and didn't come out with us so I went with Ferdinand and the young hunter. Leaving the safari car some distance away, we walked to the blind. It was early afternoon so there was plenty of time and no sign of any animals around. On hands and knees we crawled through the narrow opening. Inside there was just room to sit for the three us with our two loaded rifles, cameras, binoculars and a flask of coffee because we were expecting a long wait. Above us and a bit to the right we could see the bait. I could also smell it and the flies had started to collect.

We had been there for some time and it was getting dark when, instead of a leopard, a pride of lion arrived. We were soon surrounded and some were busy trying to get the bait out of the tree. Ferdinand kept saying, "My God, we must get out of here." He and the hunter were whispering and I could feel the panic. The hunter kept saying, "We will never get through; it is safer here." I don't know how it would all have ended, but very badly I suspect. Then I heard the sound of Stan's truck. Stan brought the International up as close as he could and then standing with his rifle trained on the lion, he said, "Get out and move very slowly towards me."

In their panic, the men pushed to get out first and ran towards the car, dropping everything on the way. There was no thought of saving women and children. I was unarmed but as soon as Stan arrived, I felt totally protected. On leaving the blind, I retrieved all the belongings that had been discarded during the men's mad rush for safety. I walked through a group of totally amazed lions and joined Stan. I can still see the baobab trees and the faint swirl of dust around the lights of the International. I can see Stan with his rifle cocked, seemingly trained on me. I could also see Stan's gun bearer with his rifle ready. I could feel the presence of the lion and knew they were watching me but I was enjoying myself. It was a feeling of euphoria and I was smiling when I got to Stan. He took off his hat and placed it on my head. Lifting my face between his hands, he said, "You are one hell of a girl and I adore you."

That night, Stan told me that he had been lying on his bed listening to the radio, when he got the strongest feeling that I was in danger. At first he told himself that it was only because I wasn't with him, but the feeling became so strong that he went and got his gun bearer and came to find me. That is why he arrived on the scene when he did. I laughed about how the two men had behaved. I can pick up vibrations from animals and I knew the lions weren't any real threat. They were being lazy. I told Stan what I had seen in Cannes during the war when I was on the Carlton Hotel balcony watching a plane bombing the harbour and people in their panic had started tearing their clothes off and rushing around half-naked. Afterwards, I had come down in the lift to find the lobby full of fainting people. Stan refused to see the incident as a joke though and we ended up having an argument about it. I don't know what was said to the men but the following day he packed up the safari and the atmosphere on the way back to Nairobi was far from pleasant.

CHAPTER
──────
50

In early 1964, my mother and Rory arrived in Kenya for their winter visit with our friend Hilda Lezard. Stan took us to Murchison Falls in Uganda and on the way we stayed two nights at a beautiful hotel in Entebbe on the banks of Lake Victoria. I was thrilled because I had managed to borrow some skis and went waterskiing. Skimming over the lake was marvellous. The water was smooth and I was enveloped in a warm spray. I was able to get close to the fishermen in their dugout canoes while being careful to avoid the nets they were casting into the lake. In Uganda, the people are very black and the fishermen in their white loincloths looked even darker. I could see the fish jumping, the birds wheeled low overhead and the shores were a tropical jungle, wonderfully green and mysterious. On the opposite side there were lovely houses and gardens going down to the water. It was a marvellous way to see the lake.

On the way to the falls, we stopped to have lunch in Masindi at the East African Railways and Harbours hotel, a low sprawling colonial-style building that delighted Rory. He was even more thrilled when we were served off heavy chinaware, embossed with the railways crest and E.A.R.&H. He was determined to have a plate for his collection. He asked the manager who looked like a retired colonel if he could possibly buy one and was very disappointed when told they were not for sale. Hilda Lezard told him not to worry, she would smuggle one out for him. To my horror, as we were paying the bill, the manager said to Hilda, "I think, Madam, you have got one of our plates in the front of your dress. I would be very grateful if you could hand it over." With great cowardice, I skipped outside and went to join Stan who was arranging our transport. My mother arrived smiling. Knowing my beloved parent my heart sank. Sure enough, as soon as we were all back in the truck, she said, "Look what I have got!" And produced out of her handbag three plates, a cup and a saucer. All to Rory's intense delight and my shame for my family's criminal tendencies.

I remember my joy at watching the scene of the trucks and safari cars loading onto the ferry which would take us over the Victoria Nile and to the falls. On the other side, the red dirt road went up a little hill and at the top was a big bull elephant browsing off an acacia tree. While Stan was unloading the lorries and my mother was admiring the wildflowers growing near one of the African huts, I went off to take pictures of Jumbo.

Suddenly, in the lens of my camera, I realised I was being charged. Stan who always seemed to have eyes in the back of his head where I was concerned, rushed up, seized hold of me and threw me through the door of one of the African huts. Its occupant screamed with rage as we burst through her doorway, particularly when the elephant started tearing strips off the thatched roof. Stan told her to shut up and then started to lecture me on my stupidity. I said to him. "Look, the elephant is about to come through the roof. Why don't you go and lecture him not me." He just laughed and said, "He'll soon get bored. Dry *makuti* won't taste that good."

Stan had shouted to the others to get into the hut nearest them and stay there. My mother was thrilled because she got some wonderful photographs of the elephant attacking our roof. I despaired of my parent. I said to her, if she wasn't pinching things she was busy recording her supposedly beloved daughter's demise. "Darling, I knew you weren't in any danger," said my unflappable parent with a grin of delight.

Murchison Falls was quite wonderful. We camped on the banks of the river and I think in all my years in east Africa, I have never seen as many elephant as we did there. At sunset, a bright orange-red ball lit the skies and the grasslands with flame, and the black silhouettes of hundreds of elephant moved across them slowly as the vast herds crossed the shallows. During the day, we would go by launch up the river. The white boat with scalloped cotton awnings contrasted with the very black faces of the crew in their navy blue tailored shorts and tops. The banks teemed with crocodile, gigantic monsters which would slither into the water at our approach, and the waters surrounding our boat were full of hippo blowing spray in our direction. Rory and Hilda were enthralled by the various trees and the vegetation on the banks and would have learned arguments about the Latin names. Back at camp they would gather their books and compare notes.

In the mornings, Stan would take us on early walks so that they could collect specimens. It never ceased to amuse me that they could walk past a herd of impala or zebra without even noticing them, so intent were they on examining a particular tree. Even buffalo would receive the most cursory of glances as an enraptured Rory, with exclamations of delight, would follow a butterfly. Their great love of nature gave life an extra dimension and I gradually came to realise that there were other beautiful facets to Africa apart from animals.

On our return to Ol Orion from Murchison Falls, my mother gave a dinner party. Joseph the chimpanzee was now quite grown up and slept in my bathroom. There was a window over the toilet but I had taken this out and built a box into the space. This is where Joseph slept. He had his mattress, pillow and blanket and could use the toilet during the night without waking me up. Joseph, like Tana, was able to open all the house's doors so he could come into my room if he wanted to. My bathroom was at the very end of the passage next to my bedroom. There were other bathrooms so it never occurred to me to warn the dinner guests not to use mine.

After dinner, Jack Block and Lee Harragin, the young lawyer married to Petal Erskine, went off to find a toilet. It wasn't long before I heard Joseph's shrieks of delight and Lee's howls of distress. Joseph had woken up to see Lee spending a penny. All wild animals are curious about things they haven't seen before. Joseph took one look and made a dive for Lee's pride and joy. Lee, with his good looks, fancied the girls so when Joseph got hold of his most treasured possession, he was distraught. When I arrived on the scene, Joseph was dancing round going "OOH! OOH! OOH!" with delight. Lee equally was dancing round saying, "Oh my God! Oh my God!" I shouted to Lee, "For heaven's sake, don't try and take it away." No wild animal likes a newly acquired possession wrested from it and I had visions of Joseph sinking his teeth in if he thought he was going to be deprived of his new toy. I ran and seized a bottle of whisky, which Joseph loved above all things, but was rarely ever allowed. To my vast relief, Joseph after a moment of indecision chose the bottle over the "toy" and peace was restored once more. Lee told me later that it was weeks before he was back to normal.

My family and I had another disastrous dinner about this same time but this time Tana was the culprit. The guests were a couple who had had to flee Poland during the war, leaving vast estates behind. Like most refugees, they still had their titles but no money. Nights are cold on the equator at 6000 feet and the Polish lady arrived in a rather sad and slightly threadbare mink jacket that was still, obviously, a treasured article. Ol Orion was kept very warm as my mother and I were hot-house flowers and so our guest left her mink jacket on the sofa when we went into dinner. During the course of the meal, I realised Tana wasn't at her usual place at my feet, nor was she under the table.

With trepidation, I left the dining room to find her. Tana was happily ensconced on the sofa, tearing up the last remaining piece of mink jacket. Bits of fur lay scattered over the room. Tana almost winked at me as if she thought this was great fun, much better than any football. I couldn't scold her for what after all was my carelessness but my heart sank as I looked at her and realised that the damage was irreparable.

I slunk back into the dining room and for the rest of the meal debated how best to break the dreadful news to my mother's guests. In the end, I took the coward's way out and sent a note over to Mummy explaining what had happened. I wrote, "Tana chewed up mink, terrible mess, what do I do?" My mother started laughing, brandished the note in the air, and said, "I have some really bad news. My daughter is too much of a coward to tell you but her bloody lioness has chewed up your mink jacket." The poor lady, quite distraught, tore out of the dining room and even confronted Tana as she tried to drag the remnants of her jacket from under her stomach. My mother put her arm around her shoulder and said, "Not to worry, come and have a brandy and we will sort it all out." Eventually, a magnificent mink coat was sent from Paris, much better than the furry disaster that Tana had disposed of.

My next birthday turned out to be another eventful evening. My mother, knowing how much I loved calypso music, had arranged for a band to come and play for us at Ol Orion. It was a marvellous night with a full moon. The garden had been lit with flaming torches on long iron stands that threw light and shadow onto all the beautiful trees. The calypso band was sensational, the peaks of the Ngong Hills towered black against the night sky and the scent of jasmine and woodsmoke vied for a place on the evening air. Dawn had come and gone and most of the guests had left, when from the jacaranda forest there came a series of piercing shrieks. Tana, having got bored with being locked in my room, had finally managed to prise the window open. She had jumped out into the trees and the first thing she had come across was a couple making love. Two of the guests had stripped off and were in the middle of a passionate interlude when Tana landed on top of them. It had terrible consequences because the lady in question went into some sort of spasm with shock and her muscles contracted so hard her lover couldn't withdraw. They were locked together in a dreadful dance of love. When I rushed over to see what all the noise was about, I couldn't make out what was happening. They were both screaming but it obviously wasn't with pleasure. Once again, I went to get my mother who had gone to bed. She decided that a doctor's help was needed.

The only good that came out of the whole story was that the lady's husband had imbibed so much of my mother's good whisky that he had fallen into one of the flower beds and some kind friend had driven him home. I don't think he ever found out about his wife's unfortunate infidelity.

CHAPTER

51

My next safari with Stan was to the Tana basin near Meru to the east of Mount Kenya and on the equator. It was the first time I had been to that area and it was such a magnificent part of the country, I immediately fell in love with it. I certainly never thought that I would eventually live there. We set off in the International with three lorries filled with all our equipment. On top of one was a cabin cruiser with two outboard engines. We had a marvellous couple of weeks and Tana was introduced to boating. It was no easy task and the first lesson took the better part of an entire afternoon. Tana was very reluctant to try this new mode of transport but rather than be left behind, she eventually, with a great deal of shoving and pushing, condescended to get on board.

Every time Tana got on board, the boat would start rocking, whereupon she would jump straight off again. Finally she caught onto the fact that with a lot of balancing with her tail, she could make it to the prow. This, in future years, was to become her favourite place and many were the times we went down the Tana with her sitting there, watching the passing parade. Her ears pricked her beautiful head and her shoulders would be outlined against the dark river. I would sit resting my back against her and from my position of comfort, would also watch the movement of the river. Tim Tom, a little Thompson gazelle I had rescued and who now always accompanied me, hated the water, unlike Tana. As a baby he had been in dugout canoes with me, but now that he was older he refused to go further than the water's edge. He would watch us get on board, then he would turn and rush back to camp.

Stan loved to fish and his line sailing through the air would have a soporific effect on me. Tana would be fascinated by the swishing noise it made as it went past us until it landed with a plop in the water. Occasionally I would wake if Tana shifted position. Also, I had to make sure that Stan didn't cheat when I was asleep and actually catch a fish. When I was with him, everything caught had to be put back.

Tana and I were good travellers together in these trips to be with Stan. Only on one occasion did we have a mishap. I was on my way to meet Stan at the Mount Kenya Safari Club at Nanyuki, to the west of the mountain. He was hunting near Marsabit, miles away in the northern frontier district, but desperate to see me he had persuaded his clients to spend a few days back at the club while they changed camp.

I was in the heart of the rich Kikuyu highlands (what had been, until independence, the White Highlands) when suddenly there was a most horrible smell coming from the back seat. I had to find a straight bit of road as we were high in the hills before I was able to stop. I got out to see what the problem was but already suspected the worst! Tana had an upset stomach. If anyone can imagine what lion shit smells like, well it is – and worse!

I let Tana out of the car and got busy with newspapers and water out of the *debes*. I had forgotten about Tana until I heard a blood-curdling shriek. A Kikuyu *bibi* (housewife) was coming along the road, with her heavy load of wood, a familiar sight in Kenya. The women carry heavy loads of firewood on their back, suspended from a leather thong that goes around their forehead. The *bibi* had seen Tana and, screaming with fear, had dropped her load and taken off down the hillside. Tana thought it was a game, promptly went after her and, for once, paid little attention to my shouted commands, pausing only long enough for me to get close to her in pursuit.

In desperation, seeing Tana about to take off again, I threw myself on top of her in a rugby tackle whereupon we both started rolling down the steep hillside. Thank goodness, it had been planted with maize which cushioned our fall a little and we ended up a tangled heap against a small thorn bush. Tana, I think, was totally amazed at my undignified behaviour and I could have sworn she thought it a huge joke and was laughing at me.

Totally winded by having a lion rolling on me, I lay stunned for a few minutes. Tana quickly recovered and stood with a bemused expression on her face. I used her neck to pull myself up and sitting on a large rock surveyed the damage to my person. I could hardly fail to realise what a mess I must be looking.

The poor Kikuyu *bibi* had long gone, her shrieks fading into the distance, and I was left to climb the hill with my reluctant lioness in tow. What a mess! By the time I got back to the car, all my bones were starting to ache and bruising was beginning to appear. I was covered in soil, my stockings were in shreds and I was bleeding and scratched.

I changed my skirt and shirt, discarded the torn stockings and did my best to wash up. Even so, when we arrived at the elegant Safari Club where we were to stay for a few nights, I could see the receptionist regarding me with grave suspicion as I approached the front desk. I must indeed have been a sorry sight, despite the roadside repairs. There was still mud ingrained in my wounds and to make matters worse, blood had seeped down my naked legs into my shoes. My face as I had already seen in the car mirror was scratched and bruised and my mouth was beginning to swell.

I watched first the expression of disdain on the gentleman's face and then his look of total horror at the sight of Tana standing so quietly beside me. I had had a special harness and lead chain made for her and used this when visiting. Whenever strangers were around I also carried a stick, thinking it would give people more confidence but the receptionist didn't look in the least reassured. He had a tramp and a disreputable lioness standing at his reception desk and was wondering how to get rid of them. I could see he was about to tell me the club was fully booked, desperate to have us gone before any guests appeared.

I hastily told him I was a friend of the American Ray Ryan who was a co-owner of the club, along with the actor William Holden. I could see the poor receptionist had severe doubts as to the veracity of this statement but was afraid to upset his boss in case it was true. Kenya was used to the strange but I couldn't help thinking that I must be a good deal stranger.

I had asked for a double bed with bath for three nights and I gave the immaculate young man full marks as, weighing up his options and looking at me with total hauteur, he asked in a plummy voice, "And the lioness too, Miss?" With great reluctance, he handed a key to the porter and we followed our luggage upstairs to the nether regions of the club, to a small room well out of the way of the grand guests. But at least it had a bath.

Unfortunately, there was only a single bed and not a particularly large one at that. Certainly there was not enough room for myself and Tana. I had to go down and get my leopardskin coat out of the car to put on the floor for her to sleep on. Thank goodness, she did occupy my coat and not the bed. Having had a bath and cleaned up, I locked Tana in the room, put a Do Not Disturb notice on the door, and went down to dinner. Ray Ryan, who happened to be there at the time, saw me enter and invited me to join himself and his guests. I felt that this must reassure the staff that I did indeed know him and was not an escaped lunatic.

It was a fun evening. Before going to bed rather late, I took Tana for a walk. I had already dosed her heavily with my diarrhoea mixture with which I was never without and hoped that the incident in the car would not be repeated. As usual, I read a book before going to sleep, this time with Tana staring at me reproachfully from her bed on the floor. Then I turned the lights off. Almost immediately, I felt a burning sensation all over my body. I didn't pay much attention until it got worse. Thinking I must have an allergy to something, I peered under my nightdress to find that I had come up in a mass of weals. I was just about to get out of bed to fetch the antihistamine cream when I saw, issuing out of the mattress, masses of wedge-shaped *dudus* (insects), which I immediately recognised as bed bugs.

Promptly stripping off my nightgown, I rushed into a bath. I was worried that Tana might have picked up a few bugs too so I tried unsuccessfully to get her washed as well. Firstly, I struggled to lift up her front end, but without her co-operation this turned out to be impossible. Finally, with a lot of coaxing I got one leg into the bath at a time but when we came to her rear end, she was adamant. It was not going to be subjected to such indignities. By now, the bathroom was a quagmire.

With clean clothes on but my body heating up because of this activity, the weals all over me started to itch with a ferocity that was astounding. Grabbing Tana, I headed once more for the front desk to request a clean new room. There was now only a night porter on duty so he had to phone the manager.

He came back to say that he was very sorry but my room was all that was available and he suggested my problems might be caused by the lioness. I replied, would he please inform the manager that the Countess de Sales (I had in fact gone back to my maiden name of Cavendish but on this occasion, felt that my title sounded more impressive) was being eaten alive by bed bugs and unless I got a clean room for the night, I would write to the papers and let them know that the famous Mount Kenya Safari Club was infested with bugs and not a fit place for any member of the public to stay in.

Several of the late night guests, drawn by the spectacle Tana and I must have made, were starting to collect and a young assistant manager who had by now arrived on the scene quickly said, "Please come this way my lady," and Tana and I were escorted into the most magnificent suite. Not only did a vase of flowers and fruit soon arrive, but he also announced that I was to be the guest of the hotel during my stay.

In front of the Safari Club there were beautiful man-made lakes and islands full of exotic water birds. The following morning I took Tana behind the lakes towards the forest so that she would not intrude on the other guests. Ever since the incident of the "dead *bwana*", I had kept my correction stick handy but I still felt it more tactful to keep her well out of sight.

We were lying under the dappled shade of a giant fig tree, my head propped on Tana's convenient stomach while I immersed myself in a book, when I felt Stan's presence. I looked up and he was standing there watching us. As usual, he had moved so silently that I had not heard his approach and Tana, knowing him well, had not thought to warn me. I felt my heart race out of control and the very air around me came alive. I wondered why his presence should always have this remarkable effect on me.

He said, "I have been watching you and thinking how beautiful you are. Maybe the Africans are right, you are part of the pride and do not belong to this earth!"

I realised that there is truth in the saying that the eyes of love are undemanding. In spite of my bruises and swollen lip, to him I was a vision of loveliness. In the distance, I heard the cool clear tones of an emerald-spotted wood dove and I felt tears very close to the surface.

Stan had a beautiful voice and, laughing as he spoke, he said, "Come, *Toto ya Simba* [child of the lion]. Let's walk down to the river."

We stood in a clearing and the filtered sun turned the forest into a haze of golden light. The raucous cry of an eagle echoed down the valley and I looked up at the peak of Mount Kenya, its snow-covered slopes white against the sky. There was a clarity of light and the slight breeze was cool on my face. In the background, I could hear the bees as they gathered their nectar from the flowers warmed by the sun and the bittersweet pain of loving was almost more than I could bear.

Stan was telling me of the heat and the dust and the arid dryness of the vast plains from which he had just come and I will never forget his words as he told me of his love and his fears that I would leave him. He said that for hours he would lie in his tent in the heat of the desert and think of me. He likened himself to a thirsty man who had seen an oasis but it was always out of reach. "The more I try to possess you the more you elude me, like this river rushing by. One day you will be gone out of my life and I will return to the desert a broken man," he said. I could not see into the future and Tana was leaning heavily against me. I could feel the heat from her body through my thin cotton dress. The day was too beautiful for such prophecies and I was certain I would not be the one to go.

CHAPTER

52

I had been down to the *duka* at Karen to collect the mail and was delighted to see a letter with a Mexican stamp. I was sure it was from Enrique de Medina who was one of my great friends from the south of France. The Marques de Medina, he lived in New York and was a dress designer, but whether he was a great one or not I never knew as he never took life seriously. When I asked him what his designs were like, he laughed and said, "awful".

He was a tall, dark, beautiful young man, with large liquid southern eyes and a continual giggle. He was gentle and kind and laughed his way through life. He was a marvellous dancer like most Spaniards and Mexicans and we went out a lot together. Given his strong Spanish accent and his great sense of fun, it was like being with an exotic sister. He was also a great friend of Rory's, so he came to Fiorentina often and we spent a lot of time in all the night-spots of the Côte d'Azur.

There had been the most appalling tragedy the previous year. Enrique had been on a world tour and had been going to come and stay with me in Kenya but for some reason the dates of his visit had to be altered. I think I was going to be away on safari at that time. He went to Hong Kong instead and, crossing a street, was run over by a bus. The driver in his panic then reversed and consequently ran over him again. The result was his leg had to be amputated above the knee.

The letter was to tell me that he had been to Germany to fit his new leg and that he was now able to walk much better, and so he was on his way to me. I was determined to give him a good time and show him Kenya. I felt terribly responsible for what had happened to him. If only, I thought to myself, I had not gone on safari and he had come to Kenya as planned, he would never have lost his leg.

Stan was brilliant about the visit and equipped a whole safari for me. He would never have done so if it had been any other man but gentle Enrique. The only thing worrying Stan was that it was the rainy season and whether I would be able to cope with the hazards that entailed. He was off on a safari to Uganda but left me his best drivers. We were taking two five-ton lorries with all the equipment and the personnel. He also arranged for his old elephant tracker and gun bearer Ismael to come with me.

Stan had organised my safari. Now I had to convince Enrique to leave his beautifully tailored shirts and trousers behind. With a great deal of reluctance on his part, I finally managed to get him to Ahmed Bros in Nairobi. I tried to conceal my mirth at his look of horror as he surveyed row upon row of various coloured khaki and dark green bush suits and shirts.

After several days of tailors and fittings, he was still complaining about the colour making him look "seeck". I tried to cheer him up by telling him that if we went on safari with all his beautiful coloured trousers, we were bound to get charged. I would have given anything to have see Stan's face if Enrique had gone prancing off, in his pale blues and greens and pink! I was once stopped from following a herd of elephant up north near the Ethiopian border because of my companion's attire. The Turkana tracker there said in Swahili, looking at my fashionable friend's white shorts and top with scorn, that if we followed the elephant with a *memsahib* dressed like that, we were certain to get charged. So we had to watch the elephant depart without us.

That wasn't going to happen this time.

Comforting the despondent Enrique who, in heavily accented English and lots of giggles was saying, "I hope I don't meet anyone; I look so 'orrible", I packed up the International. Tana had her usual position in the back and Tim Tom the gazelle was lording it on the front seat with Enrique.

Nearly all my animals were brought up on Cow & Gate's powdered milk, lime water and posho, crushed maize meal. I used to make up the formulas in the morning and have a large cool-box with me to store the bottles ready for feeding. On safari, depending on how many animals I was rearing and which were travelling with us in the car, Ismael and I would go around with bottles, instead of bullets, tied to our gun belts. Made of thick leather, the bullet slots made marvellous attachments for the formula. All the baby animals had to be fed every two hours and one could not keep returning to camp to do this.

I also decided to take Jason on this safari. He was the baboon baby I had rescued in Arusha. Mummy and I had been staying at the hotel there for a few days on our way to Ngorongoro. The baby baboon was tied to a tree and I often used to hear him screaming. People passing by were teasing him unmercifully. The night before we left, I waited until everyone was asleep and then, clambering out through my window across the roof, I went to his rescue. I was sharing a room with Mummy and while she kept watch, I did my James Bond act. Jason was not at all happy about being rescued but I didn't have the time to try and pacify him. It was a rush and grab affair and in his panic, he insisted on biting my hands. Then I had to attach him to me so I could climb back up the tree, onto the roof and into my room.

Mummy was laughing so much by the time I managed to get myself and a screaming baboon back onto the window-ledge that she was of no use to me. We then gave him a bottle of milk that we had already prepared with a few grains of one of Mummy's sleeping pills in it. Thank goodness, that did the trick. I took him to bed with me and at last the screeching stopped. How the whole place did not wake up, I don't know. We left at five the next morning and were almost at Manyara before Stan realised we had an extra passenger. We were still having a platonic relationship at the time and he was so busy trying to impress me he didn't object too strongly to this new addition to the menagerie already on board.

When travelling, Jason had to be kept on his collar and lead. Otherwise, every time we came to a stop he would insist on climbing the nearest tree. He never tried to escape though as he was terrified of being left alone. I only had to pretend to leave and he would rush down. These manoeuvres were very time-consuming, so when driving I used to attach him to the side of the International.

He had toys to amuse him and in no time he became a seasoned traveller like all my animals. When he used to see me appearing with the nappies, he knew it meant the car and he used to get wildly excited. In the camp he was always free but he never let us out of his sight. Most of the time he was sitting on our necks or trying to steal things out of the kitchen. He even cadged rides off the long-suffering Tana.

First, I took Enrique down to the Mara, one of Stan's favourite areas. Not only is the scenery magnificent, but there is nowhere in the world like it for the amount and variety of game. In those days, there were no lodges there. It was Masai country and even the Masai were scarce. Sometimes, appearing out of nowhere, one would see two or three *moran* who would always stop and pass the time of day. Leaning on their spears, these beautiful red warriors would be full of smiles showing their perfect teeth.

They were invariably fascinated by Tana and their greatest joy was to be given a lift to anywhere. The direction never seemed to matter; it was just the fact they were in a car with a lion. The journey would be accompanied by much excited chatter and laughter and a lot of hand-holding. The smell, even in the open safari car, was usually overpowering. The Masai lived on milk and blood and smelt accordingly. One of the most romantic tribes of Africa, and certainly one of the most beautiful, Europeans were very proud if they could claim to be accepted by these nomadic warriors. I know I used to feel wonderful coming into one of the villages with a load of Masai. I would proudly drive around hoping one of my friends would see me. Tana was the big drawcard but the glamour of the Masai presence in my vehicle used to wash off on me. When the opportunity arises, I think most of us like to show off. Sometimes it seemed as if I would circle for hours before anyone took the remotest bit of notice!

During Kenya's independence negotiations in the early 1960s, I had been visited by a delegation of Masai elders. They wanted me to go and explain to the queen in England that they had lived peacefully with us for so many years. Now they were worried about being ruled by the Kikuyu who had been their enemy. Their sacred mountain was Kilimanjaro, just over the border in Tanganyika, which had also been British and just been given its independence. Would I explain to her, the elders asked, that as her people and the Masai were friends, they could continue their life of harmony, if she gave them all the country of the mountain and left Kenya to the Kikuyu. I was very flattered by their confidence in me, but had to disillusion them as to my importance. They found this difficult to understand. They asked: "Does Queen not know that you live with a lion?"

From the Mara, Enrique and I went to the Loita Hills. The rains had started and the rainforests dripped, even when the sun came out. It was like walking in a shower with all one's clothes on. Enrique was ecstatic. The trees were covered in stag-horns and orchids and he insisted on my climbing up all and sundry to collect samples which he tenderly wrapped in damp moss for the journey back.

It always felt to me though as if I was taking their freedom. I dislike uprooting plants, chopping trees or taking life in any form. But with his one leg, Enrique was unable to scale any of the trees. I had also developed my fear of heights and the loveliest buds seemed to hang temptingly off the furthest branch. On our return, the trees at Karen blossomed with the most glorious selection of orchids.

Before continuing our safari, we had to go back by way of Karen to replenish the provisions, especially Tana's meat supply. It was on this part of the trip that we had our first of a series of adventures. The rain had been pouring down and we were skidding along. Although we had chains, there were no roads or tracks and every so often we had to dig ourselves out of the mire. The lorries with their heavy loads were continually getting bogged down. It was already late in the afternoon and we had been driving along the banks of a small river for a while, looking for a suitable crossing. When we finally found one, Ismael sensibly suggested we not waste any more time. With the torrential rain, he worried that soon we would not make it at all.

Ismael walked in front of my safari car with a very long stick, testing the going. The water in places came right up to the top of the mudguards and at times I felt as if I were going to be swept away by the red-brown swirling current. Having only just got ourselves across, we then had to winch the lorries over. By now, the rain had stopped and we set up a lovely campsite under some acacias.

While the men were busy erecting the tents, I took Enrique to look for dead trees to use as firewood. Driving around, I realised that we had somehow managed to get ourselves onto an island. In all directions, we were surrounded by a fast-flowing muddy stream. That was not all. We were also occupying the island with a large pride of lion. I was very worried about Tana. Thank goodness she was not in season or all hell would have broken loose. I realised that it was far too late to recross the river and that we would have to remain and hope for the best.

I had already found lots of dead branches for firewood and so I walked back to the International. I was loading them into the back when I turned round to look for Enrique. He was dragging a large dead tree behind him. His progress was rather slow as he had to manoeuvre his false leg but, to my horror, there playing like a kitten, slapping at the ends of the dead branches with her paws, was a young lioness.

I realised that if I warned him what was happening, he might panic and start running and the chances were that the lioness would forget her game and spring. Meanwhile, Enrique was laughing and joking about the weight of the tree, not realising that half of it was his extra passenger. It seemed to take a lifetime for him to reach the car and I had to keep talking to him so that he wouldn't look around.

I was standing by the passenger seat. Safari cars have no doors or sides and are high off the ground, making them difficult to climb into. I said, "Enrique, get in fast. There is a lion on your tail." He turned around and said, "Oh my God! So there is, she's divine." I wasn't prepared to waste time discussing the merits of our feline friend so without more ado, as he started climbing into the car, I grabbed him by the back of his pants and pushed him hard. He fell sprawling across the seat with myself on top, I was in such a rush to get to the wheel.

In moments of crisis everything seems to go wrong. In our hurry we landed on top of Tim Tom who was trying to escape. I had to grab him to prevent him jumping out the other side and becoming a lion's evening meal. In the ensuing pandemonium, I kicked Enrique onto the floor. Enrique was totally confused and asking, "Pat, have you gone mad?" as I lay sprawled across the front seat like a landed whale clutching a struggling Tim Tom. I had no free hand to help my poor Spanish friend out of the predicament into which I had tossed him. Enrique finally extricated himself from the floor, managed to lift his wooden leg off the gear lever and, with me telling him to hang onto Tim Tom, we drove back to camp.

Enrique was thrilled that he had been so close to a lion and bemoaned the fact I hadn't let him know at the time. He was not in the least perturbed, even when I told him that in all probability we would see a lot more of them before the evening was through. In fact, as night fell, they decided to join us.

I zipped all the flaps of my tent down and warned Enrique to do the same. I was worried that they might come looking for Tana, or that Tim Tom or Jason would escape. The noise was deafening; they killed a poor wildebeest which had probably rushed into the camp seeking protection right outside the mess tent. Lion were everywhere, roaring, grunting and scratching themselves on the tent strings until I was convinced that everything would collapse around me.

At one stage, I stuck my hand out with a microphone through a gap in the tent. A lion was making such a racket that I thought it would be a pity if I didn't record it. I didn't realise he was so close until my hand made contact with his back.

It was ages before they moved off. In the excitement of the kill, they had charged through the men's tent, which had collapsed. Some of the men had escaped up a tree where they spent a very uncomfortable night and the luckier ones had made it to the lorry. The lion had also bowled over the lavatory tent and had a lot of fun towing it around the camp. There were bits of tent all over the place and they had a lovely time with the toilet paper. They had conducted a paper chase so it was everywhere, even hanging off the low branches of the trees.

At dawn, what was left of the kill was being devoured by vultures and our pride had not moved far. Not that there was far to move under the circumstances. Our packing was done with the maximum of haste and the minimum of care. Stan would have been horrified at our unseemly departure but I didn't want to risk any more encounters and Tana, who I had not dared allow out to be clean, was getting very fractious.

The only person loving every minute was Enrique. He told me that he was sure that he was about to be eaten and that he kept thinking that if this was the way he was going to die, at least it would be very romantic.

CHAPTER

53

I then took my safari off to the Tana and used one of Stan's old camp sites high on the banks under some large duom palms overlooking the river. I had been here on several occasions and considered myself fairly familiar with this part of Kenya. There were beaches and pools. Tana loved playing chase and we would charge around splashing in all the shallow rivulets. I always kept an eye out for crocodile as there were a vast number of these huge monsters, just waiting for the unwary. Prehistoric and sinister, they would sleep on the banks, lying so still that it was often difficult to pick them out.

Tim Tom also loved these games and would go skipping along. Although he was old enough to be weaned off the bottle, he still insisted on his favourite tipple. He had grown little horns and kept practising battle formations with myself and Tana. I had put cork stoppers on them so that he couldn't get too carried away.

I always carried a large double camp bed that Tana and Tim Tom shared with me. Not that it left me much room, especially with the dogs and whatever animal I was bringing up on a bottle at the time. As I've said, I have always found that sharing one's sleep with wild animals makes them much tamer. I think it is the constant bodily contact that gives them the security they lack when they lose their natural parents.

I had been given little Tim Tom the Thompson Gazelle when he was just a few days old. His mother had been killed and this beautiful creature had been found lying in the grass. For years, he was a constant part of my life. He would sleep at the bottom of the bed so he did not interfere with Tana who lay beside me, her head on the pillow, breathing short lion puffs into my ear at night.

During our travels, Tim Tom occupied the front seat of the International. When I was driving, he would have the whole front seat to himself but when Stan was with us, he would lie next to me. He would curl up as soon as the car was in motion and remain asleep for the entire journey, only waking to be fed and to get out to spend a penny.

Once, we had left Stan in his camp on the Tana river and I was driving to Mombasa when a vulture which had been eating some carrion on the side of the street flew up into my windscreen. The noise gave Tim Tom such a fright that he leapt out of my fast moving car and I watched in horror as he tumbled over and over. Slamming on the brakes, I raced over, expecting to find him dead. He was alive but in a state of shock with a broken front leg. I wrapped him up and bandaged his leg as best I could, using some branches for splints. Then I drove as fast as possible to the vet, in tears most of the way. I was certain Tim Tom wouldn't survive. The vet in Mombasa did a marvellous job though, putting the leg into a cast. The first few days were traumatic as the little gazelle had to be carried everywhere until he got used to the cast. I had to carry him about with his leg propped up on a pillow. Then he got used to hopping around, dragging his leg sideways. Eventually, he recovered completely.

In the wild, Thompson Gazelle are very territorial and mark out their perimeters. Tim Tom, leading such a nomadic existence with me and my constant travel and safaris, used to try and mark out his territory if we ever stayed more than a few days somewhere. Unfortunately, we had usually moved on before he had really established his kingdom.

He knew everything that was happening in camp. His sense of time was quite extraordinary. He would know when early morning tea was arriving and would be up and waiting at the flap of the tent. I used to drink the tea and he used to eat the biscuits. At meal times, as soon as he saw the men put on their kanzus, he would head straight for the mess tent and wait impatiently by my chair for his two pieces of dry toast. If there was any delay, he would stamp his feet to draw our attention to the fact that he was being kept waiting. Having eaten, he would then go and lie under the table with Tana and the dogs.

The first day on the Tana this time, Enrique and I didn't go out on the river but drove around looking at game, the lovely savannah lands and the tropical vegetation. The next day after lunch, we decided to go on the river in a little boat we had. Our mechanic had checked through the outboard and it was all installed and the boat was on the water.

Getting aboard was not that easy. It was only a light little craft and fitting in a lion presented problems. Tana was used to Stan's launch, which was much bigger, but this one rocked about under her weight. She stood unhappily in the prow swishing her tail to keep her balance.

Although we had brought the boat up onto the beach so as to accommodate Tana, she refused to get on unless I went too. I would hop on board to show her and then quickly jump off again. Tana was not having any of this; every time I jumped off she followed. Finally, with everybody pushing, and our combined weight on board making it very difficult to get us off the sand, the boat was afloat. Now we had to get Enrique and his false leg on board. He finally decided it was easier to take it off.

Thank heavens I had decided to leave Tim Tom and Jason in the camp. The boat wasn't big enough for everyone. It was lovely out on the water though and Tana, the most phlegmatic of creatures, was now sprawled out on her mattress in the prow. Having removed the two front seats for her, she ended up with the major share of the boat.

Stan had often shown me on the launch how to navigate on the Kenya rivers. That means avoiding the sandbars and the hippo. The hippo were in such vast numbers, they used to look like trippers having a day out at Blackpool; large fat mothers and portly fathers wallowing and splashing with their brood of children and assorted relations. They would surface from almost under our bows, then sit half-submerged, blowing water and regarding our progress with the greatest of curiosity.

Monstrous crocodile woken from their sleep by a boat's passage would raise themselves on thick bandy legs and, descending the banks, glide soundlessly into the water and disappear, only a V-shaped ripple on the surface bearing witness to their passing.

This was the first time I had been in charge of a boat trip and I was worried that one of the hippo might surface underneath our craft and tip us into the river as they have been known to do. With all the crocodile around, I was thinking about how Tana and Enrique would cope. I was not particularly worried about myself. With all the Olympic coaching from my ex-husband Frank, I felt I could outsprint almost anything to the bank.

I was concentrating so hard on avoiding hippo and watching for the tell-tale bubbles coming to the surface, that I forgot the sandbanks. It was only when I felt the dinghy shudder beneath me that I realised disaster had struck. We were stuck fast on a submerged sand bar in the middle of the Tana River, miles from anywhere, a lioness, myself and a one-legged man. We considered all aspects of the situation for a while and tried shaking the boat loose. To no avail, we were firmly embedded.

All the time, I kept concentrating on not getting upset. The last thing I could afford in this type of situation was to have Tana pick up negative vibes from me. Enrique said, "One of us obviously has to get out and lighten the boat and try and dig ourselves out. It better be me as I have only one leg and I can feed the other one to the crocodile if they try and attack me."

He was marvellous to be with. Not only was he brave but he treated it all as a great joke and an exciting adventure. I considered this option but realised that although he might be stronger than myself at digging the boat out, I would not have the strength to heave him back on board once we were afloat again.

So, looking with trepidation at the basking crocodiles and telling Enrique to keep a careful watch, I went overboard. The water was well above my waist in parts, even though we were on a sandbank. It was only the front that was embedded as the bank shelved upwards. I had to keep diving under the water, which was muddy at the best of times.

Now, with the roiling sand, visibility was nil. With the help of a spade and coming up frequently for air, I started digging. It seemed to take hours and every now and again, I would hear Enrique shouting, "Crocodile!"

Tana started getting restless and came to lean over the side trying to see where I was. This rocked the boat and, with her weight, it almost capsized. Fortunately, Enrique had the presence of mind to throw himself in the opposite direction. Miracle of miracles, this violent activity seemed to do the trick and the boat came free. I quickly grabbed an oar-lock, as the current started taking the boat downstream. Enrique caught my other hand and tried to drag me on board but I was too exhausted to make much of an effort.

Enrique suggested I go to the stern and then braced his false leg, which he still wasn't wearing, across the motor. That enabled me to get a better grip. Then, grabbing my arm, he hoisted me on board like a flounder. Thank goodness the motor started and we were able to turn and head for camp.

By now it was evening and the stars were out. Tana was sitting in the bow watching a herd of buffalo that had come down to drink. She looked magnificent, outlined in black against the darkening sky. I watched her and the passing parade of life while the river gurgled and slapped the sides of the boat. Flocks of birds were coming in to roost on the tall trees that lined the banks, settling in for the night with a lot of noise and jockeying for position. In the distance, I could see the lights of the camp through the trees and I felt overwhelmed with love for the beauty of life and the world that surrounded me.

CHAPTER

54

I have always gotten a thrill out of driving at speed. It is like flying. In those days in Kenya though, the roads, except for the highway north between Nairobi and Nakuru in the Rift Valley, were all dirt and extremely slippery in the rain when they turned into red mud. Overtaking cars at speed was hazardous as clouds of dust would obliterate the view of the road. One such time, doing 120mph going south towards the Tsavo park and Mombasa, I didn't see a rock sticking out of the road. I tore the whole sump out of the car and had to spend three days at Mtito Andei waiting for the car to be repaired. Luckily, I was towed there by a very nice Sikh, whose car I had been passing at the time.

Stan was always lecturing me on my suicidal tendencies. He considered the speed at which I drove lunacy. That didn't stop me but I was banned from driving anything but the International in his presence. My appreciative passengers of course were my animals and my family who would sleep soundly as we hurtled down mountain passes on muddy, wet and skiddy roads.

Once as I came around a corner on the Langata road between

Karen and Nairobi, two white speed cops flagged me down. I drew into the side and, as they walked to the car, I thought that once they saw the car's occupants, I'd probably be let off. They looked inside and couldn't have missed Tana, who was occupying the entire back seat, and a chimpanzee standing on his head in the front seat. To my amazement and with total sangfroid, they wrote out a speeding ticket and never was a comment passed. I was most put out by their indifference but amused to think how coolly they had played it. I wonder if they ever dined out on the story of them ticketing a speeding lioness?

On another occasion, driving Mummy's stationwagon up from the coast, I came round a bend slightly too fast to find a herd of elephants crossing the road. The stationwagon was a cow in a skid. I was all over the place as I tried to keep the back of the car from slewing around while trying to aim for an ever-narrowing gap between the giant pachyderms. I must have had only inches to spare. I can still see the raised trunks and the screams of rage, as I hurtled towards them. God must have been looking after me that day; I made the gap without even grazing the sides of these giant animals. Then I was through and gone with the trumpeting of enraged elephants still ringing in my ears.

One of the great bonuses of living in Africa was the fact that one never knew from one day to another what type of adventure would be lying in wait. You could never drive anywhere without seeing game. Often coming home in the evening, on the road between Nairobi and Karen, I would sometimes have to make detours to avoid lion that had either made a kill and were contentedly lying there eating, or just strolling across. They had no traffic sense and were extremely discourteous about making way.

Once, I was on my way to see Beryl, driving on the lovely escarpment road between Nairobi and Naivasha, the highway that finished at Nakuru and was built by the Italian prisoners of war. Suddenly, the road in front of me was full of flamingos; they had landed thinking the shiny tarmac was a lake and were now helpless. So I had to conduct a flamingo rescue operation. Thank goodness I had a suitcase with me. I removed blouses, skirts and underwear and shoving it over their heads bundled them into the car. With most birds, if you can cover their heads and eyes, they cease to struggle. It's a good theory but like all theories it's not infallible, especially when one handles the number of various birds I do. This time it worked though and I took the flamingos on a long detour further north to Lake Nakuru so that I could release them in a more hospitable environment. I was soon wallowing around in the smelly mud of the lake with my flamingos. What I and my clothes looked and smelt like at the end of this session was unimaginable.

Arriving at Beryl's I got a typical Beryl greeting: "Sweetie, what a mess. Please don't tread on my carpet and before you have a bath, do be an angel and go to Naivasha for me. I never had the time to pick up the mail and I'm expecting an important letter."

I don't know what magic Beryl employed. I adored her and, feeling that going to collect her mail was a great honour, I rushed off to do her bidding. She only had to open those big blue eyes and put on her helpless female act and we all went to her assistance.

Another time on the road, I was with Stan and Mummy on one of our very first safaris. We were on our way to Mzima Springs on the west side of Tsavo National Park. On the side of the road we found a grey-haired farmer's wife sitting in her Peugeot stationwagon. Stan stopped to ask if she required any help and she said that her husband had been given a lift to collect some petrol. She insisted on staying with the car, so Stan set off to look for the husband. We eventually found him five miles down the road, returning with his *debe* of petrol. Arriving back at the Peugeot, imagine our horror to find it being attacked by an enraged rhino. Of the car there was very little left, but the brave little lady had climbed out through the back door and, keeping to cover, had hidden behind a tree further up the road. The rhino was so preoccupied destroying the stationwagon, her escape went unnoticed.

I also had a wonderful experience coming back from one of Stan's safaris on the Mara. I had left at dawn and had done the unforgivable, forgotten to fill up my spare petrol *debes*. Stan used to fuss so much about carrying spares of everything and when he had gone over the list with me before leaving, I had assured him my spares were already full. But, in fact, I had forgotten to fill them at Narok village on the way to the Mara.

Needless to say, I ran out miles from anywhere. I was on a track of sorts and I resigned myself to settling down for the night. I knew that if the worst came to the worst, when Stan got through to home on the radio telephone and found that I hadn't arrived, he would come to find me. With Stan, I had total confidence that no matter where I was or what happened he would be there for me. It was wonderful having so much confidence in someone, and so I never feared any situation. Without this faith in him, I could never have undertaken these thousands of miles of driving all over east Africa.

On this occasion, I had joined Tana in the back and was preparing for an uncomfortable night amongst the buffalo. A large herd was quietly grazing on the side of a lush grassy hill, totally unconcerned by me. Buffalo en masse do smell rather strong so I retired for the night with a scarf wrapped around my face.

It was Tana, who alerted me to the fact that there was another traveller appearing. I saw a cloud of dust spiralling towards us. At first I thought it was Stan but realised that his safari car could never be travelling at that speed. It was an Indian gentleman coming back from one of the Masai *manyattas* or villages. He was more astounded to see me than I was to see him. There were few people around in those days, apart from the occasional Masai. It was just hundreds of miles of vast plains, hills and the great Mara river, which gave sustenance to the hippo, crocodiles and herds of game. It was God's country and still is today, in spite of the vast influx of tourists.

I'll never forget his face when he saw me emerge from the back of the truck. I must have looked like a terrorist with my head wrapped in a cloth and a lioness about to attack. I could see he was petrified and about to leave us to our fate. Thinking quickly, I decided to do a Beryl act. I undid my scarf to show my face, uncovered my long blonde hair and, opening my eyes wide *à la* Beryl, implored his help. It worked like a charm. He towed me all the way to Narok where he had a *duka*. His lovely young wife gave me one of the best curry dinners I have ever eaten, marvellous rotis filled with dhal and spinach.

In the meantime, he had filled my tank and the *debes* with petrol. I explained to him that I only had a certain amount of cash on me, certainly not enough to fill the containers as well. He refused to take any money so as not to leave me short for my trip. He was confident in my good faith, saying, "*Hakuna matata* [no problem]. You pay, next week, next month, next year."

In those days, Narok was miles from anywhere, and the escarpment road leading up to it was just a dusty white track, covered in boulders, and winding up a cliff which was almost impossible to navigate. The truck would lurch from one rock to another and I, who hates heights, used to hope I wouldn't go over the side in the process. But I had found new friends and for years after, every time I went through Narok I would stop and have the most delicious curry lunches.

I told Stan the story, and the next time he sent his truck there for supplies, he paid my account and wrote a letter thanking them for looking after me. Stan and I often paid visits to the "super *duka*" as we called their shop and visits to these marvellous people was one of the bonuses of going to the Mara.

I had so many encounters on the roads of east Africa because I travelled so much. Returning from the Trans Nzoia district in the Rift as dawn was breaking I encountered the strangest sight, a bright pink car painted all over with metallic blue butterflies. It was parked just off the road and there was no sign of anyone. It was the first vehicle I had encountered since leaving camp at 4am. I stopped to see if there had been an accident and whether help was needed. As I came up, I could see one wheel was propped on a jack but it looked as if it was about to tumble off at any moment. The gallant blue butterflies looked forlorn under their heavy coating of dust. Asleep in the front seat of the car was the most beautiful Red Indian girl.

Hiawatha woke up as I stuck my head through the window and gracefully unfurled herself. As this gorgeous apparition, dressed in khaki shorts and shirt, rose to her feet, I could see she had a long black pigtail through which she had entwined bunches of flowers. They were by now also sadly wilted. Hiawatha was not fazed by having spent a night alone in the middle of Africa. I received a dazzling smile and in a soft American voice, she recounted how she had broken down yesterday and having no spare tyre, had been waiting for some help. I was the first person she had seen. I towed the blue butterflies as far as Kitale where again a charming Indian garage owner came to our assistance.

Hiawatha's name was Yony Waite. She was an artist whose father, a conservationist, kept a second home in Kenya. She was financing her travels by selling paintings. In fact, she is brilliant and is now famous in Kenya. She is one of the partners in the Gallery Watatu in Nairobi and her wonderful works of art adorn all the major hotels and houses.

Yony became one of my greatest friends and the guest house at Ol Orion became her home for a while. The pink car with its blue butterflies became a familiar sight parked under the pink bombax tree. While she stayed with me, Tana would appear each morning, adorned with flowers woven into necklaces.

During this time, in the early 1960s, I went to a party that Monty and Hilary Ruben were giving for a film company that had arrived to make *Mister Moses* with Robert Mitchum and Carroll Baker. I loved going to the Rubens' house. Hilary is fey, enchanting, writes books and plays and seems to live in another world, yet manages everything with the greatest efficiency. Monty is another wonderful Kenya character. He started a transport business that grew and grew and so became heavily involved with the many film companies that came out to Kenya.

I was thrilled to meet Shirley MacLaine who had come out to be with Robert Mitchum with whom she was having an intense affair. The next day I had lunch with her again at the Blocks and she was just as attractive and vivacious as she was on film. So many stars I have met were a sad letdown and some were even a disaster, shattering all one's illusions.

However this time at the Rubens I think I was the one who gave Robert Mitchum an unpleasant surprise.

There must have been a problem with transport because Monty asked me to give Mr Mitchum a lift down to Naivasha where they were filming. I drove down the escarpment at my usual speed and as we levelled out to take the last stretch of road to the lake, he said to me, "Aren't you worried that you might blow a shoe?" It took me until we reached the set to realise that he meant a tyre. As I never talk and drive, he must have thought he had been put into the hands of a madwoman. As for his companions in the back, they were probably frozen with horror.

I did once drive an American girl who went into shock and had to be resuscitated. One forgets that in the United States, after the oil crisis and until a few years ago, the speed limit on wonderful highways was 55mph. To be going along at a 120mph comes, I suppose, as a horrible surprise.

My driver at Ol Orion, Danny, used to amuse me. Whenever I had to take him anywhere (and I tried to avoid doing that as much as possible), he would lie curled up in the back seat with his jacket over his head. So I suppose Robert Mitchum, with his worry about a burst shoe, was displaying great stoicism for he certainly never asked me to slow down.

One driving adventure on the roads of east Africa I will never forget was during the great floods. I was meeting Stan at Manyara and, the road being good all the way, I decided to take my beloved and powerful Citroën and spend a few days at Ngorongoro Crater again. Scenically it is quite magnificent and also one of the wonders of the world as far as concentration of game goes. There was an added attraction: the game warden of that area had a hyena who would follow him around like a dog and I loved seeing this unusual pet.

The day after my arrival, I took the lodge's Land Rover and driver to go down the crater and was standing in the back with my head through the open hatch photographing lion when the car hit a pothole with such force that the hatch door flew up and landed on my head. Blood started pouring down my face and I saw stars. To make matters worse a large screw had gone into my skull. It was a long drive back up the escarpment and when I finally got to the lodge they didn't want to continue with their very basic first aid because they could see bits of bone. Instead, they suggested I should go to the hospital in Arusha, quite a distance away but the nearest medical facility.

There I sat in the waiting room for about half an hour but the yells coming from the patients inside rather put me off. Turning tail, I decided I would prefer to face the very long drive in my Citröen back to Nairobi and my sarcastic doctor, William Boyle, than join the screaming throng.

By the time I left, rain was pelting down. Coming up, the road had already been deep mud, but I knew it well, having charted every corner and the speed at which it could be taken when I had done the East African Safari Rally route for Pierre. Also, I had been to Manyara and Ngorongoro often. I had been driving for a few hours, blessing my front wheel drive as I passed unluckier lorries and cars that had skidded off the muddy road, when suddenly the straight stretch on which I was driving turned into a river. I think it was only desperation that got me through the next hour. The rain was cutting visibility to almost nothing, the road was underwater and I now had an appalling headache. I began to despair of reaching Nairobi.

By the time I arrived at the Athi River and saw the bridge I had to cross, my courage almost failed me. The road had been closed to traffic, there were no other cars around and it was now impossible to go back. The bridge over the steep-sided *donga*, which was normally dry, had water pouring over it. The sides of the bridge were very low and now invisible under waves of churning mud. I realised I had a good chance of being swept into the river by the force of the water. I opened all my windows, in case I ended up in the water, and of course that also let the rain pelt in. I then inched onto what I hoped was the bridge, although thank goodness it wasn't a very long one. I headed for what I thought was the middle of the road on the now totally invisible bridge by keeping my eyes fixed on the road the other side, taking infinite care to keep the wheels straight and the steering wheel from being wrested out of my hands by the current. I managed to get across but the weight of the car must have been the last straw. My back wheels had only just cleared the bridge as I accelerated when, with an almighty roar, the whole thing collapsed.

I made William's surgery but had to park on the opposite side of the road. When I reached the centre crossing, which was beautifully planted with trellised bougainvillaea, I remember looking across at the surgery's front entrance and then everything went black as I fainted. By the time I recovered, quite a crowd had collected. Everybody insisted that I had been mugged. I was drenched to the skin and my hair was matted with blood which was now dripping down my face. I kept insisting I was all right, that it was only a slight accident, and managed to get across and into the waiting room before I finally passed out altogether. William said my sub-conscious had triggered a mechanism that kept me going until I felt safe, and only then did I lose consciousness.

I wasn't feeling too happy with William that night; I had to go to a party at the Erskines and he had cut so much of my hair off, it took me ages to disguise the hole in my head.

There is a sad sequel to this story. Some time later, I had a young Frenchman staying in the house. He was madly in love with Louise Billyard-Leake, the daughter of one of Kenya's well-known families, and at the time she was living at Limuru. I had telephoned Mutete from the Karen *duka* to find out what household provisions were needed, and the young man had come onto the phone, saying his car had broken down. He just had to see Louise he pleaded, could he borrow my Citroën? It was a marvellous piece of machinery with its extra carburettor, my pride and joy. Nobody else drove it for it wasn't a car for an amateur and I was extremely reluctant to lend it.

But he was so desperate and I finally relented. I warned him to be careful cornering and that if it started skidding on the dirt road, he must accelerate because it was a front wheel drive. I loved the car dearly. It went into skids with wonderful abandon and came out of them dancing, and it was marvellous for rallies. It cornered like no other car and by souping up the already powerful engines, I had turned it into a flying machine.

Since I had brought it over from France, the Citroën and I had driven thousands of miles together, over Kenya, Tanganyika and Uganda, through deserts and floods, from plains to mountains, its heavy powerful engine and wide chassis clinging to the road. The back seats had been removed and a mattress installed so that Tana and Joseph could accompany me when I was not using the International. My animals had become speed freaks and were at their happiest when we were tearing along. Hurtling into the corners in clouds of dust, I could see them in my rear-view mirror bracing themselves as we skidded into a turn. Joseph would chortle with glee as he was thrown from side to side. Or he would jump up and down doing his chimpanzee war dance, much to Tana's annoyance. She also had to put up with the dogs lying on the back window seat, falling down on top of her.

I had a bad feeling this day about lending the car but I kept telling myself how utterly selfish I was being. I was also very fond of Louise and I could sympathise with his desire to see her. But when the telephone rang that evening, I was almost expecting Louise's news.

Jean was in hospital, very badly injured, and the car was a write-off. It was like hearing of the death of a close friend.

It was the car I had chosen and Mummy had given it to me. I also had the use of her Buick convertible (a horrible car to drive on Kenya roads) and Stan had given me a Land Rover and the International, so short of cars I was not, but I was often short of cash. Mummy on hearing the news, replaced the Citroën with the new model. It had hydraulic suspension and so later on I was able to take it to Meru with Tana.

CHAPTER

55

Once my mother had returned to Fiorentina, I used to spend most weekends with Beryl at Lake Naivasha. It was on one of these weekends that Stan came to collect me to take me up to the Mau, a particularly beautiful mountain range overlooking Lake Nakuru and its flamingos. It was a wonderful indigenous forest area and Stan had found a lovely camp-site with views over the Rift Valley. It was a dream world and walking back one evening we came across a clearing with a pond in a part of the bamboo forest. We sat on a moss-covered bank and the late afternoon sun, filtered by the trees, lit up the glade in shafts of soft amber light. Out of the wings formed by the curtain of bamboo suddenly stepped a fairy creature, the most delicate of all antelope, the rare forest bongo. I was enthralled by the elegance of this intensely shy creature and the extraordinary beauty of the scene. It stood on the edge of the lake, bathed in the golden motes of light as if on centre stage. Its lyre-shaped horns and enormous liquid eyes were turned in my direction and I could feel the breath catch in my throat, it was so perfect.

It was a paradise that changed into hell. Stan always carried a gun when we walked because of the danger from buffalo, rhino, elephant, or lion. For some extraordinary reason, this time, on seeing such a magnificent trophy, he raised his gun and shot it. My fairyland creature now lay still, blood trickling from the corner of its mouth, its eyes already glazing over. At that moment I hated Stan. Sobbing with despair, I raced back to camp, I did not want him near me; he was a killer and not the hero I had so mistakenly built him up to be. He was the idol that was shattered before my eyes and I couldn't get away from him fast enough.

I insisted on taking his car and leaving. I didn't care how he was to get back. I just knew I could not bear to have to sit next to him for that long drive home. I was feeling sick and distraught that a man I thought I loved could be so cruel and uncaring. I told him that I never wanted to hear from him or see him again and I refused point blank to listen to anything he had to say.

After my return, I refused to answer his calls. If I heard his car arriving, I would take Tana off into the forest. Weeks went by before I saw him again but during this time I would often go down and stay with Beryl. It was after one of these visits that I started feeling ill. I didn't pay much attention but I was aching and I felt as if I had a temperature. I had a light dinner and went to bed. During the night I had a nightmare so vivid that I can recall it now. I was lying on a road and a steam-roller kept going over me. It was rubbing all the pebbles from the road into my face, which was burning and stinging, and the more I tried to avoid it, the more it rolled over me.

I always had early morning tea and Mutete was told that when it had been taken in, I was still sound asleep and Tana was lying on top of me. He thought that sounded strange so went to have a look himself. Tana did not want him to come too near and was indeed lying over me and licking my face, which was raw. He said he thought I might have been dead as I looked very funny, so he called William Boyle.

William told me afterwards that when he got there, neither he nor Mutete could get Tana away from me. They tried with lumps of meat but to no avail. William said, in retrospect, it was the funniest visit to a sick bed that he had ever undertaken because Mutete then got onto his hands and knees and crawled round the bed. He said all he could see of Mutete was his white chef's hat bobbing around. Having arrived at the other side, Mutete tweaked Tana's tail and as she turned round to swipe at him, William pulled me from underneath her and I went crashing to the floor. William said there was no time for gentle handling. Grabbing me by the shoulders, he dragged me through the door which he then slammed in Tana's face.

William in his hurry to put as much distance between himself and the lioness had also shut the door on Mutete. As he said, he had himself and an unconscious girl on one side of the door and an enraged lioness and a frantic cook on the other. Mutete was banging and shouting, "Let me out! Let me out! Tana is very angry with me!" William said he quickly took me to Mummy's bedroom while he sent the houseboys to rescue Mutete.

I was delirious with a high temperature and Tana had obviously thought to come to my assistance. As the sweat poured off me, she had taken to licking my face, but as a lion's tongue is rough she had unfortunately succeeded in peeling most of my skin away as well. This was one rare time when loyal, loving Tana was not a great help!

With antibiotics, the temperature soon came down but I felt a bit weak and William insisted I stay in bed for a few days. I protested that that made me feel even weaker so Mutete constituted himself as my guardian. His main job as far as I could see was to fuss around, asking me how I felt and throwing his apron over his head in the most dramatic fashion every time I got up and went for a walk around the house. Tana was an absolute bore. She kept leaping onto the bed and lying on her back, asking for her tummy to be scratched. Every time I tried to get some sleep she would roll over, landing with her great feet in my face. She took a dim view of all this lying in bed in the middle of the day.

Although I hadn't heard from Stan for weeks, I knew he kept in touch with Mutete because I would get handed the locations of his camps every time they were changed. Just as regularly, I would tear them up. On the third day, I was feeling much better but lying in bed and still feeling rather sorry for myself when I heard Stan's car drive up. As he walked into my room, the old magic came back but I was not, as a matter of principle, letting him see that. He came and sat at the bottom of my bed and Mutete who had obviously told him what had happened arrived with a tray of tea and biscuits.

Stan said, "I shouldn't be here, but I had to make sure you were not dying." Having had his tea, he got up to leave. He had another long drive ahead of him to get back to camp. Standing at the foot of my bed, he added, "The last few weeks have been hell for me. I cannot believe that I could have been so insensitive. My only excuse is that it was a reflex action."

He added that it might help me to know that since that day he had not fired his rifle again.

I heard him speak to Mutete on his way out, and then the engine of the International start up. I realised I could not be so unforgiving, that I still loved him and that unless I hurried, he would probably walk out of my life forever and who could blame him? In my nightdress, I raced out into the garden with Tana in hot pursuit. She thought this was a wonderful new game and in her enthusiasm, nearly bowled me over as she cannoned into the back of my legs.

Stan's gun bearer, sitting in the back, saw me and the car skidded to a halt. Stan, getting out, rushed towards me and as I came to him he said, "My God, what are you doing now, running around in your bare feet and a nightgown?" I said, "Loving you. I can't let you go without telling you." He picked me up and said, "I'm taking you straight back to bed before you die on me." As he carried me inside, I asked him if he was going to come with me. He laughed, "My darling, is that an indecent proposition?"

"Yes!" I said.

Life was marvellous again. Stan was taking out fewer and fewer safaris and we were spending a great deal of time together travelling all over Kenya, Tanganyika and Uganda. It was probably the closest period that we had together.

CHAPTER

56

Tana's endless fascination with the river after which she was named kept me continually entertained. One afternoon while Stan was fishing upstream, we waded out to a sandbar, all the time keeping a wary eye out for crocodiles, which seemed to be massed on every available piece of sand. Tana thought this tremendous fun, especially when I had to dislodge a crocodile by throwing a rock at it. She chased around like an enormous kitten, slapping with her front paws at the wavelets where the crocodile had disappeared, and then leaping back to look astounded as the water splashed in her face. There was a slight breeze coming off the river and I lay down with my book to sunbathe.

We were not far from shore but it was a lovely sensation lying on a golden sandbar with the gurgle of the river in my ears. On one side there was a deeper channel in which a family of hippo were playing. One large lady filled with curiosity came up with a whoosh of water almost beside us. Tana, who was standing near me, made a lunge at the water and for one dreadful moment I thought she was about to plunge in and join them so I grabbed her tail and decided that I better keep her occupied and out of mischief. For the next half hour, I chased her around the sandbank, much to the amazement of a troop of baboons that had arrived on the shore.

A flock of Egyptian geese was soon put to flight as she charged them with gay abandon. I stopped and waited for her, awed by the power and play of muscle as she wheeled and turned and came galloping back towards me. Launching herself into the air, I saw her outlined against the sky as she hit me on the shoulder with her foot. Caught off balance, I fell in the water as she bounded away. About to pick myself up and go after her, I felt a searing pain in my leg and looking down I saw blood starting to flow and a large gash down my thigh. I had fallen near the fast flowing water on the deep side and all I could imagine was that a crocodile had made a swipe at me in passing.

Calling Tana, I raced back to camp, but having no shoes on and not paying attention to where I was going, I landed on a three-inch thorn. Tana was totally bemused by the abrupt cessation to her game and came to stand over me as I was forced to sit on a rock and extricate the thorn. Blood from my thigh was flowing freely and what with my wounded foot as well, I was in quite a bit of pain. I sat debating the problem of getting back to camp as there was still a large steep bank to climb. The hippo were in their pool below me, the screams of the baboons as they fought over some food came clearly to my ears, and overhead an eagle glided effortlessly, soaring higher and higher, caught in the thermal.

Tana looked huge as she stood over me and I could hear her accelerated breathing from the exercise. Evening approached and shadows deepened. The cry of the fish eagle circling above in the pale pink evening sky brought with it a feeling of desolation and the reality of isolation from the outside world. The air was cold against my bare skin and the feeling of death was all around me.

I needed Stan and he came looking for me as I knew he would. Back at camp, with the fuss being made over my wounds, I didn't notice that Tim Tom hadn't come to greet me. It was only when I painfully made my way to the rear section of the tent where my canvas bath was that I noticed he was missing. Stan's sleeping tents had a large area at the back with a tarpaulin floor and two flaps that could be pulled across to divide it from the main section. When we were on safari, it was this part that I made into Tana and Tim Tom's sleeping quarters. When I was with Stan, their bed was level with my head. Incongruous bed companions, the lioness and the Thompson Gazelle, but sometimes they would lie so close together, one could hardly tell them apart.

Having managed a token bath, I went looking for Tim Tom, sure that he must be in the mess tent waiting for his evening treat. But the tent was empty with only Tim Tom's slices of toast lying cold in their usual place. There was no dinner that night. Everyone went out to look for him. I watched the torches flicker as they searched the dark and knew that I would never see that beloved little animal again. Stan came at dawn to tell me that they had found Tim Tom hanging in the tree near the river where the leopard had taken him.

I think they had found him the night before but nobody wished to tell me. For days I was inconsolable and lay with my arms wrapped around Tana, weeping into her fur. I felt she was the only one who really understood how I felt. Indeed for days she also seemed to mourn Tim Tom's passing but maybe she was only picking up my distress. Finally Stan could stand my tears no longer and suggested we leave the area and go up to the Mount Kenya Safari Club for a few days. I was loath to go. I somehow felt if I stayed I could bring comfort to his soul. I imagined him lost and wandering around the camp.

Stan was quick to point out that was an absurd notion. Trying to cheer me up, he said if there was such a thing as an animal's soul, which I could see he found hard to believe, then being Tim Tom's it would certainly accompany me wherever I went just as Tim Tom himself had done.

I was young and it was my first experience of the death of a living thing that I loved. It was made worse by the fact that I had come across the men brushing away tracks, but not before I saw what Stan had set them to covering up; the marks of Tim Tom's flying feet as he had made one last desperate rush to meet me at the river. For days I felt that I had abandoned him in his hour of need and that my premonition of death as I sat nursing my wounds had been Tim Tom communicating his terror but I had not understood it. If only I had climbed that bank instead of waiting for Stan, I might have been in time to save him.

I wanted to remain alone with my grief but Stan would not permit it. Every corner of the road to the club reminded me of Tim Tom. Even climbing into the International, I found a few of his hairs lying on the green vinyl seat. I carefully put sticking-plaster over them so that they would remain forever glued to the seat on which he had lain for so many thousands of miles. For weeks the spectre of Tim Tom remained with me as we travelled the countryside. He was everywhere and yet nowhere.

From the club, Stan took me up to the lovely Loita Hills again. I had no wish to go home where there would be so many painful memories. Determined not to mope any more, I would take endless walks with a reluctant Tana. Stan was never affectionate towards her but after she had saved my life with the buffalo, he seemed to respect her ability to protect me. He insisted I was too much of a dreamer to cope with Africa on my own and had always issued strict instructions to his men that if Tana was not around then one of them must accompany me.

Now even Tana's presence didn't seem to pacify him. I could hardly walk out of his sight without him following me. The whole camp seemed to have eyes that were constantly watching. Finally, the beauty of the country and the presence of so many caring people and my faithful shadow Tana continually at my side made me realise that there was still so much to this world besides sorrow.

Once more I heard the birds sing and I would lie awake watching the dawn rise in splendour, casting aside its dark clouds and darker mountains. I would listen to Africa awakening as the sun discarded its shadows and the overnight dew dripped from the leaves of the trees.

CHAPTER

57

Back in Karen, events were catching up with me. Urbanisation was going to change my life dramatically. When we first went to Karen, Ol Orion was one of only four houses on the ridge. We were far apart and I didn't know or ever see my neighbours and one of the houses was unoccupied most of the time. The Karen *duka* consisted of just three buildings, one of which was the general store.

Ol Orion, facing the hills of the Ngong Reserve, had a large garden with a ha-ha dropping to more garden which bordered a dirt track known as Ololua Ridge Road. The road cut through the farm, and on the other side of it was the large paddock where I kept the cows during the day. One of the gates opened straight onto the reserve and the hills.

A farmer had recently come into the area and started a dairy herd. He was used to seeing Tana wandering around but he began objecting to the male lions that were starting to appear. Tana was now coming into season and during this period we would often have anxious suitors roaring around the house. I got so used to the noise of lions that I could sleep right through without noticing a thing. Once, a couple arriving for dinner said they had had to run the gauntlet of about 20 lion in the vicinity of the front door. Quite terrified, they had had to be rescued by Mutete through the kitchen door. I imagine the number of lion they saw was highly exaggerated but it's true that the lion roared unendingly, making speech difficult. It was not the most successful of evenings.

The dairy farmer became more vociferous with his complaints saying the lion were causing his cattle to abort. Although he did not mind Tana, he felt that as she was the cause of his problems he would have no option but to shoot her the next time she crossed his land. I was in despair. I couldn't bear the thought of enclosing her. She had never been confined and I couldn't face having to do so now. I decided that just as Joy and George Adamson had managed to establish their lioness, Elsa, in the wild as Joy wrote in her famous book *Born Free*, so I would do the same with Tana.

The problems were numerous. Tana was now so tame, none of the game parks I approached would take her. She'd never had to hunt for food and didn't even know how to tear the skin off a kill to get at the meat. I'd destroyed her natural immunity to skin infections because I'd shampooed her coat regularly since she was tiny. Because of her wonderful nature, Tana had become quite famous and had appeared with me on an English televison program *Tonight*, in a French documentary, and in various other programs and also newspapers and magazines around the world. Several embassies, hearing of Tana's plight, called me up asking if I would consider presenting her to their countries. India was one and Israel another. But again, these would have been zoo-like situations and I could not have stayed with her.

Finally Ted Goss, who was game warden of Meru agreed to take her. Meru had been a council game reserve and was about to become a National Park. It consisted of vast tracts of uninhabited land on the north-eastern frontier. It stretched from the plains at the foot of Mount Kenya to the Tana River in the south and east towards the Somaliland border.

Meru was ideal in many ways as it was so far off the beaten track that nobody went there. It had no lodges, no camps and no people, but it was beautiful, wild, open country with lots of water and masses of game. I felt it was meant to be my lioness's final home. Having named her Tana after the river, fate in the form of Ted Goss was giving her this opportunity to return there.

I got in touch with Thomas Hartley, always known by his nickname of Carr. (He later added Carr to his surname by deed poll, officially becoming Carr-Hartley.) He was Diana Hartley's brother-in-law, and had a large ranch at Rumuruti north of Thomson's Falls on the way to Maralal, northwest of Mount Kenya. Carr was a big game trapper who supplied animals to circuses, zoos and film companies. I asked him if he could let me have a pride of lion to set free with Tana as I didn't want her to be on her own. Carr whom I knew quite well was marvellous, refusing to let me buy them from him and insisting on donating them to me for my wildlife experiment. He said as Diana had been killed by a lion, the least he could do for her memory was to help establish a wild pride. He also suggested that I come up and choose the ones that I wanted.

His farm was not in the most beautiful part of Kenya. It was dry arid country with a few scrubby thorn trees and every time I went up there, the wind seemed always to be around, churning up the soil into clouds of dust. Going up to the house, you were always greeted by his tame rhino that was so docile that children could ride on its back. It would appear trotting towards you across the plain, but then you never quite knew whether it really was the tame one approaching or if you were about to be charged by a wild one.

Over numerous cups of tea, we discussed the introduction of Tana into the Meru reserve and all it would entail. The Hartleys were brilliant with their wildlife but seemingly oblivious to the cleanliness of their surroundings. I would try to surreptitiously wipe the rim of my cup before drinking. The chintz sofas sagged and you often had to move a young hippo or warthog from them before being able to sit down. I had learned through past experience to be careful where you placed your feet. Pet snakes lay like hosepipes all over the floor.

Carr's lions were kept in cages that looked like converted railway trucks. The backs of the trucks were closed but the fronts were open and contained by large iron bars. I chose a lovely black-maned lion and three lioness for Tana. Carr suggested I bring Tana up to his farm and he would gradually introduce her to her pride. Only when she had become familiar with them should I release her. Carr also stipulated that during this period I would have to stay away from her. Of course I could see the sense of this but I knew it was going to be a heartbreaking period. Tana and I had never been apart for more than a few days. Equally, I realised that I could not keep procrastinating or I risked getting her killed.

The dreadful day dawned when all was in readiness to take Tana to Rumuruti. I was in such despair I had not slept for nights. Loading her into the car for what was to be one of her last journeys was too terrible. Stan drove us up and it was a nightmare. The nearer we got, the more I had to fight the desperation I felt as to what was to happen to my beloved lioness. At one stage I made Stan stop, saying that I really could not continue, that I would need more time with her, it had all been too sudden and I just could not bear it. Stan soon convinced me that there was no alternative and whether it was this week or next week, the trauma would be the same.

On arrival, Carr ran a chute up to the car. At the other end of the chute was a large cage. They were going to chase her into the chute but I said no. I went and called her instead. Did Judas at Christ's last supper feel as I felt when I called her to me and then heard the noise of the trap as it fell, closing her in? Tana was imprisoned for the first time in her life and she knew it. I will never forget her face as she looked at me for comfort. She had known when I was despairing. Did she now know my treachery? The final indignity was when Carr put a long pair of cutters through the wire and severed her collar. I had always kept a leather collar on her, from which hung a large disc with her name and telephone number. Now this last little part of Tana was handed to me. The sun overhead was burning hot and I remember trying to get air and feeling sick. Then everything went black and I fainted.

Stan lent me his radio telephone when we got back to Ol Orion and from then on I made daily calls to Carr. It must have been a terrible nuisance to him but I think he understood. He told me that her cage had been placed opposite that of the lion that she was to join and although she seemed to hate the sight of them at first, she was now settling down. All that was now separating them were the bars of their cages.

Finally Carr told me that the time had come when he was going to introduce Tana to her future pride but that I was not to worry. He was going to call me later in the day and give me the news of this meeting. I sat by that radio telephone for hours, praying to God that Tana would be all right. I had terrible visions of her being torn apart by the others. I finally got my call and everything had gone well. Carr suggested that I leave them together for a few weeks so that they could form a bond before I released them all into the wilds.

CHAPTER

58

At last the day dawned when Carr considered the lion were able to be moved. He had organised large individual travelling cages with trapdoors. These, with the lion, were going down to Meru on Stan's lorries but Tana was going to drive down with us in the International.

I couldn't wait to get to Rumuruti, I was so excited at the thought of being with Tana once more. All the lorries with our provisions and tents had been loaded the night before and the empty five-ton trucks with their drivers were ready to leave at dawn. It was a big convoy all painted in the dark safari green that moved off in the early morning light.

When we arrived at the Hartleys' the lion had already been loaded into their crates and I rushed to greet Tana who was on her own in the lion enclosure, pacing up and down. As I approached the cage I could feel my heart racing. It seemed to be pounding away in my throat. Tana was there, my beautiful lioness waiting for me, rubbing her body against the bars and giving her little grunts of pleasure. I opened all the safety locks, my hands shaking so much it made me clumsy. It took me so long I wanted to tear them off in my frustration but everyone had kept well away and I had to manage on my own.

At last I was inside, and she threw herself at me knocking me to the floor. Then she was in my arms curling herself about me, her head rubbing under my chin as she rolled over me, her weight pinning me down. I buried my face in her neck. Was the world ever so beautiful? "Oh Tana, Oh Tana, I love you, I love you," I kept repeating over and over as I hugged her to me.

She had had no bath and the lion smell of her was strong. Half-sprawled on the floor, I felt suffocated with the emotion of being so close to her once more. Was ever a lion so magnificent, so loving and so perfect? I could see from behind the bars the whole scene laid out before me, the safari cars, the men in their khaki uniforms, the Hartleys and their men, and Stan talking to his driver. They were all waiting and the final act was still to be played. The cage on wheels was high off the ground and we were going to have to jump to freedom. I had not put Tana's harness on her, although I was carrying it. Now it was a matter of pride. I did not want a subdued lion in human bondage; I wanted to show Tana to all these people as the wild, free and loving creature that she was.

I opened the safety door and launched myself into space. I could feel Tana gather herself and could see the white of her stomach as she leaped over me. As I headed towards the International, she nearly knocked me over once more, so great was her joy as she bounced around, wanting to play. I don't think she could believe that she was finally free.

I raced towards the safari car with Tana in hot pursuit. As I ran, I could feel the excitement, the heady joy, the feeling of being intensely alive. I was aware of every detail. Again, I could feel Tana as she lifted off the ground to hit me on the shoulder, one of her feather-light touches from our daily game. Then she was off to hide behind the car and I pretended to look for her. I could see her crouched in the grass, her ears flattened. As I appeared, she jumped into the car, clearing the front and the back seat in a single leap of muscle and power to regain her favourite position in the back. There she lay sprawled, panting as if she had run for miles and I could see the laughter in her eyes as she looked at me. I sat with her for a while giving her lots of kisses while she lay in her usual soppy position on her back, showing a great expanse of lovely white stomach for me to rub.

Leaving Tana, I went off to watch the loading. The lions in their crates were being lifted onto the waiting trucks by a small crane. There was a lot of noise, dust and shouting mixed with the roaring of lion, and a great deal of cursing from the men who had to manoeuvre the crates into their final positions on the lorries.

At last we were on our way. The moment I had dreaded and yet longed for was about to happen. This long convoy of lion was on their final journey. I was filled with apprehension but there was no turning back. I watched the lorries file out behind us, the spiraling brown dust churned up by their wheels clouding the lonely landscape of grass and twisted thorn scrub. I wondered if any safari company had carried such an incongruous load. I thought of Stan who had worked all his life to build up this company of which he was so proud. Now it had been outfitted not for millionaire hunters, but to transport an African Noah's Ark. In his generosity, he had equipped an entire safari and because of my love for a lioness had once more put his livelihood at my disposal.

The road to Meru in those days was a rough dirt track that wound its way round the foothills of Mount Kenya before, choked with rocks and boulders, it dropped gradually down several thousand feet into the valley below. It was a long drive and we had to move slowly and with care because of the animals. So it was late when we finally arrived at Ted Goss's headquarters at Leopard Rock, which was at the entrance to the Meru National Park. This was where we were to establish our camp for the next few weeks.

Ted was a wonderful person, a tall, fair, good-looking young man dedicated to the preservation of wildlife. He was the archetype of those men, the game wardens, usually young men who were given virtual control of vast territories of land. They lived lonely lives, miles from civilisation. Vast areas of Africa revolved around the abilities of these brave and able men who served their cause so devotedly.

Stan and I took Tana and went to scout along the Rojewero River about 30 miles away. Unfortunately I never used to keep diaries, but I did scribble on bits of paper. I found this under the heading "Tana": "I am sitting on the banks of the river, my camp site is further up under a grove of duom palms. It is a hot still afternoon, not a leaf moves. I am sitting with my back to a rock under the overhang of an umbrella thorn. Underfoot is a stretch of white sand on the banks of this slow-flowing river as it makes its unhurried descent. How can I describe this country of Africa, an Africa that sleeps in the heat of the relentless overhead sun.

"I lift my head and see an enormous crocodile on the sandbank in front of me. Asleep with his mouth open, and so close I can see the rows of razor-sharp teeth from which an ibis is picking at the rotting meat from an earlier meal of putrefied flesh. The bird is busy, the crocodile at peace, not even awakening when a family of hippo surface for air. With a great deal of noise and much spraying of water, they all regard me with avid curiosity from large bulging eyes. Overhead a fish eagle screams. It is the voice of Africa. It conveys the loneliness, the savagery and above all the beauty and mystery of this harsh land.

"My toes curl into the short hairs along Tana's back. She lies at my feet, my African lioness, also taking her afternoon siesta. Under my toes I can feel the beat of her heart, or is it my own? I know no more, we are bonded so closely together. It is as if we are one. I have never experienced this total submerging of the senses into another being.

"Thoughts of the future have no part of my life as I sit watching the flow of the river. Under my sunburnt toes, Tana's hair was rough and I watched the speckles of black and yellow and the grease from her body come off onto my feet in a grey film as I rubbed her back. I watch her lying there, all white and gold, my beautiful Tana, named after the river from whence she came. Life for her is turning a full circle. The time is coming when I will have to leave and return her to the land of her birth.

"It is a decision that has caused me sleepless nights and endless tears of despair. Civilisation encroaching on our world has taken my options away. It is a choice between freedom and all its inherent dangers, or a lifetime behind bars and its inbuilt security.

"Tana, my constant companion for the last five years. I agonise over the decision that is being forced on me. How can I abandon her? Is it to her death I am sentencing her, or is it to a lifetime that will be hard, a continual search for food but she will be free. Is freedom so important? How do I know, and who can tell me? The choice is mine and I am playing God with this precious life. Oh Tana, beloved! How much longer do we have together; the world is closing in on us and we cannot escape forever.

"I go to lie beside her in the sand. I need the contact and the comfort, my arms around her, the smell of lion, the short hot puffs of her breath against my neck, and under my hand the feel of strength, of hard muscle. It is all so familiar. Her very presence soothes me and as I share her sleep, I can delude myself. After all, it will not be today or tomorrow, and a miracle could still happen.

"Although we lie in the shade, Tana and the sand feel warm and on the far bank I can see a large family of baboons relaxing with their babies as they groom each other. They give the appearance of a large holiday excursion at the seaside. The nubile females display to the dominant male who, busy with his succulent lunch, looks bored with the whole proceeding. The babies charge around on their wobbly legs, tormenting their mothers and elder siblings. So reminiscent of a scene on Brighton Beach that I laugh at the simile.

"Up-river I hear the trumpeting of an elephant but I am hot, sleepy and cocooned in safety. What predator would dare dispute territory with the king of the beasts, or rather with my beautiful somnolent queen? In sleep, I am a part of Africa, a part of this soil, a part of the shadows, a part of the sun and I cling to Tana who has given me this freedom, who has given me all this, her Africa."

We spent the next few weeks touring Meru, looking for a suitable place to release the lion. I could not make up my mind. Indeed, I really did not want to make a decision that would sever the connection with my beloved Tana. Finally Ted Goss made it for me. He told me that he did not want another hysterical Joy Adamson on his hands and I either must make up my mind to release Tana, or take her back to Nairobi. (When I was asked years later about Joy, by a woman working on a project on her, I said that Joy was easy to relate to and she was a very good artist. She was very European, Austrian by birth, very volatile, highly strung and I would say that she lived on her nerves. I am able to pick up vibrations from the people I meet, as one certainly does with animals. With Joy, she had a tremendous restlessness about her; she was definitely not a happy person... I used to wonder what drove her and her extraordinary relationship with the animals amazed me because there is no question wild animals pick up one's every vibration... It used to puzzle me at the time because I used to wonder if Elsa herself wouldn't become neurotic. I know she clawed Joy severely on several occasions whereas Tana never ever in all those years even so much as gave me a scratch. Joy's personality seemed to me so at odds with the life she had chosen. I feel she was never happy enough to get outside her own frustrations. Therefore, the wonder of that country passed her by in spite of her love of beautiful things, a quality she must have had to have painted as perfectly as she did.)

A few days before, we had seen a beautiful area on the banks of the Rojewero River, open plains with wonderful duom palms, flat-topped acacia, and game of all description. Above all, we had not seen any other lion in that particular area. I decided that Tana's future home would be this idyllic spot where the river flowed, the grass was high and the blue foothills of Mount Kenya could be seen in the distance.

Oh Tana!

That night I lay beside her for the last time. I refused to let myself sleep because I wanted to treasure every last second. There were so many little details to store in my memory. I listened to her breath, I could feel her heart beat and I couldn't stop agonising over her future. I watched the light of dawn and knew that feeling of total despair where even death would be welcome if it cut off the pain.

With daylight, I led Tana to the International. The lorries with their wooden crates were already loaded and waiting. As I climbed into the back with her, the air was cold and even my thick sweater didn't warm me. The convoy started moving. Around me were the dark outlines of the palms, the pale azure sky of dawn, the towering black mountains of the escarpment and, like toys they were so small in the distance, a herd of elephant. I noticed it all but I was in misery and my misery became my lioness's misery.

Tana could always sense my moods and she rolled over so I could lie between her front legs while she draped one leg over my shoulder and nuzzled my face as if I were a cub.

The track was long and rough with many *dongas* to cross as it headed towards the Tana. I felt the car turn onto the open plain as we drove across country heading for the river I had chosen. I could almost smell the water and I knew that I could count our time together in minutes. As we arrived, Tana understood that I was about to leave her and in her despair, she seized my sweater in her teeth. I had to open her mouth to make her release me. Bending down, I took that beautiful head in my arms for the last time. Kissing her, I backed away while I still had the courage to say goodbye.

Someone opened the door and Tana sprang out of the International, her last leap from a car into an unknown world. A zebra had been shot by Ted Goss. She was hungry as, at Ted's suggestion, I hadn't fed her for two days. We left her there, crouched over the stiff form of her prey.

I don't remember the long drive back to camp at Leopard Rock. I lay in the back on Tana's mattress and the rest of the day was a nightmare of regrets. Night came and I lay sobbing in my tent but somehow above my anguish I heard the hunting grunt of a lion. I listened and thought of Tana on her own for the first time. I wondered where she would be sleeping and if she had found the others of her pride. As I listened, the muffled grunts of the hunting lion that had been far in the distance now sounded so much nearer. I could feel the goose-pimples rise on my skin.

The flaps of the tent had been left wide so that I could watch the night. Suddenly the light of the moon was cut off by a giant shadow filling the opening. Oh my beloved Tana! She had retraced the tracks of our journey, abandoning the carefully selected pride of lion and following me back over the 30 miles or so, traversing strange land that had never been her territory. She had come home.

Tana leapt from the opening of the tent onto my bed. Her impatience to reach me was no less than mine to hold her once again. The bed collapsed and we rolled round together in a frenzy of reunion until finally the tent also came down on top of us and we were covered by thick sheets of canvas.

She and I had three more days together before Tana was returned to the wild. With Ted Goss's promise to monitor her wellbeing, I left her again. This time, we headed back to Ol Orion. Once more the radio telephone became my daily link to Tana via Ted. I was miserable.

One day, Stan came in from one of his safaris, greeting me with, "*My darling Toto ya Simba*, I've been so worried about you. I think I have good news. I've found out something. Ted Goss needs a lodge for Meru. If you are prepared to build one for the park, he suggests you come back and stop bothering him on the radio telephone."

It was the most wonderful gesture. Certainly Meru was an enormous area and there were no facilities for tourists and Ted had seen this as a way to help me as well as the park and its administration. For this I will be eternally grateful to him.

CHAPTER

59

Solange de la Bruyère was staying with me at Ol Orion when I received the news that Ted Goss had given permission for me to build a lodge. I had known Solange as a young girl when she came to the south of France from Paris to recover from an illness. Half-French, half-American, she had been Solange Batsell then and one of the most lovely and fascinating girls I have ever known. She was a great friend of Jackie Kennedy and one of the few people I knew with a character as beautiful as her face. I think this is one of the reasons that men adored her. Certainly she has been much married and enormously admired. Nowadays she lives in New York and is married to Christian Herter, a cancer specialist from a well-known New York family, and is still lovely, amusing, charming and crazy.

Now that I had the go-ahead to return to Tana, my one problem was money. When I was 21, Mummy had given me an income of £1000 a month, which in those days was enormous. As all my expenses were paid on top of that, including clothes, cars and whatever I fancied. I really never wanted for anything. But now Mummy was away and 15 years later £1000 was not what it was when I was 21, certainly not enough to start building a lodge. It was Solange who came to the rescue. She lent me £5000 so that I could get the building started.

Stan provided the machinery, the transport, the fridges, stoves and electrical equipment and I put all my own income into furnishings, labourers and day-to-day running costs.

Once more, a big procession of Lawrence Brown Safari trucks was on the road to Meru. This time, they were loaded with tents, food and workmen. The nearest *duka* for shopping would be a six-hour drive away. Not only did every nail, hammer and screw have to go by lorry but I could not leave my animals behind. Even the crowned Kavirondo cranes were brought along. Stan set up a camp for me on the banks of a tributary of the Rojewero River, and then, leaving me with men and transport, he returned to his clients on a safari. He had taken a few days off to help me get started but my impatience to get back to Tana had meant that I wasn't willing to wait until the safari ended, which would have allowed him to help with the building.

Ted Goss provided me with a gang of prisoners, assigned to him for labouring work, and I had also taken a lot of my Wakamba staff from Karen, only leaving Mutete and two of his relations to look after Ol Orion. I, who had never built anything, now had to be architect, builder and handyman. It was a daunting task but I was young and filled with enthusiasm. This was to be my monument to Tana, the place where I could live and monitor her movements and ensure her future.

I had watched the way the *fundis* had built the guesthouses at Ol Orion. Here I intended to use only the local materials. The thick bamboo growing so profusely near the river would, I felt, make marvellous walls for this hot climate and there were hundreds of duom palms to supply the *makuti* thatching. I kept telling myself that my brother was a world-famous builder of beautiful houses; surely his little sister must have inherited some of the Lindeman artistic ability and be able to erect, if not a grand building, then an African hut with at least some charm and style.

I built the lodge like an African village with my brother Caryll's Equator Farm in mind. I started with the sitting room, which I built in a large rectangle but I rounded the end walls. I like large rooms and I made this one enormous. We collected dead trees for the uprights and these were cemented into deep holes in the ground. Then I erected a double layer of bamboo for the walls. We drove far and wide collecting beautiful dead, wild olive trees to form the columns that would hold up the vast roof. Olive wood from the Kenya forests looks like wonderful carving with its silvery grey knotted and twisted shapes.

The floors were cement on which, with a giant ruler, I laboriously drew squares to resemble large tiles. I mixed green powder into the final dressing and when this was sealed and glazed, it was like marble with a high gloss. The tall steep roof was layer upon layer of the fan-like palm leaves that are one of the beauties of the duom palm. These were plaited and laid in rows, one above the other, on long sticks. The front was all open except for the columns of olive and led onto a verandah that ran the length of the room. I visualised it as a lovely place to sit and watch the river below. Beyond the river, there were endless vistas of palms, baobabs, acacias and grassland and ever-changing herds of game. To the right of the main building I built nine large rondavels with ensuite bathrooms. Mine was next to the main building and they were all built in the same style. Round like African mud huts, with steep thatched roofs, bamboo walls and individual balconies overlooking the river.

It took months of hard work. First of all, we had to clear the undergrowth and that uncovered hundreds of snakes and scorpions. There were numerous trips by lorries bringing in building materials and I always seemed to be running out of nails and cement. Then there were all the provisions needed, not only for my staff but for the labourers as well. At one stage all the prisoners went on strike refusing to work any longer. They sat around in sullen silence. Stan had loaned me the services of his old gun bearer and tracker, Ismael, telling him that his duty in life now was to look after me. I had a consultation with Ismael and my Wakamba as to what I should do about the prisoners and we agreed that they would be loaded onto the lorries and returned to Ted at Leopard Rock. We could finish off the lodge without them.

It was a great relief when they departed. I had never felt threatened by their presence but somehow, the very fact that there were so many of them left one with an uncomfortable feeling, especially when it grew dark. I sometimes found myself listening to the noises of the night and what was really only the rustling of a snake in the *makuti* roof would turn into the sinister rustling of bare feet on the prowl around my open room. In the days of living with Tana, I had never felt this insecurity and no matter how far I was from civilization, the darkness of night had held no fears.

We had now been building for several months in the area in which Tana had been released but still I had seen no sign of her. I came across the black-maned lion continually for he seemed to feel happier near the bustle and activity of the camp. Although he was on his own at this stage – and that is rare for a lion – he looked in good condition and I came across him one day with an old buffalo kill so I knew that he was able to survive without help from me.

The lodge was now ready to furnish and with the building completed I could spend my time looking for Tana. Until this point, I had taken two hours off every day to look within the vicinity of the camp but without ever seeing signs of her. Somehow I knew though that she was still alive. At times I could almost feel her presence. Loading the International with my tent and supplies, I intended to camp out until I found her and I knew that Ismael's incredible gift for reading spoor would eventually lead me to her. On the third day, he picked up her tracks. They were four days old, he told me, and she was with a young male. He even showed me where Tana had mated; by the looks of it they must have made love all day.

Over the next few days, Ismael would patiently show me Tana's tracks and although I was able to distinguish the male from the female, the spoor of a female lioness being narrower than a male's, I could not for the life of me see that Tana's was much different from that of another lioness. He tried to show me how she was bigger and how her spoor ran deeper as she was much heavier, but the depth was fractional and the width minimal to my eyes. Finally I would say yes as I did not want Ismael to feel that all his teaching was in vain. As *memsahib*, I should at least give the appearance of intelligence. However, I was now feeling very humble and this was a very debatable point.

Finally it was Tana who found us.

She must have heard the International for Ismael had just shown me the spoor marks of where they had passed by only a few hours before. She suddenly appeared on the track, trotting towards us, looking thinner and every inch a wild lioness. Now that the moment had arrived I couldn't believe it. Once more she was leaning all over me and rubbing her head against me as I buried my face in her neck. I heard Ismael shouting at me, "*Angalia, Memsahib!*" and looking up saw Tana's mate approaching.

In my excitement at seeing her again, I had totally forgotten that she would not be alone. Now her scraggy-looking mate had appeared, although approaching much more slowly than Tana had. I gave her the usual command of "stay" and hastily backed away. Discretion was the much better part of valour in this instance, and it was with relief that I found myself back in the International. I watched the male come up beside Tana to stand looking at us for a while. Then, with a huge yawn, he lay down as if too exhausted to contemplate further exercise.

At least a week passed before Tana found the lodge itself and the only way I knew she was there was that one morning one of the men came to tell me that during the night a lion had broken into the chicken run. "*Wote walikufa kabisa.*" They were all very dead. I did not need Ismael to tell me who the culprit was.

I had warned Ismael that when we found Tana, he was not to mention her to anybody. I had received so many lectures from Stan on the subject of leaving her strictly alone and I knew Ted Goss would not be too happy if he felt I was encouraging her to establish residence at the lodge. Now worried I might be asked to leave should she do so, but having no intention of not monitoring her progress and giving a bit of secret assistance should I deem necessary, I felt my best plan of action under the circumstances was not to let anyone know she was around.

I thought it would be better for her sake, and her mate's, to remove myself from the lodge for a while. Leaving Ismael to keep a close watch on her and make sure that she was not going hungry, I took this opportunity of going to Nairobi to pick up the furniture I needed. I left Meru with all the empty lorries and a lot of the staff. I gave strict instructions to Ismael about contacting me on the radio telephone in a code that we had arranged should he feel Tana's food supply needed supplementing. I had every sneaky intention of coming back with a bulk order in case it should ever come in handy.

In Nairobi, I had a marvellous time choosing the soft furnishings, buying large double beds, getting sofas and chairs covered in lovely thick printed rough cotton, white on white, to which I added the jewel-like colours of large Indian cushions. I watched the Indian *fundis* making up the slip-covers and the *kanga* curtains for the beds and the rooms and I could hardly contain my impatience to get back to the lodge and Tana. I haunted the bazaar. It was like being in India, with its streets full of artisans and shops and the smell of spices from the *dukas* selling curries and condiments in great wooden barrows outside their shops. The powders were marvellous yellows, ochres and reds and there were piles of chillies, peppers, paprikas and cumin set out in a wonderful blending of exotic colouring. There were *kikoi dukas*, sari *dukas* and cottons and silks *dukas*. I loved the jostle, the cars and the bicycles and the wonderful manners and smiles of the Indians. Nothing was ever too much trouble and if one did not have a particular item, they always had a friend who did.

I returned to the lodge with every lorry filled to capacity and the International looking like a tinker's cart, so loaded was it with hardware and pots and pans. I kept laughing all the way back thinking if only Stan could see his transport now. Not being the expert and meticulous packer that he was, I couldn't help noticing a few unseemly bulges. I never did master the art of getting the drivers to tie the ropes over the khaki tarpaulins in the neat way that Stan's safaris achieved. As for the animals who always travelled with us, we looked more like Dr Dolittle's caravan. There were animals hanging out of everywhere. I would put the young monkeys on leads for travelling, but somehow they always managed to climb out the sides and dangle from the roof.

We built bamboo four-posters around the guests' beds, which were varnished till they shone. Then we draped them with mosquito nets which were tied back in the daytime with big white cotton bows. The curtains on the beds and windows were also draped and tied back and were made from cotton *kangas*. One room would have the blue on white, another the peach on white, or the yellow or the red. No two rooms had the same colour scheme so it was easy to identify them to the staff.

One particular colouring that turned out very well was black on white. *Kangas* have very simple designs in the middle of the material and heavy borders of the same colour around all four edges. The black consisted of four large petals arranged in a square on a white background and a four-inch pattern of black rose leaves formed the border. When this was hung from the bamboo four-poster with its underlining of mosquito netting, it looked most romantic.

I also brought down some good pieces of furniture, needlework, carpets, china and Victorian paintings for the walls. All the tables had lovely bowls: Coalport, Worcester, Derby and Spode, which were filled with flowers. With the high gloss of the varnished bamboo and the gently filtered sunlight forming patterns on the green floors, the rooms glowed with an air of soft rustic grandeur.

Thank goodness Stan arrived before the lodge was entirely completed. He connected the old Victorian claw-footed bathtubs with their brass fittings and organised highly efficient heating systems for the water out of the big petrol *debes* to which pipes had been welded. They were then placed on their sides and laid on stone cradles off the ground so fires could be lit underneath. There was an abundance of dead wood and we had unlimited water from the river on which Stan had placed a ram, a type of engineless pump that brought the water up to the camp. Amongst Stan's finds in the scrapyards around Nairobi was an old diesel tractor engine. When it was started up at night, it gave us all the electricity we needed. The only drawback was that when it was switched off by the last person going to bed, it wasn't possible to switch it on again unless you were prepared for a long walk to the engine room. Therefore, as with all Kenya farms where lights are run off generators, torches by the bed were a necessity.

There was another drawback from clearing the bush. The snake population went on the rampage. They were everywhere. I kept the red tins of Fitzgibbon's snakebite kits in every conceivable place: the rooms, the car and in my bush jacket pocket.

I had one narrow escape myself. It was on a very hot day, all the men had gone off to lunch and I thought I would spend my lunch hour sitting in a cool bath with a book. I had just started to undress in my room when I became aware of a swishing sound, as if a hose was being dragged over the dry cement. I turned to look and there, coming over the open section of the half-door to my hut, was the most enormous cobra, its tail still on the floor of the verandah and its head only a few feet away from mine. I realised that if I frightened him or made any sudden movement, he would strike. The bathroom door was behind me, and very slowly, never taking my eyes off him, I backed towards it. Strangely, as I moved away from him I could almost feel his uncertainty and I knew that I had nothing to fear. I stood very still and watched him continue on his way towards a separation in the bamboo walls of my bedroom where he disappeared.

When the men came back after lunch, they caught him and, needless to say, removed most of the wall in the process. The cobra was so enormous the sack seemed almost too small to hold him. I took him over to the banks of the Tana River before releasing him. He was the largest of all the snakes I saw but they were so numerous that on three occasions, while I was sitting down, I had to lift my legs out of the way for them to slither past. We found them in the paraffin fridge, in our shoes, in the toilets and the gardens I was laying out. Each night before retiring I would shake out the mosquito nettings on all the beds before firmly tucking them under the mattresses. That formed a little island where one could sleep in peace, comfortably listening to the rustlings in the *makuti* ceiling above one's head without having to worry that an unwelcome visitor would suddenly arrive.

In Kenya, during the days of the early settlers, there was a lady whose beloved pet was a large python. It accompanied her everywhere, including to bed, where it would lie between herself and her husband, whom the snake hated. The husband suffered this ignominy for years. Eventually the lady's mother died and she had to return to England for the funeral. Reluctantly departing, she begged her husband to care for Thomas the python until her return. Tears streaming down her face at the prospect of parting from her adored snake, she boarded the train for Mombasa.

A few weeks later, the husband, having sundowners with his friends, was bemoaning the terrible responsibility his wife had left him with and expressing his hatred of Thomas who at this stage was lying asleep in his box. Amongst his drinking companions was his boss, an old colonel, who told him, "If you are half a man, shoot the damn thing." After much deliberation and further encouragement from his friends, the husband went for his shotgun and blew off Thomas's head as he lay peacefully sleeping. When his wife returned, everyone told her the same story. The python had, during her absence, pined away and died of a broken heart.

I had another horrible experience with snakes on the Tana. I was in the International, looking for my lion, when I saw a tall young herdsman coming towards me, his spear in one hand and naked, except for his *shuka* or cloth draped over him from his left shoulder, and a pair of sandals made from rubber tyres. I awaited his approach as I knew he would be wanting a lift. Most of these tribesmen from the remote areas had never travelled in a car before and cadging lifts was a momentous occasion.

I can still see him now as he jogged towards me, waving his spear to catch my attention, and with his lovely white-toothed smile. Then his expression changed into a rictus of pain as, out of nowhere, a black mamba struck. It all seemed to happen in slow motion. I reached into the pocket of the car to get my snakebite outfit, a brand new box that had never been used, but as I opened the lid, I saw to my horror, that the syringe was missing.

My blood ran cold. I realised that I was powerless to help the young tribesman. We put him in the International and I took off across country to Maua, for the nearest mission station doctor. But the drive on what was virtually an overgrown track full of rocks and boulders to say nothing of wandering game would take a good few hours. I knew we didn't have that long. It seemed no time at all though before I heard Ismael whisper to me, "*Memsahib, ninafikiri alimkufa.*" I refused to believe he was dead and it was only when we arrived at the mission station and the doctor examined him that I realised just how quickly death had come.

The sun still shone on this perfect land and the dust, the only sign of our passing, had settled behind me. I would now have to retrace my tracks, into the setting sun, leaving a young man to return to the earth from which he came. A young man with no future and an unknown past.

I later found out that one of the other young tribesmen who had come to watch the building of the lodge had, with the usual insatiable curiosity, investigated all the strange things belonging to the car. At that time, most of the tribal Africans, both men and women, had pierced ears from which would be hung all sorts of heavy objects, mostly highly decorative. Beads, porcupine quills, cartridges or whatever was the fancy of the moment. The young man had decided that the syringe would be a perfect ear decoration.

CHAPTER

60

At last the lodge was finished and I called it after my mother, Kenmare Lodge. For me that name still summons the feel of the tropics, the smell of jasmine, hot scented evening air, light cotton on warm skin, the languor induced by a cool interior after exposure to the heat outside. I love the sun and warmth and Meru had both in abundance. It was never cold. I would lie awake watching the moon rise, outlining the duom palms, black against the indigo sky. The cool breeze would come off the river below me, the water rushing to join the Tana, gurgling and babbling over the rocks and boulders lying in its path. That background sound of water was always with me, a Greig symphony in crystal tones. The back and side walls of my room were made of bamboo and instead of windows, there were simply no walls in front. Everything was built to catch the breeze and to give uninterrupted views of the magnificent African vistas.

I would lie in bed knowing that if Ted Goss at Leopard Rock was away, it would be a four-hour drive to my nearest neighbours at the tiny mission station at Maua. Myself and my Wakamba, Meru and Somali helpers were a little enclave in this vast land.

The moon would light up my room and the breeze would stir the palm fronds in the roof over my head. Safely cocooned in my mosquito net, I would listen to any rustling in the thatching and wonder if it was a snake or one of the many lizards that made it their home. I once watched a poisonous boomslang snake strike an agama lizard and I saw the poison rushing through its body, the bright blues and golds changing to muddy grey before the lizard fell to the floor in death.

As night fell, I'd hear the many sounds of Africa, the trumpeting of elephants as the herd negotiated the river, the cough of a leopard, the distant grunt of hunting lion. I would listen for that beloved deep-throated rumble that was Tana, and I'd be certain sometimes that I could hear her voice above all others. Then, splitting the night would come the bloodcurdling howl of a hyena tapering off into a mournful sobbing. Sometimes the hyena would come onto my verandah and I would see their dark shape and smell that acrid odour of dried blood.

As the night became still once more I would hear in the distance the soft voices of the Wakamba and smell the smoke from their fires. A drum would start its primitive tattoo and another would join it until the night would come alive with the pulsating heartbeat of Africa.

Night after night, I would lie listening to the voice of this vast continent, this mysterious, beautiful, cruel country. Here I was the only *mzungu* (white person) for many miles. Surrounded by all that I loved, I would wonder if it were possible for anyone to be more blessed by God's bounty than myself.

Tana's mate was not of course the one I had so carefully chosen and brought all this long distance. That magnificent black-maned lion was relegated to the females I had also brought to form a pride for Tana. She had scorned their company and had chosen instead a typical northern frontier lion, a scruffy individual with hardly any mane and what he had was yellow, the same colour as the desert. He had a large tear in one ear which made him look particularly unprepossessing. But Tana obviously was happy with her choice and after all, who was I to judge?

Meru was so far away from so-called civilization, towards the deserted country that led to the Somaliland border, that there were no roads where we were. The only way to find me was for me to give a compass point. We had to make our own tracks to the lodge. In the early days, when anyone came to visit rolls of toilet paper were tied to the trees at the crucial turning points. Somehow the visual impact of the toilet paper made more of an impression, we discovered, than any other type of marker and one that was never missed.

Stan was away most of the time. Now I was safely installed in the lodge, he felt able to go back to his safaris. He loved the idea of me being in Meru and away from everyone and any man who might take a fancy to me, even though we sometimes didn't see each other for months. The solitude never worried me. I felt I was part of the country and the country was mine. My only communication with the outside world was the radio telephone, a large box on a table with its aerial attached to one of the higher trees. It used to splutter and scream at me in the most alarming fashion until I got used to its idiosyncrasies. Once the radio telephone was switched on one could listen to all the various calls going on. Often, I used to listen to Professor Louis Leakey, the brilliant anthropologist and archaeologist, whose wife Mary was also an eminent anthropologist. At this time, Leakey was at Olduvai Gorge in northern Tanzania where the couple had made several of their controversial discoveries of early primate fossils. He was always calling up for more supplies to be sent from Nairobi. I would hear him getting highly impatient if the necessary items were temporarily unobtainable.

I grew quite expert at navigating the African bushland as I drove to and from Meru. Meanwhile Stan, as usual after two months on safari, had found some excuse to see me and this time it was a paraffin fridge he claimed that he urgently needed.

Stan used to try and get through to me daily at 10am after returning from his early morning hunt. He was on the Tana River delta when he called up to say he urgently needed the fridge. He gave me compass points and lots of instructions as to directions and his parting words were that if I got lost I was *never* to leave the car; the same thing applied should I have a breakdown. I had to be sure that all my water *debes* were full and to take provisions for four days. Stan also insisted that I stop at 10am and 4pm and contact him on the radio giving my exact location.

I did a last-minute check to see that I had forgotten nothing; Stan had told me on many occasions that it is often the little details on which one's life could depend. Ismael and Kimau the mechanic were already installed, so collecting Tim Tom II, a present from Stan after he had found him abandoned, I placed the new little Tommie on the passenger seat beside me and off we set.

I watched the sun just beginning to rise. The air was soft on my bare arms but there was already a hint of heat to come. I drove out first to look for Tana for I couldn't leave without assuring myself of her wellbeing. I found her not far from the camp, lying with her mate. I sat and watched her for a while until she got up and, yawning, started coming towards me. It was time to say goodbye and leave.

With my headlights showing me the clearings between the dense thorn thickets, we set off on our journey into the plains and hills of Africa. It was a long, slow and tortuous drive following my compass settings, climbing hills and driving in and out of *dongas* and all the time trying to avoid the thick thorns that tore at the car in passing, the hidden rocks that could tear the sump out and above all the ant-bear holes that would entrap the unwary.

In spite of all my care, by evening we were firmly stuck in one of these. The left back tyre was all the way in and we were tilted at a giddy angle. Out came the spades and the blocks of wood and canvas used for these emergencies. Even so it took us a good hour. I didn't have the art of rocking the car the way Stan could with all his years of practice. I tried but somehow it didn't work for me and so I decided we would camp there for the night. I was tired and hot and longing for my canvas bath. I strung up the radio telephone and left Kimau trying to get hold of Stan.

When he did come on, I couldn't even tell him where I was. He started fussing and said I was to stay and he would come and find me. I assured him that I was on a perfectly good compass reading and the only reason I had stopped so early was because I wanted a bath. Stan wanted to know what was wrong with Ismael for letting me behave in such a wayward fashion and for not having got us onto the Garissa road. I explained to him that Ismael had assured me that we would soon be there. Stan exploded, "How the bloody hell does he know?"

Ismael was standing by me, listening to the talking box but I don't think he understood much, given his English was limited to about five words. I said to Ismael, "*Bwana* Stan wants to know if you are sure we are heading for Garissa."

"*Ndio, naweza kuninusa.*" I told Stan not to worry, Ismael says he can smell it. He thought that was very funny and so feeling that I was still in capable hands, I signed off.

The next morning we started off at first light. We were in really arid scrub country and there was no sign of the beautiful mountains and hills we had left behind. All my concentration for the next three hours went on avoiding the small stunted trees and scrub. We saw no animals, no human beings. It was flat, ugly and very hot sandy country we were passing through. My rally driving experience was no use here; we never moved over 20 miles an hour. Relying on my compass points and Ismael's infallible nose – which in spite of Stan's scepticism I firmly believed in – we headed for Garissa.

The very first person we saw was a Somali herdsman who suddenly appeared out of the shrub with his camels and was no less taken aback than ourselves. He registered his delight at our unexpected appearance with great panache, displaying all his private parts for my edification. There was a howl of rage from Ismael and the boy quickly dropped his *kikoi* and disappeared back into the undergrowth with his camels, although he did keep turning to look longingly in our direction. I decided to put a bit of distance between us and the sex-starved herdsman. Accelerating away we soon hit the Garissa road.

We arrived in the full heat of the day. The sand shimmered under the hot sun and even the pepper trees lining the main street hung lifelessly, their thin leaves weighed down with dust from the road. A pall of heat hung over the small town of neglected houses with their tin roofs. Not even a chicken moved. The few men sitting crossed-legged in their doorways looked as if they'd welcome the arms of death just to get away from the searing heat. I headed for the one tired-looking petrol pump and took the precaution of filling all the tanks, having already used most of my spares. Even climbing down from the truck was an effort and as my hand touched the sides the heat blistered my skin. I kept telling myself that if my brother Rory were here he wouldn't notice the heat but would instead be entranced by the beauty of the people with their classic features and coffee-coloured skin and the lovely colours of the *kikois* in which the men and women draped their graceful bodies. But my beloved Rory wasn't there and I found that the dust hung on the hot breathless air, that my eyes were aching from the oven-like atmosphere. I could feel the sand in my mouth and smell it in my hair, my clothes were coated in it and the car was no longer green but layered and caked in dirty brown earth.

I wanted a cold bath and a cold bed and to rest my aching eyes but I still had hours of travel ahead, hours more of concentration and I couldn't afford to waste time longing for the impossible. I envied Ismael's and Kimau's ability, now that we were on a road, to sleep soundly in the back of the truck through this nightmare journey.

Leaving Garissa, we had a proper road to follow, so travelling was made comparatively easy. Stan's camp was near the delta and he was meeting me at the turn-off from the road to the camp. It was almost dusk when I saw his familiar figure leaning against the side of his safari car. The green sides highly polished, the canvas neatly rolled, the gun racks shining. My International, the twin to Stan's, looked as if it had been in the battle of El Alamein and I certainly looked no better.

I had started off with a scarf to cover my hair but it had long been abandoned. Although evening was almost upon us, the heat still hung on and the very earth under our feet was burning through the soles of my sandals. I could now see with horror the channels of sweat that had formed in the thick dust that coated my naked legs. I could feel the coolness of Stan's lips and the clean smell of him in his immaculate safari clothes and I felt filthy and tired and could have wept. I joked about the temperature and the dirt and climbed back into my truck. The heat of the engine rose to meet me and the dust from Stan's car enveloped us in clouds. Night fell and I followed his headlights into wave upon wave of billowing dirt. I felt that Dante's *Inferno* could not have been much different.

The camp was in the most beautiful situation as usual, on the banks overlooking the Tana, amongst thickets of fever trees, their beautiful branches shading the green tents. Stan spent the next day with me and sent the clients off with his assistant. We walked for miles along the banks of the Tana – Stan, myself, his gun bearer and Tim Tom II. In the background were the wonderful songs of the emerald-spotted wood dove, the orioles and above all the glorious white-browed coucal or bottle bird, because it sounds like water going glug, glug, glug through an empty bottle. Birds were everywhere. We were followed by a pair of pied kingfishers. They form devoted couples and do everything together and these two flew ahead of us, swooping low over the water and then returning to join us on a nearby branch. We were soon in the mangrove swamps and sandy area where I watched a whole troop of yellow baboon which seemed to be fishing for crabs.

I never tired of watching these family groups and the wonderful interrelation between such a large community. The babies were doing somersaults or playing tag and the parents that weren't fishing were grooming each other. One large female was in utter abandon, her arms and legs outstretched, while presumably her daughter went through each individual hair.

Further on, we came across a family of vervets, these wonderful sociable little monkeys. The mothers clutched their babies to their breasts, feeding and patting their offspring's heads with such love and adoration that it brought tears to my eyes.

Stan handed me his large white handkerchief. "What is it this time?" he asked. I said it was the monkeys' intense devotion to each other, their adoration of their young. I have watched a vervet mother clutching the corpse of her baby, stroking it, trying to breathe life into it, crying over it and when all else failed, clutching it to her and rocking and loving it for days until there was nothing left but tufts of stiff dry hair.

I spent two weeks at Stan's camp. It was the first time I had been on the Tana without my lioness and so I was permitted no more wonderful walks. If I left the camp now, either Stan or Ismael had to accompany me, Tim Tom II not being considered a suitable escort. It was very difficult for Stan to leave his clients, so I had none of the freedom of movement that I had been so used to with Tana. I missed not being with her and watching the passing parade of life in the bush, knowing that I was safe, knowing that nothing could harm me, and that through her I was also part of this life.

Without her beside me I felt an alien. I missed her so much that I even started to hate the life of the camp with all its restrictions. The talk of hunting over dinner would also upset me even though Stan did his best to avoid the subject. He was a brilliant raconteur and had a fund of incredible stories with which he would entertain us around the campfire at night. I knew that most of them were being told so as to keep everyone laughing and to keep conversation away from any controversial subjects.

I never stopped finding these hunting safaris a strain, mainly because I was worried about the effect my presence was having on Stan. In an ideal world, he would have had me with him all the time and for me that was an impossibility. I knew that everyone was asked not to mention shooting or killing, that trophies were hidden out of sight and that I could be responsible for ruining a client's safari. I must say they were all marvellous to me but I was very conscious of being a total pain.

I was getting more and more restless, so I told Stan that I must get back to Meru. Stan suggested that, as they were going to change camp in a few days anyhow, he would send everything ahead with his assistant and we and the clients should take a few days' holiday and go to Mombasa instead.

CHAPTER
61

In those days, to get to Mombasa from the north one had to take the ferry over the Kilifi creek. I loved watching the blackened flat wooden barge, its sides so low that one was almost at water level. There was some sort of rope and pulley system that winched us across and every time the rope came out of the water, there would be a shower of muddy droplets. The ferrymen, their skin very black and shiny, wore white cotton loincloths that were heavily stained by the oil from the barge and the muddy brown waters. They used to chant as they hauled in the rope. Often they would make up songs about their passengers. This time it was about Tana and me.

This was the first time I had crossed the ferry without her and as it happened I was sitting next to Stan and Tim Tom II was out of sight, lying amongst the luggage at the back. The song as I remember, went something like this: "*Memsahib* Simba [myself] was very angry. *Toto simba yake* [her baby lion] *amemua na amemla swala* [had killed and eaten the gazelle, Tim Tom] and for this terrible sin, she had been punished and not allowed on a holiday." This was repeated with various additions until we arrived at the other bank. I was highly amused and explained that she now had a husband and didn't need me any more.

We passed a queue of cars and ox wagons waiting to board. Coming off the ferry, the road of hard-packed red earth climbed steeply until levelling out amongst thick tropical vegetation, enormous mango and banana plantations. This red road wound its way through a tropical paradise. The huts of the Giriama villages were made of branches and red clay and often decorated with shells. The women went naked, except for short bustles of coconut palm fronds that were tied by a thong around their waists so that the little skirts stuck out behind. Over these, the women tied brightly coloured *kangas*, large backsides being considered an object of beauty. Smoke rose slowly in the soft heavy air of the coast and lots of very black and naked children with glorious white teeth would rush to the roadside, falling over the goats in their anxiety to be the first to see us. They would wave and jump up and down shouting greetings. It was a pastime of which they never seemed to tire. Some of the young girls aged no more than six and seven would be carrying their siblings so that they could watch these *mzungus* passing. The little brothers and sisters were often almost as big as themselves.

We went to the lovely Nyali Beach Hotel. Stan and I had a cottage among the coconut palms which looked onto miles and miles of white coral sand and translucent waters, beyond which were the distant waves breaking over the reef. Package tours were unknown then and the beaches were deserted except for fishermen, the guests in the hotel and the few houses that were built near the sea.

Martha Gelhorn, Ernest Hemingway's wife, had a pretty cottage on the beach which she had decorated all in white and lime green. It made such an impact on me that I have used that combination in decorating ever since. She was a very good-looking, fascinating woman and I used to enjoy my visits to her beach cottage. It was such a romantic setting for her, surrounded by palm trees and the vast Indian Ocean.

Mombasa itself was a beautiful town situated on an island. It sprawled amongst a tropical jungle of trees. In front, the old fort and opposite it, on a slight rise the Mombasa Club looked onto the palm-lined banks of the harbour inlet. Behind were the creeks of thick mangrove swamps. Down by the harbour was the Old Town, with its mosques, narrow lanes and houses with their beautiful doors and intricate fretwork balconies almost touching overhead because the passages leading to the waterfront were so narrow. Down these would walk groups of Muslim men in their white robes and embroidered caps and behind them came the ladies covered from head to foot by their black *bui buis*. It was impossible to tell whether they were young or old, rich or poor. They drifted by on their way to the docks to watch the *dhows*.

Following the monsoon winds these boats would arrive to unload carpets from Persia, carvings from the African coast, chests and spices from the south and wonderful bales of cloth from the bazaars of India. The shops in the streets of Mombasa overflowed with these exotic cargoes, as well as their own carvings, sandals, *kangas* and *kikois*. There were silversmiths and goldsmiths, copper and tin wares; it was a glorious jumble and even the streets smelt of spice and frangipani.

Mombasa was a happy mixture of various races and religions. Built in 1885, the Mombasa Club was a typical example of colonial architecture, its balconies and railings rising elegantly out of the jungle. I loved the atmosphere of the club with its green wicker tables and chairs set to catch the evening breezes, its Indian attendants clad in immaculate white uniforms with red turbans. I could imagine I had stepped out of the pages of a Somerset Maugham novel. It could have been India, Singapore, Ceylon, the Bahamas or any of the tropical countries of Queen Victoria's empire. The Club had been a meeting place for the explorers, the adventurers, the settlers, the army, the navy, the rich and famous and the poor and infamous. Now the people had changed but the buildings remained, a memorial to a bygone era.

Stan and I would sit holding hands and watching the sun set behind the jungle-clad hills and towering coconut palms. I would think of all the others before me who had sat as I did now, drinking their sundowners and watching the same sun fade from sight until only the trees were outlined against the night sky. I would watch the stars and think, one day we also will be gone and they will still be shining and throwing shadows onto this table where some other person will be sitting where I am now.

In spite of everything the exotic town had to offer it was the beaches that were the ultimate adornment. There were miles of white sand, seawater inlets, jungles of coconut palms and reefs with a myriad of jewel-like fish swimming in and out of the mountains and valleys formed by the coral. It was an exotic underwater garden and I would swim for hours, watching the continual movement of this subterranean world through my goggles.

Afterwards would come the voluptuous feeling of wellbeing from the cold shower as it washed off the salt and sand, combined with the lethargy induced by too much sun, too much water. Nothing then but to lie naked in cool cotton sheets. Mombasa has so many romantic memories for me but I am no longer young and the city also has crumbled. The fine streets lie in ruins, rubbish litters the sidewalks, the beaches are filled with tourists and hawkers. Only the Mombasa Club defies the progression of the years with its elegance. I never want to go back, memories are painful. I still want to remember the beauty, the nights of passion and the days filled with sun and sea and happiness.

I left Stan at Voi. They had set up camp there; it was great elephant country. I couldn't bear to leave him but my dislike of hunting made it unfair of me to stay. Stan, in his desire to have me near, never really understood why I couldn't adjust to his way of life. He was convinced it was because I didn't love him sufficiently. Men who are used to an enormous success with women become ultra-possessive if they feel the woman they love is eluding them. Passion is obsessive and Stan would convince himself that my desire to leave was because I had found somebody else. He couldn't believe that I was happy to be in love with him and that being the case, I wasn't interested in an affair with another man even if I went for a long time without seeing him. I wasn't concerned about his affairs though and I have found that with men like Stan, if they can't pin one down they keep on trying to do so. Through the years, Stan and I would have endless arguments about this. Never having suffered from jealousy myself, I could not understand how men always imagined sex could dominate a woman's life to the same extent that it seemed to dominate theirs.

CHAPTER
———
62

I desperately wanted to get back to Tana and Meru, but decided on a long detour so I could spend a night with Beryl. I hadn't seen her or Mummy's horses for quite some time.

It was evening as I approached Naivasha and on arriving at the house I was told that Beryl was down on the lake with the *bwanas*. It was a weekend and so both Charles Norman and Jan Thrane were with her. Setting off with my dogs into the sunset, I decided to go and meet them but as I walked I had the strangest feeling that I should return to the house with all the dogs. I retraced my steps and shut all the dogs in the car. Having done this, I felt better and decided to return to the lake but again some premonition of impending doom stopped me. I was standing by the sitting room window when I saw them approaching, three figures outlined against the fiery sunset, and Jan's doberman running out in front.

As they came nearer, I saw Charles was holding his hand, which was dripping blood. On entering the room he said, "That mad dog of Jan's has just bitten me."

Beryl went to the cabinet to get herself a gin and tonic, saying to

Charles, "Sweetie, don't make such a fuss. It's only a small bite and you are dripping blood all over the carpet. Jan, do take him away before he ruins it." Turning to me, Beryl said, "He is making such a fuss about nothing, so tiresome of him." Then, pouring her drink, she sat down and we discussed horses. Charles and his problems were forgotten.

Jan came back and said to me, "You know a lot about dogs. Would you come and look at mine? I have tied him up at the back but he has bitten several people lately and that is not his normal behaviour."

Charles, who had followed him in, said, "He should be shot."

"Do stop fussing, Charles," said Beryl. "If you don't calm down, you'd better go home."

As I approached the dog, every instinct told me to stop even though the dog was quietly sitting under the tree to which he was tied. Keeping well out of range, I noticed that his eyes seemed to have a red glaze to them. I always feel total confidence with animals but for the first time I felt no contact. It was a sinister feeling as if the animal were already dead and his sightless red eyes reflected the abyss. I suggested to Jan that the dog be taken to a vet. I felt there was something very wrong with him, that he might be suffering from some type of snakebite.

Jan took Charles to the doctor in Naivasha and so, by the time we sat down for dinner, peace had been restored in the household. That night, Jan untied the dog and took him to his room to sleep. I, in the meantime, had taken my dogs for their after-dinner walk and then retired to bed with them. The following morning at dawn, we went off for early morning gallops with Jan's dog once more tied to the tree and mine locked in the bedroom. I had taken the key in case the houseboy let them out by mistake, a precaution I never normally took.

Over breakfast, Charles complained about the terrible ache in his hand and Jan suggested taking him back to the doctor. Beryl, who had no time for anyone or any animal that was sick or in pain and an aversion to any physical weakness, was bored by this conversation. She turned to me and said, "If Charles keeps on behaving like an old woman, I'm going to tell Jan to take him back to the Kinangop."

"So tiresome of him," she kept saying, as if it were all his own fault.

I left for Kenmare Lodge and it was only several months later, when

I was next in Nairobi, that I heard the awful sequel. Jan's dog had had rabies and bit several people. One man succumbed in hospital after having himself bitten several other patients. Everybody who had been in contact with the dog had to have inoculations. In those days, that meant a series of 40 injections into the skin of the abdomen. Charles became allergic to them and ended up in hospital. Even a six-year old child had had to receive this terrible prophylactic. How lucky for myself and my dogs that I had this premonition and therefore had no contact with the doberman.

Instead I soon found myself in danger again. On leaving Beryl's house in Naivasha, I took the road which crossed over the Aberdares. It winds up and up among thick forests of trees which in those days were home to vast herds of elephant, buffalo and the lovely kudu antelope. In fact, nearing Mweiga, I had to wait for almost half an hour to let one of these herds of elephants pass. They were grazing along the verge of the road. There was some type of vegetation that they found particularly delicious and some had amassed a trunk full of wildflowers. Others browsed on the trees or ambled across the road. In the background, towering over us was Mount Kenya, its snow-capped peak like icing sugar against the azure blue sky. I sat enthralled before driving on to Nanyuki, a village that nestles in the mountain's foothills and whose *dukas* would be the last shops I would see until my return. It was at this last outpost that I always made my final purchases for the lodge before heading home.

The dirt road, which skirted forests of cedar and bamboo, clung to the mountainside and was full of rock, so one had to navigate with care. Seldom were there other cars. Just before the tiny village of Meru I would turn off and begin the long difficult descent into the valley below. The track now crossed mountain streams and I would have to dodge buffalo grazing like cattle on the lush deep grass. I would navigate around them as they stood staring, slowly chewing the cud and looking fat and docile, their heads lifted, nostrils distended, smelling the air. Most of them had enormous horns that curled at the ends. Seeing them like this, it was hard to imagine that a wounded buffalo becomes one of the most deadly and cunning of all the big game.

Night was now falling and it was getting more difficult to manoeuvre along the track. By the time I arrived at Ted's headquarters at Leopard Rock it was almost dark. As soon as I entered the park I would get this marvellous feeling of being home, the air seemed to soften, the scent of desert herbs would rise from under the tyres and there were the wonderful duom palms, now black against the moonlit sky. From Leopard Rock it was still a long drive to the lodge because of the conditions and I was now concentrating very hard, trying to follow the wheel tracks. In the headlights, I now noticed swirling sprays of thick dust that eventually got so heavy I was forced to a stop. I could no longer see where I was going. Suddenly beside me, blacker than the black night, was the towering shape of an elephant. My heart plummeted. I was surrounded by elephant. Somehow, I had driven into the middle of a huge herd.

I kept the engine running but there was nothing I could do, nowhere I could go. I waited, expecting at any moment to hear the trumpeting of an enraged bull, but the night was silent. All I could hear was the loud rumblings of the elephants' stomachs and the cracking of branches. They were so close that if I had reached out my arm I could have touched them. Terrifying and deadly, the giant shapes were all around me and the International, like all safari vehicles, was a truck with open sides. I had switched off the headlights as I stopped so as not to disturb the herd and my eyes were now accustomed to the moonlight. I watched as they browsed, realising that this peaceful scene could at any moment turn into a nightmare. I started to wonder what would happen to my animals should the International – and I – get smashed up.

With this cheerful thought in mind, I very slowly reached down to the bag at my feet and taking out pencil and paper wrote a note to Mummy and to Stan as best I could in the dark, hoping that if anything happened to me, someone would eventually find it. The dogs that were with me had their address on their collars. They also had been well schooled never to move from the car or bark when game was around. Thank goodness that training stood me in good stead now. My other worry was Tim Tom II in his usual place on the seat beside me. I couldn't see him coping on his own for long but prayed that Stan would find him before he came to harm. Having disposed of the animals' wellbeing, I settled down to observing the elephant. I could see clearly all that was happening around me.

What started out as a terrifying experience became one of the most memorable nights of my life. I felt as if it was my herd and my children as I watched these wonderful and clever animals. I was amazed at the love they had for each other. They continually used their trunks to touch and fondle, especially the mothers with their young. I could almost feel their adoration of each other and I sat there longing to be part of them so I could protect them from a future that I knew would hold only death and suffering for some of them. I could feel the tears in my eyes at that thought. Indeed, I was fortunate I couldn't see more closely into the future. In later years, these herds were almost entirely wiped out by poachers and the Shifta bandits from Somalia.

Almost as suddenly as I had entered the herd, the elephant departed. Like ghosts of the night they left, swallowed up by the trees of the forest. I felt bereft. The night was almost gone. Taking compass bearings and looking for landmarks in the dim light of pre-dawn, exhausted and exhilarated, I headed for home.

CHAPTER

63

I don't think Kenmare Safari Lodge was ever a great success. Being so far off the beaten track, tourists seldom came, although it had all the luxuries. Stan had even excavated a swimming pool out of the rocks above the river and I would lie and sunbathe and listen to the birds while the sound of the river below lulled me to sleep. I didn't need the outside world I felt so much a part of this earth, warm from the African sun. I would open my eyes and watch the waterbuck, the fat zebra or the distant elephant.

The first guests to come to the lodge were my family, bringing with them David and Pamela Hicks. My mother and brothers were always full of bright ideas and when my airplane-savvy Caryll had first come to see the lodge's setting he insisted that I build an airstrip. It was something that turned out to be quite easy to do but my team and I had never thought of it. Following his instructions we cleared the bush on a nice flat piece of ground on a rise across the river. Unfortunately it was also full of rocks and thorn bushes and these all had to be dug out by hand. Once more, we were disturbing the snakes and scorpions. That we managed to survive was more by good luck than good management

Caryll flew everyone to Meru and this was the first time the new airstrip was to be tested. I had spent a sleepless night worrying about potholes and was up early, taking all the men to help clear the runway. In fact, the biggest problem turned out to be keeping the game off the strip. Finally the plane arrived. At first it was a little speck in the sky coming from the direction of Mount Kenya but it was soon overhead, and from my position on the roof of the International I had a good view of Caryll and his passengers. Before landing Caryll made several low passes over the airstrip; I am not sure he entirely trusted his sister's capabilities as a builder of runways. I could see Mummy waving and the dreaded Tikki as usual sitting on her shoulder. I have no idea what number Tikki this was. The hyrax always looked the same to me.

I watched the final approach feeling sick with apprehension. My prayers for their safe landing were rudely interrupted by a shower of stones. As they landed, a cloud of dirt and gravel churned up by the propellers billowed out behind the plane, enveloping me in a hail of sharp pebbles and dirt. By the time the plane taxi-ed up to where I was waiting, I looked like a heavily disguised ant-hill, covered in red soil.

The humiliation of it! The door opened and my beautiful and immaculate family descended, accompanied by the gorgeous David and Pamela Hicks, all looking like a cover story out of *Vogue*: "How to be Glamorous in the African Bush". Trying to get the dirt out of my eyes and mouth, I shuffled towards them with Caryll laughing his head off.

Whenever I hadn't seen my family en masse for some time, I would be overcome by the effect of so much beauty. I would feel a frisson of pleasure, and goosebumps would appear on my arms. Each day I proudly drove them around my new territory. At this stage it was a matter of exploring for me too, as having been so busy with the lodge I had hardly moved except for the long hauls to Nairobi for supplies and to keep track of Tana. It was all very exciting and made even more so as I was now able to see it through my brother Rory's eyes.

His extraordinary eye for beauty added an extra dimension to everyday living. I had been in the area for months and had been overawed by the magnificence of the scenery with its horizons of mountain ranges, the wonderful variety of trees, the herds of game, the grasslands extending into the endless horizons of Africa. But now, driving around with Rory and David I was made to realise that the very earth beneath our feet was a fairyland. An astonishing variety of flowers and plants had been brought out by the rains. Their petals, washed free of the dust, bloomed in all their bright purity of colour. Giant white butterflies, like the most ardent of lovers, hovered and fluttered in homage.

The lodge, with Rory's expert touch, also became a place of beauty. Out came the best china, the Meissen and Sèvres and Famille Rose bowls, which were soon filled with wonderful bouquets so the lodge was filled with their warm sweet scent. I sat studying Rory's books on the wildflowers of Africa and they brought back so many memories of other books and other places and the journeys we had done together.

We could take eight couples in the *bandas* (huts) and if more came we would erect tents along the riverbank. The tours that came to the lodge would spend two to three days and there was always a mass of game to show them. There was the marvellous drive to the Tana River for a start, and Ted Goss's white rhino, which he had imported into the reserve, could always be relied on to appear out of the thorn scrub. Arriving at the river we would give them picnic lunches, sitting under the shade of the duom palms on Persian carpets placed on the sand. In the afternoon there would be trips down the river in Stan's launch. On the return journey there would always be herds of elephant and buffalo coming down to the river to drink.

There were drives across the plains where game stretched as far as the eye could see. There were hills and mountains, there were camels and deserts. The people who came to my lodge had the whole of Africa on their doorstep. Even so I felt that something was missing. I wondered if you could really feel part of this country from a car. I loved walking, and in the middle of the night an idea came to me for a scheme whereby I could safely take a lot of people on a walk amongst the animals.

The following day I put my idea into practice. Having consulted Ismael, we erected serious looking ladders and platforms in the trees beside our river. We then made a path that wound its way around these trees for about a mile upstream where the country was open and animals could be seen from a distance. I didn't want to risk anybody's life, so each time I took the added precaution of sending Ismael to scout the river bank before we started out on our walking safaris.

After a few of these walks, I cooked up another scheme to make it a bit more exciting. Once more I consulted Ismael. On our next walk, Ismael, with his rifle over his shoulder, went ahead and as usual I brought up the rear. At a selected point, Ismael gave his hand signal of danger and then pointed up to the trees. Before coming out, everybody had been carefully instructed on the meaning of the danger signals and warned never to make a noise. Soon everyone was up the trees, standing on their platforms and peering into the undergrowth below. The whisper went around that rhino had been seen. Some were even convinced they saw the leaves move as they passed. Neither Ismael nor I let on that there was not a rhino within miles. Instead, we let them experience the feeling of being close to nature and its dangers. After a suitable time had elapsed, Ismael would give the all-clear signal and everyone would climb down and head for the lodge while looking fearfully over their shoulders at the shadows cast by the sun.

My little walking safaris turned out to be a great success. Later, over meals in the safety of the lodge, the guests would recount their adventures and embroider on them. Many told me that it was the highlight of their trip to Africa, and I received letters from around the world thanking me for sharing a little part of my life with them.

When Stan arrived back from safari, I told him of our innovations. He thought it very amusing and even said he hoped that another group would come while he was around so that he could accompany us. I didn't say anything but I knew he was much too macho for that. Ismael and I continued with our walking safaris whenever the opportunity presented itself and we became quite adept at tree-climbing. We had made it all very easy so that even a child could manage, not that we ever had any. I didn't want anybody falling or finding the ascent too difficult.

These excursions continued until one day we came a cropper. We had six elderly couples from Des Moines out walking with us and were almost at our tree-climbing stage, Ismael out in front with his rifle over his arm and myself bringing up the rear. To my horror, I suddenly felt Tana's presence. I looked around and there, sure enough, was my beloved arriving at a slow jog and a little way behind her was her mate, whom we had now dubbed Mara. I was on foot, I didn't have the International and there was the group in front to be protected. I didn't know how the male lion would react but I decided to carry on, as I couldn't see an alternative that wouldn't cause a panic. We proceeded, the group now with an extra two lions, and myself praying that nobody would look back.

After what seemed hours, but was probably only 10 minutes, we arrived at the escape trees where Ismael, who hadn't realised that we had extra passengers, started his usual warning hand-signals of danger. Now as the group started climbing, everybody was naturally looking around to see if they could see where the danger was. As a result, the lions were discovered and one lady let out a shriek that could be heard in Nairobi. Slight chaos reigned until everyone reached the platform.

My great worry was that if I climbed up too, would Tana follow? I explained that these were pet lions, in the plural, and there was no need for fear. I headed up the tree and to this day I can see Tana's look of amazement at my disappearing act. She flopped down underneath to patiently wait, unable to understand my extraordinary behaviour. From time to time, she would look at me as if to say: are you quite mad? Finally I realised that she was settled for the evening and I would have to make some move to distract Mara and her. Ismael was making various gestures which I finally interpreted. I always wore a light bush jacket so I could carry the Fitzgibbon's snake kit in my pocket. I now took this off, disposed of the kit, rolled my jacket into a ball and threw it as far as I could.

Tana, delighted to be playing games once again, went after it and I climbed down and went off in the opposite direction, keeping a wary eye on lover boy who was sitting some way off under a bush. Keeping the male in the periphery of my vision, I hastily made my way back to the lodge, knowing that Tana would follow and so would Mara. Tana had picked up my jacket and in her usual fashion placed it on her head and was having a lovely time rolling around with it. Seeing me disappearing, she decided to follow and out of the corner of my eye I could see her ambling after me, dragging my jacket like kill between her front legs, her head held high.

Nearing the lodge, I told her to sit and although Mara was always a presence to be wary of, I felt enough confidence in Tana to take a little gamble and indulge myself once more in the joy of her closeness. I sat beside her in the long grass and watched Ismael lead the small party home. Tana lay in her usual position with her great head on my lap while I scratched her under her chin. Then she rolled over, her feet in the air, so that I could rub her tummy. As I watched her I remembered so many other times and other places and I tried so hard to imprint this picture on my mind as the minutes rushed past. I was as jealous of time as any lover, grudging every passing second.

I kept putting off the terrible moment of parting and watched from my grass cover as someone went to the pump-house to turn on the generator. I heard the chug-chug of the engine as the lights came on and knew my time was running out. With the onset of dusk the jungle started to awaken after the heat of the day and Tana's mate was getting restless. Taking her head between my hands I kissed and nuzzled her. As always, she brought one large paw over my shoulder and I placed my head in her neck. Beneath my cheek, I could feel the blood pulsing through her vein and in my ear I could hear the steady beating of her heart. As I knelt there telling her of my love I was filled with fear for her future. How long would she be able to cope with the hardships and the continual fight for survival? Her great body was no longer filled with flesh; I could feel the bones beneath the skin and I ached for her.

Tortured with self-doubt, I wondered if I had taken the right steps. She was no longer a pampered pet. How would she manage if there was a drought or the game disappeared? Lions have been known to go up to 50 miles a day in search of food and although game was now plentiful and she stayed near the lodge, how could I ensure that other lion would not dispute her territory and drive her and Mara off? The fear of her death or of losing her was always present.

Each morning my first waking thought was of Tana and how she had survived the night. Ismael and I would leave the camp at dawn and scout around until we found her. I could never start a new day without establishing her whereabouts and her wellbeing. Ever since Tana had found her mate though, I had drawn further and further away from her so that she could settle into her new life without my interference. It was only on rare occasions like this that I had close contact with her and I was loath to leave and return to the alien presence of strangers. I realised that this was probably the last close contact we would share and I was sure that she would soon be having cubs. I thought I could even feel them move already beneath my hands. I tried to communicate to her that my love was infinite as indeed it has been and still is after all these years. By now, night had arrived and I could feel her agitation. She was torn between her two worlds. Mara was almost beside us but because of Tana I had no fear.

I could smell the wood smoke and see the cold hard reflection of light from the naked bulbs. There was the shifting outline of people as they moved between the buildings and the distant sound of voices. I wanted to stay but knew I had to go. Rising, I walked towards the lodge with Tana at my side and Mara slowly following. Desperate to make every moment count, I tried to prolong our parting but time was running out and once I reached the edge of the lights I knew I couldn't delay any longer. It was unfair to Tana to indulge myself further. Her life was now with Mara, no matter that he was not the beautiful black-maned lion I had chosen. He was her choice and a family unit would soon be established. I consoled myself with the thought that he had a nice wide forehead and brown eyes; the characters of lions are so clearly indicated by their faces.

It was time to go. Taking that beautiful big head again between my hands I showered her with kisses. Then, taking the bush jacket that she had returned, I bundled it up once more and threw it into the night. Happy as always to be playing games, she left me to my tears. Unable to face seeing people, I went to my cottage and turned off the lights. I needed the dark to weep for my life that had passed and to weep for the future that, without Tana close to me, stretched bleakly before me.

I watched the dawn come up and setting off on my usual early search for Tana, I came across my herd of elephants. They were watering in the river. Getting out my binoculars, I climbed onto the roof of the International. The herd appeared so close through my glasses that I could even see the expression in their eyes. The first part of the herd crossed the river, climbing out and up the muddy bank, and I watched entranced as the babies, holding onto their mothers' tails with their little trunks, were hauled up the other side.

Now that the main herd had passed, the incline was not only steep but very slippery and a cow and her calf were having great difficulty manoeuvring themselves up it. To my amazement, another female elephant appeared and seeing the problem came up from behind. With baby clinging to its mother's tail and being pushed by its aunt, the three of them arrived muddied but triumphant at the top. I noticed some elephants on the top side starting to uproot trees. The bank was a total quagmire by this stage and at first I couldn't make out what they were doing. Then I realised they were making a causeway of trees and logs so that the other stragglers and the mothers with the tiny babies would have an easy task of climbing out. I watched them all safely negotiate the treacherous bank and as they disappeared I realised how privileged I was to witness this scene and I marvelled once more at the extraordinary intelligence of these great animals. It left me with a feeling that life still had so much to offer, that our earth was full of miracles and that I had been accorded this one as a message of comfort.

Hungry after my fast of the night before, I made my way back to the lodge. When I entered the dining room, the guests were just finishing breakfast and I was greeted like some sort of heroine. The story of yesterday had lost nothing in the telling. I explained that Tana was totally tame and that lion were not killers by nature, that armed with an umbrella one could walk past lion with equanimity, that only those that were semi-tame, rogues or starving were dangerous but like all cats it was their basic curiosity over something strange that might get one into trouble.

My guests had been very worried when I hadn't come back the night before but Ismael assured them through their driver that I was fine and was lying in the grass with my family. I was amazed to hear that Ismael had known exactly where I was. I had considered myself so well-hidden. What really astonished me though was the garbled explanation he had given them for my behaviour. According to his story, I was really a lioness that had come onto earth by mistake as a *memsahib*. Such people led charmed lives and no animal would touch them; therefore I was a very lucky person to have around and they all looked after me very carefully. The visitors had been highly amused by this reasoning and from the looks they were giving me, I am not sure that they didn't consider me as nutty as a fruit cake. One of the elderly gentlemen had taken a photograph of my disappearing act followed by two lion and was hoping that it hadn't been too dark to get it developed. Would I autograph a copy if he sent it to me? I never heard any more, so presumably it was never processed.

Once they departed I went to have a few words with Ismael. "*Toto ya Simba,*" he said. "*Enye wazimu kidogo.*" Everyone else called me *Memsahib* Simba, but he always referred to me as baby lion, or child of the lion: "Baby Lion," he was saying in Swahili, "you know you are slightly mad." Slightly cross, I said, "Thank you very much. What gave you such a stupid idea?"

"We all know you are not as everyone else; you live in two worlds. Even *Bwana* Mwindaji knows and told us all to look after you, as you are not like other *memsahibs.*"

This sort of logic was beyond me and I went off determined to have a word with that great white hunter but as often happened I was unable to get through. I was annoyed at the patronising way this male-orientated society had come to the conclusion that I was not all there and was now proudly keeping me under observation as if I were a half-witted child about to do something more foolhardy than usual.

There was another idiosyncrasy of mine that used to worry Stan, and that was my love of walking. Having ridden all my life, I had taken to my feet with Tana for company and Stan as my teacher. I loved to walk for miles through the beautiful ever-changing country that was Kenya. On safaris, Stan would take me on 15-mile hikes, through shoulder-high elephant grass, across waterways filled with hippo and leeches and into the most magnificent forest areas where orchids hung from the trees. It was wonderful feeling so close to the earth, and the smell of grass and flowering thorn, and then finally to be able to identify the animals by their scent.

Having taught me to walk through Africa, which I now insisted on continuing, Stan fussed. When I had Tana by my side he calmed down a bit and would say that she had much more sense than me. Now that we were at Meru and Tana was no longer with me, I noticed that whenever I left the camp on foot Ismael would accompany me. Obviously Stan had asked him to keep an eye on me. In fact, I was glad of his company and he never intruded on my dreams.

William Boyle was another one who kept on about my lifestyle every time I saw him. Over the years, he had patched me up on numerous occasions even though his foreboding that I would be eaten by Tana was never realised. When I announced I was going to join her at Meru, William gave me a long lecture in his usual rude fashion as to the size of my brain.

William did insist that before going to Meru I take a course in first aid and learn about all the basic medicines and their usage. Thank goodness I did this, as it was of great benefit. I had already realised that the distances between the lodge and the nearest habitation were such that in emergencies I would need to be able to handle most situations until I could get help. The nearest doctor was at Maua and although there might be a plentiful supply of witch doctors, I had yet to accept their beliefs. I took the first aid course and then bullied William into teaching me as much home-doctoring as possible. When I left Nairobi I took drugs, pills, potions and copious notes, a veritable arsenal of medical supplies. I found studying medicine fascinating and as I progressed was able to handle most of the simple illnesses, wounds and minor complaints. The Africans above everything loved injections and with some of the horrible festering wounds they sported, I duly obliged. They would be thrilled and awed to see how after a few days of injections and dressings, their wounds would heal to a healthy pink. I never ceased to be amazed either at their bravery and how stoic they were under the most appalling infliction of pain.

But looking back now, I can see how this over-protection from all the different people who loved me was the slow beginning of the end of my dream life. Maybe if I had been more circumspect I would still be in Kenya and maybe Beryl would not have managed to weave me – and everybody else – into her plans.

The first time the subject of Beryl leaving Kenya was broached was on my next visit to her at Lake Naivasha after the rabid dog incident. She was having her usual gin and tonic before lunch and was dressed in her blue shirt, immaculately tailored slacks and with a small handkerchief knotted at her neck. Tall and elegant, moving slowly around the room as she talked, a glass in one hand and fiddling with various objects with the other, Beryl finally said she was thinking of going to South Africa to look for a place where she could take the horses. She explained that she knew she had a top string but there was no future for them in Kenya where the stakes in horseracing were just too small. She felt it was time she made a move.

"Sweetie," she asked. "Wouldn't you like to come with me and help me find somewhere?"

"No, I certainly wouldn't," I replied promptly and emphatically. "That is the last place I want to go to."

I really didn't take Beryl seriously, thinking that she had probably just had another row with Tubby Block's manager at Naivasha. Beryl's marvellous place at the lake with its charming house, wonderful views and stables built in a large circle under giant acacias persuaded me that no-one who was also as successful as she was would wish to leave all this.

On this day, we rode down to the track and handing my horse to the syce, I climbed the tree that stood in the middle of the ring and was used as a lookout. I was having a lot of problems with my back as a result of all my falls during my life, and now from the continual jarring in the International. Up in the tree I now sneezed and my back seized up. The first time this had happened to me was when I was a young girl and cantering in Hyde Park; my horse shied and agonisingly my back locked into position. Some mounted police had taken pity and come to my rescue. This time, waiting until Beryl, who was notoriously unsympathetic to invalids, was down the other end of the track, I managed to get one of the grooms to help me down. Then half-carrying me and with me instructing him not to tell Beryl, he got me to the car. I left a message for her to say I had had to rush off. By the time I arrived back at Ol Orion where I was staying while I was away from Meru, I was unable to move and had to be carried into the house, which was infuriating to say the least.

William arrived with his usual cheerful greeting, "What bloody stupid thing have you done this time? I suppose it is that horrible lion?"

He gave me an unpleasant injection and another lecture. He was convinced Tana had landed on me and that I was lying about the sneezing. He left, patting me on the head as he went and saying, "Next time, I'll probably find you in the mortuary."

My future was gradually closing in.

CHAPTER

64

As soon as I was mobile again, I went to the kitchen to see Mutete. He was busy preparing lunch. Being a vegetarian and a born cook, he had developed a wonderful repertoire of meatless dishes. He tried so many times to show me his secrets but I am no cook. Left to me, bread and cheese and lots of cream soups would be the order of the day. I watch the patience needed to make a crème brulée, one of my favourites. Two hours later and with half the pots in the kitchen lying in the sink, this little masterpiece is consumed in a matter of minutes during the course of a dinner conversation. Thank heavens for Mutete. At least while I was at Ol Orion I was able to eat the most delicious food and have a friend with whom I could discuss all that had taken place in my absence at Meru.

Through the Kenya grapevine I was kept up to date on all the doings of my friends. Some of them would have been horrified if they knew in what detail I was made party to their most intimate secrets. The African being a great raconteur, no detail was left out and embellishments were numerous. I wanted to catch up on all the news and Mutete always wanted to know what I had been doing and how

Tana was. I was sitting at the kitchen table when Joseph arrived with one of my beautiful Sèvres cups. Climbing onto a chair, he came and sat beside us. As Mutete poured Joseph his tea, I suggested getting something less valuable for him to drink out of. I will always remember Mutete's answer: "He is so careful with everything, do not worry. He has chosen it because it has all those pretty flowers. When he eats, he always brings his own plate and it is always from your best china. He knows the difference."

Laughing, he said, "After all, he is one of your children."

Who was I to argue with Mutete's logic? He and Kimoyo adored Joseph and pandered to his every whim. I never minded because he was so extraordinarily well behaved with everyone and wildly affectionate. Encouraged, I then told Mutete the story of Ismael telling me that I was a little crazy. He smiled and said, "I'm not supposed to, but I will tell you how it all started.

"When you decided to go and live at Meru, so that you could be with Tana, *Bwana* Safari, [it was only Ismael who called Stan *Bwana* Mwindaji or the Hunter] was very worried as he realised that you would be living most of the time on your own and there would be no other women around. He wanted to make sure everyone would look after you as he knows how you love walking into the bush and are very forgetful of what happens around you. He said we all know you are very *bila uangalifu* [without care]. The *bwana* spoke to me about it and this is the story he told to those who were going with you.

"He said that a long time ago, Tana and you were mother and daughter but they got it all muddled up when you went to heaven. They sent you back as a human and Tana was left behind. She walked all over heaven looking for you until the good God couldn't bear her moans any more and sent her back to earth to continue her search. But they made another muddle and sent her back as a tiny cub. Tana made sure that you found her but realised she would have to grow up fast and become very big and strong so that she could look after you. Her *toto* was doing lots of crazy things, like driving her at terrible speeds across the face of Africa. As if this were not enough, she would take her for long walks and charge around in the most stupid fashion amongst the elephant and buffalo. Therefore, she could never relax and lie in the shade of a tree for long to recover from the mad drives,

Pat brought Enid along on her first safari with Stan.

Stan, right, loved women and he believed that if Pat didn't mind his affairs when he was away from her, then she didn't really love him. In fact, Pat was preoccupied with her animals like Tim Tom, above.

Stan was a stickler for correct, subdued dress on safari.

"You must be the most expensive girl in east Africa," said one man of Pat.

Eventually, Tana had to be returned to the wild.

Ted Goss, right, the warden at what was to become Meru National Park, agreed to take Tana but was firm about how it was to be handled. He didn't want another "hysterical Joy Adamson". For Pat, the process was heart-breaking.

Tana is released into Meru with the lure of a dead zebra.

Where Tana went, Pat couldn't resist following. She built a lodge at Meru.

KENMARE SAFARI LODGE

MERU GAME RESERVE

Nairobi Radio Call
303

Phone : { Karen 540
{ Langata 423

P.O. Box 24899,
N A I R O B I.
KENYA.

25th January.

Tana

Pat,

Please stand-by at 8.30 tomorrow morning and I will ring you then.

Will you send a bill to Mrs Kent for 6 7shillings, 33½ miles travelled in the ford, I took them out & showed them all the [...] the run.

[...] down in the ford, and has little [...] Miali's to finish the [...] new bandas

Pat named her safari lodge, above, after Enid's last title, Lady Kenmare.

So anxious was Pat to be with Tana at Meru that she didn't even wait until Stan was free, and able to help her build her lodge, this page. She headed to the park with her animals, Stan's lorries packed with tents, provisions and building materials, and some Wakamba staff from Ol Orion. The lodge eventually had all the luxuries, even a swimming pool built by Stan, but it was too distant to be a great success.

The first guests to the new lodge were Pat's family, including Caryll.

A lion brought Pat to Kenya but the other animal that changed her life there was the horse, and Enid's passion for horse-racing. Above, Beryl Markham's racehorses were beautifully muscled. Lone Eagle, right, owned by Enid, was the star.

Lady Claude Hamilton employed Masai to look after her horses.

Enid and Jan Thrane accept the cup for the East African Derby.

Enid, now showing signs of age, leads in another of her winners.

Above, Broadlands, outside Cape Town, the property Beryl Markham persuaded Enid to buy.

Any visitor to Broadlands is warned: mind the baboons.

At 79, Pat's main concern is what will happen to all her rescued animals after her death. There is Kalu, the chimpanzee, who lives on a platform at the back of the property. There are umpteen dogs, cats, birds, pigs and mischievous baboons who love the sound of smashing objects.

Pat says she is grateful to her animals for showing her the magic of life.

before having to get up and follow her crazy *toto* out into the sun and prevent her from going back to heaven before her time.

"Tana then grew into a huge and beautiful lioness and now it was time for her to find her mate, so she is asking all the *toto*'s friends to stay by her side and look after her, so that eventually they can go back to heaven together."

Mutete said, "*Bwana* Safari tells lovely stories but he is right. There is a great love between Tana and yourself. You can talk to each other without speaking; we have all seen this. Also she thinks as you think and she has saved your life. Therefore, her soul is your soul. We also are at peace with you and don't want you to leave us. Therefore we are only too happy to look after you, *Toto ya Simba*."

I was so moved by this lovely Swahili story that I could feel the tears come to my eyes. The language is so beautiful and expressive and rolls off the tongue like music. I didn't speak the grammatically correct language of the coast but the up-country Swahili, which has practically no grammar and is easy to learn.

I thought again how much I loved this man who had looked after me like a father and protected me. After the Mau Mau uprising, it was his torch that I would see circling the house at night to make sure all was still safe. He was the one who rescued my cattle when they were stolen. He was the one who always came to my assistance with the wild animals when I needed help, often at great personal risk. I felt humble and grateful that I should be surrounded by so many remarkable and wonderful people.

And I understood what Stan had done too. There would be months when I would be away from civilization as such, living amongst warrior tribesmen and wild animals. His story would give me their protection. Amongst the tribes at that time, if one were slightly odd, it was thought that the spirits had taken over the body and therefore it would be very unlucky to harm such a one. Also in the tribal culture of the Masai, a lion was the symbol of strength. Therefore, as a reincarnation of a lion, one was inviolate. Stan was an inveterate storyteller and the Africans with their puckish sense of humour were also weavers of yarns. The story of myself and Tana would lose nothing in the telling.

In those days the African was very superstitious. With some tribes, it was unlucky to die inside and one would come across the very sick or the old laid out on wooden frames for the hyena or vultures to finish off. The Rendille, nomadic people from the north, had one significant taboo I was told. If a second son was born on a moonless night, the child was laid out immediately after birth for the hyena to dispose of. If allowed to live, he would be a curse on the first son. Spitting to ward off evil was another common superstition. Witch-doctors played an integral part in all tribal lore and most of us who lived in Kenya came to accept that they had certain inexplicable powers for either good or evil.

I have watched them at work and I have seen strong men who have been cursed wither and die. Equally I have seen them cured. I have watched a witch-doctor throwing his bones and finding the thief amongst a crowd. I was also told of one of the wives who was taken over by an evil spirit. I went to her hut where she was lying on her bed surrounded by the men of her family. It was so dark inside that the figures were hardly discernible. Suddenly she became a wild thing, flailing her legs and arms, foaming at the mouth, continually talking and screaming. She would shout, the whites of her eyes rolling in her head as if pursued by the devil and trying to throw herself off the bed. It would take all the men to hold her down as she fought like a tigress. I said, "I will send for the doctor." No, I was told. This is not for white men's medicine."

Nevertheless, a doctor was summoned and it proved an almost impossible task to get the hypodermic into the vein. The doctor suggested sending her to Mathari hospital in Nairobi. I knew he had given her a tranquilliser that was supposed to have her sedated within minutes. Half an hour later, she was still just as frantic. The witch-doctor arrived, made various signs around her head and then took out some evil-smelling powder which he mixed into a paste, smearing it all over her face and forehead. The husband told me that the witch-doctor wanted to take her away until she was cured. I didn't want to interfere, though personally I gave her no chance of recovering. By now she was quiet and went with the witch-doctor like a sleepwalker. I felt that it was probably the delayed reaction of the tranquilliser. The next night she was back, although very subdued. To my total amazement, the following day she was her usual cheerful, laughing self. I was told they had rid her of the devil.

One large firm that belonged to a friend in Nairobi had so much pilfering they resorted to hiring a permanent witch-doctor. From then on nothing disappeared and it saved them a fortune.

A friend told me a lovely story of protecting her game. She was doing a thesis on eland, the large African antelope, and spent three years on her own with a particular herd. She was studying for her doctorate and left for the University at Edinburgh. After an absence of five years she returned to Kenya and immediately went off to find her herd. She found to her despair that it had dwindled to almost nothing as the eland were being speared and slaughtered for meat. She decided to consult a witch-doctor who agreed to help. Taking him to the area, she spent days with him marking out the territory of her eland herd. When they were ready, he went to work. He took one of the little pouches that he carried with him and at certain spots along the perimeter buried it just under the soil. It took them many days as it was a large area. Years later the herds were still thriving and the killings had ceased.

As a rule I never interfered with witchcraft, although I was taken on several occasions to see the results of spells. One day at Meru, an old man was brought to me. He had once helped me when the lodge was first started. Supported on either side, he now had the greatest difficulty in walking. Undoing the filthy bandages of goatskin, I found horrible suppurating gashes all over his feet. Once I had soaked the feet in hot salt water and dried them off, I realised that it looked as if someone had taken a knife and had made incisions from toe to heel. I asked how this had happened and he explained that his feet were always aching so much that he found walking difficult. A witch-doctor had made the cuts to let the evil spirits out and now he was unable to walk at all. He remembered the *Memsahib* Simba who could speak with lions and had *"dawa nguvu"* (strong medicine). I kept him and his family in one of the huts; they must have walked all of 50 miles to get to me. I put him on antibiotics, dressed his feet daily and insisted he remain in bed as I did not want any more dirt getting into his infected wounds. I noticed that he had exceptionally large and completely flat feet. When he recovered, I made him walk around while I studied his feet. I was convinced that his problem was caused by totally flat feet and not by an evil spirit.

The following day, I managed to raise William on the blower and he agreed that this was quite likely and the solution would be support shoes. This of course presented an almost insurmountable obstacle. That night I lay in bed considering my options and the following day I stood the old man on a large piece of paper and outlined his foot. Then taking my tape measure, I measured it in sections and when I had it all worked out to my satisfaction, I managed once more to get hold of William.

"God preserve me from lunatic women," he exclaimed. William was nothing if not chauvinistic. "Only an elephant would have feet that big. Get hold of some glasses and stop assing around."

Being no mathematician, I felt he might have a point. I went to take new measurements but came up with the identical size. Several days passed before I could again get hold of William who this time objected strongly to the expense of ordering four pairs of shoes when, as he said, they wouldn't fit anyhow. He would order one pair only.

When the shoes were ready, I decided to take the old man and his family all to Nairobi. He was delighted to be travelling in a car and had never been to Nairobi. It was a very long and tiring drive and being in a hurry as usual, I was swinging the International around the tight corners of the escarpment. The next thing I knew there was the most appalling smell. My passengers had all been sick! We had to find an icy mountain stream, stop the car and bring out my bottle of antiseptic while everyone washed themselves and the car.

There is a wonderful epilogue to this story of the old man, his feet and his new shoes.

One morning, back at Meru, I was up at dawn. Lion had been roaring all night very close to the lodge and I wanted to see if it was Tana or another pride. As I arrived at the safari car two shadows rose out of the night. I could smell the odour of sweat and wood smoke and see the vague outline of their spears. A faintly recognisable voice said, *"Jambo Memsahib Simba, habari?"* (Good morning, *Memsahib* Lion, how are things?) It was the younger brother of the Old Man. They said they had something they would like to show me that was not far from their village.

They were very mysterious and I could not elicit from them what we were off to see, although I gathered it was something to do with monkeys. Loading them on board, we took off on a long drive up the escarpment until the terrain became almost impassable, even for the four-wheel drive. Being no mechanic, I didn't want to damage my precious vehicle on a perpendicular mountainside so I suggested we get out and walk. It was a densely forested area so we continued on foot for about an hour until we arrived at a little village clearing. There were a few thin chickens scratching in the dry dust and a *bibi* in a short leather apron. The flesh above the thick silver bracelets decorating her upper arms was badly swollen where the circulation was being cut off. Her large pendulous breasts swung as she pounded maize into flour and there were pot-bellied children with snotty noses, the flies collecting on the mucus as well as on their eyes. It was a typical village scene, with goats walking in and out of the huts and a few old men sitting around smoking, probably *miraa*, as there were several trees in the proximity of the village. It is a stimulant and must have been one of their cash crops as I saw a bundle of newly picked leaves tied together lying by one of the huts.

On our arrival, the Old Man, proudly wearing his shoes, detached himself from the group of elders and came to greet me. The mystery of my visit was solved. He wanted to show me the *mbega*, the flying monkeys. He knew how much I loved all animals and thought it would give me pleasure to see the colobus. He had arranged this little surprise for me. I felt quite emotional at the thought of the trouble this very simple man had gone to and what the long and arduous walk just to reach me had entailed for his relations.

With a guide from the village, we set off walking up the eastern slopes of Mount Kenya. The giant forest trees formed a feathery canopy over our heads and the sky glimpsed through the branches was cobalt blue. Our path was dappled by the rays of sunlight that danced in the deep green corridors of our passage. We skirted pools and tumbling waterfalls where mists of spray hung in the air and little sunbirds, incandescent in their jewel-like colours, fluttered around the flowering yellow ochna. As I followed my guides, I was glad Stan had taught me to walk long distances and at high altitude. One gets into a rhythm and the miles pass effortlessly. Under my tennis shoes I could feel the soft earth, and the smell of wet leaves and damp soil permeated the cool sharp air. Ahead, my entourage walked with that loosed-limbed grace of the tribal African.

Podo, hagenia (East African rosewood) and pillarwood trees lined our way on the lower slopes and I was continually picking berries and flowers so that the pockets of my bush jacket were soon full to overflowing. This was another world from the plains I had left this morning and a continual reminder of the extraordinary variety of Kenya's countryside.

As we stepped into a clearing, we disturbed a male bongo and above us towered the snow-capped peak of the mountain. Climbing ever upward, we had arrived almost at the rockface when we saw the troop of colobus flying from tree to tree. As they rose into the air they were in the full light of the sun, like actors under a spotlight. They performed their aerial ballet and for their stage they had the whole majesty of Mount Kenya. No *corps de ballet* could have had such a setting and no dancer could have performed with such grace and agility. They rose soaring into the air, their long white and black coats rising with them like giant fans of ostrich feathers. They sprang from treetop to treetop, covering almost a hundred feet with some of their gigantic leaps and the branches would bend in homage to their passage. I watched entranced and was desolate as they disappeared from sight, like dancers exiting into the wings. Only the fluttering of the leaves still bore witness to their fabulous display.

I have known many people and many races but I think it would be hard to find finer people than the tribesmen of Kenya as I knew them. I admired their loyalty, sense of honour, their humour and sense of fun and above all their extreme bravery. They wove themselves into my life and never in all those years at Karen or Meru did I have cause to doubt or mistrust them.

CHAPTER
───
65

That evening on my return to Kenmare, I saw Stan's International and my heart beat fast with excitement. I rushed out of the car to meet him but the lodge was empty, with only his safari hat lying on a chair at the entrance. I went down to the river and found him sitting on the bank with his fishing rod lying by his side and a piece of wood he had been whittling discarded on the ground. I still today have a lovely little vase that he carved for me, with the most intricate design of elephants. I noticed all these details but as I neared, something in his attitude filled me with foreboding. He was bent over clutching his chest. He had for years suffered from angina and always carried his pills with him but he was now only wearing his khaki shorts and the pockets were empty. He demanded, "Where in the hell have you been?" I sped up to the cottage, shouting for help and praying that I would find the pills in his jacket pocket. Although it could only have been a matter of minutes, by the time I returned he was lying doubled-up at the foot of the rock. I could see how blue his mouth looked as I put three pills onto his tongue.

It was late evening but the heat generated by the rocks was still unbearable. Taking off my petticoat, I dipped it in the river to place over his head and got the men started on erecting a tepee-type structure from the bamboo growing near the banks to give him shade. Kneeling by him, with my fingers on his jugular vein, I could feel the thin thready beat of his pulse. My eyes closed and I prayed desperately. I couldn't help remembering another occasion many years ago at Fiorentina when Mummy was very ill with a temperature of well over 100 degrees and the doctor had despaired of her recovery. Mummy was very superstitious about the 6th of October, the very next day's date, believing it to be a day of ill omen. As I knelt by her bed, midnight was approaching and it occurred to me that if she saw the clock by her bed, it might be enough for her, in her delirium, to let go her tiny hold on life. I picked the clock up with the intention of changing the date and as I held it in my hand it changed its own date, not to the 6th but to the 7th. It had skipped a whole day and I knew then, as I lay with my head on her arm, that this precious being who I loved more than life would not be leaving me and that I had witnessed a miracle.

Now, as I was kneeling over Stan, Ismael said, "*Hapana shauri*, I think the *Bwana* Mwindaji is dead." I could feel the pulse under my fingers strengthening and didn't want to be disturbed by Ismael's dire words. In a matter of minutes, Stan started to sit up and his first words were, "What is all the fuss about?"

Feeling quite giddy with relief and not wanting him to move, I suggested that we have dinner under the hastily erected shelter. Stan joked and said, "I see you have erected a funeral pyre. Were you intending to send me up in smoke?" Ismael, who was standing nearby looking at me with awe, said, "The *bwana* was dead. *Toto ya Simba*, you have given him life."

We had a picnic as the river rushed by and the coolness it generated in the evening air was a contrast to the heat from the rocks that had been baking all day in the sun. I threw crumbs to the golden palm weavers and watched the sun setting, with wisps of clouds like streamers crossing the red sky. Even the river took on a red glow and as I watched the evening star became visible against the yellow perimeters of this African sunset. Upstream, a herd of elephant were making their usual crossing, their dark shapes looking like theatrical cut-outs against this crimson world. As they drank, raising their trunks to spray each other, even the droplets were clearly etched in relief, fiery bubbles enveloping them in a golden shower.

The following day I suggested we drive to the Tana. We set off early with Tim Tom II in his usual place, rather annoyed with me as I was taking up some of his space on the front seat, so he held us up while he fussed around establishing his territory. The result was I was almost reduced to sitting on Stan's lap. This Tim Tom was so used to having the entire passenger seat to himself he was very resentful at my usurping his rights.

We passed the usual herds of buffalo and Ted Goss's white rhino. The beauty of Meru, apart from its magnificent grasslands, duom palms and acacia trees, was in the number of streams and dry riverbeds with thick green jungle vegetation along their banks.

Arriving at the Tana, the track opened up onto a sandy beach, Stan's boat lying under the shade of the palms and henna trees near the thatched circular cottage of the boatman. He now helped Stan to put the launch in the water. The boat's canvas canopy had been erected and it all looked so clean and gay as it danced up and down on the brown ripples. You could hear the echo as they slapped against the white painted sides. I took up Tana's position in the prow so that I could watch the crocodile and hippo and as I bent down to arrange Tim Tom on his travelling cushion, I saw some of her hairs trapped in the floorboards at my feet. Memories of the wonderful times we had shared in this boat overwhelmed me and I could feel the tears rush to my eyes. Glancing at Stan, I saw he was watching me and had registered my distress. He said, "Remember that no matter what happens in the future, you have given her the chance to live a full life in her own surroundings. Surely to live a life of freedom is the ultimate option."

Stan was sitting in the stern, very tanned in his shorts and safari hat, one hand on the tiller, the other arm resting on his knee holding his pipe. I could feel his concern and thought how selfish of me to spoil such a perfect day with my sad thoughts. Behind Stan I could see the wide stretch of river and the water boiling as the hippo emerged with their pig-like grunts, watching us with avid interest. Overhead a pair of fish eagles flew, their wings and talons outstretched as they landed on the bare branches of a dead tree in which they were building a nest. The tree rose stark against the blue sky and the lush green of the jungle. Such a contrast between life and death and I thought of yesterday and what might have been. Looking at Stan, so much a part of this wild and beautiful country, I realised that life without him would be unimaginable. Even though we were so often apart, the very fact of knowing he was there if I needed him gave me confidence in myself, and therefore I never felt lonely. I could spend months on my own, leading a life of solitude that for some would be unbearable, but I was at peace with myself and this paradise I lived in because I had the security of his love.

On the way back, we were crossing the river and I was laughing at one of Stan's jokes when, looking up, I saw Tana standing on the opposite bank high above us and outlined against the deep blue sky. She was partly shaded by a large wild fig under which she and Mara had obviously been lying. She was a magnificent sight, the dappled sunlight weaving a pattern on her tawny coat, the slight breeze stirring the fawn white hairs of her chest and stomach as she towered above us like a wonderful Delacroix painting. I could hardly breathe for the sheer wild beauty of the scene.

My continual fear when I lived at Meru was that one day I would go out and would be unable to find Tana. For a long time, it was a recurring nightmare in which I would endlessly circle the vast empty plains, calling her name while the mists rose off the swamps. I would see her blurred outline but as I rushed towards her the mists would clear and I would be on my own. I think my neuroses over Tana developed soon after we arrived at Meru. It wasn't long before I received visits from some of the local tribesmen saying that Tana was killing their cattle. I couldn't see how this could be as she had always lived at peace with all mine, but it was a crime for which I knew she would be speared to death. Therefore I paid out large compensation. Another time they came to say that during the night they had lost another cow. It couldn't have been Tana as she hadn't been in that area, but I realised that it might be one of the lion that I had brought with her. So with Ismael we spent days tracking down the Hartley lions.

The male was easy to find as his territory was fairly near the lodge, and we also found the two females that I had named Sasa Hivi, "right now" and Bado Kidogo, "wait a bit". Bado Kidogo was now spending time with Tana and Mara. The females were a lot smaller than Tana and slightly darker in colour but the third one of the trio we couldn't find anywhere. She was a lion that I had named Toto (baby) as she seemed younger than the others. Always very boisterous, she had relished her freedom. I would love watching her as she chased anything that moved and she took great pleasure in practising her stalking technique, charging out at her companions who would yawn with boredom and return to their afternoon siesta. After spending so long in a cage, life to her was endlessly fascinating and she made the most of every minute.

I was in despair now, picturing that beautiful lioness lying pierced and bloodied, either dead or dying in agony. We could find no trace of her and the men we spoke to assured us that they had not killed her but the tracks of the cattle were everywhere and the rain overnight had obliterated any sign of her spoor. I felt responsible for her death, which I knew was certain. Now my fear also grew that Tana might still get the blame for someone else's crimes. Everyone knew there was a tame lion at Meru and every transgression I feared would be laid at her door. This was the very reason I had taken Tana from Ol Orion. Now, through all the time I spent at Meru, I was never convinced that there would not be some terrible drama. But when it came, it was not from Tana.

After our day on the river we arrived back at our camp fairly late and I was still in a state of euphoria. Stan, when he saw Tana towering above us on the river bank, had said, "I see it won't be long now before the cubs arrive." It confirmed what I had hoped might be happening to her. I did not remember much of the drive home as the whole way I was scheming how I could help Tana when her time arrived. The fact that she didn't belong to a pride worried me. She would only have her two companions, Mara and Bado Kidogo. Would they be capable of providing the food while the cubs were very small and Tana was unable to help? There was no way I could ask anyone to kill animals for her even if I had been so inclined. Instead, I started planning how I could get to either Meru or Nanyuki, depending on where I could buy meat in bulk from a butcher. If Tana had her cubs while Stan was still at Meru, he would never allow me to supplement her feeding.

I insisted on opening a bottle of champagne that night in celebration of Tana's pregnancy and, as I practically never drink, I went to bed feeling quite disorientated. I had marvellous dreams of litters of little Tanas crawling all over me. Next morning before dawn I had Stan out of bed and into the safari car so anxious was I to find her. He tracked her back from where we had seen her the day before and we discovered she and Mara had killed a waterbuck during the night. The vultures showed us the way and there was not much left by the time we arrived. It was near my airstrip that we found them lying up under the shade of a large palm, not far from their unfortunate prey.

I always felt very proprietorial about the landing strip, as if I had hewn it out of the jungle myself. Stan used to tease me about my use of the personal pronoun. My lion, my park, my lodge, my river, my Kenya and I suppose my white hunter? Therefore when he was being perfectly horrid he used to call me *"Memsahib* My My".

CHAPTER
66

It was lunchtime when we returned to the lodge and as we approached I had a strange feeling that something was about to happen. Maybe it was the stillness, as if something was sitting waiting. Usually there were people around. There was always some activity. Now Kenmare lay deserted, shimmering in the heat and humidity of the noonday sun.

By the time our car had stopped, most of the staff had appeared and with them three wardens. They were bleeding, dusty and dirty with their uniforms torn. That was the first thing I noticed. We were all so used to seeing them in their immaculate khakis, their shorts with razor-sharp pleats and leather cartridge belts shining, that to see them less than impeccable meant that there was something amiss. We learned that they had been in a fight with Somali bandits, Shifta, who had been armed. One of the wardens had been killed and as we were the nearest outpost, the others had made their way to the lodge. It had happened in the evening and they had walked all the way to us overnight. Stan loaded them into the safari car and we drove them to Leopard Rock. As far as I know, those were the first shots fired in what was eventually to turn into the Shifta war. It started off as a dispute about boundaries between Somalia and Kenya and the rights of Somalis, but degenerated into outright banditry, poaching and murder by the Shifta. At the time, we had no idea of the seriousness of the situation that was to develop, nor the far-reaching consequences for us and our lives, for the lodge, and for my beloved Tana. The Shifta would eventually lead to the death, amongst others, of the conservationist and author George Adamson.

It was getting dark by the time we started the return journey and for the last half hour we drove without lights. The full moon, so enormous in the clear air, hung above us like a Chinese lantern, illuminating our way through the African night. I could smell the perfume from the flowering thorns, their gossamer-thin leaves black against the midnight blue sky and forming a vault above our heads through which the stars shone diamond bright in their clarity. The beauty of our return drive, its brilliance such a contrast to the drama that had played itself out in the heat of the day, acted like a balm to the feelings that had oppressed me through the hours of daylight. I still remember my feelings of intense pleasure at the sight of my beautiful lodge, its thatched roof turned to silver, so bright was the moonlight and the river below glinted and glistened like a fairy carpet woven of moonbeams.

The enchantment of the night turned into glorious dawn as I lay awake. I had been preoccupied all night by more practical things. I was still plotting as to how to provide food for Tana in the days to come. When Stan was not on safari, we always spent every moment together. I could think of no excuse to be gone for a whole day and that is what a journey to Nanyuki and back to buy meat would necessitate. By the time I heard the rattle of cups heralding the approach of early morning tea, I still hadn't come up with a feasible solution to my problem.

The drama of yesterday was almost forgotten with the dawning of a new day and my worries about Tana. How lucky none of us can see into the future and so I could not imagine the repercussion those events would have on my life. It would be the Shifta war that Beryl would use to get Mummy – and me – to South Africa.

A few days later a safari came through, a married couple and their guide. I was delighted as I felt this was the ideal opportunity for Stan to try my game walk. The next day we set off, but this time Ismael had not been sent ahead to reconnoitre and ensure the absence of game. He was also now relegated to the rear with myself and Tim Tom II, who had insisted on coming. After about 20 minutes, Stan stopped to examine fresh elephant droppings and when he and Isamel had finished looking at all the vegetation and branches and twigs lying around, Stan said with great excitement that the elephants had just passed through. What's more, there was a bull with the herd that he had been hunting near Isiolo, north on the way to Marsabit, three years before.

I looked at Ismael in despair realising that Stan, totally absorbed in the elephants, had forgotten the reason for our expedition. All my beautiful ladders up the trees were going to be given a bypass. I whispered to Ismael that he must please tell Stan that now is the time to get into the trees. At this stage we were crossing a *donga* and tracks were everywhere. Stan was bent over the imprints trying to find the tracks of his bull. There was a bit of a conference as Stan explained that at the speed they were moving, it would take about half an hour before we caught up with the herd.

Nothing Ismael might have said would have changed Stan's mind. But how lucky I was that Stan had forgotten the original itinerary and that we did not spend wasted time up a tree. This was to be one of my last game walks with him.

There are few things in life more exciting than walking across Africa in pursuit of these magnificent animals. As one approaches, every step must be noiseless. Then there is the constant fear that the wind will change or that a false movement will alert them to one's presence. When we caught up with the herd, they were in a marshy scrub area and we were able to get to within a few feet of them.

Stan's knowledge of game and particularly elephant was phenomenal. He had lived all his life since his early teens hunting them in one way or another, first of all for their ivory, then for the early game department culling (another excuse for selling ivory), then for his clients to get the large tuskers. He had walked east Africa going where they led him and over the years he had built up an enormous respect for these huge mammals. Indeed so admiring was he that as the years went by he found it more and more difficult to be instrumental in their death. He told me of the times he had watched elephant go to the rescue of a wounded friend. Coming up on either side of the stricken animal, they would try to hold him up and lead him out of danger. He also told me of the intense love they have for one another; he had watched a cow elephant go back every year to visit the grave of her daughter. He also told me that the old very big tuskers leave the herd and when they go, two young bulls accompany them to act as their *askaris* or security guards. Weighed down by their tusks and their advancing age, they are not as mobile as the younger males and they know they are the target for the hunting safaris. The younger sons will defend their father and indeed, to such an extent do they give their loyalty and protection that the hunters often found themselves faced with the problem of having to kill one of them in lieu of their quarry. In the days of licences though, it was more than their job was worth to kill more than their quota and only one elephant was allowed on a licence. That itself cost a fortune. Stan was convinced elephant understood this, so highly did he rate their intelligence.

Stan told me the story of one of the most famous elephants in Africa, affectionately known as Ahmed. He was of a vast age and had enormous tusks. It was the ambition of every hunter to be the one to finally succeed in collecting these tusks as their trophy. Over the years, all the elephant safaris would spend time sitting on the boundaries of the park where Ahmed lived waiting for their chance. But as often as Ahmed and his two companions were seen, never were they foolish enough to set foot outside the park's boundaries. Ahmed seemed to know the delineations of the park almost better than the hunters and would appear in view, as Stan said, as if to show them all what they were missing. Then Ahmed would go to sleep in the afternoon sun with the weight of his tusks resting on the branch of a large tree. Carefully guarded by his *askaris*, he would have a snooze within a few feet of the hunters in the waiting safari party, their fingers itching but powerless to shoot anything. In those days, poachers were practically unheard of and the parks were sacrosanct.

I had my own story of the intelligence and sensitivity of elephants. The film that Robert Mitchum had come out to make in Kenya, *Mister Moses*, as far as I remember, featured an itinerant who drove his wagon pulled by an elephant across Africa. During the filming they had great problems with the elephant accepting the wagon. It was a terrifying contraption with a canopy and lots of pots and pans which made a considerable rattle as it was towed across the hard and uneven ground. Each time the elephant would be harnessed and each time she would charge off trying to escape this purgatory. The wagon would be on its side, pots hurtling all over the place. The noise was deafening and red dust lay in clouds over cameras, crew and actors.

Finally, with tempers running short, her handler felt it was time for a severe reprimand. Unfortunately, the elephant dissolved into tears, creating an even more emotional scene. The handler was distraught. He kept saying to me, "She is so sensitive. Nobody understands how traumatised she is." I helped him mop up the tears that were trickling out of the elephant's little eyes. She looked the picture of despair, even the trunk drooped in melancholy. After a great deal of kissing, patting and tidbits, he finally restored her to normal and they could get on with the filming. I have never forgotten that touching cameo, and the huge love between the elephant and her trainer.

Stan and I now watched this herd of elephants in front of us and went with them as they slowly moved ahead. I love the silence of the elephant walk with only the crashing of branches and their rumbling stomachs bearing testimony to their presence. I love the smell of aromatic herbs and fresh cut grass as the elephant choose a succulent morsel with their trunks, then bear it to their mouths with their little eyes half-closed under their long lashes, so content are they with the abundance of food and water in this paradise. At times we were so close we could have reached out to them.

We finally found the bull away from the herd. He was dozing, his tusks resting on one branch and his trunk with great abandon draped over another, his head almost hidden in the leaves. At his feet, dancing around looking for the grasshoppers and *dudus* he might have disturbed, was his little following of ibis. Stan had cautioned us before we approached to keep very still so as not to alarm the birds who would have alerted the bull to our presence. I could see Stan leaning against a tree, totally relaxed, his safari hat pushed to the back of his head, hands in his pocket, as he watched his old adversary. I thought how he must appreciate being an observer and how glad he must now be that he had lost this old bull in Isiolo. I silently prayed that these elephant would realise that they were in a safe haven and if they remained in our park they would always be out of reach of the hunters' bullets.

Miles overhead, I could see the B.O.A.C. Comet, a tiny dot moving across the sky, leaving a vapour stream in its wake, which then merged into the snowline of the mountain as the plane made its way across Africa to the cold shores of England. I tried to imagine the passengers as they got their last look at Mount Kenya. I could picture them all strapped to their seats heading for London, a faceless crowd with their own lives and loves and identities and I was separated from them not only by distance but by a different world.

I could see Stan looking at me as I followed the plane's progress. I knew it was time to go as there was a long walk back to the lodge but I didn't want to leave this peaceful scene. I wished it had been just the two of us. Once Stan, Tana and I had followed a herd like this for three days. I think for him it was a form of relaxation, taking me amongst the herds and turning from hunter to teacher. It was the only life he knew but he always had great compassion for animals.

The walk back to the lodge was superb. There was a little breeze that helped cool the air and in the late afternoon light, the mountains turned a deep hazy blue and the snow was clearly visible. During the course of the day we had covered between 10 to 15 miles and the visitors were beginning to feel the effect of so much walking. It was decided that Stan would stay with them and Ismael, Tim Tom and I would return to camp and send back the safari car. I had insisted on going back as all the dinner arrangements had to be taken care of and because I had made no provision for such a long day out, nothing had been organised. Stan was not happy about this but as I kept assuring him, Ismael and I would often go on long game walks when he was not around. The only difference now was that he would only be a few miles away, not a few hundred.

Smiling to myself as we passed all my ladders on our way home, I thought how shoddy my little outings were and how unjustifiably proud I had been of my "mini safaris". In comparison, the grandeur of what we had just witnessed and the magnificence of the terrain we had traversed bore no resemblance to the plastic fare that I had been offering. I knew that Stan was amused by my *mise en scène* and had probably intended to participate in the fiction as he'd promised, but once faced with the reality he would have been unable to pretend to escape danger by rushing up a tree. Any man who has the courage to face a charging lioness and to call her bluff and not fire was not the person for my parlour games!

I often thought Stan and my brother Caryll had this in common. Neither was foolhardy and both were very conscious of every aspect of a situation. Once having taken every precaution as they saw it though, they would then have absolute confidence in themselves and their ability to handle any eventuality. They would plunge into a crisis and get great satisfaction and enjoyment out of a situation that would be deadly for anyone without their own nerves of steel.

The main reason in fact that I had wanted to return to camp was to ensure that we had another vegetarian meal. I knew perfectly well that everyone at the lodge was quite capable of organising our dinner without my interference, but my devious mind had finally worked out a plan whereby I could convince Stan that we would need another deep-freeze and a large supply of meat. The advent of this little group had given me just the excuse I needed.

We retired to bed after having eaten a perfectly delicious spaghetti supper but nevertheless, another meatless meal for the visitors. I explained to Stan that as we had so little warning when people were coming, we would have to get a large paraffin deep-freeze to enable me to store the meat for just such an eventuality, therefore avoiding in future the embarrassment of giving people such a limited menu. He said he could see that obviously the one freezer wasn't enough, but how had I managed up to now as he hadn't noticed any shortage of anything before? I said quickly that I had had to send the driver on frequent journeys and a new freezer would circumvent that necessity in future.

To find the right freezer, we eventually had to go all the way to Nairobi. That was even better for me. Stan dropped me off at Karen on the way, as by this time it was much too late to go shopping. He was to pick me up from Ol Orion the next morning. I took this marvellous opportunity to get up and rush into Nairobi at the crack of dawn. By going in so early and by the back entrance to the butcher, I was able to fill an enormous tin safari trunk with meat for Tana. It was so huge it filled the whole back of the little jeep I was using, another present from Stan. I rushed home as it was essential to get back before he arrived to pick me up. In fact I only just made it before hearing the International coming up the drive. As I ran through the kitchen, I told Mutete to get the trunk out of the jeep and loaded onto the International. I told Stan that I was taking a case full of books that I had packed for the lodge. He was in a hurry to get started but I had to insist on having a cup of tea and some toast. I didn't want him to see Mutete and the boys struggling to get that heavy trunk transferred from one car to another.

Feeling very devious, I assured myself that Tana's good health was well worth all this subterfuge. Mutete had cleverly covered the trunk with my raincoat and safari blankets so that it didn't look obvious but my heart sank when I saw the amount of space it was occupying. I wondered how we were going to get a large deep-freeze in as well. I had visions of Stan wanting to repack it, so as to make room for everything else. He did look at it as he climbed into the driving seat and asked, "Are you sure you need so many books?"

I was in a state of real nerves by the time we left. I thought Stan would hit the roof if he found out what I had been up to. Not only because of all the lies but the fact that I had given a promise on going to Meru that I would not interfere in any way with Tana, that I would not cushion her as she adapted to the wild. I was not only breaking this promise but lying like a trooper in doing so.

We found what we were looking for in the backyard of an Indian friend of Stan's who collected second-hand junk and scrap. The yard covered a large area on the outskirts of Nairobi and Stan loved going there. It was where he had found practically every piece of machinery used at the lodge, from engines to pumps. The journey home to Meru took a very long time and with the heavy weight in the back we had to progress very slowly over the rocks. To make matters worse, I had to keep stopping to make excursions into the undergrowth. Like an elephant, when upset I always had tummy problems.

At one stage I was racing to get behind a large bush and ran straight over a large puff adder. I was going so fast it missed me by inches. I laughed afterwards as I told Stan of my experience. I seemed to be spending my life on collision courses with snakes. I kept finding them in my shoes, in the fridges, under the table, in the sitting room, on the verandah and finally I even found a large cobra curled up on the mosquito net of my bed. It was there when I woke up one morning and was so big that in the half-light I thought it was Tim Tom. The Cavendish coat of arms is topped with an entwined snake, so I began to feel there must be a reason for this. I am probably protected from them! It's a nice idea, though not a very practical one.

Once again it was the middle of the night when we arrived at the lodge and I was up well before dawn again to get my meat packed away and out of sight. Then I sent Ismael and the driver off to start the feeding program and hoped they would be safely back at the lodge before Stan realised that some of the transport was missing.

After breakfast we went to look for Tana and when we found her I felt all the lies had been worthwhile. She looked so sleek and pleased with life as she finished off the remains of the Nairobi meat. I was thinking happily to myself how any day now I would come and find her with her cubs. Meanwhile Stan was leaning forward, his arms on the steering wheel, smoking his pipe. It was a very relaxed scene until my euphoria was blitzed. Stan had started to look in the pocket of the car for his binoculars. Fortunately we were in my car and more by luck than good management I hadn't brought any. He had no way of getting a closer look at what was interesting him so much. He said to me, "I can't figure out what they have killed. It's like nothing I have ever seen."

I cursed my stupidity. I should have realised that with his hunter's eye he would pick up details that would pass other people by. I could still see bits of meat clinging to a large bone and it all looked perfectly normal to me but he said he couldn't see any hair or skin and the bone looked like that of a cow. He said, "Without my binoculars I can't be sure. I hope to God it's a buffalo as otherwise there will be serious trouble."

I realised he thought they might have killed one of the African *ngombes* (cattle) but he was still puzzled as to the lack of other evidence. He drove closer and soon picked up the tracks of my International. Within minutes, he had formed his own conclusions as to what had been going on.

He turned to me and said, "Darling, I think you'd better tell me what you have been up to. I suppose I was dragged off to Nairobi to help in this totally illegal activity?" I must say he took it all very calmly and by the time I had finished my story there was not the row that I thought there would be. In fact, now that it was a *fait accompli*, he accepted the fact that he had been made an illegal accomplice and found it very funny. He said, "As far as that bloody lioness is concerned, you have no scruples. But that you managed to con me into your underhand schemes is carrying things a bit far."

It was in a very lighthearted mood that we returned to the lodge and I felt such relief that I could now openly carry on with my feeding program.

After lunch Stan went off to fix up the freezer. It was not in the best of condition but he was amazingly proficient with any type of machinery or electrical fitting. He had installed all the appliances at the lodge, from pumps to engines, and I don't think there was any gadget that he couldn't make work. Although the freezer smelt awful when I opened the lid to look inside, it wasn't rusty and with a coat of paint would look like new.

I was sitting on the verandah writing a letter to Mummy when I heard a loud explosion. I rushed round the back and saw Stan coming towards me, blackened and charred. The freezer had blown up but with amazing good luck and quick reflexes, he had realised that there was a leak and had started to roll away seconds before it exploded. He was badly burnt but it could have been a lot worse. I got his pills and put him in a bath of water while I went off to make a thick paste of bicarb soda. The burns were mainly on his chest and there were a few small ones on his thighs. He had been wearing shorts at the time and although it looked terrible at first, he had come off comparatively lightly. I refused to let him out of the bath until the paste was ready so he complained like mad that I was trying to give him pneumonia. I wanted to take him to the mission hospital but he adamantly refused to go. Nor could I get hold of William on the radio telephone because it was making too much noise and I didn't want Stan to realise what a panic I was in. When one is miles from anywhere and a crisis like this happens, one feels so helpless. On top of which I blamed myself entirely.

It had its lighter side though, as Stan was never serious for long. Although the burns must have been agony, he never complained except for the fact he was unable to go outside into the sun. On the third day I was sitting on the bed doing his dressings when he said to me with a very serious and puzzled expression on his face, "My darling My My, do tell me who he is. I won't make a fuss and I will disappear peacefully."

I said, "What on earth are you talking about? Who is who?"

"Your secret lover," said Stan. "He must be really something. I have led a fairly eventful life so far, being charged by elephant, buffalo, leopard, lion, rhino, but that is like having a picnic on Brighton Beach in comparison to spending a few weeks around you."

Stan started counting on his fingers. "The last time I was here you tried to poison me." He was referring to the fact that because I had been brought up during the war, everything was precious and I hate waste. All machinery at the lodge worked off paraffin, which came in large tin *debes* or cans and it always annoyed me that so much was wasted with paraffin being left in the bottom. One day, I went around draining all the *debes* and filling a large soda-water bottle with the dregs. I then stuck the bottle on top of one of the large fridges so that it could be used next time paraffin was needed. Somebody came along, thought it was water and put it in the fridge. As was bound to happen, Stan, very thirsty after working outside, filled a glass and as he swallowed, realised the mistake and managed to spit out most of it.

At the time, I thought he was about to choke to death, he was hardly able to get his breath. Now he said, "This time, I have only been here a few weeks and you cause me a major heart attack by disappearing up Mount Kenya with God knows who. As that wasn't successful, you concoct a devious little story to get me to buy a deep-freeze with a serious leak. Now I am on my deathbed with third-degree burns and you would never guess who is the only nurse around!"

I told him to "Stop being such an ass and be grateful for small mercies," but we were laughing so much by the time he had completed his list of woes that he had forgotten all about his burns. In fact the more we realised how close he had come to death on each occasion the funnier it seemed.

I had been feeding Tana and her friends every three days for the last two weeks. I could see the cubs were imminent, she was so large. Stan was getting peeved at my long absences from the lodge and now really was cross that I was interfering with nature to such a degree. He couldn't wear a shirt because his burns were too sore and, while healing very well, he still couldn't go out in the sun. At least one good thing was that he had turned the verandah into a workshop and all the machinery at the lodge was getting repaired and overhauled.

The day came when I couldn't find Tana. I rushed back to the lodge in despair, convinced she was dead but Stan assured me that she would be giving birth. I longed to believe him but was not totally convinced and kept haunting the other two lion, Mara and Bado Kidogo. I would watch them from the International through my binoculars. It was only on the fourth day, after having made life for everyone else a misery, that I found her. There she was, lying in the sun with three minute cubs. I was crying with relief and with pride and joy, she looked so wonderful and so happy. She was lying on a ledge of grass halfway down an outcrop of rocks. The babies looked small and frail as they tottered on their little legs, scrambling to get to the milk. I stayed there for so long, lost in admiration of my beautiful family of lion, that Stan eventually came out to find me. I had forgotten time or that he might be worried at my long absence but when I saw his safari car arriving I was thrilled that he would be able to share this incredible experience with me. I had forgotten how painful Stan's burns must be in the heat or how inconsiderate it was of me to have stayed away all these hours. I now had somebody who would understand my excitement. As I climbed into his car I couldn't wait to tell him that he was right and that releasing her had been the true miracle, that my doubts as to the wisdom of what I had done were over, there would be no more sleepless nights as I lay tormented with misgivings. He had understood her needs so much better than I.

I watched a Bateleur eagle wheeling in the invisible currents of the air, black against the turquoise sky, floating effortlessly above the valleys of silence and dark shadows and I knew part of me would always accompany that lone figure in its flights over this mysterious and beautiful terrain. I realised that freedom to all of us is a prerequisite of life.

As soon as Stan was better he had to leave on another safari. He tried very hard again to get me to go with him but I was caught in a trap of my own making. I had to keep the food supplies for Tana going and if I left the park there was nobody I could trust with this mission. Pleading my dislike of being foisted on his clients, which he well knew, I remained at Meru. However I set about a program of gradually tapering off the meals so that by the time the cubs were eight weeks old I had stopped altogether. I hated this period and would have given anything to have been able to discuss my misgivings with someone who could have advised me. Sleeping very badly I would agonise over the cruelty I was inflicting on Tana and her family. I would spend day after day following the pride in my International and smoking cigarette after cigarette. I had set myself a program but now I was hating myself for enforcing it.

One morning when I went to find Tana. I found them with a fresh kill, an old buffalo bull that I knew well. He had been turned out of the herd and had joined up with the zebra for company and protection. I had seen him around for a long time. He had lost the tip of one of his horns and he was gradually losing his sight and it was this poor old vulnerable bull they had killed. At least I knew they were once more able to take care of themselves.

CHAPTER

67

A few days later, I left Meru for Nairobi to pick up my glorious mother who was coming over from Cap Ferrat for one of her visits. It was with intense excitement that I went to meet the plane, praying that she hadn't been so late she had missed it. Lone Eagle, the racehorse that she shared with Jan Thrane, was favourite for the East African Derby. At this stage of his career Lone Eagle was unbeaten and was the Kenya glamour horse. Mummy had also purchased his dam Xylone, Kenya's champion broodmare. She lived to the venerable age of 41 and on the day of her death she refused to go into her box. As everyone was used to pandering to her slightest wish, she was left to wander around while everyone got on with their chores.

Xylone lay down under a huge willow tree on a nice bit of lawn and everyone thought she was resting. But by the time it was decided that enough was enough and her groom should go to shut her in for the night we found that she had died. She was buried under that same tree. In the stud in South Africa that we eventually ran, we had 28 of her descendants. One or another of them had won almost every major race in the country including the greatest race of all, the Durban July.

On this East African Derby day, we all went to the races in our very best clothes. Mummy looked incredible in an ice-blue Dior creation with a large feathered hat to match. Even I was forced into a hat, which I cannot bear and Beryl, who naturally was with us because she trained Mummy's horses and we were staying with her at Lake Naivasha, had condescended to get into one of my dresses for the day. In all the years I knew her, the only time I saw her out of her trousers was when she borrowed a dress from me for just such an occasion. The race was everything we could have wanted. Under a brilliant ride by Buster Parnell Lone Eagle won by three lengths and there was great celebration in Tubby's box afterwards.

Beryl was already fixed on her South African plan, unbeknownst to me. On my last visit to her she had kept telling me about a wonderful farm she had discovered there and how my mother and I should go and see it. I hadn't paid much attention, never really thinking she was serious. Beryl had been having a lot of trouble with her horses at Naivasha – their muscles were seizing up – and she was convinced that a curse had been put on them. All sorts of tests were carried out and eventually the cause was found. It was the seepage from the lake water in the bore-hole that was poisoning the horses. From then on Beryl had to import all their drinking water in large tankers. Once this was sorted out they started on their triumphal progress once more.

Apart from this problem I had also heard through the grapevine that Jan had definitely found another girlfriend. Looking back, I am sure that Jan decided to seize Beryl's new interest in South Africa as an opportunity for him to get on with his new life. Certainly, he and Charles became very supportive of Beryl and encouraged her desire to move. The plan at this stage, from the way they had been talking when I was down on previous visits, was that Charles would find a partner and buy the farm in South Africa, Beryl would take the horses and Jan would start a dairy farm. At the time, listening to them, I had left them to their dreams and returned to Meru.

After the Derby win Beryl was in great form and suggested that Mummy seriously consider going shares with Charles and Jan in the purchase of the farm she had found east of Cape Town. It was called Broadlands and she painted a magnificent picture of the historic farmhouse, with the Helderberg mountains behind, overlooking

Gordon's Bay and the green paddocks in front filled with beautiful thoroughbreds.

That night, when I got Mummy on her own, I squashed any ideas she might have had of purchasing yet another farm. "Darling," she said, "you are such a little spoilsport. There is no harm in just having a look." All this time later I remember so well saying very firmly, "You go if you want to, but I have no intention of ever leaving Kenya."

From Beryl's house we went to have lunch with the Delameres at their family estate Soysambu at Elementeita in the Rift Valley. Diana Delamere was a beautiful woman of my mother's age but it was a much harder beauty. It was she who had been married to Jock Broughton and who had been having an affair with Lord Errol when he was murdered over 20 years before. Now she was married to Tom Delamere, son of the Lord Delamere who had been so vital in Kenya's history. Very blonde with large, cold, rather protuberant blue eyes, she had none of the softness and sense of fun that Mummy had and was not in the same league as far as looks. I think I was a bit prejudiced too as I had heard talk of how she had no time for unwanted racehorses and a bullet would end their careers very rapidly when they had ceased to be useful. I know Groombridge, their stud manager and jockey, used to be in despair at times as some favourite horse of his bit the dust. Another unattractive side to her character was that she was very penny-pinching, certainly as regards to the horses. For example, she would never buy lead-reins, except for the races. I suppose her methods were eminently practical but meanness and racehorses don't make great bedfellows and I think although her horses loved their racing they never reached the heights they could have.

Diana, one always felt, was very conscious of her looks where Mummy never was, but it was a very glamorous lunch party. In the early days Tom Delamere had been one of Beryl's lovers (as had Joss Errol) and I think this is where his interest in racing started. Seldom does one sit down with one famous beauty, let alone three. I am appallingly bad at smalltalk so I let the conversation wash over me as I observed these famous ladies.

Mummy as usual was behaving extremely badly, flirting like mad and I thought to myself, *Oh my God, here we go again, another lover.* This time he was an ambassador from one of the Mediterranean countries and so a lot of hand-kissing was going on. Beryl was behaving in a much more dignified fashion. She was trying to get Jan to agree to something that was obviously important to her. I watched her throwing all her charm at him but her left hand was crumbling the roll on her side plate and I realised that whatever it was, she was finding a certain resistance. Seeing me look at her, she said, "You do agree, don't you, sweetie? You are always so sensible about these things."

What I was being sensible about I had no idea but I agreed as that was clearly what was required of me. I think it was probably a dreadful mistake that I hadn't paid attention to what was going on. By the end of the weekend Beryl had talked my mother into buying another five horses, all the top racehorses in her yard. Afterwards I gathered that is what they had been discussing at the lunch.

We spent a night after that with the Hamiltons at Nderit. Mummy and I often used to stay there. Lady Hamilton was truly remarkable, with flaming red hair and an exquisite complexion, and she surrounded herself with the Masai. She would float amongst them in robes in their own colours of red and ochres. Her house was a fairytale of exotic splendour, a perfect setting for this fascinating woman. Lady Hamilton, or Genessie, used to lend me her horses and her Masai syce and with this red-robed but otherwise naked warrior I explored the lakes of the Rift. I always kept a wary eye out for pythons that might be asleep in the trees and might wrap themselves around me as I rode underneath. Genessie had warned me that this had once happened to her.

When we arrived this time, Genessie was looking more than ever like Elvira out of Noel Coward's *Blithe Spirit*, trailing around the house in her Masai-red chiffons and scarves. She reminded me of Mummy's other great friend, the explorer Freya Stark. They were both great eccentrics, loved camels, Arabs and charging around deserts. The only difference was that Genessie was very good looking and Freya was not, in spite of her long hair which she wore in a swathe over the side of her face to disguise the fact that she had only one ear. The *on dit* was that it had been chewed off by an Arab in a moment of passion, although the truth is she had almost been scalped in an accident with factory machinery when she was a little girl.

I don't know of anyone else besides Genessie who had ever succeeded in domesticating the Masai. They were such a proud race and considered us whites vastly inferior beings. Genessie had Masai women in the house while the rest of us had houseboys. She had succeeded in putting her ladies into flowing red cotton robes too, so that they did not appear at the table with bare breasts. I always thought it was such a pity how, after independence in Kenya, the Masai started to adopt clothes. I suppose you can't have politicians running around in the altogether with only a red sheet for modesty, but the glamour was gone.

Back at Karen after the races life with Mummy remained very social, a far cry from life at Meru. We saw a lot of my friends and had lunches and dinners, went to films and the theatre, as well as playing endless bridge games. It seemed as if virtually every famous person in the world was visiting Nairobi at the time and film companies were out in force making epics with Kenya as a background. Meanwhile the residents themselves were leading their usual fascinating lives. They were an intensely glamorous polyglot society, wild, fantastic, but never boring.

The New Stanley Grill was the smartest place in town. How smart they considered themselves I had not realised until I went there one evening with Ferdinand Liechtenstein, the prince who had proved to be such a coward on safari. He had asked Mummy and myself to dine. She was playing bridge but said, "Pat would love to go." So I was sent off to make dinner conversation, which she well knew I always dreaded.

When Ferdinand met me in the foyer, he was looking extremely glamorous with his silver hair, black trousers, black Dior silk rolled-neck jersey and white dinner jacket, the very latest Côte d'Azur fashion. It was not good enough for the New Stanley though. "I am very sorry, sir," the maitre d'hôtel said, "but ties are obligatory." Even my explanation that Ferdinand was a prince and the smartest clubs in Europe would be proud to have him dressed in this, the latest of fashions, had no effect on this gentleman. I don't think he would have let Mr Kenyatta himself grace his dining room in this state of what he considered undress. I was now determined we were going to get in. I went and called Tubby, explained the situation, and in no time at all we were being ushered to the best table. How satisfying to have influential friends.

Mummy and I went up to Treetops for a night. I had been going there ever since the original tree, when one had to take sleeping bags. Now they had lovely rooms built around the tree and if one was lucky and visited at the right time of year the branches running through the bedroom might be full of flowers. I always adored going there and again, if one is extremely lucky, baboons will also come through the bedroom windows looking for food. Sitting on the verandah at night after a delicious dinner, one would see herds of elephant, buffalo and usually some rhino.

One day we went and had lunch with Lady Pamela Scott whose historic farm Deloraine was at the foothills of the Londiani volcano, near Rongai, on the western edge of the Rift Valley. The farmhouse today is always described in terms of its wonderful colonial architecture. Her father, Sir Francis Scott, was the younger son of the Duke of Buccleuch and had brought his family out to Kenya when his daughters were very small. He was totally uninterested in farming and, so the story goes, incapable of handling finances as he had never ever done so. For a while he steadily went broke.

Finally realising that he could no longer afford to keep a manager on a farm that was losing money, and becoming more interested in politics anyway, he decided to hand the running of it over to his daughter Pamela who was then only 18. Being a remarkable girl, she learned to do the veterinary work as well as branding, dipping, fencing and dairy farming. With a workforce of over 100 Africans and their families to help her, she carved the farm out of the forest and ended up with a famous herd of Ayrshire which she subsequently crossed with Sahiwal, to establish a hardier breed and a strain more able to resist the numerous tick-born diseases. She was tireless in her desire to better the education of children in her area. She never married and remained dedicated to turning the farm into a prosperous commercial unit, which she succeeded admirably in doing. She also was a very good equestrian and in her youth often rode as a jockey at the professional race meetings. She was a rather mannish woman and I found her slightly terrifying.

Eventually I made my way back to Kenmare Lodge after our social festivities to find an atmosphere of unease. The staff were worried about the escalation of the Shifta activity in the area and I was told that some missionaries had been found buried alive with their feet sticking out of the ground. How true this story was I couldn't vouch for. None of the staff had actually seen this occurrence but the story was rife and they believed it.

I didn't pay much attention knowing how everything was likely to be embroidered. Indeed, I didn't say anything about the Shifta to anyone as I couldn't really see them having much effect on my life. How wrong I was. The weeks of socialising I had just had in and around Nairobi proved to be the first faint sounds off-stage of the next act of my life.

CHAPTER

68

Tana's cubs grew from playful kittens to juvenile delinquents. One day I watched with delight one of them stalking a large white butterfly, eyes tense with concentration. He crouched in the long yellow grass but patience was not his virtue and the excitement was too much. He leapt into the air trying to grab it with his paws only to watch it flutter away as he charged up and down in hot pursuit. I tried very hard to keep away from them and would spend days at a time busying myself with the lodge and walking in my grove of pawpaw trees. I hated waste as I've said, because of my wartime background, so had saved all the pips from the fruit. We ate and then planted them in the sandy soil of the river. The hydraulic pump that Stan had installed did a sterling job, pumping up gallons of water for the garden and the lodge. It was all a wonderful lush green and everywhere was the sweet smell of frangipani and jasmine. The honeysuckle and bougainvillaea ran riot all over the buildings, bright against the cerulean blue of the sky.

In the heat of the day I would sit in the shade of my own little jungle with the wonderful smell of damp, hot earth and watch the monkeys as they feasted on the fruit. It was deliciously cool. The irrigation channels gurgled and the river tumbled over the rocks. I would take tidbits to feed the weavers and rollers and my garden of Eden would become a symphony of colours as these birds fluttered and chirped in their scramble for food. So many wonderful lazy afternoons were spent watching my little bit of Africa flourish and blossom in the heat of these long summer days.

How often people would ask me, "Are you not lonely or bored out there on your own? What is there for you to do all day?" My days were so full that I would wake each morning with a sense of excitement. As dawn broke the country would come alive. Shapes would emerge out of the shadows. The birds would call their greetings as the sun rose slowly until the plains were lit with its brilliance. When I woke I didn't know what was ahead. This was a time of living free, of discoveries, of living with the herds and troops of animals through those long hot days when the plains and forests belonged to the animals and the human population was insignificant.

One day, I had been up since dawn watching a leopard that lived near the lodge. On my return, I was told that the Shifta had burnt Stan's boat on the Tana and had taken the boatman prisoner. The *askaris* had followed their tracks south and had then lost them. We were overjoyed when, a few days later, a naked, exhausted man arrived at the lodge. It was the boatman who had managed to escape during the night and had fled back to the camp. He told us that the bandits had stripped him and tied a rope around his waist, then forced him to carry their belongings. He had walked for days with a rifle prodding him on and in terror of his life.

From then on everything seemed to change dramatically. Now there were always *askaris* about, heading off in one direction or another, and I was warned not to go far from the lodge. The lodge itself was like a frontier outpost in the Wild West and getting the lorries in and out for provisions became a problem. Sometimes we had to get an escort to accompany them. My wanderings over the countryside became almost an impossibility. I never mentioned any of this to Stan but finally news drifted down to him of the unrest in the area so he packed up his safari so he could be with me. The day before his arrival, I had watched from a long distance a running battle from the lodge but the whole drama had such an air of unreality. The figures were so far away it was as if I were watching them running across the stage in a play.

Then Stan arrived and the very fact of his presence gave me such a sense of security that I couldn't really imagine life had changed in any way after all. One soon learns to adapt to any situation. I knew the people of the area and I felt almost sure that Ismael who was a Somali was a member of the Shifta and as he was always loyal to me, I felt safe. The men who had come to the lodge with me also chose to stay, although I had given them the option of leaving and returning home. Their loyalty was unquestioned; I had no fears of being surrounded by enemies. My only worry was: how would all this affect Tana? Stan became more and more reluctant to track her down, saying that I must leave her to live her own life, assuring me that the Shifta had no designs on eliminating the lion population. I knew he was right but her safety was a continual source of anxiety. As time went by though, even this fear subsided and life resumed its dream-like quality.

Apart from the boatman and a few skirmishes, we saw nothing further of the Shifta. I accepted that there were bandits in the area but their shadow had no substance for me. Instead there was the reality of my everyday life and the love Stan and I had for each other.

Stan had another safari and this time he refused to allow me to stay at the lodge on my own. In any case, Mummy was arriving from Europe shortly anyhow, so I came back to Karen and as usual was amazed at how Mutete always managed to keep Ol Orion running so perfectly in my absences. He always did. I would arrive out of the blue, only telephoning him from the *dukas* at Karen so that I would know what supplies to bring, and by the time I arrived at the door, he would be there with his beautiful smile, his khaki shorts and shirt pristine, with his white apron and white chef's hat. All the staff would greet me, with a lot of hand-shaking and "*Jambo. Habari?*", laughing and talking. I just felt so thrilled to see everyone again.

I would enter the sitting room to find it full of flowers, the parquet floors shining and the floral slipcovers on the sofas and chairs, newly washed and starched. Beyond were the open mullioned windows and stretching behind them the garden, still beautifully tended with the sweeping herbaceous borders going down to the ha-ha and the lovely blue Ngong Hills in the distance. And everywhere were the trees, with their climbing roses which tumbled and flowered. As I close my eyes, I can smell the beeswax and flowers. I can see the pale olive green walls stippled by the sunlight. I can hear Mutete's soft laughing voice, all the sounds, the scents and the beauty that was Kenya.

It was on just such a day, the garden and the house wrapped in the soft sunshine, that I received the telephone call that was to finally deliver what Beryl wanted. Joseph came tumbling in followed by Kimoyo telling me the doctor was on the telephone. It was William asking me to come and see him. I asked him, "Why so mysterious?" But he insisted that I come in as he wanted to talk to me.

I went the following morning. As I sat in the familiar waiting room overlooking Delamere Avenue I thought that it could only be that I was about to receive another lecture on my lifestyle. When I was shown into his rooms, I gave him a peck on the cheek and said, "I suppose I am about to receive one of your gloomy lectures." Looking over his glasses at me, he said, "Sit down. I have to have a serious talk to you.

"I don't think you realise but Enid has a bad heart and the altitude here is a danger for her. As long as you live in Kenya though, nothing will stop your mother coming out. I have to warn you that it is putting her life at risk. I understand from Enid that she is very keen to buy a share in this farm in Cape Town. It is at sea level and I think you should consider the advantages of this."

It was not until I got back to Ol Orion and had time to think over what William had told me that I realised the full implications. When faced with the fact that I might be instrumental in causing my mother's death, I had no option. The love I had for this beautiful fragile being mattered more than anything else in my life. She was all things to me, my child, my mother and my friend and without her I felt my world would have ceased to exist.

I know William genuinely believed my mother had a serious heart problem and certainly she found breathing difficult when she was in Kenya. In fact, the truth is she had developed a dangerous allergy to a drug that had been prescribed for her arthritis. This was discovered only later by a doctor in South Africa and consequently that did save her life. So maybe fate as well as Beryl had taken a hand.

It was years later that I learned that Beryl had convinced my mother that living as I did amongst the Shifta was suicidal, and that Stan was so worried about my safety that he had moved down to be with me. Beryl told Mummy she was sure that he would finally divorce Ronnie and we would get married. None of my family, especially Rory, approved of Stan and the thought that he might consider getting a divorce filled them with despair. Beryl now suggested that getting me to the Cape would solve all these problems.

William produced the trump card.

CHAPTER
69

When Mummy arrived she was not looking well but as she never ever complained, it was almost impossible to find out about her health. It was a subject she would never discuss. She was always filled with energy. Like a child, she lived life to the full, surrounded by her toys – her paints, her needlework and her animals. Everything to her was an adventure and it was like watching a wayward child reaching out to everyone in such a generous, loving way one couldn't help but be enchanted. It was only because I constantly worried about her that I could pick up the signs.

Rory and I bullied Mummy unmercifully. We always considered it was for her own good. One of the reasons I eventually became her chauffeur was that I considered her far too dangerous behind the wheel. Every now and again she would escape my clutches and take off, foot flat on the accelerator, and I would die a thousand deaths until her return. She had one meek friend who she talked into going with her on one or two occasions with the result that the poor lady ended up with shingles, so terrified was she.

Mummy and Rory both had the same quality of innocence. The

dark spots of life were discarded and not allowed to intrude on their existence. They saw the world through a golden haze and if you were lucky enough to be part of their magic circle they took you through into that fairyland where life was always fun and always filled with beauty. The reverse simply wasn't tolerated, or perhaps noticed.

This time, when Mummy and Beryl brought up the subject of a trip to the Cape, I was no longer able to refuse. We spent three days in South Africa and they were a nightmare. The Cape seemed to be total suburbia. Even Broadlands, the stud they had in mind to buy, straddled a main highway and although it had a lovely British occupation period house – the transition from Cape Dutch to English Colonial – and was scenically quite spectacular, in my jaundiced eyes it was the antithesis of everything I held dear. It was another south of France, admittedly one that was less populated and with somewhat grander scenery, but there were none of the vast horizons of Kenya. There was no game. There were cities and towns. It was all I had managed to escape. It was civilization.

Mummy, with wide-eyed wonder, saw only the beauty of the new property and its surroundings. She saw where the swimming pool would go, right outside her bedroom window. There was no garden but she was already planning large herbaceous borders and lawns. But above all, what really sold Broadlands to her was a potential croquet court. A large, perfectly flat area of grass to the side that would need no alteration. When she was told that there was a thriving croquet club in the area, I knew she wanted this property. Mummy was a brilliant player and although there was a croquet lawn at Fiorentina nobody had ever played with any enthusiasm. It wasn't one of the games of the Côte d'Azur. It was a hangover from her Australian upbringing. All the Lindemans played croquet and although Mummy had tried to instill in us a love of the game, only Caryll was a willing participant.

By the time we returned to Kenya, she had signed an option on the farm and paid a deposit. Charles was supposed to have paid half of this but at the time, and after all the promises, he had some reason as to why he was not able to do so. Needless to say, none of the partnerships were ever realised. Mummy was left buying Broadlands and financing the entire removal of Beryl and her racing establishment.

Jan did come down and help settle the horses in. He stayed with Beryl, who had taken over the manager's house, and he set up a jersey herd as he had planned. But instead of running the farm as was originally intended, he found a manager and then returned to Kenya where he eventually married the lady of his choice. Charles never came at all, and so all of Beryl's plans collapsed around her. Much to her chagrin.

This was yet to be played out though. All I knew was that my life had turned into a claustrophobic nightmare from which there was no escape. On my return I had to tell Stan of my decision and he came with me to Meru to pack up the lodge that I had built with such happiness. Now I was abandoning Tana at a time when possibly she needed me most.

I can still see her as I went to say goodbye, lying on her back, surrounded by her family, contented and at peace. Or was this how I wanted to remember her? I don't know any more. I didn't truly realise I would never see her again, and if I had known that, would I have had the courage to leave? What fate befell this golden creature that was my other self?

More than 20 years later in Cape Town, I went to see a clairvoyant. He told me some amazing things about Mummy and Rory that nobody else could have known. Then, half-rising out of his chair, he said, "Oh, my Lord! Oh, my Lord!" His head started swivelling around and he cried, "I don't know what is going on, this has never happened to me before." He sounded breathless and disturbed. There was total silence. I didn't know what to expect. I rather thought some evil spirit might have been conjured up and I also nervously looked around.

In a faint voice, he said, "There is the most amazing thing occurring. A huge lion, no, a lioness, it is a lioness, an enormous lioness, has walked in." He kept repeating himself and I noticed he was gripping the side of his chair with one hand. His head turned and his blank eyes were looking at me. "She has walked over to you, she has gone to lie by your side, she is so close to you... so protective of you... she is guarding you so carefully, she won't even let the doctor near you."

Only I knew of Tana's protectiveness and how she had once prevented William Boyle getting to me, and it was a story long forgotten. Nobody could have told him about Tana; she was part of my youth, my life in Kenya. People in Cape Town didn't know about it. After all, by then there were plenty of other stories that people told each other about the wild animals and the racehorses and training that formed part of my daily life at Broadlands. But nothing of my present life was even mentioned at that clairvoyant's session.

I can only think that as Tana and I were so close in life, so even now in death she has remained with me. For all these years, I have had to live with the knowledge that I deserted her and Joseph. They have haunted my dreams and I have wept bitterly thinking of their love and dependence on me and how I betrayed that trust.

At least Tana was free in the wilds. I feel far worse about Joseph. He went to a friend of Stan's who had a farm on the slopes of Kilimanjaro and I sent Kimoyo with him. I had to give my beloved chimpanzee away because without my supervision his love of children finally got him into trouble. The owner of one of the houses on Ololua Ridge nearby had a daughter-in-law to stay and she brought her small baby. How Joseph discovered this fact, I will never know. Maybe he had heard the baby cry on one of his bicycle rides with Kimoyo to the Karen *duka*. Anyhow, later on, he made his way there, climbed to the second storey and seized the baby out of its cot. Thank goodness its cries alerted its mother who was able to rescue it from Joseph's tender care.

Afterwards, I heard that the friend who had taken Joseph moved to Dar-es-Salaam where he opened a restaurant. Then I lost all my papers and addresses and now I have no idea of his name. If he had a restaurant, Joseph would have had to have been enclosed and that thought has haunted me ever since. I went to Tanzania every year after that but could find no trace of him. Maybe I never tried hard enough; horrendous things so often happen to these incredible animals and maybe I couldn't bear knowing.

I kept Ol Orion and the staff going for several years as I refused to believe I would not return to live there, and I left the lodge at Meru fully furnished too with a few of the Somali staff to run it. I was sure that the Shifta was a temporary setback and I would not have to remain in South Africa for long, that I would eventually be able to spend six months of the year at Broadlands and six in Kenya when

Mummy was back in France. One of my dearest friends told me that he had taken a safari to Meru later and it was like a ghost town. Even the beds were still made up. For a long time, I went back to Kenya every year and that same friend takes me on flying safaris. I go everywhere but never to Kenmare Lodge.

When Mummy finally sold Ol Orion, she bought Mutete a little hotel in Machakos, the old up-country post just south of Nairobi. Kenya has changed altogether. I have not been back to Ol Orion since either but Karen is so built up that where lion used to kill on my road there is now a housing estate.

On my last trip there several years ago, I drove some friends from Nanyuki to Subukia and I said to them ahead of the trip, "For the next three hours, we will be travelling through wonderful tropical forests." But the country I had once known so well was unrecognisable. There was hardly a tree to be seen except in the distance. This terrible cutting down of trees has led to soil erosion which has then led to drought. Africa is now full of rubbish too. The saying goes that its national flower is the plastic bag because they are everywhere.

It isn't just the decimation of the forests that has filled me with despair; the animals have disappeared too. In my day, there were few people but game was everywhere. Herds of magnificent elephant, buffalo, zebra, wildebeest as well as the lion and cheetahs and all the smaller animals. Now, with the ivory poaching, the horrific deaths from thousands of snares, the killing for food, the disappearance of the forests and the over-grazing by cattle, the wildlife is vanishing. For Africans, having children is very macho and so there is huge overpopulation too. Greed, corruption and the rapacious nature of man is destroying this universe.

And what of Stan? In all those years together, we had never discussed marriage. I had never wanted or expected it of him but the night before I left for South Africa, he came to me and asked, "If I get a divorce will you stay?" But marriage was never an option for us and could never have been. When I married Frank a second time, Caryll spent two hours on the lake persuading me to go through with it. Stan spent four hours trying to talk me out of it. But he was always far too possessive of me, and in any case I would never have broken up his marriage. I couldn't have had that on my conscience.

Stan insisted on leaving with me to see me settled at Broadlands. We left by ship, for every extra day was now precious. We arrived in Durban and then drove to the Cape but even when I finally saw him off on the plane back to Kenya I never realised it would be four years before I saw him again and then it would only be for a few hours. I was visiting Nairobi and we had driven up to the Ngong Hills. He begged me to marry him and come back to Kenya for good. I never saw him again; it was Tubby who told me of his death.

Stan had given me so much. Together with Tana, we had camped and walked and driven over all of east Africa, from Uganda to Tanganyika. He had shown me a new world, as if he were opening the pages of a treasured book. He had revealed an Africa that was magical and mysterious, a continuous delight. Kenya, a land of memories, where my dreams became reality and my life was an eternal summer.

EPILOGUE

Beautiful Enid, Countess of Kenmare by her fourth and last marriage, died in 1973 after spending the last years of her life at Broadlands successfully overseeing the training and breeding of racehorses – and putting her money on them. She and Beryl Markham fell out soon after her move to South Africa and Enid persuaded her daughter to take over as trainer for her horses. Pat's husband Frank introduced her to the legendary Australian horse-trainer Tommy Smith and she also studied with the vet Percy Sykes who taught her to make her decisions about her horses based on analysing their blood samples. Broadlands then produced champion after champion, including Miss Lindeman and Swan River.

Meanwhile, Rory had sold Fiorentina and moved back into Le Clos. One day in summer, with tourists flooding the Riviera, he found himself stuck for three hours in a traffic jam on the increasingly crowded Moyenne Corniche. That was enough for the aesthetically sensitive Rory. He sold Le Clos too and moved to Menerbes in Provence where he created another beautiful home from an old farmhouse. He died in 1985.

The memory of these two deaths still causes Pat great pain. Pat remembers coming back to Cape Town after visiting Rory who by then was very weak from AIDS, with a nurse watching him night and day. One morning, Pat had just finished the early morning gallops at Broadlands and had walked into her bedroom when she saw Rory sitting at her dressing table. She says, "He looked magnificent. No longer a skeletal figure but well and healthy, dressed in a blue shirt with a black sweater. The one thing I particularly noticed was the whites of his eyes. They had the healthy bluish look that one often sees in a child. He told me he felt wonderful and that I was not to worry any more. Then he got up and went out of my bedroom door. Halfway through, he turned back and said, 'You can tell Sidney [Sidney Teperson, the family doctor] that you won't need to come next week.'" At the time, all this seemed normal to Pat who says she remembers a feeling of euphoria, a glow of happiness that lasted for days, but when her doctor later heard of it, he said, "I have had another experience like that with a patient. Don't tell Pat but it means Rory is dead." Hours later, says Pat, she received the call from France telling her that.

By the end of her life, Enid was unable to stand up straight because of the back injury she had suffered decades earlier when she had fallen badly from her horse while out hunting. She was also in great pain from a hiatus hernia. In spite of that, Pat remembers her mother being terrified of being given pain-killers, a legacy of the time she had been given morphine after her riding fall. In those days, morphine was given readily to patients in pain and, like many in her circle, Enid had become addicted. Pat says Enid later went to a clinic determined to cure herself and did so. But it meant she had a horror of ever becoming addicted again. As her daughter says, she regarded it as an unbearable weakness.

Pat's brother Caryll, Lord Waterpark, has had a distinguished career back in Britain pursuing his great passion, aviation. He visits Broadlands every year and stays for several months helping with the property. At one stage, there were 300 racehorses but those days are long gone and Pat has also had to sell off much of the surrounding land.

Pat now shares her large home and grounds with 35 dogs, nine donkeys, 10 cats, 12 baboons, 22 vervet monkeys, eight goats, two bullocks, two pigs, 26 mice (rescued from the cats and kept in a separate building), umpteen birds and one much-loved chimp called Kalu. All the animals – not just the mice – have been rescued from terrible circumstances. Frank spends part of the year in Sydney, Australia, and part of the year in South Africa where he has learned to share Pat with her animals and whichever baby baboon is being nursed in her bed. Pat is up at 5am each day, preparing the dogs' breakfasts. Afternoons are spent with Kalu and she recently wrote: "How many women of almost 80 have the privilege of experiencing this unconditional love of a so-called wild animal? How many women can lie on the sunbaked earth of Africa, surrounded by all my rescued animals and not feel blessed by God?"

EDITOR'S NOTE

Several years ago, Pat was in Johannesburg for the yearling sales when she discovered that a restaurant buffet featured live lobsters. Aghast, she immediately rescued all several dozen of them from the diners – by paying the restaurateur three times their worth. Pat told me she had watched lobsters in the Mediterranean doing their mating dances and decorating their holes in the rocks. Who could eat such a creature? Before putting her rescued lobsters in the hands of couriers who would take them in tanks back to the coast, to the sea and freedom, she insisted that a couple of the vets who she usually used for her horses check their health. "They had to get out their stethoscopes," she told me, with a glint. "And of course, the only time these gentlemen had inspected lobsters before was when they were sitting on a plate between a knife and fork."

Patricia Cavendish O'Neill is a born story-teller and someone who, if she had lived a different and less-privileged kind of life, might have authored a dozen best-sellers. But what she has written here is prize enough. This is Pat's book in Pat's voice, full of larger-than-life people and anecdotes like the above. I have endeavoured to check all that I

can while necessarily keeping in mind that this is how Pat remembers her life; these are her memoirs.

In my editing, I am indebted to a number of people – Elissa Fidden, Andrew Barnett, John Glen and Keith Janes – who have helped with the fact-checking, accuracy and authenticity. And to Professor Peter Gray who had done so much work already on providing background material on the characters and events mentioned. Like Pat, I have also used a number of books for checking and cross-referencing and these are quoted at times. They are listed in the following bibliography.

SHELLEY GARE

BIBLIOGRAPHY

George Adamson. *My Pride And Joy* (Collins Harvill, 1986)

Lord Birkenhead. *Walter Monckton – The Life Of Viscount Monckton of Brenchley* (Weidenfeld and Nicolson, 1969)

Robert Calder. *Willie – The Life Of W. Somerset Maugham* (William Heinemann, 1989)

Roderick Cameron. *The Golden Riviera* (Weidenfeld and Nicholson, 1975)

Roderick Cameron. *My Travel's History* (Hamish Hamilton, 1950)

Anne Cox Chambers, editor. *Remembering Rory – A Collection Of Tributes* (privately published by Anne Cox Chambers, 1987)

Robert B. Edgerton. *Mau Mau – An African Crucible* (The Free Press, 1989)

James Fox. *White Mischief* (Jonathan Cape, 1982)

Barbara Goldsmith. *Little Gloria... Happy At Last* (Macmillan, 1980)

Joanthan Guinness with Catherine Guinness. *The House Of Mitford* (Hutchinson, 1984)

C. David Heymann. *Poor Little Rich Girl – The Life And Legend Of Barbara Hutton* (Hutchinson, 1985)

Edwin P. Hoyt. *The Vanderbilts And Their Fortunes* (Frederick Muller, 1963)

J. A. Hunter. *Hunter's Tracks* (Hamish Hamilton, 1957)

Elspeth Huxley. *White Man's Country – Lord Delamere And The Making Of Kenya, Volume II* (Macmillan, 1935)

Elspeth Huxley, editor. *Nine Faces Of Kenya* (Collins Harvill, 1990)

Molly Izzard. *Freya Stark* (Hodder and Stoughton, 1993)

Max Lake. *Vine And Scalpel* (Jacaranda Press, 1967)

James Leasor. *Who Killed Sir Harry Oakes* (Houghton Mifflin, 1982)

James Lees-Milne. *Beneath A Waning Moon, Diaries 1985 – 1987* (John Murray, 2003)

Mary S. Lovell. *Straight On Till Morning – The Biography Of Beryl Markham* (Hutchinson, 1987)

Beryl Markham. *West With The Night* (first published by Houghton Mifflin, 1942)

Robert M. Maxon and Thomas P. Ofcansky. *Historical Dictionary Of Kenya* (Scarecrow Press, 2000)

Leonard Mosley. *Castlerosse* (Arthur Baker, 1956)

Richard Murphy. *The Kick* (Granta, 2002)

Christopher Ogden. *Life Of The Party – The Biography Of Pamela Digby Churchill Hayward Harriman* (Little Brown, 1994)

Margaret Pringle. *Dance Little Ladies – The Days Of The Debutante* (Orbis Publishing, 1977)

Pamela Scott, edited by Philip Mason. *A Nice Place To Live* (Michael Russell, 1991)

George Malcolm Thomson. *Lord Castlerosse – His Life And Times* (Weidenfeld and Nicolson, 1973)

Errol Trzebinski. *The Kenya Pioneers* (William Heinemann, 1985)

Errol Trzebinski. *The Lives Of Beryl Markham* (William Heinemann, 1993)

Errol Trzebinski. *The Life And Death Of Lord Errol* (Fourth Estate, 2000)

Gloria Vanderbilt and Thelma, Lady Furness. *Double Exposure* (Frederick Muller, 1959)